Mexican Americans
Across Generations

Mexican Americans Across Generations

Immigrant Families, Racial Realities

Jessica M. Vasquez

NEW YORK UNIVERSITY PRESS

New York and London

NEW YORK UNIVERSITY PRESS
New York and London
www.nyupress.org

References to Internet websites (URLs) were accurate at the time of writing.
Neither the author nor New York University Press is responsible for URLs
that may have expired or changed since the manuscript was prepared.

Library of Congress Cataloging-in-Publication Data
Vasquez, Jessica M.
Mexican Americans across generations :
immigrant families, racial realities / Jessica M. Vasquez.
p. cm.
Includes bibliographical references and index.
ISBN 978–0–8147–8828–8 (cl : alk. paper) — ISBN 978–0–8147–8829–5
(pb : alk. paper) — ISBN 978–0–8147–8836–3 (e-book)
1. Mexican Americans. I. Title.
E184.M5V344   2011
973'.046872—dc22   2010041976

New York University Press books are printed on acid-free paper,
and their binding materials are chosen for strength and durability.
We strive to use environmentally responsible suppliers and materials
to the greatest extent possible in publishing our books.

Manufactured in the United States of America
c   10 9 8 7 6 5 4 3 2 1
p   10 9 8 7 6 5 4 3 2 1

Much gratitude and love go to my family, who have believed in me, supported me, and encouraged me in my educational and career endeavors: Dorothy Mullison-Smith, David Vasquez, Earl Smith, Jason Vasquez, and Isabella Vasquez. I dedicate this work to my family, including my grandparents: Wendell and Ethel Mullison, who, academics themselves, appreciated my bookishness and gave me the gift of daylilies; and Manuel and Lucy Vasquez, who were staples of my childhood and whose own tale in part inspired this intellectual quest.

Contents

Preface   ix

Acknowledgments   xiii

1   Introduction   1

PART I

2   Thinned Attachment: Heritage Is Slipping through our Fingers   33

3   Cultural Maintenance: A Pot of Beans on the Stove   64

4   Tortillas in the Shape of the United States: 91
    Marriage and the Families We Choose

PART II

5   Whiter Is Better: Discrimination in Everyday Life   127

6   Fit to Be Good Cooks and Good Mechanics: 163
    Racialization in Schools

7   As Much Hamburger as Taco: 194
    Third-Generation Mexican Americans

8   Conclusion: Racialization despite Assimilation   229

    Methodological Appendix: 245
    A Note on Sociological Reflexivity and "Situated Interviews"

    Appendix A: Respondent Demographic Information (Pseudonyms)   257

    Notes   261

    Bibliography   269

    Index   283

    About the Author   301

Preface

Since 1924, Old Spanish Days Fiesta has been an annual summer celebration in my home town of Santa Barbara, California. The aim of the nearly week-long event is, according to its official website, to "celebrate the traditions handed down from Spain, Mexico and the California Rancho period." This festive affair includes a historical parade, a children's parade, rodeos, nightly dance performances, and *mercados* (outdoor plazas) filled with bands, dance troupes, and Mexican food vendors. The highlight is the evening dance performances, known by English and Spanish speakers alike as Noches de Ronda (Nights of Serenade), held on a stage outside of the town's red, Spanish-tile-roof courthouse. The audience stakes out spaces on the lawn early in the day for prime viewing of the elegant dancers who don elaborate costumes and perform Spanish flamenco, Mexican *ballet folklórico,* and Aztec dances.

Looking back, I realize that most, but not all, of the dancers were Latino/a, primarily of Mexican descent.[1] I remember being a teenager chewing on a *churro,* enraptured by the dancers, and musing about how it came to be that most of the dancers on stage were Latino. Given the demographic makeup of Santa Barbara, one would expect a rough split between non-Hispanic white and Mexican-origin participants. Another point of curiosity for me was the question, Why do some Mexican Americans engage in culturally rich traditions and art forms whereas many others do not? Many Mexican Americans and non-Hispanic whites happily watched the performers. While being an audience member is arguably a form of engagement in one's heritage for Latinos, certainly there is a range of involvement in Fiesta as a cultural activity for those whose heritage it is intended to represent and celebrate. So, I wondered, why are some people strongly identify with their racial/ethnic background whereas others are not?

My nascent interest in social groups—and particularly in race/ethnicity—was piqued when I attended college on the east coast. While I loved my native state of California, I was eager to become familiar with another part of the country. My informal education began even before I moved into my college dorm room in Princeton, New Jersey. As soon as my mother and I sat down for our first dinner after arriving at the Philadelphia airport, we noticed that I was the only dark-haired person dining in the restaurant that night. This was my first experience of feeling like a cultural and phenotypic outsider. This had never happened in my home town in southern California, of course, since I was a cultural insider to both mainstream white and Mexican American cultural worlds. In California, I enjoyed cultural trappings that I now realize are hybrid but are nonetheless (and importantly) embraced in that environment: my family and I had piñatas and pin-the-tale-on-the-donkey at birthday parties, we had Sunday barbeques at my grandparents' house with chili beans and apple pie, and we attended Presbyterian and Catholic churches to honor both of my parents' religious upbringings. My physical appearance lent itself to this bicultural status as well—pale skin, brown eyes, dark brown hair. In a town that is 78 percent white, 13 percent "some other race," 4 percent "two or more races," 2 percent black, 3 percent Asian, and 33 percent Hispanic/Latino (of any race),[2] I literally "looked" like most of the town, fitting comfortably into the two predominant racial/ethnic populations of white and Latino.

Also during my freshman year at Princeton University (1994), debates about Proposition 187 were raging in California. Proposition 187 was created to deny basic social services, including health care and education, to undocumented immigrants. In my intermediate Spanish language class—which should have already been an indicator that I am probably not a Mexican national fluent in Spanish—other students identified me as the person who would "know" about the Proposition 187 debates. They barraged me with questions about what *life in Mexico* was like and what my stance was on the California proposition, clearly expecting me to speak from the perspective of an undocumented worker as opposed to a U.S. citizen. When I left for college, I had no idea that in New Jersey, three thousand miles away from my largely Hispanic state of California, some would see me as an "all-or-nothing-Mexican." This shocking categorical rigidity moved me to understand the power of race and the forces that shape our perceptions of our racial identity.

I became involved in a *ballet folklórico* dance group in college. Previously, there had simply been no need for me to actively preserve or promote any particular aspect of my background. My environment reflected who I was, both non-Hispanic white and Mexican American. Placed in a different social milieu, where the student and faculty population was predominantly non-Hispanic white, I desired a connection to cultural elements that were natural to me in southern California but lacking at college on the east coast. If "necessity is the mother of invention," then desire for a taste of home in college was the inspiration for my dancing. In this way, social situation did bear on the activities I was engaged in. If that was my personal experience, does that tell us anything about the broader experience of racial and ethnic identity? Tuning in to C. Wright Mills's notion of the "sociological imagination," I began to ponder how individual experience is linked to the broader context of historical timing, structure of society, and institutions. This book is an academic research endeavor that seeks to discover the social influences that shape the way Mexican Americans, over family generations, experience and explain their social identities.

When giving presentations on this research I am frequently asked the question, "Where do you fall in the spectrum of 'thinned attachment' to 'cultural maintenance'?" As will become clear, I use these terms to describe people in terms of the strength of their knowledge of and commitment to their Mexican heritage. Portraying these two ways of being as opposite ends of a continuum is useful because it suggests the existence of a wide intermediate space. Many later-generation Mexican Americans are somewhere in this in-between zone where they can be selective about the traditions and practices they wish to keep while living fully acculturated "American" lives that are indistinguishable from those of other native-born Americans. As boring an answer as this may be, I too exist somewhere in the middle of these conceptual categories. English was my first language and, while I learned a few basic Spanish words as a child, I had to take Spanish classes in high school and college in order to hold a conversation. I love Mexican food and know how to cook scrumptious Mexican meals, though I happily cook a variety of cuisines. I graduated from an Ivy League university, clearly a marker of academic success and comfort in American institutions. As a Ph.D. holder and a university professor, I am a product of, and deeply embedded in, America's educational system. I am unquestionably American. Yet, I focus on Latinos as my primary research area. More than attempting to maintain a particular version of a culture—there should be no line drawn between so-called Mexican and American culture because of the fluid and intermixed nature of culture—I am concerned with increasing understanding about race relations, immigration, and American culture.

Taking the idea of the sociological imagination seriously, this book examines the way individual experience is shaped by the structures of historical moment and social organization. We are products of our eras, our families, our religions, our educations, and more. As we watch news programs that shed (politically spun) light on debates about immigration, policy change, and on-the-ground racial dynamics, it is important to consider the larger context in which we live. Taking the case of multigenerational Mexican American families, we should ask how their lives are shaped by their families, racial and political discourses, and everyday experiences. As people conform to, contest, or creatively navigate racial dynamics, social expectations, family ideologies, and cultural beliefs, how are they and those around them changed? How do families share ideas about history and identity across generations? How do belief systems and cultural practices maintain or transform over time? Who do immigrants and their descendents become after decades—indeed, generations—in the United States? This book takes on these questions and shows the crucial role that race, family, and sociopolitical milieu play in the lives we live.

Acknowledgments

I would like to gratefully acknowledge the financial support I received from the University of California-Berkeley, the National Science Foundation, the University of California Institute for Mexico and the United States, and the University of Kansas. I would like to thank the inspired scholars who challenged and encouraged me, advancing the theoretical depth of my questions and the intellectual rigor of this book: Michael Omi, Ann Swidler, David Montejano, Sandra Smith, Joane Nagel, Joey Sprague, Bob Antonio, Kelly Chong, Tanya Golash-Boza, Yajaira Padilla, and Jorge Perez. Many thanks go to my steadfast writing group partner and ongoing collaborator, Christopher Wetzel. For thought-provoking and detailed comments on the entire manuscript, I deeply appreciate the investments of Ilene Kalish, my editor at NYU Press, Tomás R. Jiménez, Edward Telles, and two anonymous reviewers. Colleagues and friends who provided feedback on my scholarship, in its various stages, also deserve recognition: Cinzia Solari, Jon Norman, Keyvan Kashkooli, Jennifer Randles, Jennifer Sherman, Osagie Obasogie, Eréndira Rueda, Katrinell Davis, Laurel Westbrooke, and Kevin and Karen Lucas. Thanks to numerous other friends and fellow sociologists with whom I have conversed over the years, for your support, questions, and feedback have also helped shape this book.

Appreciation also goes to the many people who shared their heartfelt stories with me and whose tales appear in this book. It was my privilege and my challenge to work with and represent their life stories. I warmly recognize Timothy Brennan, whose confidence and pride in me has been with me since my first research trip. I deeply appreciate my longtime friends, or "fictive kin," whose love and friendship sustain and nourish me, especially Kim Clarke Arce, Carrie Clough, and Rebecca Miner. Most importantly, I am grateful for and recognize the support and love of my family, to whom this book is dedicated: my mom, dad, step-father, brother, grandparents, and niece.

To discover yet another ethnic group that is showing signs of assimilation would be nothing out of the ordinary if it were not for the widespread belief that Mexican Americans were "unassimilable"—forever alien to the American way of life—and predestined for low social status. The general experience of immigrant populations in the United States was rarely if ever projected to this minority. . . . *[T]hese stubborn notions are in need of revision.* (Grebler, Moore, and Guzman 1970: 10; emphasis in original)

Threads of nativist hostility from earlier eras remain resonant with much of the American populace. For example, in the late 1800s and early 1900s, when the United States instituted restrictions on Asian immigration,[2] the Mexican migrant labor that became a necessary reserve army of labor in the wake of all these legal exclusions was met with nativist antipathy (De Genova 2005; Gutiérrez 1995; Montejano 1987). Vigilante groups like the Texas Rangers who aimed to subordinate Mexicans through intimidation and violence have found a contemporary incarnation in paramilitary groups like the Minutemen Militia. According to anthropologist Leo Chavez (2008), the Minutemen Militia is a prime example of the "Latino threat narrative" discourse in action. The Latino threat narrative is a racist, xenophobic, nativist discourse that "posits that Latinos are not like previous immigrant groups, who ultimately become part of the nation [because they are] unwilling or incapable of integrating, of becoming part of the national community" (2008: 2). In this reductionist and fear-laden rhetoric, all Latinos are viewed as immigrants (who, in reality, comprise 39.8 percent of the Hispanic population in the United States [Pew Hispanic Center 2007b]), an invading force that is destabilizing national unity. In news press articles, the metaphors used to discuss immigration are exceedingly negative and fear arousing, including references to floods, tides, invasions, takeovers, sieges, diseases, burdens, animals, forest fires, and criminals (Santa Ana 2002). Latinos are figured as a threat to the nation due to a language, culture, fertility, and race nexus fearfully referred to as the "browning of America."

Using interview data rather than emotion-driven ideology, *Mexican Americans Across Generations* investigates the racial identity formation and incorporation trajectories of three-generation Mexican American families in California. *Mexican Americans Across Generations* explores the primary question, How do first-, second-, and third-generation Mexican Americans come to their sense of racial identity? Secondary questions follow: How does a sense of race get transmitted or transformed through three generations in a family? Outside of the family, what other social arenas affect one's sense of racial self? As racial self-perception is an indicator of assimilation, what integration patterns predominate?

My research finds that Mexican immigrants, their children, and their grandchildren become increasingly embedded in U.S. institutions and ways of life with each successive generation. However, there is substantial variability in the ways members of each generation experience and express their racial identity and cultural legacy even while successfully navigating U.S. institutions and appropriating U.S. culture. I develop a framework to understand this. "Thinned attachment" describes families whose commitment to and familiarity with their Mexican heritage wanes over time. By contrast, "cultural maintenance" describes those families that continue Mexican cultural practices, Catholicism, and the Spanish language through all three generations. Family ideologies, teachings, and memories (often in the form of family stories) are vehicles that transmit content of identity intergenerationally. Each generation's racial identity style—or palette of racial identity options—is informed by both "appropriated memories" (inherited from others) and "personally acquired memories" (developed from direct experience) (Mannheim 1936). Forces beyond the family, including public spaces, educational systems, peer networks, religious institutions, and occupations, also powerfully shape racial identity and assimilation trajectories.

As Mexican immigrants and their families deal with what it means to be Mexican American, my research offers a case study into the processes of racial identity formation and assimilation—the process of adaptation to a host country. Racial identity formation is the interactional process whereby an individual negotiates the racial component(s) of his or her social identity. Through interactions with other individuals and institutions, people negotiate the social ascriptions (such as race) imposed upon them and, in response, develop an understanding of and ways to navigate these social categories. The patterns of incorporation discussed in this book are far from a story of simple dilution with each passing generation. Instead, this work problematizes notions of uncomplicated and unavoidable eventual assimilation into the U.S. mainstream in a way that forsakes forbearers' racial and cultural identity.

Whether Mexican Americans, or Latinos generally, are a race or an ethnic group is a fraught question in the social sciences, in politics, and within the group itself. Scholars debate the definitions of "race" and "ethnicity," as well as their application to Latinos. Prevailing usages of the terms "race" and "ethnicity" conflate them.[3] Due to the socially constructed nature of race and ethnicity and their various applications through history, there is contemporary disagreement over the distinction. For instance, regarding Mexican Americans, some view this group as a race (Acuna 2000) whereas others view it as an ethnicity (Macias 2006; Skerry 1993; Smith 2003) and still others argue in favor of the term "racialized ethnic group" (Golash-Boza 2006; Telles and Ortiz 2009). I think of Latinos (including Mexican Americans) as not simply an ethnic group but a "racialized ethnicity." I favor this term because Latinos, the umbrella category that encapsulates people hailing from Latin American countries, are often treated as a separate racial category, despite being listed as an ethnicity on the 2000 U.S. Census.

"Racialized ethnic group" honors the notion that Latinos can be racially black or white (or Asian or Native American Indian) as well as underscores the highly racialized experiences that this population undergoes. Many interviewees referred to their experience as one of a subordinated racial group rather than one that is merely distinguished by ethnicity or culture. Race is understood to be (and is experienced as) biological and unchangeable, rather than something you can choose (Blauner 2001). Currently, there is a renewed debate about the biological basis of race, fueled by the fact that it is commonplace to use skin color as a proxy for race (Duster 2003). The commonsense understanding of race is that it is inherited, innate, and unchangeable, whereas ethnicity is understood to be cultural, a matter of shared traditions such as customs, language, or food. One issue this book explores is the degree to which Mexican Americans experience themselves as a race as opposed to an ethnic group, whether this experience changes generationally, and what accounts for any persistence or change.

As for terminology used in this book, I use "race" as a label imposed from outside by the ways people treat one another. I use "ethnicity" to refer to culture that is embraced or "chosen" (Gans 1979; Waters 1990). Race can be understood as a human group that is "socially defined on the basis of physical characteristics"; "the selection of markers and therefore the construction of the racial category itself . . . is a choice human beings make" (Cornell and Hartmann 1998: 25). Note that there is more genetic variation *within* supposed racial groups than *between* them (Cornell and Hartmann 1998; Duster 2003; Obasagie 2009). This highlights that the lines dividing racial categories are social divisions rather than genetic or natural ones. On the other hand, ethnicity relies on self-definition whereas race is an ascriptive characteristic, assigned to people by others. Ethnicity is "subjective," relying on individuals voluntarily to claim group membership, and holds that a "distinctive connection" based on "common descent" (Cornell and Hartmann 1998: 17) unifies the group. Importantly, there is overlap between ethnicity (elective self-definition) and race (imposed) even here, in that ethnic claims often refract what others tell us we are: "although an ethnic identity is self-conscious, its self-consciousness often has its source in the labels used by outsiders. The identity that others assign to us can be a powerful force in shaping our own self-concepts" (Cornell and Hartmann 1998: 20). This overlap not only reveals the shared terrain of these terms but also shows the interactional nature of self and society.

As scholars, politicians, and the public deliberate the "who are we?" question of national identity, it is imperative to take an empirical look at the impact of Mexican immigration on these debates. Who do Mexican immigrants and their successive family generations become after settling in the United States? Do they assimilate? If so, what routes of racial and cultural incorporation do they take as they assimilate into U.S. society? How do families transmit concepts of culture and racial identity across generations? Samuel Huntington's (2004b: 230) polemical work argues that "contiguity [of sending and receiving countries], numbers, illegality, regional concentration, persistence [of immigration waves], and historical presence" combine to make Mexican immigration distinct from previous immigration from Europe, Asia, and Latin America. Rather than simply presuming or fearfully exaggerating the impacts of Mexican immigration and immigrants on America, my book offers a detailed perspective on people's subjective experiences of immigration and settlement. The degree to which Mexican Americans experience their ancestry as an ethnicity—diluted in each generation and ultimately an "ethnic option" (Waters 1990)—as opposed to experiencing it in terms of separation, subordination, and racialization, is precisely what this book investigates empirically.

I interviewed members of middle-class families in part to determine whether and in what ways these economically successful and structurally integrated Mexican Americans are racialized. Are Mexican Americans more likely to assimilate and view their heritage "symbolically" (Gans 1979), like previous waves of European immigrants, or will racialization forestall that option? Portes and Rumbaut (2001), focusing on the first and second generations, argue that due to low human capital, nativist hostility, racial discrimination, and a reactive counterculture, Mexican Americans will probably experience downward assimilation. Yet, time plays a key role in the assimilation process, and my research extends to the third generation. While a segment of the Mexican American population is part of an urban underclass (Dohan 2003; Sánchez-Jankowski 1991; Vigil 1988), another segment has experienced upward mobility (Alba 2006; Perlmann 2005; Reed, Hill, Jepsen, and Johnson 2005; Smith 2003). Mexican American upward mobility adds optimism to this group's assimilability—ostensibly, at least. Thus, determining whether and in what ways middle-class Mexican Americans are racialized reveals much about Mexican Americans' ability to assimilate rather than stand apart as a racial "other." A focus on middle-class Mexican Americans is interesting because it is precisely this class-privileged group one would expect to be able to assimilate. Working one's way up the socioeconomic ladder is a yardstick of assimilation; upward mobility is considered "making it" in America. Middle-class Latinos are "considered to be the most successful members of their group and, thus, to face little (or less) discrimination" (Feagin and Cobas 2008: 41). Both popular lore and academic writing suggest that social acceptance and first-class citizenship will be awaiting those who achieve middle- or upper-class status. The fact that class status does not shield middle-class Mexican Americans from the effects of race underscores the salience and gravity of race, even among the economically fortunate, even among the U.S. born. Even this relatively class-privileged group has embittering, racializing experiences that highlight their status as outside of the white[4] mainstream. This book is therefore as much about achievement of upward mobility and middle-class status as it is a story about "racialization despite assimilation."

Racial identity formation and assimilation occur concomitantly through everyday practices and experiences. This book deals with the experiential process of racial identity and assimilation, distilling key moments and everyday decisions people make that significantly influence the process, speed, and direction of assimilation. As a general trend, as each generation takes on more "American" self-descriptions, they also take on more "American" modes of life and cultural behaviors. "American" is in quotation marks here—but not hereafter—to point out that "American" is a universalizing concept that unfairly simplifies the regional character of the myriad American identities and overlooks the hybrid nature of identity, which includes region, religion, ethnicity, and so forth. Considering the variety of racial options and American identities lived out by third-generation Mexican Americans, this is not an oversimplified story of gradual, straightforward assimilation. Given the middle-class status of the families in my sample, neither is this book a tale of "segmented assimilation" or integration into an already stigmatized subgroup (Portes and Rumbaut 2001; Portes and Zhou 1993). Mexican American identity is not yet an "ethnic option" (Waters 1990), as it is for white ethnics. Indeed, all three generations experience a high degree of racialization in numerous social arenas. Thus, the story that unfolds here is not simple and straightforward but instead follows a "bumpy-line" (Gans 1992a) and branches in a number of directions.

Theories of Assimilation

"Racialization despite assimilation" is an innovative approach to think about the way race informs integration trajectories and also to demonstrate that to be racialized and to be assimilated are not exclusive and opposite states of being. Focusing on the institutional and interactional experiences of immigrant families and their offspring, I examine the life course trajectories of Mexican immigrants, their children, and their grandchildren. I examine the daily decisions and key moments wherein acculturation and integration take place. By analyzing experiences (rather than life outcome measures) across three generations, I am able to distill patterns by which both assimilation and racialization occur. It is through everyday decisions, encounters, and experiences that individuals and families move toward, resist, and reshape patterns of assimilation.

Traditional or "straight-line" assimilation theorists assert that assimilation–the process of adaptation to a host country—is the inevitable destiny for immigrant groups (Gordon 1964; Park, Burgess, and McKenzie 1925). Anglo-conformity has historically been the most prevalent assimilation theory, assuming the "desirability of maintaining English institutions (as modified by the American Revolution), the English language, and English-oriented cultural patterns as dominant and standard in American life" (Gordon 1964: 88). This perspective is predicated upon an assumption of European superiority. Gordon does not complicate his analysis with concerns such as gender, class, culture, historical timing, or structure of opportunity in the host country. The final, inevitable destination of Gordon's theory is assimilation, earning the nickname "straight-line assimilation."

Straight-line assimilation theory was developed in response to the "great migration" of the late 1800s and early 1900s. These immigrants, primarily from Southern and Eastern European countries, over time assimilated into mainstream American culture because they could eventually make claims to whiteness. While portrayed by many as generalizable, straight-line assimilation theory is limited by the characteristics of the mostly European[5] immigrant population and the historical moment (education was not crucial and jobs that paid a living wage were more accessible). European immigrants' assertion of whiteness was facilitated by the cessation of migrant flows due to restrictionist laws, making the Mexican American population an interesting case because of its continued influx of newcomers, or "immigrant replenishment" (Jiménez 2008; Jiménez 2010).

Acculturation is no longer the surest path to successful economic incorporation, as the straight-line model suggests (Bean and Stevens 2003; Zhou and Bankston 1998). Instead, "casting off one's immigration identity can lead to downward mobility—a concept that directly challenges the dominant sociological paradigm of straight-line assimilation" (Lee and Bean 2004: 227). In this light, "selective acculturation" (Portes and Rumbaut 2001; Portes and Zhou 1993) and "accommodation without assimilation" (Gibson 1988) offer a way to hold on to supportive strands of native culture while simultaneously accommodating to the new culture.

Segmented assimilation, as a revision of straight-line assimilation theory, accounts for a variety of assimilation outcomes and addresses what "segment" of society a group is incorporated into (Portes and Rumbaut 1996; Portes and Rumbaut 2001; Portes and Zhou 1993; Rumbaut and Portes 2001). This theory posits that different levels of human capital facilitate different acculturation outcomes (Portes and Rumbaut 2001; Portes and Zhou 1993). This theory accounts for the possibility of downward assimilation (or assimilation into a marginalized or stigmatized subgroup), noting that assimilation into the middle-class mainstream is hardly a certainty (Gans 1992b). Segmented assimilation posits three possible outcomes: integration into the white middle class, assimilation into a poverty-stricken underclass, and economic advancement along with preservation of immigrant community values (Portes and Zhou 1993: 82). This theory was developed in response to the 1965 Immigration Act that loosened immigration restrictions, allowing for an influx of in-migration from Asian and Latin American countries.

Building on segmented assimilation's insight that race is central to the incorporation process,[6] I refine bumpy-line assimilation to argue that spouse/partner, personal traits (phenotype and name), gender, and social position are crucial to integration processes and outcomes. Rather than predict precise endpoints of the assimilation process—into the mainstream, into a marginalized subgroup, or into an economically advanced position while continuing immigrant values—bumpy-line assimilation acknowledges a gamut of possible assimilation outcomes that do not follow a linear pathway (Gans 1992a). Bumpy-line assimilation allows for immigrant families to be included in the mainstream on various levels (education, linguistics, occupation, culture) while *also* maintaining ethnic cultural values, beliefs, practices, and social circles. In this conception, to be assimilated and to be culturally thick or thin are compatible positions. Bumpy-line permits a both/and identity formulation—both American and Mexican. Bumpy-line does not forecast the same process or outcome for an entire migrant ethnic group. Allowing for variation, I refine bumpy-line theory by highlighting the elements respondents reported as central to their experience of feeling either included or excluded in the greater American society: spouse/partner, personal traits (phenotype and name), gender, and social position. Secondarily, one's cultural toolkit (English/Spanish language ability and American/Mexican cultural fluency), social context, institutions, and citizenship status also direct Mexican Americans' life experience, opportunities, achievements, limitations, barriers, and identity options.

Assimilation is an incremental process that can branch at numerous points and lead to a multitude of experiences and outcomes, ranging from assimilation with white dominant culture to cultural maintenance to an unpredictable process that includes reversals, turns, branches, and bumps. Assimilation is incremental and intergenerational, a product of everyday decisions (Alba and Nee 2003). Integration into the dominant society is a *process,* one that influences the self-concept of those undergoing it (Kibria 2002: 197). This "modern assimilation theory" critiques straight-line assimilation theory as a form of "Eurocentric hegemony" because it uses white, Anglo-Saxon Protestants as the reference point, which allows no room for the positive roles of racial and ethnic minorities. Modern assimilation theory argues that immigration will result in the "cultural reshaping of the mainstream" (Alba and Nee 2003: 282) and that the mainstream will eventually include previously excluded populations (although power holders will still probably remain whites). Similarly, others have suggested that the people who comprise the mainstream, as well as the boundary lines between groups, are shifting due to demographic changes spurred by immigration (Kasinitz, Mollenkopf, and Waters 2004). As assimilation occurs and the U.S. mainstream changes, it is imperative to discover how immigrants and subsequent generations of their families understand and enact their racial and cultural positions in the United States.

Assimilation theory to date overestimates the linear direction of incorporation processes and "exaggerate[s] the consistency and uniformity in direction to which assimilation occurs across a wide range of social dimensions" (Telles and Ortiz 2009: 284). Even segmented assimilation theory, which accounts for differential levels of human capital, is short-sighted in that it presumes discrete, unitary responses and outcomes among groups. Segmented assimilation contends that U.S.-born second- and third-generation

Mexican Americans have a primary loyalty to their coethnics, are "locked in conflict with white society," and join a "reactive subculture" to protect their self-worth (Portes and Zhou 1993: 88–89). Revealing a class distinction, my research shows that this does not hold true for middle-class Mexican Americans. The question remains: How do race, ethnicity, class, and generation shape the life experiences of immigrants and their descendents who achieve middle-class status?

This book builds on assimilation scholarship by disentangling generations in order to examine intergenerational incorporation trajectories. By interviewing three-generation families (grandparent, parent, child), I can identify different types of multigenerational integration pathways that comprise a range of assimilation possibilities. Pursuing the critique that "assimilation, or the lack of it, can occur at quite distinct paces and even in an opposite direction," this book demonstrates the "bumps" and directional splits within generations that exist along the road of assimilation (Telles and Ortiz 2009: 284). This book builds on the undertheorized concept of "bumpy-line" assimilation by acknowledging both the variety of incorporation experiences over generations and the ways in which trajectories can take unexpected turns and swerves.

Theories of Identity: Race, Gender, Family, and Generation

The social-psychological work on identity development is extensive (Breuer and Freud 1966; Briggs 1992; Cooley 1998; Erikson 1968; Erikson 1980; Erikson 1985; Freud 1938; Freud 1961; Mead 1934; Schachtel 1959a; Schachtel 1959b). Families, as well as other primary groups such as neighborhoods, play groups, or community organizations, are the "nursery of human nature"; they are fundamental in the formation of the social nature and ideals of an individual (Cooley 1998: 180). Yet, little of this scholarship rigorously interrogates the intrafamilial processes by which people claim racial/ethnic or national group membership. Existing literature also lacks information about how racial identity and feelings of national inclusion or exclusion change over time due to interactions within family generations. This social-psychological literature leaves open the question of the processes by which racial identity and integration into the U.S. national imaginary develop and change through the life course and family generations.

Both inside and outside the family unit, race is a critical component of social identity. Rather than consider race an immutable and ascribed category, I consider it flexible, contested, negotiated, and situational. Identities are "strategic and positional" (Hall 1996: 3) as well as contextual. People still think with reference to both categorical and relational group memberships when trying to draw the boundaries of their identity. While adhering to the premise that identities are partial and positional (Hall, Morley, and Chen 1996), I employ an interactionist approach that holds that culture occurs and identity ("presentation of self") is manufactured in social interaction (Goffman 1959). However, so as not to overstate agency, the possibilities of action or self-assertion must be understood and contextualized in relation to institutional and cultural structures. People assert agency from within particular opportunity structures and situations of constraint. Accordingly, one critique of segmented assimilation is lack of consideration of the dynamic processes of race and gender: "Reducing race and gender to elements of the assimilation process . . . deflects attention from 'the ubiquity of racial [and gender] meanings and dynamics' in everyday life experiences, as well as in institutional practices" (Lopez 2003, quoting Omi and Winant 1994).

"Difference is an ongoing interactional accomplishment" (West and Fenstermaker 1995: 8). From this perspective, race is not a preexisting social identifier that has a constant and unchangeable meaning. Instead of viewing race and its effects as "objective, factual and transsituational," this standpoint posits that properties of social life such as race, class, and gender "are actually managed accomplishments or achievements of local processes" (Zimmerman 1978: 11). This perspective disrupts the notion that modes of difference (such as race) are natural and immutable. Overturning the idea that ascriptions such as race and gender have an essential nature requires that we view these social elements as constructed and maintained through social interactions. West and Fenstermaker (1995: 25) write, "Conceiving of race and gender as ongoing accomplishments means we must locate their emergence in social situations, rather than within the individual or some vaguely defined set of role expectations." If race is an everyday interactional accomplishment, the question becomes, What aspects of social life bear on the creation of a(n inherently dynamic) racial self? My respondents reported that family life, schools, peer networks, religion, workplaces, and public discrimination were all significant in shaping their racial selves and, consequently, their feeling of being *a part of* or *apart from* the U.S. mainstream.

Race does not merely operate on the social-international level, however. Race structures societies in eminently important ways. Critical race theory applies insights from social science—namely, that race is a social construction—to the law. It aims "not merely to understand the vexed bond between law and racial power but to *change* it" (Crenshaw, Gotanda, Peller, and

Thomas 1995: xiii, emphasis in original). Concerned with racism, racial stratification, and discrimination, critical race theory suggests that judicial rulings can be shaped by social phenomena, such as race. The law is not objective and impervious to human subjectivity and influence; the law is a social construct.

Race is in part a legal construction. The law has been manipulated, in particular in its definition of whiteness, in order to defend a racial hierarchy. The law has had a hand in creating, sustaining, or changing racial definitions. Racial categorization, especially of whiteness, carries serious legal ramifications, notably U.S. citizenship. Haney López (1996) cogently argues that racial prejudices and preferences are encoded in the law, which, in turn, affects social organization on a large scale and day-to-day lived experience on a small scale. As a concrete example, the legal system actively *colored* the U.S. population through immigration, naturalization, and marriage laws. Recall that one had to be deemed a white person in order to immigrate to the United States, as established by the 1790 Naturalization Act. This stipulation was challenged through court cases, wherein we witness the elevation of a "common knowledge" understanding of race (you know it when you see it) and the repudiation of scientific rationale when science failed to justify racial boundaries that pleased the court. Admitting to the United States only persons defined as white had two direct racist consequences: first, it defined American citizenship as synonymous with whiteness; and, second, it directly shaped the marriage pool and reproductive choices (Haney López 1996: 15). Laws excluded nonwhite races from the country and even stripped women of citizenship if they married ineligible men. Given this legal history that privileges whiteness, whiteness can be viewed as "status property" in that it is protected under American law and carries public and private societal benefits (Harris 1993). The law has played a leading role in manipulating the phenotypic appearance of the U.S. population and erecting a racial hierarchy.

The law colored or racialized the U.S. populace. These legal beginnings are "past in present" (Collins 2004) in that they influence racial ideas and discourse centuries later. Historically, commonsense beliefs about race were encoded in law, which spurred and substantiated ideology. Law both constructs and legitimizes race. Once laws regarding race are institutionalized and legitimated, they feed racial ideologies that penetrate societies and naturalize racial constructions and the racial order (Haney López 1996). We hear echoes of these racialized laws in today's public and legal concerns regarding who should be admitted to the United States. An undercurrent of this conversation is about measuring the worth and fit of populations—foreign and native-born alike—against the U.S. "imagined community" (Anderson

1991) that was legally prescribed to be racially white. This book details how racialized legal restrictions reverberate in the day-to-day lives of American citizens who, to varying degrees, feel included or excluded from society on the basis of their interactions with institutions and other Americans.

Like race, gender is a social construction that nonetheless has material, emotional, and psychological consequences for the way life is experienced (Anderson and Collins 2007). Intersectionality literature shows how gender, race, and class are "interlocking systems of domination" (Collins 1991). By examining race, class, and gender from a unitary perspective (rather than an "additive approach" where one axis of difference is considered central and others tacked on), one sees how these systems of privilege and oppression interconnect and have a "multiplicative" effect (Collins 1991; Collins 2004; King 1988). Feminist "standpoint epistemology argues that all knowledge is constructed in a specific matrix of physical location, history, culture, and interests" (Sprague 2005: 41). Knowledge comes from a vantage point and is therefore partial and historically specific. Black and Third World feminists argue that "standpoints promise to enrich contemporary sociological discourse" (Collins 1986: 5) because they unearth marginalized voices and provide important supplements to existing knowledge (Sudbury 1998). The literature on intersectionality and feminist standpoint theory claims that contextualizing the source of knowledge and listening to viewpoints from a variety of social locations lends insight into a society's organization and minority women's empowerment (Anzaldúa 1987).

The literature on gender and migration holds that international migration refashions gender ideologies and gender roles among the migrants and causes migrants' children to negotiate between "old" and "new" world norms (Hondagneu-Sotelo 1994; Jones-Correa 1998; Pedraza 1991; Smith 2006b). In what Hondagneau-Sotelo (2003: 9) calls the "third stage of feminist scholarship in immigration research," gender is seen as permeating "practices, identities, and institutions." While it is important to avoid essentializing and homogenizing sending and receiving countries and viewing their inhabitants as undifferentiated, gender and generation play a significant role in the way gender relations in families are constructed and reconstructed in new national contexts (Barajas 2009; Barajas and Ramirez 2007; Smith 2006b). As intersectionality and standpoint epistemology insist, racialized and gendered life experience produces a particular situated knowledge and outlook (Anzaldúa 1987; Collins 1986; Lopez 2003; Moraga and Anzaldúa 1983; Ruddick 1989).

This book examines racialization and assimilation processes and the way they operate or rebound in families. The family is an organic unit that boasts an opportunity to trace racial lineages, experiences, ideologies, and practices through three generations. Multigenerational families are an underutilized unit of analysis for studying race and assimilation. Typically, when multigenerational families are studied, life outcomes rather than life experiences are emphasized and two- rather than three-generation families are studied.

The family is a cornerstone of identity development. The family is a key source of factual family-history information and a wellspring of informal education on "what it means to be" or "how to be" of a particular heritage. Karl Mannheim (1936) theorizes the intergenerational transfer of knowledge as formed by both "appropriated memories" (those taken over from someone else) and "personally acquired memories" (those created directly from knowledge gained through one's own experiences). Both appropriated memories—such as lessons handed from parents to children that constitute background knowledge—and personal experience ("the only sort of knowledge which really 'sticks' and . . . has real binding power" [Mannheim 1936: 296]) are critical to knowledge creation. Childhood is the "primary stratum of experience" upon which worldviews are drafted, "all later experiences tend[ing] to receive their meaning from this original set" (Mannheim 1952: 298). Thus, human consciousness is formed by an "inner dialectic," and worldview formation is always constructed with reference to the primary stratum.

Generations share a "particular kind of identity of location, embracing related 'age groups' embedded in a historical-social process" (Mannheim 1936: 292). Generations are subject to common dominant social, intellectual, and political circumstances. The insight that race is a negotiation between generations (or cohorts), shaped by historical eras, motivates this book. I put assimilation theory in dialogue with Mannheim's generational analysis of history and knowledge transmission. By centering on multigenerational families, I am able to investigate intergenerational communication within a family. I probe the experiential and family-memory aspects of race to discover how people discuss and negotiate the content, meanings, boundaries, and constraints of Mexican American identity. Using this conceptual apparatus, we can deepen our understanding of the way historical context and family generations bear on racial identity formation and assimilation processes.

The focus on race across generations is compelling because the political meaning and definition of race is historically contingent. As discussed, Mexican Americans have alternately been considered a race and an ethnic group. Not only have boundaries around racial categories changed over time, but also the meanings attached to racial groups are dependent on historical context, generation, and family influence. Indeed, scholars utilizing a "racial-generational approach" have discovered that political styles of, perspectives on, and involvement in ethnicity change generationally, and often in reaction to the wider political climate (Cohen and Eisen 2000; Takahashi 1997).

This book is situated at the intersection of identity, race, gender, family, and generation literatures. Studies on generations tend to obscure the influence of family, research on families often loses the generational analysis,[7] and social-psychological research does not necessarily contextualize individuals in their social locations. The family, identity, and race literatures leave unanswered the question of how the life experiences and ideologies of the parent generation affect the beliefs and practices of the next generation. My book is motivated by the realization that life experience does not end with the single individual who lives it. Rather, life experiences can profoundly influence other family members through shared values and principles, and through shared memories and stories. Since neither identity nor culture is static and unitary, individuals have some creative agency as they sift through storehouses of familial knowledge and try to make meaningful both inherited and first-hand knowledge about racial identity and their place in U.S. society.

Why Study Mexican Americans?

The question of where the Mexican-origin ethnic group, or the larger Latino umbrella category, fits in the U.S. racial landscape is an important one. Latinos are perceived as occupying racial terrain somewhere between blacks and whites, somewhere in the "racial middle" (O'Brien 2008). Scholars have long focused on the black-white binary in the United States (Blauner 1989; Blauner 2001; Carmichael and Hamilton 1992; Collins 1991; Collins 2004; Conley 1999; Fanon 1967; Feagin 1991; Fredrickson 1981; Gilroy 1987; Gilroy 1993; Ignatiev 1995; Lieberson 1980; Massey and Denton 1993; Oliver and Shapiro 1995; Thernstrom and Thernstrom 1997; Wilson 1987). Only in the last couple of decades has scholarship moved beyond this emphasis by focusing on the burgeoning Latino population, widening the black-white dichotomy into the multitiered image of a "racial hierarchy" (Chavez 2008; Davila 2008; De Genova 2005; Flores and Benmayor 1997; Foley 1997; Gómez 2007; Hondagneu-Sotelo 1994; Jiménez 2010; Marrow 2009; Millard and Chapa 2004; O'Brien 2008; Oboler 1995; Williams, Alvarez, and Hauk 2002). Recently there has been a surge of literature on Latinos, an increasingly visible population. Some scholarship investigates the contributions of this segment and other work is born out of fear of the "browning" or "Latinoization" of the United States.

There is a dearth of work in the sociology of race literature on the subtleties and contradictions of how Mexican American identity (or Latino identity) flows through family generations. The bulk of the scholarship on Latino families to date concentrates on immigration, settlement patterns, revised gender dynamics (Griswold del Castillo 1984; Hamilton and Chinchilla 2001; Hondagneu-Sotelo 1994; Hondagneu-Sotelo 2001), and the role family and cultural background play in youths' academic achievement (Kao and Tienda 1995; Kao 1998) or disengagement (Ogbu 1990; Ogbu 1994; Valenzuela 1999). Recent portrayals of the rising second generation (Portes and Rumbaut 1996; Portes and Rumbaut 2001; Rumbaut and Portes 2001) carefully detail experiences of acculturation, language acquisition, academic performance, ambition, and discrimination, yet focus solely on the first and second generations. Questions of identification swirl around selecting pre-prescribed options on the U.S. Census (Rodriguez 2000) or battling against the limiting nature of ethnic labels and calling for political action through self-definition (Oboler 1995). While some literature traces the history of Mexican American experiences in the United States utilizing age cohorts within ethnic groups as units of analysis (Montejano 1987; Sanchez 1993), none grounds its generational analysis within family units for a nuanced portrait of the transmission of racial identity and culture.

Mexican Americans have a rich and complicated history in the United States, starting from the fact that the Treaty of Guadalupe Hidalgo in 1848 to end the U.S.-Mexican War meant that the United States not only annexed one-third of the territory of Mexico (all or part of present-day California, Arizona, Nevada, Utah, Wyoming, Colorado, Kansas, Oklahoma, and New Mexico) but annexed Mexican citizens as well. It has been argued that the international border along the Rio Grande was drawn to usurp as much land from Mexico and as few people as possible. At the time of the treaty, a U.S. senator is quoted as saying, "We do not want the people of Mexico, either as citizens or subjects. All we want is a portion of territory, which they nominally hold" (De Genova 2005: 218). From the outset, there was resistance to incorporation of the Mexican people: the United States avoided according citizenship rights to Mexican inhabitants of the newly annexed territories, nullified their Mexican land grants, marginalized and discriminated against them, circulated ideologies of inferiority, and effectively introduced the notion of Mexicans as second-class citizens. After the war, land ownership moved from the hands of Mexicans to those of Anglos, followed quickly by a division of labor that was delineated by race, a dual-wage system in which Mexican Americans were paid less than Anglos for the same work, residential segregation, occupational displacement, school segregation, and political disenfranchisement (Gutiérrez 1995; Montejano 1987; Sanchez 1993).

The U.S. relationship with Mexican immigrants has been marked by racial dominance or "internal colonialism." Robert Blauner (2001: 22) argues, "The colonial order in the modern world has been based on the dominance of white Westerners over non-Western people of color; racial oppression and the racial conflict to which it gives rise are endemic to it." The dominant group secures its superior position through the exclusion and exploitation of other groups. Even if ostensibly offered greater economic opportunities in the United States, Mexican nationals have historically been pawns of the U.S. government. The U.S. federal government heavily recruited Mexican laborers during times of U.S. economic boom and forcibly expelled them during the Depression of the early 1930s. In the 1930s and 1940s, when Mexican American youth were attaining an ethnic consciousness, combating xenophobia, and arguing for dignity in the United States, the United States embarked on another round of drafting cheap Mexican labor through the 1942 Bracero Program, only to expel suspected illegal workers through Operation Wetback of 1954 (Gutiérrez 1995).

Since 1848, Mexican Americans have been negotiating their relationship with other Americans in U.S. society. Even before California's statehood in 1850, fierce debates were waged over where to draw the racial lines, a boundary that would determine who would and would not be extended the franchise and citizenship rights. Mexicans were deemed "white" and extended citizenship (although the legal enforcement of this decision was shoddy), while California Indians were deemed "nonwhite" and ineligible for citizenship (Almaguer 1994: 9). The legal system—or, more specifically, the white power holders who have historically determined law—has itself constructed the definition of "whiteness," a term whose definition has changed through time in tandem with nativist political agendas. Furthermore, the judicial system has both bestowed and revoked "whiteness" and its attendant legal privileges upon various populations at different times (Haney López 1996). Mexicans are one of many groups that have been jostled with regard to the question of whiteness and legal status.

Each generation of Mexican Americans has had to develop a self-conception vis-à-vis white mainstream America. The labels Mexican Americans have applied to themselves have changed through time and generation (Buriel 1987) and are sensitive to nativity, language, length of residence in the United States, and social context (Hurtado and Arce 1986). Labels include, nonexhaustively, "Mexican American," "Chicano," "Xicano," "La Raza," "Hispanic," "Hispano," "Latino," "Mexicano," "Chicano-Mexicano," and "Tejano" (Oboler 1995). I use the term "Mexican American" to refer to my respondents because that is the name that they overwhelmingly used in reference to themselves.[8]

The U.S. Census's changing policies about racial and ethnic categorization over time speaks to the socially constructed quality and overall tenuousness of racial categories. Racial classification of Hispanics[9] has historically varied greatly. As a prime example, the U.S. Census definitions of "Hispanic" have changed throughout history (Bean and Tienda 1987). In 1930, "Mexican" was categorized as a separate "race," a racial category that had never been used before and has not been used since. In 1940, a linguistic definition was used—"persons of Spanish mother tongue"—a term that misses those whose "mother tongue" is not Spanish yet whose heritage is Hispanic. In the next two decades, 1950 and 1960, Hispanic surnames were privileged ("persons of Spanish surname"). This practice eclipses those who are Hispanic but do not bear a Spanish surname, such as a person whose mother is Hispanic but who possesses a non-Hispanic father's surname or a woman who marries a non-Hispanic man and adopts his surname. In 1970, in response to Hispanic pressure for a Hispanic self-identifier, a subgroup was asked about their "origin" and then given several Hispanic-origin options on the questionnaire. For the 1940–1970 Censuses, Hispanics were "white" unless they appeared to be Indian or Negro. Missing the opportunity to hear how survey respondents racially/ethnically identified themselves, the Census enumerators— who were mostly white—determined who was white (the default, unmarked category), Indian, or Negro. For the most recent three Censuses—1980, 1990, 2000—"Hispanic" is an ethnic category, so Hispanics can be "of any race" they choose (Rodriguez 2000: 102).

Even the U.S. Census, a government agency, has been inconsistent regarding the classification of Hispanics. Over four decades, from 1940 to 1970, Hispanics were counted according to three different criteria: linguistic in 1940, surname in 1950 and 1960, and origin in 1970. Furthermore, there is clear indecision as to whether Hispanics constitute a separate race (as in 1930), are part of the "white" race (as in 1940 to 1970), or are best considered an ethnic group within an overarching racial category of their choice (1980 to 2000). As of the 2000 Census, four primary racial groups are designated: white, black (African American, Negro), American Indian or Alaska Native, Asian,[10] as well as "some other race." "Spanish/Hispanic/Latino"[11] is the only ethnicity that can be selected in addition to a racial category, making it possible for a Hispanic person to be of any race. This historic indecision, how-

TABLE 1.1

*Hispanic and Total Population, by State**

State	Percent Hispanic	Total Population (Million)	Hispanic Population (Million)	Mexican Origin** (as percent of Hispanic population)
New Mexico	44%	1.98	.87	52%
California	36%	36.76	13.21	83%
Texas	36%	24.33	8.59	85%
Arizona	30%	6.50	1.89	89%
Nevada	25%	2.60	0.64	78%
Florida	21%	18.33	3.75	16%
Colorado	20%	4.94	0.97	71%
New York	16%	19.49	3.15	13%
New Jersey	16%	8.68	1.38	14%
Illinois	15%	12.90	1.92	78%
Utah	12%	2.74	0.31	75%
Rhode Island	12%	1.05	0.12	6%
Connecticut	12%	3.50	0.41	10%
Oregon	10%	3.79	0.39	83%
Idaho	10%	1.52	0.15	89%

* Only states with 10 percent Hispanic population or greater are shown. Data represented in the "total population" column comes from Census 2008 population estimates. All other data come from the 2007 American Community Survey, as tabulated by the Pew Hispanic Center.

** These "Mexican origin" figures are disaggregated from the "Hispanic population" numbers. Data Sources: www.factfinder.census.gov and www.pewhispanic.org.

ever, reflects popular culture as laypeople and scholars alike are at odds over whether Hispanics are a race or an ethnic group. Some argue that the emerging racial order is "black" versus "nonblack," implicitly marking blacks as the racial outcasts (Warren and Twine 1997). Since Latinos are in an intermediate zone between blackness and whiteness (According to today's U.S. Census categories, Latinos can be racially black or white.), the question of whether Latino-ness is or is not "racialized" is especially interesting.

Today, Mexico is the leading country of origin for both legal and undocumented immigration into the United States. According to the Pew Hispanic

Center's tabulations of the 2007 American Community Survey,[12] of the forty-five million Hispanics residing in the United States in 2007, 64.3 percent (or over twenty-nine million people) were of Mexican origin.

In 2000, "California celebrated the millennium as the second mainland state (after New Mexico) to become a 'majority-minority' society" (Davis 2000: 2). In 2007, California's population was 36 percent people of Hispanic origin, compared to the national average of 15 percent. Of California's thirteen million Hispanic residents, 83 percent are of Mexican origin. Nativity status varies, with 59 percent of Hispanics in California being U.S. born and the remaining 41 percent being foreign born.

California is the leading state of residence of legal permanent residents (LPR) in 2004, estimated at 3.3 million or 28.5 percent of the total LPR population in the United States (Rytina 2006).[13] "Mexico was the leading country of birth of the LPR population in 2004 because legal immigration from Mexico far exceeds that of any other sending country, and Mexicans have historically been among the least likely LPRs to naturalize" (Rytina 2006: 4). Contemporary undocumented immigration to California from all sending nations is estimated at one to two hundred thousand per year, with Mexico as the leading country of origin. Further, immigration to California has increased five-fold, from 1.8 million in 1970 to 8.9 million in 2000 (PPIC 2002). Thus the question of whether and how Mexican immigrants will integrate into American society as a distinguishable racial group or as an assimilated "ethnic option" has become urgent politically, culturally, and sociologically (Portes and Rumbaut 1996; Portes and Rumbaut 2001; Rumbaut and Portes 2001; Skerry 1993).

As the demographics of the United States, and in particular the southwestern states, change due to the continuing influx of Mexican immigrants, concerns over American culture and belonging simmer. By understanding who these Mexican immigrants and their families (in this study, the U.S.-born children and grandchildren who are full-fledged U.S. citizens) are, we begin to better comprehend the complexities not just of immigration and assimilation but of American culture. With the exception of the Native American population, the United States has historically been a nation of immigrants,[14] a fact the nation tends to collectively forget. As nativist sentiments rise during periods of noticeable immigration from Asia and Latin America, it is probably best to recall that most of the "white American mainstream" was once part of an ethnic immigrant group, many of whom were considered "nonwhite" at time of entry and not immediately embraced for reasons of racial or cultural foreignness. Questions of the "assimilability" of current waves of Mexican immigrants can be answered in part by looking at the recent past and deciphering the racial incorporation trajectories of Mexican immigrants who arrived between 1922 and 1962 (Median year of arrival of my first-generation respondents was 1950.). Mexican immigrants who stayed in the United States and raised their families in the United States offer a window through which to view assimilation and racialization. As we will see, race is central to their experience, just as it is a chief concern in passionately contested immigration debates. "Recognizing that race and racism are centrally involved in determining which groups are accepted into America's mainstream . . . and which ones are considered its perennial and potential threats, is especially paramount for contextualizing the current immigration debate" (Davila 2008: 170).

Research Questions

This book speaks to the demographic shifts that the United States has undergone due to a continuing influx of Mexicans and their U.S.-born descendants.[15] The implications of minority populations or so-called majority minority states—that is, where the population of the state is predominantly minority—are often examined in terms of life outcomes such as educational level, job attainment, language acquisition, and income level. What is often overlooked is the larger question of identity: Who do these immigrants become after decades in the United States? Who are their children and grandchildren? How do the second and third generations identify racially? Especially given rising intermarriage rates with each generation (Bean and Stevens 2003; Murguia 1982; Schoen, Nelson, and Collins 1977), the fact that Mexicans most commonly intermarry with whites (Jiménez 2004), and the general tendency for upward mobility through the generations, third-generation Mexican Americans may be able easily to meld into mainstream America. What factors shape Mexican Americans' racial identity choices? More broadly, how are Mexican immigrants and the families they build in the United States incorporating into the U.S. racial and cultural landscapes?

Scholarly attention thus far has been devoted to both first- and second-generation immigrants in the arena of life chances, outcomes, and assimilation/acculturation patterns. Thus far there has been a failure to make within-family racial identity linkages among the first, second, and third generations in a way that highlights intergenerational communication. Quantitative studies unveil broad trends and yet this in-depth qualitative study sheds light on *how* and *why* people make choices, are influenced by their family's perspectives, and are limited or privileged by their sociostructural position. This study adds the complexity and nuance that lies behind outcomes such as diminished Spanish language ability over time, increased intermarriage with non-Hispanic whites over generations, and a transition from "Mexican"-oriented to "American" labels over time. Linking the fields of race, culture, and family, my findings speak to both racial identity formation processes and Mexican American assimilation into U.S. society. This study of Mexican American families refines assimilation theory by uncovering incorporation patterns that span three generations and by highlighting the key points at which this process is pushed forward, diverted, or reformulated.

The Study Participants

This book assesses the complex process of racial identity formation in three-generation Mexican American families. I located my research in California because it is the state with the largest Hispanic population. California has the second largest percentage of Hispanics (32.4 percent) of all fifty states, but with its 35.9 million total population, California has by far the largest Hispanic population in the United States (12.5 million) (2000 Census). I sought out three-generation Mexican American families, beginning with Mexican immigrants who are now grandparents. The first generation is comprised of Mexican nationals who immigrated to the United States, the second generation consists of the U.S.-born children of the Mexican immigrants, and the third generation includes the U.S.-born grandchildren of the Mexican immigrants. The respondents in my sample were difficult to locate due to the ethnicity, generation, family-relation, geography, and age[16] specificity of my criteria. This three-generation-family research design fills the noted empirical gap of taking generation-since-immigration seriously (Telles and Ortiz 2009: 3), distinguishing among immigrants, their children, and later generations. My research design allows for an analysis of the way Mexican Americans' experiences with race are influenced by both generation-since-immigration and the particular historical periods in which respondents live.

I conducted sixty-seven in-depth interviews in twenty-nine three-generation families roughly split between northern and southern California. The bases for my northern and southern California fieldsites were the San Francisco Bay Area and Santa Barbara/Los Angeles Counties, though the families I interviewed were dispersed around those locations within approximately a 100-mile radius. The northern- and southern-most interviews in the northern California fieldsite took place in Vacaville and Carmel, respectively, and the northern- and southern-most locations in the southern California field-site were Lompoc and San Diego (conducted by phone). All families had at least one generation residing near the primary fieldsites. I chose these two urban centers because, in migrations north from Mexico, the Santa Barbara/Los Angeles counties have historically been key destination areas. Los Angeles is the most populous city in California and is the second largest city in the United States (second only to New York City). Thirty-eight percent of Santa Barbara County's 403,000 population is Hispanic and forty-seven percent of Los Angeles County's 9.88 million population is Hispanic.[17] The largest urban region in northern California is the San Francisco Bay Area, which I included in order to capture those who settled further north of the U.S.-Mexico border. San Francisco, not including the suburbs and East Bay, is the fourth largest city in the state. I made contacts primarily in three counties in the Bay Area region: San Francisco, Alameda, and Contra Costa Counties, these three counties combined being home to over three million people. Fourteen percent of San Francisco County is Hispanic, 21 percent of Alameda County (home to Berkeley and Oakland), and 22 percent of Contra Costa County.[18]

The fact that I worked in two urban regions in California allows for more confidence in my findings. If I had concentrated my interview efforts in one region, readers might wonder if the responses were suffering from a particular regional effect. The single difference that emerged from families that originated from the two locales was that those who resided in southern California were more prone to be actively involved in the Chicano Movement and have positive associations with the term "Chicano." Recall, also, that since I interviewed three generations per family, family members did not necessarily reside in the same vicinity, blurring distinctions between the two fieldsites. Families I initially contacted in one of my two fieldsites sometimes had family members in other California cities whom I traveled to meet.[19] I focused on urban areas for the purpose of contacting middle-class families, who are more likely to live in urban regions than rural ones. A focus on the middle class is valuable because we would expect the more economically privileged to gain acceptance by the mainstream. Yet despite their upward mobility, many Mexican Americans still experience barriers to first-class, complete citizenship. Further, contrary to the predictions of assimilation theory, socioeconomic advancement does not determine a loss of Mexican cultural identification, showing that one can be both structurally assimilated and culturally connected to an ethnic heritage.

I employed a theoretical sampling strategy, followed by snowball sampling. I contacted families that fit my racial, ethnic, and generational profile by working through Hispanic chambers of commerce, Catholic churches, and high schools in various cities near my two selected fieldsites. I sent letters of inquiry and followed up with phone calls to the principals of twenty-one high schools, heads of thirteen Hispanic chambers of commerce, and twelve priests of Catholic churches. That initial outreach phase yielded four high schools, eight Hispanic chambers of commerce, and no churches as primary organizational contacts. I worked closely with the organizations that responded to my inquiry in order to attain interview respondents. Upon invitation, I had meetings with high school administrators, spoke with teachers, and made requests for study participants in classrooms. For those Hispanic chambers of commerce that responded favorably to my request to be introduced to three-generation Mexican American families, I met people by attending their local mixers and community events. I had telephone conversations to follow up my letter of introduction with priests of Catholic churches, yet these religious organizations did not produce any interviewees. Priests were protective of their parishioners, and the few referrals I was given did not generate successful contacts. I also used contacts at the University of California–Berkeley, asking colleagues (who were teaching assistants) to announce a description of my study and ask for volunteers to contact me. While Berkeley is renowned as a hotspot for political activity, the four (out of twenty-nine) families that were recruited from this connection represented a small portion of the overall sample and probably do not bias the findings. Once I made contacts in the various communities in both northern and southern California, I proceeded with a snowball sampling strategy, asking interviewees for referrals of others whom I might interview. Table 1.2 lists how I obtained introductions to families included in the study.

TABLE 1.2

*Sources of Respondent Pool**

	High Schools	Hispanic Chambers of Commerce	U.C. Berkeley	Catholic Church	Email Chain**
Initial Contact	5	10	3	-0-	-0-
Snowball (Referral)	4	2	1	-0-	4

* Numbers in each cell refer to an entire family (n=29) rather than an individual (n=67).
** Some people responded to email announcements that friends or colleagues forwarded to them; the origin of these forwarded emails was unclear.

TABLE 1.3

Respondent Summary Table (29 Families)

	N	Male; Female	Median Age	Age Range	Adolescence (age 10-20 yrs.)
Total*	67	34; 33	-	-	
Gen 1	8	2; 6	83	65-88	1927-1960
Gen 2	30	15; 14	59	38-73	1942-1987
Gen 3	29	17; 13	28	17-45	1970-2005

* Auxiliary Interviews (not counted in total N): Two spouses at second-generation level.

At least fifty-eight people declined to be interviewed because they did not fit the profile I was seeking or they did not wish to participate. The vast majority of the sixty-seven interviews were conducted in person and one on one. All respondents were either first generation (Mexican nationals who immigrated to the United States), second generation (the U.S.-born children of the Mexican immigrants), or third generation (the U.S.-born grandchildren of the Mexican immigrants).

As seen in table 1.3, the age range of the first generation is sixty-five to eighty-eight (median age is eighty-three); the age range of the second generation is thirty-eight to seventy-three (median age is fifty-nine); the age range of the third generation is seventeen to forty-five (median age is twenty-eight). Thirty-four interviewees were male, thirty-three were female, and the vast majority were middle class. I defined middle class through a number of different factors, including (1) if household income met or exceeded $57,000 (This is the average of all median household incomes for all eleven counties of California in which interviews were conducted.); [20] (2) if respondent possessed a college degree or above, or (3) if respondent held a managerial or professional occupation. If an individual possessed any of these qualities, I considered him/her middle-class. A few older-generation individuals fell into a lower income bracket and there were a couple of wealthy exceptions.[21] I oversampled middle- and upper-middle-class families, which affects the generalizability of my findings. As Feagin and Sikes (1994) found in a study of middle-class blacks, class status can act as a shield (though hardly a foolproof one) against discrimination. Middle-class status also provides resources with which a victim of perceived discrimination can seek redress through legal means, such as hiring lawyers and building court cases. Middle-class Mexican Americans may be perceived as sufficiently successful or assimilated so as not to be the target of race- and class-based xenophobic rancor. If money indeed "whitens," the personal and family narratives presented in this book, and the findings drawn from them, may very well be underrepresenting the harsher realities and more rigid boundaries met by working-class and lower-class Mexican-origin people (Bettie 2003; Dohan 2003; Murray 1997; Rumbaut and Portes 2001; Sánchez-Jankowski 1991; Telles and Ortiz 2009; Valdez 2006; Vigil 1988). It is very telling about the state of race relations in the contemporary United States that my middle-class Mexican American respondent pool reported racialization, discrimination, and contests of racial/ethnic authenticity. The arguments in this book will demonstrate that despite the middle-class bias in my sample, my Mexican American interviewees undergo racializing treatment despite their socioeconomic status, which suggests that the everyday reality for the less class-privileged is much harsher.[22]

Of the twenty-nine families I interviewed, all fit the first-, second-, and third-generation profile, although not all three generations in each family were available for interviews. Once I conducted an interview with the initial contact in a family, that person usually facilitated introductions to other family members. The eldest generation (first generation) was often the most difficult to access because they were often in frail health or reclusive and their offspring were vigilant about safeguarding their health and privacy. Due to the difficulty of gaining access to first-generation immigrant grandparents (due to their ill health, protective younger family members, or their death), I concentrated recruitment efforts on the second- and third-generation members.

The Interviews and Data Analysis

My method of in-depth interviewing aimed at eliciting focused life history narratives of my respondents. My interview schedule focused on issues of family and racial identity, but the open-ended questions provided enough latitude to prevent presumptions about the location of important identity work. I began each interview by asking for a narrative about the individual's biography, and then asked about his or her family's history. While the family is the center of gravity for my research, respondents also described other institutions and interactive spaces that affected their experiences of race. I conducted the majority of the interviews in English, and two in Spanish.[23] The semistructured interviews lasted from one to two and a half hours. I tape recorded and transcribed all of the interviews, allowing me to use verbatim quotations rather than mere recollections. I took fieldnotes immediately following interviews, attempting to capture intonation, speed of speech, body language, and my own rapport with and reaction to the respondent.

A life history narrative approach allowed respondents to select the instances and sites that were pivotal to their experience of race. I probed for "magnified moments" (Hochschild 2003) (either prideful or shameful) when interviewees' awareness of their racial self was intensified. Considering that "social life is itself storied" and that "'experience' is constituted through narratives" (Somers and Gibson 1994: 38), life history narratives are an appropriate way to try to gain insight into how people comprehend the social world and navigate their way through it.[24]

Chapter Layout

Part 1 of this book consists of three chapters that look at the three-generation families "vertically," that is, from first to second to third generation. These chapters follow the racial and cultural incorporation trajectories of two Mexican American three-generation families. Chapters 2 and 3 each highlight a family that typifies one of the two primary modes of incorporation ("thinned attachment" and "cultural maintenance") into the United States. Each chapter shows how, and by what mechanisms, the content of racial identity changes or maintains itself through family generations. Chapter 2 describes an upwardly mobile, "thinned attachment" family that has been assimilationist in its integration into the United States and has weakened its attachment to its Mexican heritage. Chapter 3 follows an upwardly mobile family that preserves its Mexican cultural knowledge, tradition, and pride. This chapter highlights the importance of historical moment in influencing racial identity and assimilation. Chapter 4 highlights the way marriage is a branching point that often leads either to the assimilation pathway of "thinned attachment" (in the case of exogamy) or "cultural maintenance" (in the case of endogamy). I argue that assimilation is occurring along a "bumpy-line" (Gans 1992a) partially due to marriage patterns. Assimilation is happening at different speeds and along different courses and, in contrast to chapters 2 and 3, I show how intergenerational family knowledge can flow "up" the family ladder, from younger to older generations.

Part 2 uses social themes and generations, rather than families, as its organizing principle. Chapter 5 uses a generational analysis to examine situations of discrimination, showing which sites and modes of discrimination are common across all three generations and which are unique to specific generations. I examine how perception of discrimination, coping mechanisms, and resistances are generationally patterned. In chapter 6, on education, I argue that schools teach—both formally and informally—that race is a vital feature of the way people are categorized and treated. I analyze how parents (mostly second-generation in my sample) refer to their own experiences in their natal families and in schools (especially with regard to gender and racial discrimination) as they craft parenting strategies to encourage their children's education. Chapter 7 considers variation in identity and assimilation among third-generation young adults, children of both intramarried and intermarried couples. Current literature concentrates on life outcomes of this generation whereas I analyze how these Americans conceive of their racial identity and investigate the social dimensions that bear on this process. The conclusion discusses how my findings revise assimilation theory and considers how the life stories presented in this book shed light on the meanings and complexities of immigration, race, and American culture.

Part I

Thinned Attachment

Heritage Is Slipping through Our Fingers

First Generation: Maria Montes

Sixty-five-year-old Maria Montes is a devout Catholic, bilingual in English and Spanish, and the matriarch of her family.[1] One of six siblings, Maria emigrated from Mexico when she was four years old with her mother and sister, while her brothers stayed in Mexico. Maria's mother chose to immigrate in part because one of her brothers and her eldest son were already in the United States and encouraged her to move. They crossed the Rio Grande River and took the train into the United States. Upon arrival, she worked in the fields picking potatoes and green beans and then at the packing house. Maria would join her mother in the fields when she was young or would be under the care of her older sister, a "second mother" caretaker for her. Twelve years later Maria's mother brought two of her other sons over to the United States. Maria weaves her immigration tale:

> Back then it wasn't as hard as it is [now]—immigration. You just come and go—so they just went across the river and came over here. . . . I remember I had that faraway vision of myself being on top of one of my uncle's shoulders. . . . So they just walked by. It wasn't deep. I was on my uncle's shoulders and we passed and were all excited, because we were coming to the United States! We were all excited. They make it sound so wonderful, you know? You're going to have a wonderful life over here. It turns out it's not that easy as people think that it is. So my mother had a hard life trying to rear us. [She was] being a mom and a dad because she never remarried after my dad died.

As with all first-generation respondents, Maria's family's emigration from Mexico was economically motivated. Once here in the United States, her family's hopes for life being automatically "wonderful"—as some returning migrants' stories had them believe—were dashed. They worked hard in order to gain a financial foothold in their new country:

> My mom really worked hard. And we worked pretty hard, too. Because every summer vacation we'd hit the fields. We'd pick walnuts, we'd pick grapes. . . . We were going to have to help her so that she could be able to maintain the household. Because it's very hard to feed so many people.

When she was a child, Maria's family was poor. Maria reveals a common conflation of race and class:

> We didn't have much. We used to use hand-me-down clothes because my mother could barely make it, you know? I used to wear her shoes to school. I used to be ridiculed. I used to stuff them [the shoes] with newspaper and I used to feel really embarrassed. Because I was a Mexican, they thought that we dressed that way [because] that's the Mexican way.

As others mistook class for race, Maria had to battle her lower-class status and her misunderstood Mexican identity. Due to an expanding economy, even with a lack of education Maria was able to secure a well-paying office manager job for a small manufacturing company. Now, in her older age, Maria has achieved a stable middle-class status, even owning more than one property in Santa Barbara.

Even while processes of adaptation to the United States compel some distance from her home country, Maria deliberately attempts to instill pride in her children and grandchildren about their Mexican heritage:

> We're Mexican and we have to be proud of the fact that we come from Mexico and never be ashamed that you are from Mexico. I said, "I know there are lots of people that look down on Mexicans, but you have to be proud. That's what we are." . . . I'm not ashamed to say that I'm a Mexican. . . . Like [my granddaughter] Jillian: she has white blood and Mexican blood, so she'll be proud of both of them.

Maria makes a conscious choice to instill racial pride in her offspring. Despite her intentions, however, structural surroundings that promote American ways of life pulled her family toward Americanization. The choices that Maria makes (and the lifestyles of the two generations that succeed her) combine with the local environment, creating hybrid identities and cultures. This interlacing of cultures through both conscious choice and natural accommodation shows that Mexican Americans are "mestizaje," a racial and cultural intermixture (Macias 2006), who live a "distinctive . . . third way of life . . . rather than simply an amalgamation of Mexican and American cultures" (Keefe and Padilla 1987: 7).

Maria's experience typifies a survival mode of parenting prevalent among poor first-generation immigrants (and to a lesser extent some second-generation individuals). A survival mode of parenting exists in those families where the parents' focus was on providing for their family economically rather than self-consciously supplying their children with a strong sense of culture. In this conception, culture can be seen as something of a luxury, although I do not mean to imply by "luxury" that culture is only found in locales of high culture (museums, literature, operas, theaters) as some scholars imply (Bourdieu 1984). Certainly, culture is found in food, traditions, religion, family knowledge, and storytelling, some of which exist to varying degrees in all families. Even given a notion of culture that encapsulates both elite and common (or highbrow and lowbrow) sources (Griswold 1987; Levine 1988), families struggling for economic survival had less free time to endow their children with this cultural backdrop.

A survival mode of parenting often leads to spotty transmission of cultural knowledge. Recalling that she was a single mother for a while after her divorce, Maria offers an image of the survival mode of parenting:

> It's hard to bring family up. . . . You don't have that much time to spend time with your kids and you're working, and you come home and you've got to do the cleaning and you've got to do the cooking. [When] . . . my kids were growing up I didn't spend much time with my kids. . . . Because to survive you have to have two families working . . . especially when you work at low jobs where you don't get that [well] paid. [A]t the beginning that's where we were—at the packing house, any place where we could . . . at least [get] money coming in to be able to support the family. . . . Back then we didn't get involved much with the kids.

As a working-class mother, Maria adopted a parenting style of "accomplishment of natural growth," wherein the children's time was largely self-organized and parents conceived of their duties in terms of providing food, clothing, shelter, safety, and love (Lareau 2002; Lareau 2003). Because of a constant struggle to provide basic necessities, Maria did not have spare time to endow her children with cultural lessons or an overabundance of family knowledge. Without conscientious instruction on Mexican culture and Spanish language, the structural environment of American institutions looms large and teaches children American cultural behaviors.

One element of Mexican culture that markedly declines through generations is Spanish language skills (Portes and Rumbaut 1996; Portes and Rumbaut 2001; Rumbaut and Portes 2001; Telles and Ortiz 2009). Spanish was overtly discouraged in education during the schooling years of the second generation. Further, immigrant parents tended to want their children to be poised to take advantage of opportunities in the United States, which would require English proficiency. Some families actively encouraged the wholesale adoption of English at school and at home; others attempted bilingualism; and still others maintained Spanish as the primary home language. While most families in my sample lost Spanish fluency by the third generation, the families range along the full spectrum of language preference and usage.[2] Maria offers a response to the question "how important is the Spanish language to you?" in a way typical of those who would have liked to preserve Spanish in theory but had difficulty doing so in practice:

> It is really important that we continue to . . . maintain our language. . . . I wish with all my heart that my kids would know it more and would pass it on to their kids. . . . Little by little they keep forgetting the Spanish . . . and they lose it. It's so sad, because it's so important that they have that language that comes with our heritage.

While Maria upholds the value of Spanish language, she did not enforce Spanish at home and her children therefore are not fluently bilingual.

Just as Spanish usage changes after generations in the United States, so too do traditional gender dynamics (Hondagneu-Sotelo 1994; Smith 2006b). Gender and gender dynamics also help drive thinned attachment. All of the first-generation women I spoke with complained that their husbands were patriarchal and domineering. The second generation also noted the subjugation of their mothers, their sisters, or themselves at the hands of overbearing patriarchal fathers. As Hondagneu-Sotelo notes, Mexican immigrant women benefit from the United States' more egalitarian gender role expectations because it affords them more voice and liberty. Hondagneu-Sotelo (1994: 98) writes, "After immigration, marriage patterns that once seemed set in stone may shift . . . and new living and working arrangements change the rules that organize daily life . . . [such as] more egalitarian gender relations in household divisions of labor, family decision-making processes, and women's spatial mobility." Most interviewees wished to dispense with *machismo* (a rigidly patriarchal gender ideology and set of behaviors).

Maria actively engaged the process of acculturation that leads to thinned attachment. She suffered under a controlling and abusive first husband and consequently discouraged her granddaughter, Jillian, from marrying a Mexican.[3] While she issued this advice in the form of a joke, her granddaughter got the message. I asked Maria, "As you advise your children—and now your grandchildren—in choosing someone to marry, how important is it to you that they marry someone who is of Mexican background?" She replied,

> Well, I don't really think that it's important that they have to be Mexican. In fact, I tease Jillian and I tell her, "Keep away the Mexicans! Macho guys!" . . . My two daughters have married white [men]. I think that they should look for someone that they're compatible with . . . that they love each other. And whether they're American, Mexican, Chinese—whatever. . . . Steer clear of the Mexicans! [Laughs]

I asked her, "And that's because you don't like the macho guys?" She responded,

> I just teased her on that. There are lots of nice Mexican men, too, that make wonderful husbands. Wonderful. But unfortunately, in our culture it tends to be more where the men want to have the power over the women. And they could go to extremes, you know? They're boss. . . . That's the way it is with Mexican men. But they're changing. I think that they're changing. The new generation is not coming out as bad as . . . when we were young.
>
> The men, they always have the pants and they're the ones that have to boss. And the woman just has to be submissive and do whatever they want. [T]hat's why I tell her to keep away from the Mexican macho guys! Macho guys, I tell her! [Laughs.]

In this discussion of marital advice for her female children and grandchildren (she did not comment on advice she gave her sons), Maria oscillates between unprejudiced principles of equality and her visceral reaction against "Mexican macho guys" that is due to her own aggrieved experience. In her scholarship on love, Swidler (2001) argues that multiple framings of a single issue can coexist side by side and be called upon at any time. Swidler uncovers two common tropes of love that are employed by married couples as they explain their love story and ensuing marital life. The "mythic love" narrative serves to uphold and romanticize the institution of marriage in contemporary America. Alternatively, "prosaic realism" is a framing that people employ to discuss the day-to-day life of a marriage, a love that is often ambiguous, gradual, uncertain, and banal (Swidler 2001). Often the same individual will use multiple framings at different times to explain his or her behavior, feelings, or life in general. Maria exemplifies the way people can employ different narrative framings in quick succession. Maria uses the trope of "mythic love" that forefronts compatibility, love, and equality with no regard for race. She also issues admonitions against Mexican men that are in direct reaction to her own unhappy marriage with a Mexican man. In this way, culture writ large and personal experience (culture writ small) organize Maria's lines of thought and action as she considers the welfare of her offspring.

Despite her stereotypical image of Mexican masculinity, Maria points out that gender dynamics are changing for the better with the new generation of young men. She cites her son and her grandson as examples of Mexican men who would be good, helpful partners. Maria's observations are in concert with Arlie Hochschild's (1989) work on family life and work-life balance after the feminist revolution of the 1970s and women's entrance into the labor force. Hochschild outlines the family archetypes of "traditional," "transitional," and "egalitarian," family forms that range in gender-equality operating norms (Hochschild 1989; Hochschild 1997). Maria notes change she has seen as generations are each reared in a historical context different from the one prior:

> Look at my grandson. Even my son . . . he's not the macho guy, you know? . . . There's a lot of young boys now . . . that are really nice. Heaven forbid that a man helps his wife washing the dishes or helping with the kids, way back when. . . . And nowadays you see it a lot, where the husband helps the wife. They clean the house. They cook for them. They help them a lot. I mean, you're equal. The wife is going to work—why shouldn't the husband help around the house?

Within Maria's own three-generation family, she sees gender and marital dynamics change from traditional to egalitarian. Maria is pleased by this revision of gender roles. When I asked what about her culture she would like to see changed, she harkened back to tearing down traditionalism and *machismo* and replacing it with gender equality: "Yeah, you wear pants, but I wear pants, too. So we're equal. . . . Let's bring our children [up] to realize that man and woman, it's nice to help each other out. These are women's chores? There's no difference between women's chores and men's chores—you know? We're a family. We're here to help each other." While Maria is unsettled by the slow detachment from Mexican culture her family is undergoing, she is also simultaneously pleased.

While Maria is saddened to see some of that connection to her homeland slipping, she is gladdened to perceive a shift in the macho male ways that had oppressed her. While Maria instills in her progeny knowledge of their Mexican heritage, her references to Mexican culture often switch into "distilled" (Kibria 2002) forms or universal principles. When I asked "what about your culture or your experience do you want to see transmitted to your children and grandchildren?" Maria began by shielding them from prejudice, saying they should "never be embarrassed of what [they] are." She then moved to platitudes about success and independence: "Never give up. Dreams are so important. I mean—what is life if you don't have dreams? . . . Never give up. There is always a tomorrow. And as long as there is a tomorrow, there is hope." Maria has instructed her offspring in life lessons as well as some Mexican culture. Rather than dwell on preserving particular Mexican traits, in part due to her survival mode of parenting, Maria reared her children to combine both Mexican and American cultural features.

While Maria was complicit in her family's thinned attachment trajectory in that she deemphasized Spanish language and traditions, these linguistic and cultural accommodations were necessary for her family's upward mobility in the United States. She did not shirk her Mexican culture for lack of emotional commitment but rather loosened those ties for pragmatic reasons. To the limited extent that Maria is trying to re-infuse her family with Mexican culture, this could very well be a response to her observation of her offsprings' thinning attachment.[4] As we will see as I profile the next two generations, Maria's family develops a thinned attachment to Mexican culture. This is due to increased generational distance from Mexico, egalitarian gender ideologies, intermarriage at the second generation, a religious conversion, and heterogeneous peer networks. Thus, the Montes/Rosenberg family's thinned attachment occurs as a result of conscious choices of accommodation as well as the sway of structural surroundings.

Second Generation: Tamara (Montes) Rosenberg

Tamara Montes, whose married surname is Rosenberg, is the daughter of two Mexican immigrants and was born in California. Despite her American citizenship, Tamara says she describes herself as "'Mexican' just because my parents were from Mexico." But, she adds, "I'm not trying to make a political statement either way." Claiming a hybridized racial space, Tamara remarks,

"I don't know that I identify with being an American or Mexican." While American by birthright, Tamara experiences racialization, which marks her as a particular brand of American: "Mexican" or "Latina." Undergoing "racialized assimilation" that does not allow her to be simply "American" (Flores-Gonzales 1999; Golash-Boza 2006; Golash-Boza and Darity 2008), Tamara learned her first lesson in racism and segregation when she was in elementary school. Realizing that she was never invited over to her Chinese best friend's house, she asked her friend about this and her friend reported, "Well, my mom doesn't want me to hang out with Mexicans because Mexicans are dumb." Even today, "People will talk to me in the grocery store . . . in Spanish. And I'll think to myself, 'God, do I look Mexican?' Of course I look Mexican!" While it is problematic to reduce "looking Mexican" to some stereotypical image because that image belies the diversity of physical appearance of Mexicans (Macias 2006; Oboler 1995), an issue that will be explored in chapter 7, Tamara knows that being perceived one way or another influences the way people interact with her. Indeed, racial categorization imposed by others (often based on phenotype) pushes people to claim that racial ascription (Waters 1990). There is a "*complex interplay* among the different aspects of an individual's ethnic identification," which is in part what leads people to change ethnic self-titles throughout their life cycle (Waters 1990: 23, emphasis added).

Tamara's childhood years were lean: "I don't think I ever realized that we were poor. I remember . . . having hot chocolate and bread for dinner. [I didn't] realize that it was because we didn't have food." Tamara saw her parents work really hard and eventually achieve a stable occupation and a middle-class status. She credits belief in the American Dream—a central American ideology (Hochschild 1995)—for her parents' optimism:

My parents were really hard working. And I think that's the underlying lesson—that if you work hard—the American Dream—you get ahead. The typical immigrant dream. And my parents lived that. . . . My dad ended up owning a little mom and pop grocery store. . . . My mom [was] able to purchase her own house. Not only one—she owns a few properties. And ran a business. Raised her kids. So just work ethic.

Her parents' work ethic and an expanding structure of opportunity were the keys to their ability to live the American Dream. Just as the ideology of the American Dream runs strong in contemporary American discourse and fuels immigrants' optimism (Kao and Tienda 1995), so too does the ideology of American individualism (Bellah 1986) and the philosophy of "pulling oneself up by one's bootstraps." In the Montes family, the American Dream invigorated their work ethic. This work ethic, in turn, became the tool that helped them achieve their aspirations. While the philosophies of the American Dream and American individualism work in tandem in this instance to reinforce one another, the down side of this individualistic logic is the potential to blame those who do not succeed by claiming they lack personal qualities that lead to success.[5] These same individualistic philosophies, however, if applied to a less upwardly mobile family, could be used to obscure structural barriers that impede individual agency.[6]

As will be explored in chapter 6, education has a tremendous influence on the way students perceive their racial/ethnic background. Many second-generation Mexican Americans, like Tamara, grew up in a Spanish-speaking home and learned English in school. English language acquisition is part of being educated in the United States and is a critical part of the acculturation process, some of which occurs inevitably as families set up long-term residence in the United States. Tamara recalls the difficulty of acquiring a new language, especially when scoring badly on tests made her question her intelligence and deflated her self-esteem: "I can still remember the vision of being in first grade and sitting at this table and putting my head down and thinking, 'God, I must be so stupid because I have D's and F's.' I think it was because I didn't know English. So of course what would I get?" Tamara learned English as her mother reinforced its usage at home.

Tamara was the only female of her generation in her extended family to go to college. Higher education was not expected in her family. Her parents had less than junior high school educations, thus lacking the knowledge and resources to prepare her for college. Because her parents were unfamiliar with the fact that a large percentage of college students accept scholarships and loans in order to attend colleges and universities, her father felt that this was a blow to their family pride. Tamara explains,

> Going to college . . . wasn't something that you did. I mean, my dad gave me a really tough time when I went away, because he felt like . . . scholarships [meant] that I was getting welfare. And that was a real blow to his being able to provide for his family. . . . I remember the conversation: "That's really bad that you're taking . . . welfare." . . . It's like, "Dad, it's not welfare. It's a scholarship because of your grades." . . . I didn't talk to my dad for a year because he felt like I had really blemished the family name by accepting money from these organizations.

Tamara's high school counselor provided her with some of the cultural capital that her natal family could not: "I was incredibly lucky, because I had never thought of going to college and it wasn't a vocabulary that was in our family. It was the high school counselor who called me [and advised me]."

Tamara's peer networks changed dramatically upon matriculation to college. Her family and educational cultures continued to clash once she began college at the University of California at Davis. Once in college, Tamara comprehended for the first time the racial, economic, and cultural disparities between UC-Davis, with its large contingent of "cowboys and rednecks," and her family and community back home. In Santa Barbara, her family was incredibly "tight-knit." They were incessantly attending "weddings, baptisms, and confirmations." In Tamara's words about her youth in Santa Barbara, "In high school . . . everyone that I hung out with was Mexican. So there wasn't any reason to have any political connections or try to say, 'I am Mexican.' I mean, you just hung out with people. I don't think I ever realized that I was only surrounded by Mexican people."

In contrast, at UC–Davis in the mid-1970s Tamara, as a Mexican American, was a numerical minority. Her changed social context in college exposed her to negative stereotypes. Some college peers had misconceptions about Tamara's personality based on her outward performance of self and femininity (her hairstyle and make-up). Tamara recalls a conversation in college:

> "Your hair was ratted. And we thought you had razor blades in your hair or something." The stereotype that they have of me was that I was . . . prone to being aggressive or violent. And, "You are ironing your jeans? My God—no one irons their jeans. . . ." And I'm thinking, "Well, everyone I know does!"

Tamara's appearance that coded her as an "insider" in her home town did not translate well to UC–Davis, where she was interpreted as an "outsider," marginal to the mainstream student culture.

Tamara discovered that she lacked middle-class cultural knowledge in the college classroom as well. While her family provided her many other sources of knowledge, their lack of money and modes of cultural consumption left a gap in her "cultural toolkit" (Swidler 1986) that only became noticeable upon matriculation to college:

> I recognized what an incredibly different background that I had, in terms of not having. . . some things that an Anglo family who has money [has

access to]—museums, those kinds of things. . . . There were certain expectations that when you came into UC–Davis you would have certain experience that I didn't have. So you just had to kind of make up for that.

In response to this race- and class-based discomfiture, Tamara became active in MEChA, a Mexican American student group committed to visibility and social activism. Only in college did Tamara feel the need to assert a Chicana identity because it was threatened by her lack of community:

> At UC–Davis [there were] the cowboys and the rednecks. And then there's not that many Mexicans. They had a particular view of who you were, what you did. . . . It was really lonely because you would stand out. I think that was the first place where I ever saw racism. I think one Cinco de Mayo we had some kind of event in the plaza. And we had names scratched on the booth that were just kind of nasty. Like, "Go home, beaners."

Tamara's involvement in MEChA and claim to a Chicana identity in college thickens rather than thins her attachment to Mexican culture. This was a very intentional response to a situation in which she felt community was lacking and racial tensions ran high. She chose to find community through a Chicano student organization rather than a preprofessional organization or sorority chiefly because it was along the racial/ethnic axis of her social identity that she felt marginalized and maligned. Interestingly, she drew attention to her Chicana identity rather than obfuscated it. Within my entire sample of second-generation interviewees, responses to racial slights and exclusions were mixed. Tamara's response represents the substantial portion of interviewees who met racial animosity head on (for example, some interviewees became active in the Chicano Movement) while others lied to obscure their racial heritage and tried to pass as a white ethnic. Unlike Marcus Lopez, whom we will meet in the next chapter, Tamara only became involved with a race-based group during her college years. Marcus and others, by contrast, held fiercely to their race-based activism, considering it more of a long-term calling as opposed to a shorter-term reaction to a situation of power imbalance. This variability of responses to racial inequality demonstrates that the process of assimilation is not uniform but variable and "bumpy" rather than linear.

Like education, religion is an institution that was powerfully influential in Tamara's racial/ethnic identity development. Tamara was raised Catholic and went to Catholic school for nine years as a child. As an adult, she grew distant from the religion of her youth and is now nonpracticing and married to a Jewish man. Nonetheless, upon considering her natal family life she found that her racial heritage and Catholicism were woven together: "I think at the root of all of it [Mexican culture] was the church. A lot of activities revolved around something happening at the church—whether it was the wedding, whether it was the baptism." The church was a centerpiece of her religious, racial/ethnic, and family life. Tamara's commitment to the Catholic church began to wane when she was twelve years old, when her parents divorced. The Catholic church prohibited divorce, threatening excommunication, and Tamara's mother took that command seriously and stopped going to church at the time of her divorce. Maria "paid a huge price in terms of being ostracized. Her brothers and sisters wouldn't help her because it wasn't the Catholic thing to do." Maria's "excommunication" from the Catholic church and banishment from her family of origin fueled Tamara's cynicism and eventually toppled her Catholic faith. (The family used the term "excommunication," yet it is unclear whether or not she was technically banned from the church.) Tamara traces the major moments of her questioning:

> The Bible says you can't get divorced. And [my mom] really believed that. . . . How can you believe in a religion that thinks you're going to go to hell? There has got to be something wrong with this! . . . When my parents got divorced it totally upset the apple cart. . . . All of a sudden [my mom] couldn't be Catholic because she was excommunicated. And she was going to hell. . . . I always challenged [Catholicism] anyway. So . . . it was easy to say, "Well, there is obviously something wrong with this."

Her parents' divorce marked Tamara's departure from the Catholic church.

A religious conversion from Catholicism to Judaism moved Tamara, Gregory, and their three children along the thinned attachment pathway. Tamara felt an ideological incompatibility with Catholicism, in particular its mandate against divorce and church members' withdrawal of support of her mother during her divorce. She therefore supported the family's embrace of Judaism, her husband's religion. Even though Catholicism was a big part of the way Tamara understood her Mexican identity when she was younger, the elements that comprise her Mexican identity have changed with time. In contrast to her youth, when being Mexican and Catholic went hand in hand, by age forty-seven, she and her children are Mexican American and Jewish.

Between Tamara's youthful observations and her mother's more conscious lesson-giving instruction, Tamara has two different models of the way a woman can wield power. Along with her own "personally acquired memories" (from first-hand experience), Tamara inherited "appropriated memories" from her mother's experience (Mannheim 1936), both of which shaped her racialized and gendered identity. Experiencing Mexican *machismo* in her relationships with her father and a college boyfriend, she learned that domineering male authority impeded her freedom and sense of self. She admits that there was a time when she thought "there would be no way I would ever marry someone who wasn't Mexican," that in so doing she "would be a sellout. . . . And yet here I've done that." She struggled with what loyalty to her Mexican heritage meant, especially if that loyalty was contradictory to loyalty to her gender. Tamara felt that marrying a non-Mexican man allowed her to escape narrow expectations of her as a woman and a wife. She was engaged to a Mexican national in college and found his understanding of womanhood, manhood, and their potential marital life together to be discordant with hers. With her husband Gregory she sidestepped those racialized understandings of gender: "I didn't feel like I was getting squeezed or being told that I couldn't do this, or expectations of what a Mexican woman was supposed to do. It wasn't there at all." Plus, Gregory being an Anglo "reborn hippie from the '60s" meant that he had already acquired the liberal thinking that exploded the gender boundaries she found so constricting.

Tamara analyzes the sense of comfort her life with Gregory provides where her gender identity is concerned:

> [Gregory] didn't . . . have the same background or the same traditional values. But I didn't see that as a negative. In my family those traditional values I think really held women back. And so Gregory was just this avenue, this vehicle to not have to deal with any of that. And Gregory was really accepting and very loving. And always encouraged. . . . Whereas . . . [before] I was engaged to someone who was from Mexico . . . and we were constantly having these discussions about what the roles would be, and how threatened he felt because I was doing certain things. Or what the expectations were. That was a constant dialogue, where it wasn't with Gregory. . . . I think on some levels the stereotypes [that] the Catholic church and Mexican men had . . . were negative values for me. . . . It gets back to my mom saying, "You have to learn to take care of yourself." That was such a clear message.

Taking her mother's counsel to heart, Tamara interpreted the refrain "taking care of yourself" to mean out-marriage for her. While certainly not all Mexican-origin men exhibit the macho version of masculinity Tamara found so threatening, she felt she could not take that gamble. Similarly, not all U.S.-born non-Hispanic white men are gender egalitarian, as Tamara's reactionary logic suggests, but she nonetheless succeeded in finding a similarly minded mate in Gregory.

Guarding the fate of her gendered self by marrying a non-Mexican cost Tamara some friendships and raised questions about her racial allegiance. For many, exogamy spells a lack of commitment to one's heritage and an inevitable watering down of cultural traits. Tamara suffered some backlash from her friends: "I think I probably lost some friends who would never have considered marrying an Anglo. Because you kind of sold out because you did. And I did the same thing—if I'd see someone with some Anglo it was, 'Uh-oh, they sold out.' Oh, wait a second, I did too!" Tamara ruptured expectations—both familial and community—by marrying a Jew rather than a Mexican. But she was conscientious about her decision, aware that gaining some distance from Mexican culture did not mean a wholesale rejection of Mexican culture. Instead, she opted to actively pick and choose the elements of her background to retain and to discard. She reasoned that distance from her Mexican culture was not deplorable if it facilitated a healthy sense of gender, feminism, and marriage for her.

Tamara learned lessons not just about race and ethnicity from her mother but about gender as well. Self-reliance, perseverance, and a strong work ethic were key lessons that Maria spoke of trying to instill in her children, and by Tamara's account, she heard that instruction loud and clear:

> I think my mom's biggest lesson was just an incredibly strong work ethic. And, as a woman, you had to be able to take care of yourself. . . . I couldn't count on anyone else but myself to take care of . . . myself and my family. . . . A woman had to be able to take care of herself and not depend on a man to do that. And . . . if you really worked hard you could achieve whatever goal you wanted to.

The life lessons Maria endowed her children were also lessons about gender. Maria was ever mindful of telling her daughter not to be oppressed by male authority.

Like her mother, in selecting Mexican cultural elements to pass on to her children, Tamara became a participant in the thinned attachment process. She filtered out undesirable elements and preserved valuable ones. In so doing she actively enacted "distilled ethnicity." According to Nazli Kibria (2002: 160), "distilled ethnicity" occurs when "ethnic culture and identity are pared of nonessential components down to their core essence." Parents teach children only the "basic values" about the family's race/ethnicity. This reflects a high degree of acculturation to middle-class America because that is all parents can or want to pass on to their children.

The value of family was passed on intergenerationally as part of this distilled ethnicity. Referring to her natal family, Tamara remarked, "what I learned from being Mexican is just a sense of family. That you're there for your family no matter what." She has taught her children this lesson, noting that geographic proximity to her mother (they live twenty minutes away by car) made possible a close relationship among all three generations: "Since they were born the kids have always gone to their Grandma's house at least once a week. And when they were smaller—three and four times a week. And so they've learned that sense of family." Family events involved getting together for meals: "We used to go to my mom's twice a week for dinner. And it would be my sisters and my brother, and all of their families, and some of my cousins . . . and so it would be twenty, twenty-five people every Thursday." After contemplating what she hopes her children will hold on to, she declared family as "always there, no matter what . . . [it is a] safety net." Allowing for sibling differences but hoping for family unity, Tamara pronounced in an imagined conversation with her children, "You might not appreciate each other's perspective sometimes. But . . . in the end you are the only ones that will be the copresidents of your siblings' fan club!" By focusing on family bonding, Tamara is maintaining one symbolic attachment to her Mexican heritage. However nearly universal the tenet of family and family values might be, Tamara endows that value with Mexican meaning.

Each generation confronts different struggles regarding their racial background. Tamara consciously bucked marital and religious expectations, yet she embraced other elements such as "Thursday dinners" with her family and Mexican food. Tamara recognizes that her half-Mexican, half-Jewish children are presented with a different host of identity concerns than she confronted. While she and her husband have afforded them a class-privileged lifestyle that includes the expectation of college education, this trend of upward mobility and assimilation has come with the consequence of a racial "identity crisis," to use their children's own words. Tamara considers how a third-generation Mexican American identity can be confounding:

[Racial/ethnic identity struggle] wasn't something I ever had to deal with. I was just Mexican and that was it. And [my children] really struggle with what it means. And as they go through their journeys they'll decide how important it is and where they want to be. I'm hoping that they embrace both and that they realize they have an incredible history.

Tamara spoke of Andrew as "embracing both" the Jewish and Mexican cultures, explaining that Andrew was the one who pushed the family to connect with his father's Jewish faith. Immediately after that assertion she claimed, "Andrew loves being Mexican. He has all kinds of blankets and little tchatchkes that he keeps because that's who he is." Unintentionally illustrating the cultural mix in her home, Tamara uses the Yiddish colloquialism "tchatchke" to refer to her son's Mexican trinkets.

Third Generation: Jillian Rosenberg

Jillian, a twenty-year-old student at Yale University, is the eldest daughter of the Rosenberg family. She is Mexican (from her mother's side) and Jewish (from her father's side). Jillian has medium-brown hair, light skin, and dark hazel eyes with a bit of an almond shape to them. She is short, petite, and very well spoken. She says people variously think she is "all Mexican, all white, or something else." Some people approach her speaking Spanish while others are shocked when she reveals she is part Mexican.

By measures of structural and behavioral assimilation, Jillian is integrated into the U.S. mainstream. Several factors contributed to her assimilation: her parents' upward economic mobility and firmly middle-class standing, her educational achievement and trajectory, her English language fluency (and loss of Spanish fluency), and her adoption of middle-class values (work ethic, career aspirations) as well as the bicultural norms practiced by her family.

Jillian's expression of thinned attachment is not an inevitable consequence of her structural assimilation, as chapter 3 will make clear. Jillian's relaxed relationship to her Mexican heritage is due to both familial and institutional forces. Due to her family structure and orientation, class privilege, educational segregation, "appropriated memories" from her mother and grandmother, and college experience, she is living out a race-sensitive but not Mexican-centric life. Jillian expresses a "thinned attachment" to her Mexican background in that it is not central to her life. She does not assert and practice her Mexican-origin identity, nor does she find it instrumental in facilitating or limiting her opportunities. Reasons for her thinned attachment include being raised in a bicultural home with an assimilationist orientation, embeddedness in American institutions, being non-Catholic, and bearing a last name that does not identify her as Latina (Murguia and Forman 2003).

Her mother's exogamy (which bestowed upon her the white ethnic surname "Rosenberg") and her grandmother's admonitions against marrying a Mexican man have conditioned Jillian with a largely assimilationist mindset. A hallmark of "thinned attachment" is the fact that she is aware of her cultural background yet not bound to it (by herself or others).

In grammar school, Jillian rejected her Mexican heritage, even typecasting other Mexicans (often lower-class Mexicans) according to mainstream negative stereotypes. She reasoned that her allegiance to whiteness was due in part to the fact that, as the "norm," she found it "unproblematic." Her Jewish ancestry is the "taken-for-granted" or "background" or "norm" of her identity, as well as the invisible benchmark for society. Jillian's tacit rationale for obscuring her Mexican identity and highlighting her white identity probably involves being able to garner certain benefits of white privilege, such as uncontested enrollment in high school in Gifted and Talented Education (GATE) classes that were racially segregated. She observes, "growing up I was trying to navigate between two worlds but more trying to keep myself out of one of them as much as possible. It's gotten more complicated in college." Her mixed heritage is alternately a source of flexibility as well a wellspring of "identity crises."

In a social and educational context of whiteness, Jillian "naturally" assumed that she was white. Jillian explained the logic by which she deduced she was white in elementary school:

> In all of the GATE [Gifted and Talented Education] classes, everyone was white. There is a really clear-cut distinction between the white people and the Mexican people. If you are a Mexican kid, you were in ESL [English as a Second Language] classes or not very intelligent. . . . It was like, "Are you Mexican or are you white?" I look a lot more white than I look Mexican . . . and I was in the GATE classes with all the white kids, so I was white.

Complaining about the "unbelievably distinct boundary between white and Mexican kids," Jillian found no room for her mixed-race heritage. Due to her school achievement, tracking placement, class privilege, and peer group, she identified as white. Circulating in predominantly middle-class white circles, Jillian was exposed to and adopted some stereotypes of Mexicans. Jillian identified as white in elementary school, yet it is unclear whether she did so because she did not perceive stereotypes of Mexicans as applying to her or because she *did* make that connection and opted for whiteness in order to escape being typecast. For instance, Jillian reflected, "I had really awful stereotypes of what Mexican people were like too, like all Mexican people are gardeners and maids." She laughed uncomfortably as she admitted, "[there was always] the half of me that I had to hide. I was always so embarrassed of that; I was soiled in some way because I had Mexican blood in me."

The low social value that society places on Latinos influenced Jillian's retreat from her Mexican heritage. Food, as a cultural signal of her ethnicity, came to symbolize shame and substandard performance for her. In answer to my question about when she first understood the concept of race or ethnicity, she described a situation that occurred when she was eight or nine years old:

> I played piano for my whole life. We used to have performances and competitions. For one of them you had to memorize five to ten pieces and you'd play them in front of a judge and . . . you'd get a scorecard back. . . . I was performing my pieces in front of a judge and I just really freaked out and messed up all of my songs and got really off track. The guy was trying to calm me down and talk to me and he said, "Did you have anything to eat today for lunch?" I was like, "Yeah, I did." He said, "Well, what did you eat?" I had had a burrito. [Laughs.] And for some reason I was deathly ashamed to say that. But I couldn't think of anything else to say, so I was like, "I had a burrito" [meek, quiet]. "A burrito?" [curious, surprised] I'm sure he wasn't even talking about race or anything, but for some reason that really stuck in my head. "Oh my God, what if he thinks I'm a gross little Mexican kid who can't get her songs right?" . . . I was really embarrassed about being Mexican at that time and I felt there was a big distinction between me and him, this white guy. I was so ashamed of my little burrito.

Food can flag ethnic difference. Just as it can fortify ethnic identity and rejuvenate family bonds (Di Leonardo 1984; Macias 2006), so too can it draw boundaries between mainstream and periphery. Despite being so young, Jillian understood that Mexicans and their customary burritos carried social signals with which she did not want to be associated. Here Jillian plausibly suffered from "stereotype threat" (Spencer, Steele, and Quinn 1999; Steele and Aronson 1995; Steele, Spencer, and Aronson 2002), where one feels one is at risk of confirming a negative stereotype about one's group, the stress of which leads to underperformance. During this time in elementary school she was in advanced classes with white peers and she felt pressure (and perhaps desire) to be white. She was struggling with social and institutional messages about the extant racial and ethnic hierarchy. Because classes were segregated by race (she reported she was one of five Mexicans in all of the GATE classes), in order to remain in her GATE class without being suspect, she felt pressure to deny her Mexican heritage in favor of her white ancestry. In these years she was struggling with anxiety about how to reconcile two distinct ethnic backgrounds into one complete identity. By admitting that her lunch was inconsistent with mainstream food culture, she increased her social distance from whiteness, and that only amplified her sense of frustration and inferiority.

In her youth, Jillian distanced herself from her Mexican background due to multiple forces: educational segregation (to be in GATE classes she must be white), society's low estimation of the Mexican population (making her burrito shameful and her whiteness unproblematic), her grandmother's and mother's oppression within patriarchy and Catholicism, and a racially politicized college experience that uncomfortably highlighted her mixed heritage. Jillian experienced her whiteness as unproblematic because it is accepted as the norm in U.S. society. Whiteness is a location of structural advantage (racial privilege) within a hierarchy; it is also a set of cultural practices that are typically unmarked and unnamed (Frankenberg 1993: 1). While whiteness usually constitutes an invisible norm, it is in fact a salient organizing characteristic of white people's lives. Given the benefit of racial privilege, those of mixed heritage may be tempted to side with their whiteness because, as Jillian said, it is "unproblematic." Furthermore, there is external pressure for one's attitudes, behavior, and racial identification to match one's physical appearance and name. As Julie Bettie (2003: 85) found in her work with Mexican American and white high school girls in California, "one's race performance was *expected* to correspond to a perceived racial 'essence,' marked by color and surname." For light-skinned, brown-haired Jillian *Rosenberg*, this conceptualization of race performance expects her to "pass" for non-Hispanic white (Jewish).

Because of Jillian's "wanting to pass for white" in grade school and being perceived as such because of her physical looks and other signals such as class status, demeanor, and educational attainment, it is no wonder that she feels she is "part of dominant or mainstream U.S. culture." As corroborating testimony, note that she does not feel like she has encountered discrimination. A sign of her assimilation, she "thinks she passes for being white pretty well" and therefore avoided the blunt end of discrimination. Yet, even her "passing" is inconsistent because she feels "hyper sensitive to [race], like [she] expect[s] to be discriminated against."

Familiar with her family history, Jillian was aware that patriarchy and strict Catholicism did not serve her grandmother and mother well. The two women above Jillian in the family line experienced gender oppression as a result of their cultural and religious ties. Therefore, they raised Jillian with far looser cultural and religious bonds, resulting in her thinned attachment to Mexican culture and her stern opinion that she would not marry a Mexican man or practice Catholicism.[7] Recall Maria's divorce from her physically and verbally abusive alcoholic husband and Tamara's need to escape patriarchal expectations of gender by marrying a Jew and attending college. Jillian recalled family stories about her grandmother's life:

> She was the first person in her entire family to get a divorce and her entire family did not speak to her . . . some for six years, some for ten years. No one would go near her. She didn't have any help. She was raising three kids on her own. Even in the neighborhood . . . rumors were spread about her. . . . People would be telling [my mom] to her face that they were all going to hell [because my] mom got divorced. It must have taken so much strength to be able to do that—she is a really, really religious person, very Catholic.

Negative associations of Mexican culture and Catholicism as detrimental to an egalitarian gender identity were passed down three generations in the female family line.

Jillian's first-hand experiences only advanced the thinned attachment to Mexican culture with which she was reared. Jillian's insider knowledge regarding the gender restrictions that her forebears claimed Mexican culture imposes on women vis-à-vis power dynamics in marriages, circumscribed educational opportunities, and a gendered division of labor pushed her even further from Mexican traditionalism. Noting that both her grandmother and mother are somewhat "black sheep" in their own natal families because of behavior that defied gender norms (divorce and out-marriage), Jillian described her traditional Mexican kin:

> I think, actually, that a lot of the misconceptions I grew up having about Mexicans were from [my family] because they are a very, very traditional family. My mother would kill me if she heard me say this. The women stay around and cook and have no jobs and the men go out and come back and kick their feet up and demand beer and food. No one goes to college and you should be married and having kids at my age [authoritative tone]. It's really, really, really traditional.

She described her family's reaction to her mother refusing to abide by gender expectations of marrying a Mexican and remaining in the domestic sphere:

No one would ever say outright, "I can't believe you married a white guy" [and yet] I always felt like we were the black sheep of the family and it was some sort of disgrace that my mom married a white guy. My mom has always been the black sheep because she went to college, too. She actually had goals and did something. They always felt like, "What is this woman doing, running wild and going off to college and trying to do something with her life?"

Seeing both strict gender expectations and her mother's defiance of them, Jillian continued along the pathway paved by her second wave feminist mother. Acutely aware of her family history and not open to the possibility of variance within the totalizing term "Mexican culture," Jillian feared being "pigeon-holed" into a gendered role that she didn't want:

The subservient wife. You pop out the kids and you make dinner and keep the house clean and keep him happy. [One side of my family] . . . is very, very, very traditional and I always felt like I didn't get any respect. Even when I was a senior in high school and I was going off to an Ivy League school and I had done really well for myself and I had a lot of accomplishments . . . I felt like I was never going to get any respect from them. Like I was betraying my culture by trying to go off to college and do something with that.

A much-disputed research finding suggests that for some minorities educational success equates to "acting white" (Matute-Bianchi 1986; Ogbu and Fordham 1986) and betraying one's cultural background. The "acting white" critique is not only about race and ethnicity but about class as well, for it suggests that those who become educated will no longer be able to relate to—or will perhaps act as if they are superior to—their more humble roots (Kadi 1996; Lewin 2005). Feeling this pressure, Jillian struggles with commitment to her goals that are supported by her immediate family and the traditional race and gender roles that her wider kinship circle expects of her. In order to liberate herself from gender constraints, Jillian distanced herself further from the rigid gender roles of her extended Mexican family.

Jillian's pathway of thinned attachment continued upon her matriculating to Yale University in New Haven, Connecticut, and moving out of her family's sphere of influence. First, her college attendance was in part a function of her middle-class status and her family's acculturation, or changed cultural patterns and values that match those of the host country. A mark of structural assimilation, or "entrance into cliques, clubs, and institutions of [the] host society" (Gordon 1964: 71), Jillian's Ivy League college education signals her membership in mainstream U.S. society. Indeed, her Yale University education is in many ways a perfection of an ideal, considering the premium most middle-class whites place on an Ivy League education. This isn't simply going to college; this is attending an *elite* institution.

Jillian's college experience included racialized encounters. These situations belie her smooth and wholesale acceptance into an elite, historically white university. While Jillian was made aware of her racial background in college in a new way and took on a "Mexican American" label more willingly because of her new "politically correct" college atmosphere, she did not actually renew any substantive connection to it. While her Mexican heritage was "symbolic" to the extent that it did not overly determine her life outcomes, it was not symbolic in the pleasurable and voluntary way that Gans (1979) predicted. For Jillian, being of Mexican descent was an integral feature of her life because she struggled on a regular basis with the question of what being half-Mexican and half-white meant.

Recall that Jillian comfortably saw herself as white through most of her growing-up years, although this perception was periodically troubled. In college, social context further complicated her story of racialization, because Jillian's Mexicanness was exoticized at a predominantly white, Ivy League campus. Due to a confluence of factors (having checked "Mexican American" on her college application, residing on a politically aware college campus that values "diversity," and experiencing renewed connection to Mexico due to recent family travels), Jillian began to accept "Mexican" as a descriptor. Her move toward "Mexican" was only partly voluntary, however:

> I think I started saying "Mexican" since I'd gone to Yale, because now it's "cool" to be Mexican [wry tone]. It definitely is weird. I feel weird that I don't have nearly as many issues with being white and Jewish as I do with being Mexican. I think I probably use Mexican and Mexican American. . . . As much as I say that being white is an identity, it does feel like more of a vacancy. There is really not anything to explain there. With Mexican it's like, "It's this and this and this." There is not really anything to confront with being a white person.

Whiteness, for Jillian, is easier to identify with because it is "unproblematic." Because the white race is the majority race in the United States, whiteness does not need to be explained or defended.

If Jillian is assimilated, how does she live out her Mexican culture? She experiences a "thinned attachment" to Mexican culture. She is both symbolically and practically attached to Mexican traditions and knowledge, but tenuously and loosely so. With regard to Spanish, which is often used as a marker of cultural maintenance, Jillian remarked, "I have a good vocabulary but bad grammar; I don't know how to put a sentence together. It was my first language and I lost it. It's really important, but I haven't been able to make time to actually do it because I have two majors and I'm pre-med." Jillian lost Spanish at a young age and has never recaptured it because her home life did not reinforce it and her school life is overwhelmed with other academic concerns.

Never pointing to any Mexican traditions as strongholds in her life, she experiences her Mexican identity primarily due to her commitment to her family. When I asked what she likes about being of Mexican descent she responded,

> I think the most important thing to me is the importance of family. That is just so, so, so important to me. I'm really glad to be a part of a culture that appreciates that. I think it's the culture that is most focused on the family. It's just really important to me. My mom chose to live here [in Santa Barbara] because she wanted to be near her mom and I want to live here as well and let my kids have the same kind of relationship that I got to have with my grandma. . . . And I've never met anyone else who has felt that same way; everyone else is like, "oh, God, I want to get as far away from my parents as I can." . . . I've just been raised and learned that your family is there for you no matter what, you can't escape them, you are related by blood, and they are there for you and that's that. . . . I really love everyone being together and getting to share moments together.

Aside from Jillian's commitment to her family—which she and her mother both attribute to Mexican culture but which is, in fact, valorized across many ethnic cultures (Di Leonardo 1984)—she is only loosely connected to her maternal grandmother's homeland. Jillian's thinned attachment is demonstrated by the many ways in which she is distant from Mexican traditions and belief systems and even actively moving away from them. Specifically, she is opposed to patriarchal family forms and *machismo,* is not Catholic, and does not think she will marry a Mexican American. She reflected on the aspects of Mexican culture that she does not like:

> The traditional family structure. Odd that the thing that I like the most is also the thing that I dislike the most. I don't like the traditional "man goes

out and works and the wife stays home and cooks and doesn't really do anything." I really don't like that. I [also] really don't like a lot of the really strict Catholicism.

Jillian has distaste for Catholicism, which she considers synonymous with Mexican culture. Upon discovering that her Caucasian boyfriend was Catholic, she exclaimed, "I didn't know that whites were Catholic! I thought it was just Mexicans." From this vantage point, Jillian's move away from Catholicism is yet another way in which she is moving away from traditional Mexican culture.

Just as her mother avoided what she saw as pitfalls of a traditional culture that violated her gender equality ideals by marrying a non-Mexican, Jillian is also headed in that direction. When I inquired as to her ideas on marriage, she replied with certainty, taking her grandmother's woman-to-woman advice to heart:

I am like 99 percent sure that I won't marry another Mexican. Which makes me really sad because my kids will be only one-fourth. But my grandma—she's like, "*Mija* [darling], never date a Mexican man. They are nothing but trouble. Stay away from the Mexican men."

I asked her, "Why do you think she says that?" She replied,

I think that she has a very traditional view of them as well and doesn't want me to be in that role, a subservient role, and doesn't want me to fall into the traditional structure like that.

Jillian holds strong convictions about gender equality that she sees as largely incompatible with Mexican manhood. Furthermore, she notes that most Mexican men she encounters are not "marriageable" in her sense of the term. That is, they have not been on the same assimilationist and upward-mobility trajectory as she. In a prospective marriage partner, matching education, family structures, and belief systems are of utmost importance to her. In this equation, while she bemoans the potential loss of Mexican culture through intermarriage, it will probably not be retained:

What are the chances of me meeting a Mexican man who doesn't want a traditional family structure and who is well educated and has my similar beliefs and values and someone that I'm attracted to on top of that? What are my chances of that? It's probably a really cynical view to have, but if I'm honest with myself, that's really how I feel. . . . Because all of my serious relationships have been with white guys, I just feel like that's where it's going to end up. And it does make me a little bit sad because I want my kids to be able to share that kind of culture and history that I do. It does make me sad that they would only be one-quarter, but maybe that just means that I have to make a better job of filling that culture in them.

Jillian romanticizes some aspects of Mexican culture (such as family togetherness) while disparaging others (patriarchy and traditional gender roles). She makes life choices that avoid what she sees as the downsides of her Mexican heritage. By resisting patriarchal family forms, rejecting Catholicism, and dating non-Mexican men, she is on a trajectory that will further assimilate herself and her potential offspring, the fourth generation. Recognizing that her "thinned attachment" will probably result in exogamy and that a consequence will be her future children's even further distance (generationally and culturally) from Mexico, Jillian is disheartened and vows to rejuvenate Mexican culture for her children. However, the likelihood of this occurring in any meaningful way is dubious. Intermarriage is more likely to occur among Mexican American children with one non-Hispanic parent than among those who have two Mexican-origin parents (Telles and Ortiz 2009: 281). Without the support of a partner who can contribute knowledge and emotional support to Jillian's aims, her children are in all probability going to continue the assimilationist and thinned attachment course that her grandmother, mother, and she and her siblings have charted.

Jillian's Mexican heritage has been problematic for her, producing "identity crises" at various times in her life. While she did not discuss this directly, it is plausible that her struggle with how to cohere her "fragmented" identity also motivated her thinned attachment. The two extremes (and accompanying crises) Jillian experienced in terms of her Mexican identity were dependent on context: it was "dirty" and something to actively estrange herself from when she was younger, and in college it is exoticized by her east coast college peers as "not just white." Because whiteness is often the "unmarked and unnamed" standard (Frankenberg 1993) and is a trait shared by the majority of the U.S. populace, Jillian's Mexican side provides her a noticeable racial identity:

I've had identity because of my Mexicanness. White is the norm. Anything you add on top of that is going to cause problems or issues. My dad [Jewish] has a lot of history with his family, with the Holocaust, and so there is definitely that history, but I almost don't associate that with white history. It feels like there is no "white history." There is the history of our country and all that, but it doesn't feel like there is as much history there as with other cultures. Odd. . . . I guess it is because it's such an odd conglomeration of everything. Mexicans are from Mexico. Whites are from *everywhere*. Maybe it's because growing up, it was okay that I was white. I never had any issues with that. I never felt like I had to hide it or be really proud of it. I don't feel like it has as much attached to it, which is sad because I don't want to feel like half of me is really significant and has all these issues to work out and the other half of me . . .

For Jillian, her whiteness is an easily acceptable identity feature because it is the national norm. Mexican identity, however, provides distinction (positively and negatively, depending on social context) and therefore "causes issues" for her. She struggles with how to combine two seemingly disparate racial heritages. Jillian hopes that her future children will have an easier time coalescing their identity features than she has had, which they probably will if she marries a white man as this will strengthen their connection to whiteness. She refers to an acculturated "distilled ethnicity" (Kibria 2002) as she ponders what she would share with her children about her background: "I'd want them to have a sense of their Mexican heritage . . . and the big emphasis on family." As much as Jillian, and other third-generation Mexican Americans, may want to preserve their cultural heritage, this may not be possible without sustained and conscientious striving. After declaring that she wants to "preserve all of it," Jillian conceded, "I feel like it's slipping through our fingers." The pull of her assimilationist, upwardly mobile, and thinned attachment reality seems inconsistent with her preservationist sentiments.

Social Forces Driving Thinned Attachment

The thinned attachment trajectory, as evidenced by this family but also practiced by a third of families in the sample, is characterized by loosening commitments to their Mexican heritage and increasing attachment to American cultural behaviors. Several features are key in routing families toward thinned attachment, including religion, gender and gender ideologies, peer networks (including social context and educational experiences), family memory and teaching, marital partner, cultural toolkit (namely, language), and phenotype. A survival mode of parenting in which parents focus on providing the basics for children and lack time to supplement their children's knowledge of family history is one way attachment to Mexican culture weakens. Parents not teaching children Spanish or maintaining it in the home has a direct effect on with whom Mexican American children can communicate and what kinds of cultural knowledge they can obtain. Many families expressed a *desire* to continue the use of Spanish in the family but they either lacked the vigilance to implement that commitment or could not counteract the centrifugal force of English that surrounded them in public spaces and institutions.

Changing gender dynamics and gender roles also contribute to thinning. In the move from a more traditional and patriarchal system in Mexico into a more transitional/egalitarian system in the United States, a thinning of Mexican ways of life can be a byproduct of conforming to new structural surroundings (Hondagneu-Sotelo 1994; Smith 2006b). While U.S. residents do not unilaterally exhibit more equal gender relations than residents of Mexico, national context can condition cultural behaviors, such as gender norms. Some Mexican Americans (namely, women in all three generations and many men in the third generation) made purposeful decisions to adopt the ideology and practices of gender equality, advancing thinned attachment.[8]

Diminishing devotion to Catholicism also contributed to cultural dilution. The vast majority (69 percent) of Mexicans in the United States identify themselves as Catholic (Pew Hispanic Center 2007a: 13). In many families' narratives, Mexican culture was very much intertwined with Catholic religious traditions. Despite this general devotion to Catholicism, the Rosenberg family, in its attachment to Judaism, represents a twist to the trend of "Latinos, over time . . . changing religious preferences toward those of the larger non-Latino community [Protestant/Christian]" (Chavez 2008: 63). The families that remained practicing Catholics usually retained a strong sense of Mexican identity whereas those families who converted to other faiths (Jehovah's Witness, Seventh-Day Adventist, Judaism) did not. Mexican culture and Catholicism have a mutually reinforcing relationship; it appears that when one weakens, so does the other.

Improved economic status occurred for the vast majority of my sample—both thinned attachment and cultural maintenance families—and so upward mobility does not determine level of cultural identification and commitment. Upwardly mobile families oftentimes moved into higher-socioeconomic-status neighborhoods or geographic regions that were predominantly non-Hispanic white. These families became enmeshed with middle-class, mainstream American culture, losing daily contact with coethnics and thus forfeiting a source of cultural reinforcement. Yet, not all upwardly mobile families experienced thinned attachment; some remained very culturally attuned and committed.

Educational attainment is heavily influenced by generation (and class). All first-generation immigrants had "junior high or less" levels of education whereas their children's modal educational attainment was college degree.[9] The third generation is well on its way to a college degree being the minimum educational attainment, with a sizeable portion of individuals seeking postgraduate degrees. While educational attainment is not crucial to one's racial self-concept or incorporation pattern, the social context of school is important. Both the racial demographics of the school campus and its racial atmosphere play an important role in racial identity development. The way people calibrate their responses to racialized educational settings steers their racial identity development. For instance, Mexican American respondents who attended a school with a sizeable portion of other Mexican Americans felt supported by their surroundings and social networks. As a consequence, this social environment allowed them to hold onto and practice their cultural heritage. On the other hand, if students attended a school where they were a minority population, encountered unwelcoming peers and institutional indifference, they were more likely to either resist schooling and/or use thinned attachment as self-defense.

Exogamy is another pivotal factor in thinned attachment. Intermarriage is commonly viewed as an indicator of assimilation (Gordon 1964; Kalmijn 1998; Lee and Bean 2004; Murguia 1982). But intermarriage also has decisive consequences for the racial, social, and cultural position of the offspring of such pairings. Exogamy is both an indicator of and factor leading toward assimilation. Those who intermarry with European-descent Americans in the second generation[10] have a far greater propensity to adopt American traditions and outlooks and loosen the grip on Mexican ones. Telles and Ortiz (2008b: 281) found that children with Mexican-origin and non-Hispanic white parents "were less likely to know Spanish, were more likely to intermarry themselves, identified less with their Mexican origin, and were more likely to call themselves Americans." Exogamous marital choices can either be interpreted as a consequence of structural assimilation (as traditional assimilation theory predicts) or a deliberate choice (as in cases where a Mexican American woman wants to escape rigid gender expectations). A Mexican American's out-marriage with a European-descent American further reinforces American culture within the family unit. As demographers remind us, "intermarriage increases the size of the Hispanic population through the addition of people who have one Hispanic parent and who were identified as Hispanic. . . . While not yet large, a nontrivial and growing proportion of Hispanics are 'part-Hispanics'" (Lee and Edmonston 2006). Alternatively, Mexican American intramarriage supports a family atmosphere that includes some Mexican orientations such as Spanish, food, tradition, and values. Marriage is thus a heavily influential ingredient in the cultural recipes for either thinned attachment or cultural maintenance.

How likely someone is to loosen his or her sense of Mexican identity is also influenced by personal features that make that identity more evident to others, such as skin tone and surname. Physically, thinned attachment families, especially by the third generation, are lighter in skin tone than cultural maintenance families. Phenotype changes in the third generation are partly due to intermarriage in the second generation. Skin tone and surname affect the way people are perceived and treated by others as well as how they self-identify. While the preponderance of my sample had Hispanic last names, those who did not were invariably in the thinned attachment category. As a result of phenotype and surname, this population is more accepted by the dominant society and therefore has an easier time acculturating (and, conversely, has a harder time preserving ethnic culture).

It is due to structural and cultural influences as well as the choices of everyday life that one develops a thinned attachment to a natal culture. Deliberate choices can enact thinned attachment, even if the decision itself is not based on a desire for cultural distance. The structural and cultural conditions of American life can sway immigrant families toward cultural assimilation as well. "Assimilation occurs while people are making other plans, as it were" (Alba 2006: 292), as people attempt to improve their lives. Recall that a sizeable portion of my sample represents the other possible incorporation outcome of cultural maintenance, so American culture does not inevitably overwhelm immigrants and overtake their native cultural traits. Indeed, while assimilation models often assume that upward mobility is achieved at the expense of shedding non-U.S. traditions and cultures, upward mobility can also occur by *adhering* to the values of that culture and preserving a high degree of ethnic involvement (Zhou and Bankston 1998). This illustrates an exception to the assumption that assimilation requires immigrants to jettison their homeland's culture and value system in order to achieve academic success and socioeconomic upward mobility.

The portrait sketched here is in the spirit of a Weberian "ideal type" (Weber 1978). I have described how thinned attachment families appear in the aggregate, using the Montes/Rosenberg family as a rich illustration.

For each family characteristic described above that contributes to thinned attachment, there is a range of possibilities that can combine to yield a similar result but due to different "configurations of causes" (Ragin 1987; Ragin 1994). Thinned attachment and cultural maintenance represent two poles on a spectrum of incorporation possibilities. Families do not need to fit neatly into these two categories, but may instead lie along the continuum that exists between thinned attachment and cultural maintenance.

The Montes/Rosenberg family demonstrates how each generation in a family makes both conscious and unconscious choices to move away from Mexican culture. In this "thinned attachment" pattern, the cultural linkage to Mexican traditions weakens with each succeeding generation. Families such as the Montes/Rosenberg family who experience thinned attachment do so as a result of focusing their attention on the United States and steering their attention away from Mexico. Thinned attachment refers to individuals who do not consider "being Mexican" a significant portion of their social identities. Instead, they demonstrate a relaxed expression of Mexican cultural traits and inconsistently attempt to preserve a meaningful Mexican identity for themselves or their offspring.

This chapter focused on a mixed-race family because of the high degree of marital assimilation among Latinos by the third generation; Latino intermarriages with whites exceeded 50 percent in the third generation during the 1990s (Lee and Bean 2004: 222). Furthermore, among my interviewees, the three out of four second-generation interviewees who intermarried with whites were on the thinned attachment pathway, buttressing the argument that marital partner plays a significant role in the incorporation trajectory of a family.

Thinned attachment refines assimilation theory. Straight-line assimilation theory is overly deterministic, assuming that incorporation requires total shedding of native culture. Thinned attachment allows for "distilled" cultural elements to be passed on, even while assimilation occurs at other levels. Thinned attachment elaborates assimilation theory by examining the mechanisms that propel the incorporation process, adding nuance to our understanding of integration patterns and racial identity formation over generations. Racial/ethnic self-concept and degree of attachment to a cultural origin are highly contingent on generation, family orientation, social context, historical era, and personal features such as phenotype.

Structural assimilation does not inevitably lead to thinned attachment, as we will see in chapter 3. Thinned attachment, accompanied by a high degree of structural assimilation, is one of the two modal patterns of incorporation of Mexican immigrant families into the United States. Some of the same factors highlighted in this chapter, with different content and in different combinations, can produce a qualitatively different outcome. The next chapter explores the second of the two main paradigms of incorporation and racial identity development found among my upwardly mobile middle-class[11] sample. Chapter 3 showcases two families who demonstrate the cultural maintenance trajectory. These complementary chapters refine assimilation theory by uncovering key points at which assimilation advances, reverses, stalls, or changes direction. The concepts of thinned attachment and cultural maintenance emphasize the intergenerational transmission of culture and racial meanings that occurs within familial, institutional, and historical frameworks. Taking this chapter and the next as two sides of the same coin, we can see how a diversity of identities and outcomes can be exhibited by three-generation Mexican-origin families that one might at first glance consider a single homogeneous group.

Cultural Maintenance

A Pot of Beans on the Stove

Our lives represent, in C. Wright Mills' (1959) phrase, the "intersection of biography and history." While we may be only dimly aware of the historical currents that are shaping our lives, we can rest assured they are.

—Doug McAdam, *Freedom Summer*

Racialization is an ideological process, an historically specific one.

—Michael Omi and Howard Winant,
Racial Formation in the United States

When I arrived at the Benavidas home in the Oakland hills, my respondent's wife, Melissa, gave me a tour of the front portion of the home, saying her husband would join us in a minute. The house was immaculately decorated, boasting art on the walls from Spain, Mexico, and Ecuador, as well as southwestern art hand crafted by Melissa's father. As Melissa ushered me into the kitchen, she laughed, saying tongue in cheek, "Not to be a stereo-typical Mexican family or anything, but we've got to get the beans on!" We both laughed. She followed up with, "Well, really, we usually do have a pot of beans in the house."

We already see a contrast between the Rosenberg family and the Benavidas family; the Benavidases are immersed in Latino culture in the form of art decorating the home and the pot of beans on the stove. To complement the last chapter on "thinned attachment," this chapter presents an alternative model of assimilation into U.S. society: "cultural maintenance." In contradistinction to the thinned attachment families, the cultural maintenance families have preserved many elements of Mexican culture while still making

swift adjustments to U.S. culture. While families in both models have assimilated in terms of structure (mainstream schools and occupations), economics, and civic participation, they vary in their levels of adoption of U.S. culture and continued adherence to Mexican culture. This chapter argues that
the same factors that influence a thinned attachment outcome–namely, marriage, gender ideologies, and religion–when configured differently, can produce a cultural maintenance outcome. The "cultural maintenance" trajectory
of assimilation occurs most often when racial/ethnic in-marriage, Catholicism, and traditional (or transitional) gender ideologies persist in the second
generation. Cultural maintenance helps us rethink assimilation theory by
adding an understanding of the way retaining cultural values from a sending country can help rather than hinder acclimation to and success in a new
national environment.[1]

While socioeconomic status does not noticeably vary between the two
groups, the thinned attachment and cultural maintenance models diverge
in several ways (see table 3.1). Marriage (endogamy versus exogamy) at the
second generation is a primary influence, causing families to branch toward
either cultural maintenance or thinned attachment. Cultural maintenance
families have far higher intramarriage rates, more traditional gender ideologies, and higher rates of participation in civil rights activism, and they are
also more often practicing Catholics than their thinned attachment counterparts. Family memory and personal traits also vary: cultural maintenance
families display strong adherence to family history, are more often Spanish-
surnamed, and possess darker skin tones and more non-European features
than do thinned attachment families.[2]

TABLE 3.1
Points of Divergence

	Thinned Attachment	*Cultural Maintenance*
Marriage	Exogamous	Endogamous
Gender Ideologies	Transitional/Egalitarian	Traditional/Transitional
Religion	Catholic or Nonpracticing/ Converted	Catholic
Spanish	English monolingual to Bilingual	Bilingual
Personal Traits	Spanish surname or Non; European phenotype or Non	Spanish surname; Non-European phenotype
Social Context (Peers)	Heterogeneous/ White	Heterogeneous/Mexican

This chapter highlights the Lopez family, who experienced the Chicano Movement as a watershed moment wherein racial consciousness peaked, and the Benavidas family, who were committed to their Mexican identity prior to the 1960s. As we shall see, historical context heavily influences the way people understand themselves racially. First-generation immigrants confronted Americanization, deportation, and recruitment programs whereas the second and third generations experienced the civil rights movement and the affirmative action eras, respectively.

The Importance of Historical Era in Biography and Identity

First Generation, Juan Lopez:
Americanization, Deportation, and Bracero Programs

The Lopez family illustrates a "bumpy" process of assimilation (Gans 1992a): influenced by the sociopolitical context of their respective adulthoods, the first generation is assimilationist whereas the second and third generations emphasize cultural maintenance. Juan, the 84-year-old who immigrated with his family as a child in the early 1920s, is staunchly assimilationist in outlook except for his desire for his children to marry coethnics. His 57-year-old son, Marcus, was an avid supporter of the Chicano Movement and disagrees with his father on several political issues because of his generational status and altered racial consciousness. Marcus's 35-year-old son, Antonio—who goes by "Antonio" at work and "Tony" in social circles—fluidly operates with both Anglos and Mexican Americans as a bilingual county deputy sheriff in Ventura, California.

History bears significantly on the way people choose to express their racial identity. Waves of recruitment and deportation vacillated with the United States' labor needs. "Americanization programs" (1915–1929) provided vocational and civic training in order to mold immigrants into "good Americans." These programs targeted Mexican women because, as wives and mothers, they were seen as gateways through which to influence the cultural values of spouses and children (Sanchez 1994). These Americanization programs encouraged immigrants to abandon their natal traditions and conform to the American industrial order (Sanchez 1993). Soon thereafter, the Mexican government established "Mexicanization programs" to invigorate ethnic consciousness and nationalistic fervor, with the goal of enticing Mexican expatriates to return to Mexico. These émigrés had learned new skills in the United States that the Mexican government hoped could be put to use in Mexico if they "won back" these Mexican nationals (Sanchez 1993: 122).

The United States began deportation programs after the stock market crash of 1929. The government forcibly removed the formerly "cheap, mobile labor" during the Great Depression (Sanchez 1993: 213) in a program called "Operation Deportation" that operated from 1930 until 1942 (Almaguer 1994). With economic prosperity fading in the United States, many Mexicans also voluntarily left. The 1920s-1940s was a period of segregation between Anglos and Mexicans. Much like the Jim Crow segregation between blacks and whites in the South, this southwestern segregation was marked by rules regulating contact between Anglos and Mexicans. The division of labor was delineated by race: Anglos were the landholders and Mexicans were the laborers. A racial discourse of Anglo ethnocentrism and an ideology of Mexican racial inferiority supported and rationalized this segregation (Montejano 1987). The Bracero Program (1942–1964), a Mexican contract labor program aimed at filling the wartime labor shortage, again recruited Mexican workers during a time of U.S. labor need. This historical background gives a context to the periods Juan lived through in southern California.[3] Juan's youth and young adulthood took place between the 1920s and the 1950s, a time when assimilation paradigms and labor recruitment and deportation programs ordered the relationship between whites and Mexicans in the United States.

A first-generation immigrant, Juan did not go beyond the second grade in grammar school and never learned to read or write. Juan did manual labor for years and was a security guard for nearly thirty years at a Mexican American cultural center. During World War II, Juan served for the United States in New Guinea for five years. He maintains that he never faced discrimination. His manual labor and security jobs were within his ethnic community, which lessened his subjection to racial discrimination.[4] Owing to gratitude stemming from this "dual frame of reference" (Ogbu 1994), Juan would not criticize Americans who were affording him opportunity in the United States. As we will see in chapter 5, Juan's narrative of gratitude and limited criticism is strikingly similar to the perspectives of other first-generation immigrants his age with comparable immigrant, class, and work histories.

While Juan married a Mexican woman, only one of his four children (two boys and two girls) married a Mexican-origin individual. Concerned less with the race of his children's spouses, he cared more that they "get along." Juan was nonchalant about what he wished his children and grandchildren to preserve about their Mexican heritage. Juan's parenting style was fairly assimilationist; he was laissez-faire about instructing his offspring in Mexican culture. Juan said that there was "nothing in particular to preserve about Mexican heritage except Spanish . . . but it was up to his family whether or not to speak it."

Second Generation, Marcus Lopez: The Chicano Movement

Marcus, one of the Lopez family's second-generation sons, married a Mexican American woman[5] and was highly active in the Chicano Movement. In contrast to Juan, with his lukewarm commitment to Mexican cultural maintenance, Marcus agitated for Mexican American "cultural citizenship" (Flores and Benmayor 1997) during the Chicano Movement. "Cultural citizenship" refers to establishing a space where Latinos can be "both" Latino "and" American, thereby permitting Latino cultural expressions to enrich the country. A Brown Beret[6] in the 1960s, Marcus experienced a maturation of his racial consciousness due to the social movement that legitimated racial expression and incited mass mobilization for racial justice.

Marcus grew up on a lemon orchard, where his father was a ranch hand and his mother was a lemon picker. One of his jobs as a young boy was to help out his dad in the orchard, getting up before dawn to do the "dirty job" of lighting the "smudge pots" that were used to warm the orchard to avoid frost on the lemons. Another mark of working-class status is Marcus's memory of his mother "drawing lines of nylons on the back of her legs with mascara" to make it appear as if she had on real stockings and was fashionably dressed. Marcus's parents did not impress upon him any reverence for his Mexican heritage. They took a laissez-faire approach to adapting to the United States, neither jettisoning nor preserving their Mexican culture: "They were just happy to have what they had and be where they were. My parents didn't stop it [Mexican culture], but they didn't perpetuate it. Whatever happened happened."

Although Marcus was raised knowing he was Mexican American and did not identify strongly with that background until the late 1960s, others imposed a racial and ethnic identity on him. For example, a racist high school counselor, a gatekeeper of school success, blocked Marcus's educational progress. Only retrospectively did Marcus see as racist his high school counselor's remark that "all [Mexican] people were good for were to be cooks and mechanics." Despite Marcus's mother's desire for him to continue his education, he joined the U.S. Marine Corps at age seventeen and eventually earned his General Education Diploma (GED).

It was in military service that Marcus learned about prejudice from white Texans. He reflects,

> I didn't realize there was prejudice. I knew that people didn't like black people, but I didn't know there was prejudice against Hispanics or Mexi-

cans. At the time I thought, "Well, I'm not black, so . . ." But I didn't realize there were prejudices until I got into the service. . . . My first exposure to prejudices was in the company I was assigned to because I came across [white] Texans. To them I was a bean-burner, a wetback, "come take my boots off, boy," "did your mom teach you how to make tortillas? Because I like tortillas." That was the first time I was exposed to actual prejudices and racism. I was kinda hurt by it. "You know, I'm an American."

Based on this experience of racial hatred in the military, Marcus perceived his high school counselor as a racist. Marcus clearly links his experience of prejudice with becoming politically active and joining the Brown Berets during the Chicano Movement. I asked Marcus, "How did those experiences with the counselor and the Texans in the Marines affect you?" Marcus responded,

It made me very angry. Angry enough that when I got out of the service, I joined the Brown Berets. I wanted to make change. The Brown Berets were equivalent to the Black Panthers. They would do change even if it meant violence. I didn't know if I could be violent, but I knew I could make change. The person that probably impressed me the most and really solidified how I felt was César Chávez. I met him and I became [one of] his bodyguard[s] . . . when he was in California visiting Cuyama, Nipomo, Santa Barbara, and Bakersfield. I got to know him fairly well. . . . We were his [armed] bodyguards. There was a lot of threats against him, a lot of death threats.

As a Brown Beret, Marcus helped poor migrant Mexican agricultural workers and their families by setting up shelters and clinics that provided food, clothing, and medical care. The California chapter of the Brown Berets with which Marcus worked also organized MEChA (Movimiento Estudiantil Chicano de Aztlán) at several college and university campuses, as well as set up local community cultural centers.

Marcus's increased racial pride and confident "presentation of self" (Goffman 1973) is based in part on the civil rights movement:

I know there is a difference between the way you present yourself, the way you carry yourself, no matter if you are Hispanic or not, that perpetuates awareness to somebody else. . . . I learned this in communication class. When you look at someone and you have eye contact with them and you say, "My name is Marcus Lopez," they tend to kind of like, "Okay." There's a difference between [that and] "my name is Marcus Lopez" [nervous, eyes downcast]. . . . I've learned to . . . just project . . . "I know who I am, who are you?" . . . If I detect any kind of a racial thing I just don't participate in that person's mind game. . . . The power of presentation is a very powerful thing. I'm not sure if that was a defense mechanism that grew over the years. . . .

Defense mechanism or not, Marcus's more assertive presentation of self is a consequence of not just a communication class but also a post–civil rights period that allows space for the pride and confidence of ethnic/racial minorities.

Another ramification of the civil rights movement was the creation of multicultural education curriculum in the 1970s (Yamane 2001). Multicultural curriculum legitimated the study of ethnic/racial and gender groups that were previously shunned by disciplinary canons.[7] This impact of the civil rights movement affects the education of students today. Marcus commented,

I thought [Mexican American art class] was the greatest thing in the world. . . . I didn't know that the Aztecs really did [discover] astrological things, I didn't know that the Mayans invented the [concept of zero]. You assume it's the Chinese or somebody, you know? Mayans and their agriculture, they grew crops with irrigation systems before the Egyptians knew how to irrigate with the Nile. Wow. That really got me going, as far as learning. I even took Black Studies classes to understand black people a little more.

Marcus sees multicultural classes as a way to learn more about himself as well as a way to become acquainted with other groups. Indeed, multicultural education raises levels of understanding across groups and therefore lowers distrust, heightens egalitarianism, and underscores commonalities while encouraging appreciation of differences (Astin 1993; Duster et al. 1991; Giroux 1992; Schoem and Hurtado 2001; Maher and Tetreault 1994; Nieto 1999; Vasquez 2005). In sum, Marcus sees that racial tensions have eased since the 1960s and that "we're accepted a little more but not quite a part of the mainstream."

For Marcus, as for many others, a key to Mexican American identity is to "remember who you are and have pride." He added, "You don't have to carry a piñata to show you are Mexican." His definition of Mexican American identity allows for acculturation and shedding of some traditional Mexican symbols. Similar to thinned attachment families, Marcus's family insisted that "keeping the importance of family" is a keystone of what it means to be Mexican American. More so than other respondents, Marcus emphasized his Mayan and Aztec roots that underlie Mexican culture.

When I asked Marcus how he would respond to his father's claim that he never experienced discrimination, he said that his father "felt he owed the white man loyalty because his life was better here [than in Mexico]." In contrast, Marcus discerned racist joking that went undetected by his father. He used his own consciousness-raising experiences to open his father's eyes. Marcus related a conversation in which he and his father were called "wetbacks" in a grocery store: "They're not laughing because they like you, they're laughing because you are different and you are not what they like."

The Chicano Movement raised Marcus's racial consciousness but did not inspire his father. Juan's relationship to the United States solidified before the Chicano Movement, during a period of Americanization programs and government-sanctioned cycles of Mexican labor recruitment and deportation. Juan was unmoved by the Chicano Movement because he was loathe to criticize a country that had given him upward mobility. Marcus's and his father's perspectives are distinguished by their generation in the United States and their respective relationships to the civil rights fervor of the 1960s. Nativity, generation, and historical era during their "coming of age" largely determined both Juan's and Marcus's relationship to the civil rights movement. Marcus's commentary on his father's indefatigable work ethic sets the stage for a generational difference between him and his father regarding relationship to the United States and racial pride:

I think my dad's biggest accomplishment is living to be eighty-four [chuckle]. 'Cause, he worked hard. All his life. . . . I think all of his fingers had been broken at one time, and still going to work. I don't think I ever remember him being home. He'd go to work sick. . . . I remember one time he smashed all his fingers trying to change a plow apparatus on the tractor. It slipped and the bars came down and smashed his fingers. That happened early in the afternoon, [yet] he worked all afternoon, then he came home and . . . he soaked his hand in ice water, wrapped it up, took some aspirin. Didn't even go to the doctor. The next day he went back to work, he just put tape around his fingers. I knew all his fingers were broken. When he came home his hand was just all crumpled up. I remember him taking his fingers and going like this [he tugs on each finger from the tip, one at a time] and just straightening them out. I don't know if you noticed, but his hands are all [makes a mangled pose with his hand]. They healed, but they healed deformed.

Marcus proceeded to tell a similarly dreadful tale of the tractor rolling over his father's foot and yet the next day he "wrapped his foot and . . . tied his boot real tight" and limped to work. While Marcus admired his father's work ethic, the two maintained political differences.

Nation of birth, citizenship status, and generation marked Juan's and Marcus's political styles. Marcus reflected on the political philosophy that drove his father's tireless work ethic:

> He thought that he owed everything to the white man for what he had. He felt compelled that he had to go to work. . . . He owed them for the life that he had. . . . He felt that the life that he had was better than what life would be in Mexico. I used to tell him, "What are you doing this for? They don't care about you!" So he and I just had big differences. [He and I used to get down into] knock-down drag-out fights about . . . me being a Brown Beret . . . I was "ungrateful" and all of that; "they're just radicals, they don't love this country!" We had big differences.

Juan felt a sense of debt and obligation to the country into which he immigrated whereas Marcus felt that he had a duty to fight for equal rights and representation. The first generation paid its debt of gratitude by means of a robust work ethic whereas the members of the second generation felt their responsibility was to shore up "cultural citizenship," combat subordination, and attain first-class citizenship status.

As argued in the previous and following chapters, marriage is a key element in influencing a thinned attachment or cultural maintenance pathway of incorporation. Keeping in mind that there is a spectrum of incorporation possibilities, most thinned attachment families out-married while most cultural maintenance families in-married. For Marcus, "All of [his] relationships have been with Hispanics" because he desired cultural similarity. Marcus followed the advice of his parents to "stay within [his] own, stay with a Mexican girl," as both his first and second wives were Mexican (mother of his first son, Tony, and his second son, respectively). Marcus's parents advised him, "white girls treat you bad." It is unclear precisely what that means—whether they felt white girls are too independent minded and not subservient enough to be good wives, or whether they conflated race, religion, and culture and

TABLE 3.2
In- and Out-Marriage by Sex and Generation

Female In-Marriage	Female Out-Marriage
G1: 6 (All)	G1: 0
G2: 12	G2: 1
G3: 2	G3: 1

Male In-Marriage	Male Out-Marriage
G1: 2 (All)	G1: 0
G2: 12	G2: 3
G3: 1	G3: 4

Notes:
1. Missing Data: G2: 1; G3: 22
2. "In-marriage" includes all Latino national origin groups.

feared their son might partner with a non-Catholic, non-Mexican woman. This male in-marriage provides a rich gendered contrast to the female out-marriage seen in the previous chapter on thinned attachment. Note that I am *not* making a gendered argument about which sex is more likely to marry endogamously versus exogamously. Table 3.2 demonstrates that there is no clear gender divide regarding who in-marries as opposed to who out-marries. Similar to national data estimates that 65 percent of Hispanics marry endogamously (Kalmijn 1998: 406), even to the fourth generation (Telles and Ortiz 2009: 265), my study found that in-marriage was the most frequent coupling at all three generational levels for the entire sample.

Preference for in-marriage is the chief way Marcus's parents pressed for cultural preservation. While they may not have stressed "Mexican culture" per se, they were committed to promoting intramarriage in their children (although only one of four children actually followed this advice). While Marcus believes it is desirable to have ethnic/racial commonality with a partner, he does not see ethnic matching as a necessary ingredient for a happy marriage: "I've seen mixed marriages where there is a clash of cultures . . . and I've seen mixed marriages where they've blended real well. I've seen both." Although it is not a "deal-breaker," Marcus also prefers that his two sons marry Mexican (or Hispanic) women.

The vast majority of cultural maintenance families are Catholic in all three generations. While Juan and his grandson Tony are Catholics, Marcus professes holding American Indian religious beliefs. Marcus reveres not just his Mexican predecessors but his Native American and Aztec ancestors. He remembers that Mexicans were born of the Spanish conquest of the Aztec and indigenous civilizations with the arrival of Hernan Cortés in Mexico City (then Tenochtitlán) in 1521.[8] Marcus's religious beliefs are not so much a departure from Catholicism as they are an attempt to return to belief systems that predated the arrival of the Spanish conquistador's Catholicism in the "New World."

Another factor that distinguishes cultural maintenance families is an emphasis on racial pride. Marcus propounds a racial pride that is not ostentatious but is incorporated into his outlook. Marcus counsels his children to continue feeling this pride: "I tell them . . . to remember who you are and be proud of it." Even given this commitment to Mexican pride and representation, cultural maintenance families are not immune to attenuation of Mexican cultural knowledge that is a byproduct of cultural and socioeconomic adaptation to the United States. As parents—of any generation—invest time and energy in career advancement and socioeconomic achievement in order to increase the life chances of themselves and their children, they have less time to continue cultural traditions. Marcus describes this cultural forgetting:

I think it's important to keep it [Spanish] to ensure that the culture stays. There is a lot of tradition that even I don't know about, that I've forgotten, that my mom and grandma used to teach us and tell us about. [My brother] keeps alive making tamales on Christmas Eve, for the family. [He] does it every year; my mom taught him. Again, it's to get the family together. It took me a long time to get back to that, or to realize that. I got too career oriented.

While Marcus regrets the dearth of time he spent at home, he was frequently away from home in order to secure his family's financial well-being. The household division of labor between Marcus and his first wife was traditional in that he was the breadwinner and his wife was in charge of childrearing and other domestic concerns.

In order to solidify his family's place on a middle rung of the socioeconomic ladder, Marcus worked diligently as a supervisor in a growing corporation. Focusing his effort on his occupation and hopes for integration into the U.S. middle class, Marcus made few attempts to secure cultural knowledge for himself and his children. A gender analysis would indicate that Marcus, as a man, was probably inclined to leave the food, feasts, and festivals to a female spouse because such cultural activities would fall under a woman's domain within a traditional household division of labor (DeVault 1991; Di Leonardo 1984). "Women are often constructed as the cultural symbols of the collectivity, of its boundaries, as carriers of the collectivity's 'honor' and as its intergenerational reproducers of culture" (Yuval-Davis 1997: 67). In this conception, women carry a particular "burden of representation" (Yuval-Davis 1997: 45) as symbolic bearers of collective identity (Kurien 2003). Women are imagined as mothers of children (or whole families) that they nurture within a national or cultural framework.

This gendered logic that positions women as carriers of culture may have also played into Marcus's parents' advice to marry a Mexican woman rather than a (non-Hispanic) white woman. If Marcus married a Mexican woman, under a patriarchal home set-up at least, his wife would be in charge of raising children within their shared Mexican culture. This way, Marcus could continue with his career aspirations and rest assured that his children were receiving cultural instruction from his wife, the implicitly designated carrier of culture. This is one reading of Marcus's parents' counsel and his own adult actions that accounts for how his gender influenced his life. Whether deliberate or not, Marcus was active in the public sphere, gaining a financial foothold for his family, until his retirement. In his late fifties, having provided economically for his family, Marcus took early retirement to spend more time at home. Now he can be found baking in his newly remodeled kitchen, awaiting the arrival of his teenage son from high school football practice.

Marcus reflects on how his devotion to his family through dedication to his career allowed for cultural forgetting. Now, in the early days of retirement, he relishes enriching his cultural knowledge. Still, he is somewhat abashed that these are skills he must learn rather than simply intuit. Marcus comments,

> You know what the sad part is? . . . I'm taking a cooking class this month to learn how to make salsa. . . . The guy giving the class is a white guy. [Laughs.] . . . I want to learn how to do salsa, how to make a good *carne asada* [flame-grilled beef], a good *chile verde* [green chile stewed pork], a good *chile Colorado* [beef with red chile sauce], good *carnitas* [braised pork].

Marcus is trying to counteract his cultural loss through active learning and practice. Interestingly, since Mexican food has crossed over into American mainstream cuisine (Davis 2000), it is possible for a "white guy" to teach a man named Marcus Lopez how to make salsa.

Third Generation, Tony Lopez: Affirmative Action Era

Tony is second generation on his mother's side (his mother emigrated from Mexico) and third generation on his father's side (his paternal grandparents emigrated from Mexico). Tony's maternal grandparents were extremely influential in his life: "I spent more time with my [maternal] grandparents than with my own parents when I was young. . . . They were pretty much my world."[9] Thus, a good portion of Tony's cultural knowledge flows directly from Mexican grandparents as well as Mexican intramarried parents.

Tony's maternal grandparents heavily influenced his racial/ethnic identity. His maternal grandfather hailed from Spain and his maternal grandmother was born in Mexico. Both grandparents persistently emphasized that Tony was "Hispanic . . . because 'Mexican' was a dirty word. 'Mexicans' were field workers." This claim, interestingly, focuses on one grandparent from Spain and omits the history of the spouse originally from Mexico. It simultaneously obscures and denigrates the history of Tony's paternal grandfather from Mexico. Tony explains how his maternal grandmother "converted" from "Mexican" to "Spanish": "My grandma was born and raised in Mexico, but she still considered herself Spanish.[10] I think it was . . . because Mexican was a dirty word, a lower caste. . . . My grandmother considered herself educated because she could read and write, so she even considered herself Spanish. . . ." Tony was taught that since they "were supposedly descendents from more educated upper-class, [they] were 'Hispanic.'" To this day, Tony says, he will "even catch myself correcting people: 'You're Mexican?' 'No, I'm Hispanic.'"

Unlike most other cultural maintenance third-generation Mexican Americans, Tony reports that because of his physical appearance (pale skin and dark hair) he is often perceived as white, most often of Italian descent. He feels socially accepted by the mainstream. Reasons for this feeling of inclusion probably include his light skin color and middle-class status. He is an American mainstream cultural insider in that he does not fall into lower-class Hispanic stereotypes such as having a "heavy accent, capped teeth, really bad dentistry, thick dark hair, dressed kind of a mixture, maybe outdated. . . ." Tony has an "ethnic option" (Waters 1990) and can pass because he is phenotypically ambiguous, flawlessly bilingual, middle class, and behaviorally mainstream. In Tony's words, "I have an easier time blending in and I think a lot of it has to do with [the fact] that I don't fit a lot of stereotypes." Tony conflates race and class in this narrative, yet it is in part due to his middle-class status that he escapes intense discrimination. Social acceptance facilitated by his light skin color, his middle-class status, and his profession as a county deputy sheriff probably shield him from overt discrimination.[11]

Tony's maternal grandparents emigrated from Mexico due to poverty in the 1920s. They chose to reside in Santa Barbara because a cousin was already living in the area. Tony's maternal grandfather was a carpenter by trade, but because he spoke so little English he could not join the union and practice his skill. He ended up working as a dishwasher at a hospital for over thirty years. Tony's maternal grandmother worked in the same hospital for approximately twenty-five years, cutting vegetables. In a manner similar to that of Maria Montes, profiled in chapter 2, Tony's immigrant grandparents were prudent with their minimum-wage earnings and bought a house at a time when the Santa Barbara housing market was not inflated. Tony marvels at his grandparents' financial success: "I never realized until I turned about fifteen or sixteen . . . that my grandfather was a dishwasher and my grandmother was a vegetable cutter." Around that age Tony inquired as to his grandparents' job responsibilities:

> My grandpa said, "I come [to the hospital] every day at four in the morning and I wash all the dishes. I do it for eight hours a day. Five days a week. Till one o'clock in the afternoon." He never referred to himself as a dishwasher; he referred to it as "I help make the hospital run." . . . Without him doing what he did, things would stop. My grandmother would cut the vegetables for the dishes, the soups, the salads. . . . I was so proud of them. I would never be embarrassed to say [they] were just a dishwasher and vegetable cutter. Everyday, it would amaze me, they would iron their uniforms. Every day. Nobody saw them. They wore smocks. They wore the cleanest uniforms and they ironed them every day and they shined their shoes. That just kills me. Talk about taking pride in what you do.

Service industry workers can garner an extra degree of dignity and self-respect by discursively professionalizing their work (Solari 2006). Here, Tony's grandparents made rhetorical and behavioral claims of "making the hospital run," viewing their minimum-wage jobs as integral to the functioning of a professional enterprise.

Tony's maternal grandparents who helped raise him had a traditional household marked by a gendered division of labor: "It was the traditional old-world family: the woman was the housewife and did the inside things and the guy did the outside work." On his father's side of the family this tra-

TABLE 3.3

Spanish Language Ability in Cultural Maintenance Families (18 Families)

	Less Than Conversational	Conversational	Fluent	Number
Gen 1	0	0	100% (n=5)	5
Gen 2	5.2% (n=1)	31.6% (n=6)	63.2% (n=12)	19
Gen 3	22.2% (n=4)	61.1% (n=11)	16.7% (n=3)	18
Total:	11.9% (n=5)	40.5% (n=17)	47.6% (n=20)	n=42

TABLE 3.4

Spanish Language Ability in Thinned Attachment Families (11 Families)

	Less Than Conversational	Conversational	Fluent	Number
Gen 1	0	0	110% (n=3)	3
Gen 2	9.1% (n=1)	36.4% (n=4)	54.5% (n=6)	11
Gen 3	81.8% (n=9)	18.2% (n=2)	0	11
Total:	40% (n=10)	24% (n=6)	36% (n=9)	n=25

TABLE 3.5

Spanish Language Ability in Total Sample (29 Families)

	Less Than Conversational	Conversational	Fluent	Number
Gen 1	0	0	100% (n=8)	8
Gen 2	6.7% (n=2)	33.3% (n=10)	60% (n=18)	30
Gen 3	44.8% (n=13)	44.8% (n=13)	10.3% (n=3)	29
Total:	22.4% (n=15)	34.3% (n=23)	43.3% (n=29)	n=67

ditional gendered division of labor also prevailed, providing Tony a coherent picture of what home life is supposed to look like. Tony adds, "both of my grandmothers were good cooks of Mexican food," noting the role that women traditionally play in passing on cultural aspects through "feeding the family" (DeVault 1991). These traditional gender ideologies that were comfortable to Tony contributed to his cultural maintenance.

Tony's Spanish fluency is due in part to his maternal grandparents: "They could speak a little bit [of English], but they always spoke Spanish in the household. So my first language was Spanish, then I transitioned to English when I got into school." As can be seen in table 3.3 on cultural maintenance families, the majority of third-generation Mexican Americans in this category is conversational in Spanish.

Tony is a fluent Spanish speaker because he grew up speaking Spanish with his grandparents. As a comparison, none of the third-generation Mexican Americans in the thinned attachment category are fluent Spanish speakers and the vast majority are "less than conversational." Table 3.5 breaks down the Spanish language knowledge of the entire sample by generation. This table shows that, in accordance with literature on native language retention among immigrants, Spanish language knowledge dwindles with each succeeding generation (Portes and Rumbaut 1996; Portes and Rumbaut 2001; Portes and Zhou 1993; Rumbaut and Portes 2001). In a study located in Los Angeles, California, and San Antonio, Texas, that spanned five generations since immigration, findings reveal that virtually all Mexican Americans are proficient in English in the second generation but that Spanish persists in the fourth generation and only declines sharply in the fifth generation (Telles and Ortiz 2009: 209). Low parental education is associated with Spanish retention (Telles and Ortiz 2009), which could explain my small sample's rapid English acquisition and loss of Spanish skills, since the vast majority of the second generation (87 percent) achieved at least "some college" education, with some earning a doctoral degree (see table 6.1).

Spanish language ability is both a contributing factor and an outcome of the cultural maintenance category. Spanish language ability is part of a "feedback loop" for the cultural maintenance families: Spanish knowledge leads to the ability to create and maintain social networks and traditions that are Mexican oriented. Because cultural maintenance individuals tend to marry endogamously (arguably as a result of shared language, social networks, ideologies, and traditions), they tend to produce cultural maintenance offspring to whom they teach their shared culture, including Spanish. This "feedback loop" is not as influential for thinned attachment families. In this case, while Spanish language ability at the second generation *does not vary* between the cultural maintenance and thinned attachment families, the third generation's linguistic proficiency helped to determine the family's incorporation trajectory. For thinned attachment families, while the second generation is largely conversational or fluent in Spanish, intermarriage with whites at the second generation leads to Spanish loss at the third generation because the non-Hispanic white parent can rarely speak Spanish.

Though occupational discrimination is well documented (Bertrand and Mullainathan 2004; Pager and Quillian 2005), affirmative action has opened up occupations to some members of minority groups since the mass mobilization of the 1960s. Tony was actively recruited to be in the Ventura County sheriff's department, a fact he attributes to affirmative action policies. Like others who feel they have benefited from affirmative action policies, and as shown in other studies (Macias 2006: 62), Tony quickly justifies his job placement by saying he works hard. Expressing a sentiment unheard of a generation earlier, Tony says he believes that his race has been advantageous to his career:

> As far as getting into new jobs, new promotions, new positions, I think because I'm Hispanic and because I'm willing to work hard, I think [my race] has kicked open a lot of doors for me. I think that I've been given a lot of chances based on not just the fact that I'm Hispanic but that I work hard and that I get things done.

Tony believes his Mexican background has been an asset to him on the job because he began his career after policies issuing from the civil rights movement began to take effect and because he lives in a largely Mexican American town. The demographics of the area, at 37 percent Hispanic, insulate him from the harshest of racial obstacles. Tony refers to the mix of Hispanics and whites in the greater Ventura area and how his heritage and Spanish language give him an advantage on the job: "I think right now Hispanics are taking over Ventura, white people are going to be a minority. We [county sheriff's department] teach people who don't speak Spanish; we send them to [Spanish] classes. They pay me extra because I speak Spanish. I look at being Spanish as . . . being ahead." Tony believes that his background and language ability were big "selling points" for him since he can communicate with both white and Hispanic community members in an official capacity.

Like many cultural maintenance third-generation individuals, Tony feels "a lot of pressure" to represent the Hispanic community. Tony, more so than most, is in a job that highlights his bicultural and bilingual skill sets, so he is more obviously a representative of the Mexican community. Some thinned attachment individuals also felt the need to positively represent their Mexican heritage through their successes. For all third-generation individuals, the pressure to achieve academically, financially, and occupationally is a reaction to being identified as Mexican American and the imposition of negative stereotypes that come with that label. Tony explains, "[I am] representing the Hispanic community and [I] just don't want to mess up. . . . I want to be a good role model and be available and help everybody. I want to carry my people up to the next level." Tony continues, referring to the negative stereotypes that he is working against:

I hate being around other deputy sheriffs who immediately label Hispanics as field workers. So I really promote that all they need is a chance. There is always going to be a population of bad or not so good [people]. It's the same with white people. I try to reach out as much as I can. . . . It's important for me to carry myself a certain way and make sure my name [badge] is displayed prominently. . . . Being in uniform I can help a lot.

Tony considers his race and Spanish ability to be an asset on the job. He is both a liaison between the white and Hispanic populations as well an advocate for the latter.

Since Tony secured his job in a post–civil rights era and during a period of affirmative action hiring, his workplace is set up to allow him to maintain his Hispanic culture on the job. A cultural maintenance incorporation trajectory is promoted by Mexican Americans in his community and is more widely accepted by society in the new millennium than it was in his father's and grandfather's young adulthood. Additionally, by financially rewarding his bilingualism, Tony's work structure encourages him to continue on his cultural maintenance pathway rather than divert him toward thinned attachment. Tony's fluency in Spanish is a tool in his "cultural toolkit" (Swidler 1986) that facilitates his claim to a seamless and coherent Hispanic identity.[12]

A cultural maintenance trajectory does not preclude progressive ideals. Tony, like most of his third-generation peers, was frustrated with patriarchy: "I think there is still some old traditional families that are not going with the times and I hate to see the women subservient and speak when spoken to. I don't like that, and I see that a lot, being a deputy sheriff." As interested in preserving and representing his Hispanic heritage as Tony is, he hopes to "equal it out." Disturbed by the enforced subservience of women that persists in some Hispanic homes, Tony strikes a balance between preserving tradition and adopting more egalitarian gender practices. Cultural maintenance does not require entrenchment of tradition to the detriment of gender equality.

Tony is currently unmarried with no children, leaving open the question of how he and a prospective partner will raise their potential children, the fourth generation. While Tony believes keeping Spanish is "extremely important," his openness to exogamy may hamper the possibility of a Spanish-speaking household. Tony considers how important racial matching within a marriage is to him:

I don't have any strong traits that mandate that a Hispanic woman would be the only person that would understand where I'd be coming from.

Personally, I'd like to marry outside the race because I want to learn about that other culture. . . . I wouldn't want to marry somebody based on the fact that she's got to be Hispanic and we've got to share the same traits and keep it going. . . . Yeah, that's nice, but I don't see that as important.

Yet, it's "unbelievably important" to Tony that he pass on Spanish to his potential children, not just as a marker of their heritage but as a linguistic asset in a globalizing world.[13] Along with most respondents, Tony desires to preserve the importance of family, manners, respect, and food. Tony specifies what he means by Mexican food: "real Mexican food: *menudo, tamales*; not *chalupas* or *churros*."

Tony has maintained his Mexican culture for several reasons. First and foremost, he had two parents of Mexican (or Spanish) descent and a close-knit extended family on his maternal side that reinforced his parents' ideologies and cultural teachings. Thus, two family generations—his parents and grandparents—could reinforce other Mexican-oriented elements such as a traditional gender ideology, Catholicism, Spanish, strong family memories, and cultural traditions. Having a strong relationship with his maternal grandparents (and consistent but infrequent contact with his paternal grandparents) also promoted a strong family memory. Hearing stories directly from his grandparents about their lives in Mexico, rather than hearing them indirectly through his parents, enlivened the significance of Mexico to him and his family.

The Civil Rights Movement:
The Benavidas Family as a Comparison Case

The civil rights movement did not affect all Mexican American families in the same way or to the same degree. Thinned attachment families were less involved in and affected by the civil rights movement largely because they were less highly identified as Mexican American and did not necessarily perceive the racial politics of the time as a potential benefit to them. However, engagement in the civil rights movement varied even among cultural maintenance families. Another family, the Benavidas family, is an example of a cultural maintenance family who was sympathetic to, but not highly involved in, the movement.

Class position seems to be the primary factor determining whom the civil rights movement incited to race consciousness and whom it did not. A family's middle-class status at the time of immigration can "afford" the family the opportunity to live out its cultural way of life without the same challenges as lower- or working-class families. In contrast to all other families I interviewed who became middle class in the second generation, the Benavidas family was middle class at the time of immigration. This class privilege granted them the freedom to display cultural and racial pride without heavy scrutiny from their neighbors and peers. While class distinction was not a guarantee against racial prejudice, it was certainly a buffer. Because of the class privilege of a middle-class immigration, the Benavidas family did not partake in the civil rights movement in the same way that their working-class Mexican American brethren, such as the Lopez family, did. The Benavidas family, who were class-distinct from those most involved in the mass mobilization of the 1960s, offers a different view of how the cultural maintenance paradigm can be lived out.

Second-generation Benjamin Benavidas's youth involved the factors that lead to cultural maintenance. He lived in an East Los Angeles ethnic enclave in his childhood, occasionally spent summers in Mexico, was raised Catholic, and was raised speaking Spanish at home and English at school. Residing in an ethnic enclave allowed Benjamin and his natal family to easily maintain cultural distinctions without pressure to assimilate. Marriage is as key a gateway for cultural maintenance families (endogamy) as it is for thinned attachment families (exogamy). As with most of his cultural maintenance second-generation peers, Benjamin married a Mexican American woman.

Catholicism reinforces a cultural maintenance lifestyle. Benjamin commented on the fused nature of Catholicism and Mexican identity: "we would celebrate anything that related to the Catholic Church. . . . The Catholic Church was part of being Mexican. It's inextricable. Mexican traditions . . . went along with what was happening with the Catholic Church." A study of Mexican immigrants in New York City highlights immigrants' devotion to Catholicism—in particular Our Lady of Guadalupe, the patron saint of Mexico—not only as a religious practice but also as a means to create community and public life in the United States (Galvez 2009).

Parenting style also plays into the racial/ethnic identity formation of the children. Benjamin comments,

We never were pressured to assimilate. . . . My mom is a Mexicana and had maintained dual citizenship. . . . We never really gave in to assimilation. . . . My kids are like that too . . . sort of nonconformist in that we don't go along with the crowd so you can establish your own identity.

Knowledge of family history, or family memory, plays a key role in perpetuating a sense of history, "roots," family and ethnic pride.

Benjamin uses the term "a child of the Southwest" to describe his identity, incorporating both his and his wife's family history and sense of place (his wife's family goes back several generations in Arizona). "A child of the Southwest" is inclusive of racial intermixture and is grounded in a territory that has remained constant beneath national boundary drawing. While Benjamin asserts a Chicano—as well as Mexican—self-title, it is not highly connected with the political content that produced the term in the 1960s.

Benjamin only made one reference to the civil rights movement during our interview. He mentioned it not as a personal watershed moment, as did Marcus and others, but as a historical period of hope. When I asked what he wished for the next generation, Benjamin referred to the hope and promise of the 1960s:

I would like to see the cycle broken where Mexicanos have been beat up for generations and generations and get here [United States] and get beat up more. . . . Be able to lift yourself up and fight back. . . . The only time that I've seen that successfully happen is when César Chávez . . . was able to organize people who were powerless and to take on one of the most powerful industries in the country. I saw . . . there was a sense of pride and a sense of dignity. . . . That was a point where I felt things could turn around.

Benjamin experienced the civil rights movement from a different social location than Marcus Lopez. More distanced from the Chicano Movement because of his class privilege, Benjamin saw the 1960s as a time when people hoped to "turn around that whole [terrible] dynamic" of exploitative migrant labor. The civil rights era did not figure prominently in Benjamin's narrative because his family already possessed a degree of social, financial, and cultural capital for which the movement was agitating. Yet, even while the Benavidas family was not involved in the Chicano Movement, they benefited from the progressive reforms it urged. Like Tony Lopez, third-generation Caitlyn Benavidas thinks that affirmative action policies may assist her in securing a job because she "brings a diverse element" to the workplace. When she ponders whether she was a beneficiary of affirmative action, Caitlyn is quick to note that she also "has a bachelor of arts from University of California–Riverside," much the same way Tony stresses his job-related qualifications.

Influence of Historical Context across Three Family Generations

All three generations in the Lopez family understood what it meant to be Mexican American slightly differently. For Juan, born in Mexico, his racial/ethnic claim was "Mexican," without hesitation. For Marcus, suffering racial discrimination in high school and in the U.S. military led him to become a Brown Beret, a Chicano Movement activist. His social activism sprang from his commitment to being treated as a first-class U.S. citizen, equal to his non-Hispanic white peers. Due to gains in equal opportunity employment policies, Tony, the third generation, viewed his biculturalism and bilingualism as an asset rather than a disability. Tony's self-title of "Hispanic" over more Mexican-oriented options reflects society's historical legacy of anti-Mexican feeling and his grandparents' defense mechanism of calling themselves "Spanish."

Takahashi's (1997) work regarding Japanese immigrants and their families found that one's "political style" is a result of political context (particularly racial milieu and discourses) plus biography. Each generation has a particular set of political styles that are patterned reactions to contemporary political climates. Generationally marked political styles reflect transitions in political and racial consciousness. Takahashi discovered that first-generation immigrants from Japan (Issei) embraced conservative race politics and, due to their lack of U.S. citizenship, adopted a defensive political style in their encounters with law and courts (Takahashi 1997: 24, 198). The second-generation Japanese Americans (Nisei) who came of age in the 1920s and 1930s were assimilationist and accommodationist. However, the third-generation Japanese Americans (Sansei) who came of age in the '60s and '70s, the same coming-of-age period of my second-generation Mexican American respondents, pursued protest politics. Both the Sansei and second-generation Mexican Americans engaged a politics of confrontation and mass action modeled after the Black Power movement. As these studies show, historical period can have a significant and direct impact on a generation's political strategy, racial awareness, and national identity.

The progression in the Lopez family's racial/ethnic identity claims, and the content of those claims, was greatly influenced by historical period. Juan, Mexican by birth, was on U.S. soil during the time of Americanization programs that aimed to eliminate cultural dissimilarities between immigrants and natives. He was also present during periods of U.S. government–sponsored recruitment and deportation of Mexican workers, carried out according to the labor needs of the United States. Grateful for a chance at upward mobility, Juan demonstrated his patriotism and reflected the racial discourses of the time by being assimilationist, with a hint of preservationist instinct regarding marriage.

As Marcus demonstrates, the Chicano Movement was a watershed period for many Mexican Americans.[14] The civil rights movement, of which the Chicano Movement was a part, was a critical point that marked a change of course for the racial identity formation and cultural expression of U.S. minority groups. Through raising their own consciousness as well as the awareness of non-Hispanic whites about their presence, rights, and culture, many Mexican Americans more freely expressed their racial identities during and after the civil rights era than before. One does not need to be an activist in a social movement in order to reap its benefits. Nonetheless, activists are more likely than others to remain political as a result of their participation, in part by virtue of their stronger organizational and social network affiliations (McAdam 1988).

The Chicano Movement, as performance, can be viewed as a collective action that "highlights the common official values of the society in which it occurs" and thereby rejuvenates the society's morality system (Goffman 1973: 35, 69). The social movements of the 1960s reinvigorated racial/ethnic groups' identity, sense of entitlement, and need for recognition. If culture is performance, as some scholars argue (Bellah 1986; Goffman 1973; Hochschild 1983; Wedeen 1999), the civil rights movement performed the culture of rights and belonging. Individuals establish their sense of self through practice and interaction: "This self itself does not derive from its possessor, but from the whole scene of his action. . . . This self . . . is a *product* of the scene that comes off, and is not a *cause* of it" (Goffman 1973: 252). The Chicano Movement helped shape the self by providing discourses of racial resistance.

It is a credit to the civil rights movement and affirmative action era that Tony feels that his race has boosted his employment opportunities. Unlike his father, whose educational progress was clearly stymied by racial discrimination, a fact that incited his Chicano Movement activism with the Brown Berets, Tony's prime career-building years followed the civil rights movement.

Marcus's activism in the Chicano Movement also contributed to Tony's cultural maintenance inclination. Marcus's staunch representation of his race/ethnicity informed the principles he taught his son. Further, awareness of his father's activist history strengthened Tony's belief in the importance and value of retaining Mexican culture in the United States. This story of activism or outlook in the parent generation being passed to the next generation is representative of a phenomenon present in cultural maintenance families. In all but two cases of second-generation cultural maintenance individuals, the children carried on the ideologies taught to them by their parent(s). Among the five second-generation individuals (one woman and four men)[15] who voluntarily claimed activism in (as opposed to merely sympathy with) the Chicano Movement, all of the children interviewed were living out a culturally aware and highly identified lifestyle.

Sociopolitical era influences self-identification choices. Some Latin Americans emphasize their Spanish roots in order to be closer to whiteness, or at least ally themselves with a country that has a long history of global dominance (Oboler 1995). Others choose to affirm Latin American and indigenous roots and resist official definitions imposed from above (such as by using the self-definition "La Raza," literally meaning "the race" or "roots," rather than the government-sanctioned term "Hispanic," used first in the 1980 U.S. Census). Tony prefers "Hispanic" because it derives from the Iberian Peninsula in Europe and is perceived as superior to other options. The current racial hierarchy is based on a "pigmentocracy." Highlighting skin pigmentation as the key variable to racial worth, pigmentocracy is the idea that "miscegenation throughout the colonies, racial classifications, social status, and honor evolved into a hierarchical arrangement" based on skin tone (Oboler 1995: 21). In such a system, white skin denotes high status and honor whereas dark skin is associated with physical labor, conquered peoples, and slavery. Therefore, it is strategic to claim a self-title that denotes light skin and connotes racial privilege. Tony's ethnic/racial claim reflects the profound influence of his maternal grandparents and is incongruous with that of his father, who underscores his Native American and Aztec heritage. This generational contrast in racial/ethnic labels exposes three key elements. First, the calculated use of terms, such as "Spanish" or "Hispanic," can be a way to access racial privilege. Second, the self-conscious use of political labels, such as "Chicano," can be a way to claim (nonwhite) racial pride. Third, historically dependent discourses of race, and families' reactions to those racial politics, shape racial and ethnic self-understandings.

Comparing Thinned Attachment and Cultural Maintenance Families

Like thinned attachment families, cultural maintenance families are upwardly mobile and structurally assimilated into the U.S. mainstream. The difference is that they retain a high degree of cultural affiliation and identification with Mexico and a Mexican American community. Straight-line assimilation theory suggests that cultural assimilation is a gateway to other forms of assimilation, yet upward mobility and a strong Mexican American identity are not mutually exclusive. The concept of "selective acculturation" (Gibson 1988; Portes and Rumbaut 2001; Zhou and Bankston 1998), a part of segmented assimilation theory, does not adequately capture what is happening in these middle-class Mexican-origin families' lives. "Selective acculturation" holds that immigrant parents and their children (either foreign born or U.S. born) undergo a learning process "embedded in a coethnic community of sufficient size and institutional diversity to slow down the cultural shift and promote partial retention of the parents' home language and norms" (Portes and Rumbaut 2001: 54). Cultural maintenance, as seen in this chapter, differs in that most often these families achieved middle-class status and moved out of coethnic communities by the adulthood of the second generation. The examples of selective acculturation are based on research on relatively small ethnic enclaves, such as Sikhs in southern California (Gibson 1988), Vietnamese in New Orleans (Zhou and Bankston 1998) and California (Thai 1999), and the pre-1980 Cuban exile community in southern Florida (Portes and Rumbaut 2001), where highly organized, well-integrated communities create and maintain social networks and institutions. In contrast, my interviewees existed in a middle-class context. This upward mobility often led to out-migration from ethnically homogenous Mexican-origin neighborhoods, meaning that these Mexican American respondents did not have the same density of coethnic social networks as those communities that exhibited "selective acculturation." This class distinction foregrounds socioeconomic status as an important axis of difference among immigrant families. Furthermore, "selective acculturation" theorizes only the first- and second-generation family links, not attempting to explain the cultural allegiance of the third generation, which, as we have seen, can persist.

While thinned attachment and cultural maintenance are archetypes, they are best envisioned as two ends of an incorporation *spectrum*. Factors, or "bumps," in the process of integration that lead toward a cultural maintenance trajectory include endogamous marriage/partnerships, Spanish surnames, dark skin tone and non-European phenotype, Catholicism, traditional gender ideologies, strong family memory, and participation in civil rights activism. Differences between the thinned attachment and cultural maintenance patterns that begin in the second generation widen in the third generation.[16] Cultural maintenance individuals recount family memories of ethnic pride more frequently, they more often have Spanish surnames and non-European or ambiguous physical features, they are more often Catholic, and they hold more traditional gender ideologies than thinned attachment individuals. While nearly all families interviewed lived in racially integrated neighborhoods, some cultural maintenance families lived in or in closer proximity to majority-minority neighborhoods than some thinned attachment families. While I have little data on the marriage patterns of the third generation, current dating and marital choices (as well as value systems) suggest that cultural maintenance third-generation individuals will either in- or out-marry whereas thinned attachment third-generation individuals have a high probability of continuing their parents' pattern of out-marriage. In sum, racial/ethnic awareness and cultural allegiance pervade the family life, social life, and practices of Mexican American cultural maintenance families more than for those who are thinly attached.

By highlighting patterns of association, we see that *different constellations of elements* lead to particular pathways of incorporation. There is no single causal mechanism leading to a trajectory; rather, there are *different constellations* of strong and weak elements that lead people to a particular pathway. While different elements combine to promote either thinned attachment or cultural maintenance, these two categories are distinctive as "ideal types" that represent two types of incorporation trajectories. The concept of "family resemblances" is useful here:

Things within one category bear numerous resemblances to other things within that category, as well as to things in other categories. It need not be the case that all things within one category bear any one resemblance to each other; some resemblances may be taken as more important to category membership than others; some members of one category may be more paradigmatically located within that category than other members of the same category by virtue of possessing more of the more heavily weighted characteristics of resemblance; consequently, category boundaries are fuzzy. Borders between . . . categories, then, are zones of overlap, not lines. (Hale 1998: 323)

While "thinned attachment" and "cultural maintenance" were the most common modes of racial incorporation and self-understanding, these two models are "ideal types" that highlight common trends. Thinking of "thinned attachment" and "cultural maintenance" as two ends of a continuum rather than discrete, dichotomous categories is useful to understanding the nonexhaustive nature of these models. There is a middle ground between these two trajectories and variation within them.

Cultural maintenance families, more so than thinned attachment families, concertedly "remember their roots." They do this by holding onto traditions, religion, and cultural beliefs, and by preserving and transmitting family history. While these orientations may have predated the civil rights movement, that period of heightened racial mobilization helped create the space for a cultural maintenance assimilation pathway and racial identity formation process. The civil rights movement facilitated this cultural maintenance trajectory of racial incorporation into the United States by fostering an environment of multiculturalism and appreciation of diversity.

Elucidating the complex interplay between biography and historical context, Takahashi discusses Japanese Americans:

> [Their] personal decisions and collective actions were made within specific historical contexts where economic and political forces, as well as cultural and ideological realities, were at play. . . . As historical actors, their efforts to shape their destinies emerged from a complex of generational and racial processes and dynamics that intersected with their lives. (Takahashi 1997: 197)

As a result of the civil rights era, minority-oriented social networks blossomed, commitment to social justice and "cultural citizenship" (Flores and Benmayor 1997) strengthened, and multicultural ideologies burgeoned. Given this historical background, second-generation Mexican Americans were empowered to embark upon a cultural maintenance pathway in a way that was more supported by society at large than ever before. Cultural preservationist instincts became proclaimed and enacted more fully in the second and third generations than in earlier periods.

The intersection of history and biography produces profound effects. During the civil rights and affirmative action period racial and ethnic minorities have been empowered to proudly claim nonwhite racial identities. Only a generation earlier Americanization, deportation, and recruitment programs hampered possibilities for ethnic pride. While not formative for all second-generation Mexican Americans, the civil rights movement was a "bump" in the road of assimilation that motivated people to challenge the definition of "American" and claim racial and cultural dignity. It is in part due to the civil rights movement of the 1960s that Mexican Americans in California in the new millennium can live out an upwardly mobile and cultural maintenance paradigm simultaneously.

Chapter 4 challenges the common notion that family instruction moves unidirectionally "down" the generations from older to younger by exploring family formation and its consequences, illustrating how thinned attachment and cultural maintenance pathways are not linear but susceptible to change. The microlevel processes of marrying a life partner can have tremendous influence on multiple family generations in terms of identity and cultural practices. The choice of marital partner, so often considered a purely individual decision in American society, has ramifications that extend far beyond the couples who say "I do."

Tortillas in the Shape of the United States

Marriage and the Families We Choose

Marriage is a central component of assimilation. Marriage patterns, in particular frequency of intermarriage, are a basic yardstick used to measure assimilation. Marriage has historically been understood as a way to preserve or alter the racial makeup of society. Antimiscegenation laws that banned interracial marriage and interracial sex were enforced until ruled unconstitutional in the 1967 Supreme Court decision *Loving v. Virginia*. "Anti-miscegenation laws . . . were both a response to increased immigration from Asia [and Latin America] and a reflection of persistent concerns regarding racial purity and the nature of American citizenship" (Sohoni 2007: 587). While marriage patterns have been the subject of heated popular debate and legal battles, we know less about the role marriage plays in the subjective experience of race among the marital partners and their children, which is the subject of this chapter.

Intermarriage[1] is a measurement of social distance between groups in that it is a legally recognized union that codifies a socially sanctioned heterosexual family, including children who may be adopted or born into the family. Intermarriage of majority and minority group members signals acceptance of an out-group (Bean and Stevens 2003: 152; Rosenfeld 2002). Marriage in general and intermarriage in particular are traditionally viewed as indicators of assimilation. I argue that marriage is particularly important because it can motivate either thinned attachment or cultural maintenance tendencies. Rather than merely be seen as an indicator of an outcome (assimilation), marriage should rightfully be viewed as a factor that drives the direction and speed of assimilation. This chapter asks, How does marriage—both within and outside of the Latino group[2]—contribute to the process of Mexican-origin people's integration into U.S. society? In other words, how does marriage influence ethnic culture retention, transmission, and change? I argue that marriage (that is, whether one marries a coethnic or a non-Hispanic white)[3] heavily influences the process of assimilation.

Considering the complex and strong force that marriage exerts on the ethnic culture of families and its multigenerational ramifications, marriage may best be viewed as a "bump" in "bumpy-line" assimilation. Herbert Gans (1992a: 44) argued for "replac[ing] what has often been described as straight line theory with bumpy line theory, the bumps representing various kinds of adaptations to changing circumstances—and with the line having no predictable end." As will be uncovered in this chapter, marriage is a critical juncture that precipitates both redirections and recommitments to American and Mexican cultures. As families consider "what kind of families they will be" at the point of marriage and cohabitation, we can see how marriage is highly imbricated in ethnic culture, identity, and assimilation.

Recall that in the two previous chapters a family with intermarriage at the second generation was highlighted as a prime example of thinned attachment whereas a family with an intramarriage at the second generation was used to illustrate cultural maintenance. I chose those families because they demonstrate key features of each typology and because they were representative of other families in their respective incorporation trajectories. Marriage is a key factor in shaping thinned attachment and cultural maintenance outcomes.

The table below illustrates the marriage patterns of the second-generation Mexican American cohort. All first-generation immigrants in my study married either Mexican nationals or Mexican Americans. As we saw in chapters 2 and 3, parents raise their children with varying degrees of commitment to their ethnic heritage, and the children accumulate their own formative experiences as they grow to adulthood. Due to heightened structural and spatial integration, marriage in the second generation is increasingly with the dominant racial group. Population studies have found that intermarriage rates rise with each generation (Bean and Stevens 2003; Murguia 1982; Schoen, Nelson, and Collins 1977), Mexicans most commonly intermarrying with whites (Jiménez 2004). The number of intermarriages between Hispanics and non-Hispanic whites is on the rise, from 527,000 in 1970 to 1.4 million in 2000 (Rosenfeld 2009: 70).

We see from table 4.1 that there is a clear pattern of in-marriage for both men and women, particularly for those who are enacting cultural maintenance. Out-marriage was the less common option, with all but one of those people on a thinned attachment course. While intermarriage increases with each generation, this process is slow, with nearly two-thirds

TABLE 4.1

Second-Generation Marital Patterns by Thinned Attachment and Cultural Maintenance Lifestyles and Gender

	Thinned Attachment		Cultural Maintenance	
In-Marry (Endogamy)	Women	Men	Women	Men
	1	5	11	8
Out-Marry (Exogamy)	Women	Men	Women	Men
	1	2	-0-	1

* Data from one second-generation respondent (female) is missing.

of fourth-generation Mexican Americans marrying endogamously (Telles and Ortiz 2009: 265).

Marriage is a useful barometer of integration, especially when we view "intermarriage patterns as *reflecting* and *generating* processes of incorporation" (Bean and Stevens 2003: 196, my emphasis). Understanding marriage as an entryway to the incorporation patterns I have identified (thinned attachment or cultural maintenance) hinges on viewing marriage as an input or a cause. However, marriage or marital choice is also an effect in that "more than likely, intermarriage is selective of those who are already more assimilated" (Telles and Ortiz 2009: 281). For instance, Chicanos most likely to marry Anglos were those with anglicized forenames (John instead of Juan, Martha instead of Marta) (Murguia 1982). Since identities and relationships are dynamic, gender ideologies, cultural toolkits, and religion can both influence a marital choice *and* be an outgrowth of a marital choice. In-marriage has consequences for language, cultural behaviors, religion, racial self-titles, and phenotype that predispose married couples and their offspring toward a cultural maintenance pathway. These same factors, if valued highly, may predispose an individual to select a spouse who mirrors him or her on these racial and cultural elements. The same logic applies to out-marriage and the (preexisting or subsequent) tendency toward thinned attachment. In this way, marriage is best viewed as a feedback loop, a part in a motor that perpetuates (or changes) cycles of thinned attachment or cultural maintenance. However, marital choice does not strictly determine a family's incorporation trajectory, or vice versa, as marriage and integration processes are complex. A constellation of factors can influence the incorporation pathway and racial identity development of a family, yet marriage is among the most influential.

Marriage is a gateway to assimilation trajectories. As a critical juncture in people's lives, marriage is a decisive point of change. Marriage partners will either match or disagree with one's own ethnic background and/or cultural commitments. The ethnic culture that a marital partner brings into the home will have consequences for the way ethnic identities and attachments will be defined and the way everyday life will be organized. Marriage marks a key moment of negotiation and redefinition of family life as a couple embarks upon "settling down," an identity-defining exercise in which they decide what their adulthood will look like and consider (and practice) how they will rear children. Certainly, a marriage decision does not restrict one to a particular cultural life course, but it does influence the way one arranges one's life and teaches one's offspring.

Family ideologies and teachings tend to be envisioned as moving one way "down" the generational ladder from parents to children. The parent-child nexus is the most frequent site for storytelling that teaches the younger generation (Thorne 2000: 54). Yet, the passage of didactic teaching is not limited to a one-way flow from parent to child, teacher to pupil (Mannheim 1936). The accumulated experiences of the younger generation, if communicated to the older generation, can in fact alter the older generation's thoughts and actions. As an example, a younger generation's marital choice may revivify ethnic attachments that, in turn, may work their way "up" the generational chain and influence older generations' cultural practices.

In this chapter I first consider how intramarriage with a fellow coethnic tends to result in ethnic re-identification or cultural resurgence. These are deeply gendered processes in which women predominantly reported an inclination to learn about their native culture—a culture shared with their marital partner. This process of cultural relearning affects the life of the re-identified wife/mother as well as the lives of her children, her spouse, and, surprisingly, her parent(s). This renewed cultural commitment and learning can stall cultural assimilation without inhibiting structural assimilation. Next, I discuss how the racial/ethnic background of a marital partner and his/her ideology and general cultural orientation impact Mexican American and non-Hispanic white intermarriage relationships. Incorporation patterns and racial identity formation are such complex processes that marital partner is influential but not deterministic. Finally, the concluding section argues in favor of a "bumpy-line assimilation" that acknowledges the presence of detours, branches, and reversals on the road of assimilation—a road without a predestined or final destination.

Moving up the Generational Ladder:
Intramarriage and Cultural Resurgence

Beatrice Madrigal, a 62-year-old second-generation woman, lived behind a meat packing plant in southern California where two of her aunts worked when she was young. Beatrice's mother was born in the United States and her father came over the border with his family with legal papers in 1926 when he was in sixth grade. A divorced mother of two daughters, Beatrice is on an assimilationist pathway despite the fact that she lives in a predominantly Mexican town. While she is conversant in Spanish and fluent in English, she feels that her cultural background is empty and insignificant. She remarks that, in terms of Mexican culture, she "[has] nothing to pass on to [her] kids." Indeed, her parents did not encourage her to retain Mexican traditions: "[My mother] would say, 'if you want to learn how to play castanets, if you want to learn how to do folklórico, then that would be fine.' But she didn't say, 'we come from here, this is our ancestry.' No, no, none of that." Beatrice's parents focused on financially providing for the family and were indifferent about passing on an ethnic culture. They did not talk about life in Mexico because they relocated to the United States in order to have a better life, and focusing on a prior era in Mexico diverted their attention from "making it" in the United States.

Like all immigrants I interviewed, Beatrice's parents came to the United States in order to capitalize on the greater opportunities and to build a better life for their children. Holding on to the American Dream of upward mobility, Beatrice's parents bought a house because they saw home ownership as the capstone of middle-class achievement. Her motto to her two daughters was, "Buy a house, buy a house, buy a house," which they both succeeded in doing. Educational achievement is also part of the American Dream; both of Beatrice's daughters graduated from college and one went on to law school. Beatrice has worked at the same elementary school—currently as a school-yard monitor—for twenty-two years. Displaying her hearty work ethic, she wants to achieve upward mobility for herself and her family without government aid: "We're proud Mexicans, we don't want handouts."

Similar to Tamara Rosenberg in chapter 2, Beatrice explicitly did not want to marry a Mexican because she wanted to avoid the patriarchal tendencies that she saw in the Mexican community. Casting aside these intentions (and probably also finding her choices restricted because of living in a largely Mexican town), she ended up marrying a Mexican man. However, he eventually left her for another woman. Beatrice reflects,

BEATRICE: I wasn't looking to marry in the culture. I wanted somebody not in the culture.

JMV: How come?

BEATRICE: Because of a few things I'd seen, I said, "Gee, if I marry into the culture, this is the way it's going to be." [The] father has the say, that father is the law . . . it doesn't make a difference what [the] mom says. When I saw [that] happened [at his] house I said, "Oh, I don't think I want to marry a Mexican." What happened with his parents, he also followed that pattern. It's like, "Wait on me, I come first." Oh my god, what did I do? When I married my husband and started having my family, he wanted his plates first and then my kids'. He played that macho "me first."

JMV: What were some of the things you wanted to avoid when you were in your not wanting to marry a Mexican phase?

BEATRICE: I tried to avoid the demanding man: "Do this." I used to see the man not letting the woman work. Why not? Because she's supposed to be home taking care of the kids. What happens if you don't have any kids? Then stay home and take care of the house. Oh God. [A friend] said, "Just go with your feelings, with the flow." Well, the flow got me a Mexican. What I didn't want to get into, I got into.

Despite her intention to out-marry, Beatrice married a Mexican man who only confirmed her fears of male domination and female subordination. In spite of her marriage with a coethnic, she retained her assimilationist sentiments, never teaching her children Spanish or imparting Mexican traditions.

Reyna, Beatrice's 35-year-old daughter, ties the origins of her mother's assimilationist tendencies to her grandmother's acculturation goals and perceived discrimination. Reyna comments,

My grandparents probably said, "I want my daughter to do well in the United States and we need to become more Americanized." And so I think my mom learned that from my grandparents. . . . [And] because of the discrimination that occurred . . . in the 1950s my mom dropped off her cultural values. . . . She didn't want me to experience [discrimination] so I think that's why she said, "I'm going to try and acculturate my daughters as much as I can."

As a protective move against racism, Beatrice raised Reyna without the trappings of Mexican culture. Reyna believes that her mother raised her speaking English in the home because of her own experience of discrimination based on speaking Spanish in school:

Spanish is [my mom's] first language and they held her back [in school] and she said they would be scolded if they spoke Spanish [in class]. They sent letters home to my grandmother saying, "Try not to [speak Spanish], your child needs to learn English." And so my mom probably thought, "I don't want my children to grow up like that. I want them to . . . be like everyone else." So I think that is why she didn't [teach] us Spanish.

Reyna's parents did not teach her Mexican culture. Reyna considers:

Religion—which is important to a lot of Mexican families—we didn't practice a lot of traditional Mexican holidays that deal with Catholicism, like the day of the Virgin of Guadalupe [patron saint of Mexico]. . . . My mother-in-law [celebrates] Mexican holidays that are tied in with Catholicism. My parents didn't teach any of that to us. What else did they teach us? Nothing. Mariachi music? No. . . . The food became more Americanized. . . . They didn't know about Mexican history [or] Chicano history . . . so they didn't teach any of that to us.

The single cultural ritual Reyna recalled engaging in was making tamales at Christmastime. Rather than pass on language skills or cultural knowledge, Beatrice instilled the importance of family in her daughters, a value she claims as distinctive but that, in reality, is one not solely prized by Mexicans. When I asked Reyna what her mother taught her about what it meant to be Mexican American, she cited the emphasis on family: "What my parents taught me about being Mexican wasn't so much about the food you eat or . . . the history of Mexico. They taught us that family is really important . . . ; family is going to be there for you. Friends come and go but your family doesn't."

Lacking Mexican-specific cultural moorings intensified Reyna's sense of living between two worlds: "I have no identity. I'm in between. I don't fit here and I don't fit in either culture. So I'm looking for something." She filled this void by seeking out Mexican cultural knowledge and relationships: "I'm just trying to recapture everything. Go back to where my grandparents came [from]." Reyna, who was not raised speaking Spanish and is not conversant in the language, encountered Mexican immigrant students in college, some of whom chided her for not speaking Spanish well and, on that basis, questioned her ethnic authenticity (see Vasquez and Wetzel 2009). Interactions with first-generation Mexicans her own age cut both ways: while they sometimes drove a wedge between herself and more recent arrivals, interactions also provided opportunities to learn more about her ancestral culture.

Reyna "recaptured" a meaningful ethnic identity by marrying a Mexican national. She met her husband, Rudy, in college in southern California. Rudy immigrated to the United States with his family when he was eight years old. Like most respondents who married other Mexican-origin people, Reyna felt cultural comfort with her partner and relished the opportunity to learn more about her background through him. Because of her internal motivation to "recapture everything," it was very important for Reyna to marry within her ethnic culture. Marriage to Rudy reinvigorated Reyna's sense of Mexican identity, supplied her with practical knowledge about Mexican food preparation and traditions, and provided a sense of roots.

Yet gender ideologies and national context complicate this picture. While there is intranational variation in gender ideologies and practices (Barajas and Ramirez 2007), Mexico is generally understood to be more patriarchal than the United States. The level of a society's industrialization has consequences for gender egalitarianism; egalitarian attitudes toward women are more widespread in postindustrial societies than in less modernized countries. Thus, a move from Mexico to the United States yields changes in attitudes, mores, and laws that reflect socioeconomic development and cultural modernization, including increased gender equality (Inglehart and Norris 2003; Norris and Inglehart 2001). Within multigenerational families that experienced a migration from Mexico, "traditional gender attitudes lessen with generation-since-immigration and from parents to the children" (Telles and Ortiz 2009: 205–6).

For all that Reyna learns from her husband's Mexican family, her life is conditioned by America's egalitarian gender ideals, which are generally more democratic than those predominant in Mexico. Reyna was born and raised in this national context, and Rudy, while born in Mexico, spent most of his youth and young adulthood in the United States.[4] Because he was raised primarily in the United States, Rudy's gender ideals were heavily influenced by his new country of residence. Indeed, international migration has been shown to refashion gender ideologies and gender strategies among adult men and women alike (Hondagneu-Sotelo 1994; Smith 2006b) but arguably has an even greater impact among youth still in their formative years.

Like national context, the passage of time and the period into which generations are born alter gender norms. Reyna, a 35-year-old, third-generation Mexican American woman, was raised in a U.S. context that had already experienced first- and second-wave feminism. Given this sociopolitical environment, it was "natural" and socially acceptable (and even promoted) for her to pursue an education and a profession. Contrast this with the gender expectations of Rudy's older Mexican parents. Reyna's interactions with her parents-in-law are complicated due to their conflicting gender ideologies and expectations, which are conditioned both by generation and by national context.

Specifically, Reyna's Mexican-national in-laws expect her to enact an ideal of traditional womanhood (subservience and service to men), a gender outlook and practice that she does not normally embrace. They expect her to behave according to a submissive female role that the traditional patriarchal family system assigns to her. Although she and Rudy's gender strategies correspond and are relatively egalitarian, she feels she is negatively evaluated by her husband's family and constrained by their gender rules. In direct opposition to the gendered and racialized expectations of a Mexican-origin woman, Reyna refuses to serve her father-in-law dinner first or to make herself invisible in the kitchen at family gatherings. While she is happy with the role she has outfitted for herself on an everyday basis with her marital family—she is a college-educated wife, mother, and career woman—when that role is set in relief against traditional patriarchal expectations, she becomes unnerved, believing that her in-laws think she is an "oddball" for being an "aggressive working woman." Reyna explains her position and feelings:

> Another uncomfortable experience as a woman has been—I love my husband's family—but it's a little uncomfortable there because I don't fit the typical . . . I don't want to say the typical Mexican woman from Mexico. . . . There's some [women] that do have careers but from where [Rudy's] family is from, a poor community, a little *puebla* [town], I can't identify with them at all. . . . We don't have a lot of similarities. . . . The women are very passive . . . they're very dependent on the man and I'm not used to that.
>
> In my family you have potluck [parties] because nobody should have to be stuck in the kitchen cooking. Men and women mingle. And in my husband's family, women are in the kitchen and the men are outside. And when the women are finished cooking, they feed the men and they stay in a group. Why are the men over here and the women over here and that's the whole night of the party? And I don't understand that; I just don't like it. Things [like] that do get me very upset and I don't want to say anything because that is the way they are raised and it works for them. Men will tell their wives, "Get me this, get me that." . . . Why can't you just get up yourself? And my father-in-law, I love him to death but he's very *macho*. . . . I feel uncomfortable—he's always telling his wife what to do and "get this for me."

Reyna contrasts her social position and gender ideologies with those of women and men where Rudy's family comes from. As a U.S.-born, third-generation Mexican American working mother of two children, Reyna has far more progressive gender ideologies than her in-laws. These conflicting gender ideologies and practices put Reyna in a tricky position as she tries to remain true to herself while also wanting to be accepted by her husband's family. Reyna prefaces the following vignette by telling me that she and her husband are egalitarian when it comes to who serves whom at the dinner table—either they will serve themselves or they take turns serving each other, offering to replenish each other's plates if one gets up for a second serving. Reyna sketches a picture of clashing gender roles and expectations when she is with her parents-in-law:

> One time we were at a barbeque and the food was right here and [my father-in-law] was sitting right here and everybody got up and fed themselves. My father-in-law was sitting there . . . and sitting, and sitting. My mother-in-law asked him what's wrong, and he goes, "Who's going to feed me?" And then my mother-in-law said, "Your daughter-in-law." And I was sitting next to my father-in-law and I was all, "The food is right there." And he didn't even look at me. . . . That just makes me uncomfortable. And so as a woman I just feel they expect women to act a certain way and I don't do it so it's uncomfortable to me. A lot of times I want to stand up for the women.

Raised in a post–second wave feminist sociopolitical environment in the United States, Reyna asserts her equality, even among her husband's natal family, which adheres to far more traditional gender roles than she does. Reyna's father-in-law, who has much to gain from enforcing traditional gendered power relations, polices her conduct and tests her. He tries to publicly shame Reyna by showing how she does not submit to the gendered rules he thinks suitable for a Mexican-origin woman. However, all he succeeds in doing is to make Reyna uncomfortable and demonstrate that she is a different kind of Mexican-origin woman than those who typically surround him. As this illustration makes clear, there are multiple ways one can "be" a Mexican-origin woman, and this social location is invariably influenced by nation of birth, upbringing, generation in the United States, age, class status, education, and employment status.

Reyna "goes back" to her ancestral culture through her husband and his immediate family members, yet this process includes disputes over gender roles. All of Rudy's natal family members are Mexican nationals and have transported Mexican customs, beliefs, and ideals with them to their homes in East Los Angeles. Reyna credits her husband with fostering her journey of "return":

> When I met [my husband] in college . . . he'd [say], "You never had this?" I would tell him the way my mom made it and he would say, "That's not the real way. Come to my house." And so I would visit him and his mom would cook . . . and share what my culture was really about. They would invite me to *posadas* [Christmas festivals]. Those were good experiences.

Reyna constantly learned about her heritage through attending family gatherings with her husband. Through going to a baptism on a ranch in the San Bernadino area where they had a rodeo, she learned a bit about her husband's early life on a ranch and the lifestyle he had in Mexico.

Reyna's desire to fill the void of her cultural knowledge was so strong that she actively sought to marry a Mexican. Unlike some who saw Mexican culture as containing negative elements to avoid, by marrying a coethnic Reyna saw an opportunity to (re)learn positive cultural features that she felt were woefully absent in her life. Reyna articulates her long-standing desire for intramarriage:

> I think I knew that I would always marry someone of my culture because I knew we had to have commonalities. . . . My husband knew about certain music . . . or whatever and he could relate to this area. After I took the Chicano studies class is when I said I want to marry someone [Mexican]. Especially someone that had an interest in their culture. He's from Mexico and that is what I want to learn about—to know my culture—so he could help me. He could share some things about Mexico, what I was missing. You know, the food, the history. And just us being in MEChA [a Mexican American/Chicano student organization] too . . . we had the same ideals.

By marrying Rudy, Reyna attempted to "recapture" Mexican identity for herself. Now she enacts Mexican practices in order to pass them on to her children: "I try and be around people that can teach me and so then I could teach my children. If I don't, they'll just forget who they are or who their grandparents were or how we got here." With the help of her husband, Reyna is reviving Mexican traditions and the use of Spanish in her children, the fourth generation. Reyna discusses what she wishes to transmit to her children:

I would like to teach them everything that I had learned in my Chicano studies class. . . . I would like for them to learn Spanish. My husband was speaking to them but because his friends speak English and I speak English . . . they prefer English. . . . I would like them to know about cooking certain foods but mostly about the history . . . their ancestors, even up to the Mayans and the Aztecs.

As a mother, Reyna is concerned with raising her children with the cultural knowledge that she lacked as a child but that she felt was important to her identity.

As the Madrigal family illustrates so well, ethnic re-identification may have the consequence of stalling or even reversing acculturation processes. It is not coincidental that Reyna's "retraditionalization," or study and adoption of cultural practices, followed the "symbolic moment" of marrying her Mexican national husband (Kelly and Nagel 2002: 276, 280). If "'symbolic moments' . . . provide the impetus, emotional power and motivation for individuals to begin a journey of ethnic re-identification," Reyna's marriage to Rudy certainly qualifies as such a moment (Kelly and Nagel 2002: 282). This critical juncture that prompted ethnic re-identification also reinvigorated ethnic traditions in generations both younger and older than Reyna. The "retraditionalization" that affects Reyna, her mother, her daughters, and perhaps even her husband, keeps Mexican traditions alive in a way that wholesale assimilation would not support. As Kelly and Nagel (2002: 277) found among Lithuanian Americans and Native Americans, "ethnic re-identification can slow [assimilation] by injecting resources, energy and meaning into ethnic institutions, practices and affiliations."

Individual ethnic renewal involves "matters of personal identity and the groups with whom one identifies and associates" and may be motivated "during the course of bringing up and socializing children" (Nagel 1996). A person who was not previously ethnically identified can experience a surge of interest in acquiring knowledge for the purpose of rearing children. Nagel (1996) refers to this as "reverse cultural transmission" or "reculturation," where "the passing on of family history and traditions to one's offspring can prompt a non-ethnically-identified parent to learn about his or her ethnic ancestry and take on a new ethnic self-awareness." Desiring to teach their children about their ethnic roots motivates these parents to return to or rediscover their ethnic ancestral heritage. This process of becoming more ethnic is inspired by the younger generation in that parents desire to provide a refurbished and stronger ethnic identity than they themselves had in their youth.

It is typical to think about passage of knowledge "down" the generational ladder from parent to child, yet the two-way dynamism of family interactions challenges us to consider the effects that the junior generation has on the senior one. We infrequently consider the cultural knowledge that moves "up" the generational ladder from child to parent. Through her marriage to a Mexican national, Reyna not only restored her knowledge of Mexican culture and equipped herself to transmit this knowledge to her children but passed this on to her mother as well. Reyna's mother, Beatrice, readily admits learning Mexican cooking fundamentals from her daughter's mother-in-law. Beatrice comments on how she learned how to cook Mexican food from both her mother-in-law and her daughter's mother-in-law:

> When I married I didn't know much about cooking. I learned [how to make tortillas] from my husband's mother. . . . They looked like the shape of the United States, but they were edible. My mother never did that. . . . I'm gradually going back to the way my ancestors cooked. . . . I don't know how that kicked in. Maybe that's part of my Mexican coming out: make tortillas, tamales, *taquitos*, or *horchata*. I learned from Rudy's mom because I didn't know how to make *horchata*. It's her that's helping me go back and do it the way my ancestors did it. . . . When my mother passed away I thought, "Oh God, who's going to make tamales?" . . . Part of me, that Mexican part, wants to be that Mexican, I don't want to lose it. I felt I was getting too Americanized. . . . Being around Rudy's mother—she's from Mexico and became a citizen—how she cooked didn't change, she still has that technique. She stretches the tortilla like this, then she throws it, then she turns it [demonstrates with hand motions]. I'm learning through her the Mexican way.

This passage illustrates the desire to learn traditional ways when one realizes that they are at risk of dying out when an older generation passes away. Instead of succumbing, Beatrice actively worked to acquire customary ways of cooking by seeking instruction from her daughter's mother-in-law. In this way, culture not only moves "down" through generations but laterally through marital partnerships and then "up" through generations. Incidentally, as Beatrice undergoes this elective ethnic renewal or "retraditionalization," her point of reference remains the United States, as is evident in her quip that her homemade tortillas come out in the shape of the United States—her American hands produced imperfectly shaped but edible tortillas, a hallmark Mexican food staple.

Women, far more than men, reengaged with Mexican culture in adult-hood, often in connection with marrying a Mexican national or Mexican American. It is revealing that young adult women (engaged or newly married) more often described a willful reconnection with Mexican culture. Women are traditionally viewed as carriers of culture. Women, imagined as wives, mothers, and keepers of traditions, carry a particular "burden of representation" (Yuval-Davis 1997: 45). A number of married and engaged women strengthened their attachment to Mexican culture upon marriage with a Latino man or upon bearing children.

Twenty-five-year-old, third-generation Samantha Diaz deepened her connection to Mexican culture after beginning a relationship with her Mexican American fiancé, Roberto. While Roberto is also third-generation Mexican American, he maintained Mexican culture more strongly in his life than had Samantha. Samantha highlights how her relationship with Roberto marked a turning point in her cultural life: "For me, it just makes things a lot simpler . . . [to have found] someone of the same race and same religion." Samantha continues to explain how her bond to her Mexican background has changed due to her relationship with her fiancé:

> SAMANTHA: Another landmark that had to do with race was when I started seeing my fiancé. I dated white boys previously and I saw that [Roberto and I] had a connection and I related to him so much more than I had anybody else. I go to family functions with him because I connect: we're loud, we like to laugh, our religion is the same, [and] our ideas are the same. I really didn't think it would make that big of a difference but being the same race has a pretty good plus side. If I were to be with some-one else, I know it could fit, but there are just certain things with me and my boyfriend that just fit so much better.
>
> JMV: How has your affiliation changed since seeing your Mexican boyfriend?
>
> SAMANTHA: I think it's changed in that I've become more open minded. It's simple things. I'll even try salsa when I didn't like it before. I didn't like hot food before and that's typical Mexican—salsa and hot foods go hand in hand. I'm interested in Roberto's friends and their lives and habits and will ask them about it. I'm interested because I see that that's what I'm supposed to be, but . . . I'm different still. I'm third generation, I'm pretty far back, and I'm me.

Here we see Samantha become more "typically Mexican" in that she now eats salsa and seeks out information about Mexican cultural ways. Yet, she struggles with a tension about precisely what a Mexican is "supposed to be." She acknowledges that thinking about Mexicans as monolithic is fallacious and eclipses the lives of people like her who are later generation. Despite this internal questioning about authenticity, Samantha has clearly used Roberto and his friends as resources who supply her with intimate knowledge about Mexican culture. Significantly, Samantha's relationship with her fiancé prompted her to learn more about her Mexican background than ever before. No doubt enjoying their cultural similarity for its own sake, Samantha is also, intentionally or unintentionally, positioning herself to fulfill the female-designated role of being a "bearer of culture" as a prospective wife and mother.

Further along in her relationship with a Latino man than Samantha, Yolanda Segura, a 48-year-old second-generation Mexican American woman, is wife to a Puerto Rican man and mother of four daughters. Yolanda had the "luxury of being home" with her children while her husband worked full-time. As a stay-at-home mother, she actively spent time "cultivating" (Lareau 2003) her children as she transmitted Mexican cultural knowledge to them. Yolanda remarks on her childrearing practices:

> I love being Mexican. . . . I love speaking Spanish. I love the culture and the food. And so I've passed it on to my [four] girls . . . and how important family is. My husband is . . . Puerto Rican-American; he was raised in the United States, very, very *Americano* in his ways. I was able to stay home with our girls so [I've passed on] all my traditions. So they consider themselves *Mexicanas* first.

Acutely aware of popular depictions of beauty and the "aesthetics of racism" (Harris 2009: 2), Yolanda teaches her daughters about racial diversity and challenges standard Eurocentric notions of attractiveness:

> I remember reading books to [my girls] . . . the traditional classics [like] Snow White. I would call it Snow Brown and I would [say] she lived in Mexico. . . . Whenever we would play Barbies, it would be "I'm Teresa, *no hablo Inglés*. [I don't speak English.]" I always told my girls, "Look at how beautiful you are. Your color. . . . Be proud of who you are. . . ."

As a mother and "bearer of culture," Yolanda socializes her girls to be proud of their racial and cultural heritage and to be critical of mainstream beauty ideals that do not reflect their own image.

Because women are viewed as symbolic bearers of collective identity, Samantha's and Yolanda's heightened identification with Mexican culture during their courtship, marriage, and childbearing years is particularly meaningful in terms of how gendered roles and responsibilities carry forward cultural ties.

Intermarriage: A Critical Juncture Leading to Thinned Attachment?

All of the Mexican immigrants married other Mexican nationals (or, in one case, a Mexican American). The vast majority of second-generation Mexican American men and women I interviewed intramarried. I define intramarriage or in-marriage as union with another Latino, not necessarily a Mexican-origin person specifically, although most spouses belonged to this ethnic group. Of the second-generation interviewees, twelve men and thirteen women married a person within the same ethnic group and only four married outside their ethnic group. Clearly, the propensity of the second generation is in-marriage with a coethnic.[5] Nationally, "relatively low rates of intermarriage among first generation foreign-born Hispanics have counterbalanced higher rates of intermarriage among native-born Hispanics, particularly among third- and higher-generation Hispanics" (Lee and Edmonston 2006). This amounts to only 8 percent of foreign-born Hispanics intermarrying, compared to 32 percent of the second generation and 57 percent of the third-plus generations (Edmonston, Lee, and Passel 2003). The families I interviewed follow this trend of increasing intermarriage over the generations.

In the limited circumstances where out-marriage occurred in the second and third generations, it is a decidedly gendered phenomenon. In both the second and third generations three men and one woman (for a total of six men and two women) out-married with non-Hispanic whites. Aside from the Montes-Rosenberg family previously discussed in chapter 2, Timoteo Ponce, Albert Schultz, and Milo Contreras were the second-generation Mexican American men who out-married with non-Hispanic white women. This section discusses how they and their third-generation children, Gabriel Ponce, Rex Schultz, and Renata Contreras, move from cultural maintenance in orientation to increasingly thinned attachment.

While intramarriage with a Latino/a typically leads to high incidence of cultural maintenance and intermarriage with a non-Hispanic white fosters thinned attachment, marriage does not automatically *determine* the cultural allegiances and practices of the married generation and their offspring so much as *influence* them. Ideology plays a large role in how strongly or weakly parents attempt to instill a sense of Mexican culture in their children and how receptive the younger generation is to this message. Examining the second and third generations of the intermarried Ponce, Schultz, and Contreras families demonstrates that they range from a cultural maintenance inclination (Ponce family) to a thinned attachment and symbolic ethnicity stance (Schultz family) to active distancing from patriarchal elements of the Mexican community (Contreras family).

Timoteo and Gabriel (Gabe) Ponce are part of a large Mexican family with relatives living in close proximity. This closeness feeds Gabe's Mexican identity. Gabe maintains his Mexican culture in his ideology of multiculturalism, diversity, and desire for minority political representation. Yet, in practice, he engages few traditions outside of claiming a "Mexican American" title. Drawing on a commonsense understanding of marriage as a way to branch toward or away from one's ethnic background, Gabe expresses a desire to "return" to his ethnicity through marriage with a coethnic.

Gabe's father, second-generation Timoteo Ponce, always "remembers" who he is and where he comes from. As a high school principal, he has successfully assimilated both economically and occupationally. His family has seen a strong three-generation rise in terms of education, occupation, and social mobility and feels that money has been key to his advancement and acceptance. Timoteo's parents were migrant farm workers in the Imperial Valley, following the sugar beet crops for work. Timoteo's natal family "celebrated all the Latino or Mexican traditions . . . we had *quinceñeras* [ceremonial fifteen-year-old birthday parties], *bautisos* [baptisms] . . . , we did the Dieciséis de Septiembre [Mexican independence day] festivals, we did Cinco de Mayo." Timoteo distinguishes himself from Mexican nationals, making it clear that despite his cultural activities he is an American citizen: "I'm very, very Mexican. But I'm not a Mexican from Mexico. I'm a Chicano from California."

I asked Timoteo how integrated into U.S. culture he feels. He responded by immediately noting the resistance to his inclusion that he feels from the mainstream despite his middle-class status:

> If I were a different color and had blue eyes and stuff, I'd be a *gabacho* [white guy]. I understand it [the American racial hierarchy] that well. My wife is French-Canadian, so my kids are mixed, if you will. I listen to Mexican music every morning—*cien punto tres*, 100.3, *radio romántico*. We eat Mexican food. But, we also go to the Four Seasons, we go up to the city to plays. We do all that kind of stuff.

In this complex response, Timoteo asserts that he could be totally assimilated except for being racialized due to his physical characteristics. Aside from being categorized as an "other" by outsiders, he participates in both Mexican and American cultures: he listens to Mexican music (which he code switches to Spanish to tell me) and eats Mexican food, yet he stays in expensive hotels and enjoys high-brow urban American culture.

Timoteo discusses his choice to marry a French-Canadian, saying that there was little calculation, as far as race or ethnicity is concerned, regarding who he married and how he counsels his children on whom to marry:

> TIMOTEO: It just happened for me. I wasn't looking for a French-Canadian. I just met a girl. Most of my other girlfriends before that had been little Mexican girls. But when you go to school you meet people.
>
> JMV: How do you advise your children on marriage?
>
> TIMOTEO: I didn't. Let 'em bring whoever they decided to bring. I've never been too pushy on that.

While Timoteo engages in Mexican culture on an everyday basis, through music and food, he chose to marry a woman outside of his ethnic group. While I only interviewed one of Timoteo's two sons, he discusses how they have traveled divergent paths with respect to their assimilation into the dominant culture:

> Our kids were raised middle class. In that sense, yeah, they became mainstream. I've got a *guerito* [light-skinned one] and a *moreno* [dark-skinned one]. . . . The guy that's fair, Gabe, the oldest . . . he's very much into the Mexican thing. Ramón is . . . different . . . he's a yuppie, lives in Huntington Beach, married to an Italian girl. He became more assimilated. I still keep my foot in the other side and so does Gabe.

Timoteo's narrative demonstrates the important point that not all children of the same parents travel along the same incorporation trajectory. Despite being raised by the same parents under the same circumstances, the extent of the brothers' involvement in "the Mexican thing" diverged. Interestingly, in this case, skin color does not determine cultural commitments: it is the fair-skinned son who holds onto Mexican culture and the dark-skinned one who out-marries and is "more assimilated" and does not "keep [a] foot in the other side."

Timoteo's son, Gabriel, has a Mexican American father and French-Canadian mother. A rather heavy-set man with dark, wavy hair, dark eyes, and a goatee, Gabriel says he is often perceived as white instead of Mexican-origin. As a child, he accompanied his father to United Farm Worker rallies and Luis Valdez plays, his Mexican identity formation resulting from a process rather than an epiphany. Aside from facilitating formative experiences in his youth, like attendance at Mexican-oriented rallies and cultural events, his parents "didn't really push [him] to identify as Mexican. I just did it, I just was." "Ponce" is not a typical Hispanic surname. Neither Gabe's last name nor his light skin color signal his background, allowing him to "pass" for non-Hispanic white and obviate discrimination based on race. While these factors could easily lead to thinned attachment, Gabe instead feels that "we need to be able to maintain an identity as a culture."

As far as family traditions in his youth are concerned, like many other third-generation Mexican Americans, Gabe grew up with a few trademark traditions that were more symbolic than substantive, such as tamales at Christmastime. Like the vast majority of third-generation Mexican Americans in the United States, Gabe is not fluent in Spanish. His mother does not speak Spanish, so he did not acquire the language at home. A decisive factor in Gabe's racial identity formation is his large Mexican extended family. I asked, "How is it that you identify so strongly with your Mexican side?" He responded,

> I think it's pretty simple: I grew up with my dad's family. That's who I had my experiences with. Nobody in my mom's family was speaking Italian or eating Italian food or anything like that. We spent most of our time with my dad's side of the family. . . . I just think it was more exposure. Not necessarily that I don't like being Italian too, it's just that I was more exposed to [my Mexican side].

Here we see a pretty classic "down the generational ladder" knowledge transmission process. Parents and adult extended family members teach the youth about their heritage and culture as they go about their daily lives.

Gabe is unmarried but would like to marry another Mexican American so that there is a common base of knowledge and there would be little need for cultural translation. Pointing out the linkage between Mexican identity and Catholicism, Gabe expresses the importance of having a foundation of similar experiences:

> I would really like to marry a woman who is Mexican. Not Argentinean, not Chilean, but *Mexican*. . . . I would like to do that. I think it's like me

and women who are Catholic. I grew up Catholic. . . . The fact is that if I meet a woman . . . who went to a Jesuit school, a Catholic school, we have similar experiences immediately.

Gabe clearly prefers to marry a Mexican woman, implicitly assuming that she would also be Catholic.

Gabe's desire to marry a Mexican-origin woman comes from his longing for cultural similarities and common experiences. Whether conscious or not, Gabe pragmatically wishes for a coethnic marital partner in order to reinvigorate, rather than merely maintain, Mexican traditions in his future children. Passing on more traditions than he grew up with is unlikely to occur in any substantive way unless he partners with a Mexican-origin woman because he alone lacks an extensive storehouse of knowledge about Mexican culture. Regardless of whether Gabe's desire for intramarriage results in marriage with a Mexican-origin woman and strengthening of Mexican cultural ties in the succeeding generation, we see in the example of the Ponce family that despite intermarriage in the second generation, the resulting offspring are not predetermined to embark upon a thinned attachment pathway.

Ideology plays a large role in how committed people are to their racial/ ethnic backgrounds. While the Ponce family sought to retain traditional cultural elements in their lives, the Schultz family was more oriented toward assimilation. Second-generation 65-year-old Albert Schultz was raised to be "an American" and, ashamed of his Mexican background until he earned a middle-class lifestyle, he disassociated himself from Mexican culture. As a blonde-haired, very pale-skinned man, he was commonly perceived and treated as non-Hispanic white. Albert raised his son, Rex, without cultural maintenance sympathies. Thus, as parental ideologies are transmitted from one generation to the next, they provide perspectives that the younger generation can either accept or challenge. In the case of the Schultz family, Rex lived out the thinned attachment pathway begun by his father.

The parent-child transmission of ideology began with Albert's mother, who raised him with assimilationist goals: "My mother wanted me to assimilate. . . . My mother always used to tell me, 'Eres Americano. Aquí estamos en los Estados Unidos, eres Americano.' ['You are American. We are here in the United States, you are American.']" Albert's mother instructed him in his American identity while using the Spanish language. Spanish was Albert's first language, but he lost it in his English-speaking school. In fact, Albert's earliest memory of racial difference was when he was learning the Pledge of Allegiance in English. Importantly, Albert was learning about nationalism as he was acquiring the English language, and it was at this precise moment that he recognized how racial/ethnic distinctions are sometimes bound up with language ability.

Albert describes the traditions in his natal home as well as the tension he felt between Mexican and mainstream American cultures:

> At home we spoke Spanish. . . . There were always beans being cooked. I can always smell *los frijoles de la olla* [a pot of beans] and rice and vinegar on the salad. The traditions are closer to me now than they were then. . . . I was growing up in an Anglo society, so I was a little embarrassed to be Mexican. Not until later on in my life did I become proud of the heritage that I developed.

The culture clash he felt between himself and mainstream America in terms of both race and class led him to deny being Mexican throughout high school. He views the United States as predominantly white and middle-class, obscuring both racial and class diversity. Albert explains,

> The embarrassment came [when] sometimes my parents wouldn't be able to speak English. . . . My mother would go to PTA [parent teacher association] meetings or parent-teacher conferences and she spoke broken English. Even though she was very light-complected it would be broken English. I would feel a little embarrassed about that. I'd feel embarrassed that I didn't have what other kids had. They were better off than me. All through high school I denied being a Mexican. My mother being light-complected, they thought she was from Spain.

Once Albert was educated and firmly in the ranks of the middle class, he felt he was out of danger of slipping into the grips of deleterious stereotypes. "Making it" educationally and socioeconomically allowed him to claim his background as he had never done before.

Albert thought he would marry a Mexican woman because of "the culture and the togetherness," but he ended up marrying an Italian woman. Albert prizes the "closeness of the Mexican family" and is trying to give his children, who were raised in a middle-class home, an understanding of what it means to be "real poor and hav[e] dirt floors" so that they appreciate what they have. That said, he wanted to "give [his] kids something better than [he] had" and so, following in his parents' ideological footsteps, he promoted assimilation and thinned attachment in his children. While Albert never outright stated that assimilation and Mexican culture are irreconcilable, that seems to be his working assumption because, while others of his generation held onto cultural attributes and structurally integrated, Albert only exhibited and appreciated his Mexican background *after* he achieved economic success.

Rex Schultz, Albert's 32-year-old half-Mexican and half-Italian son, looks like a European-origin American. When we described ourselves to each other before our initial meeting at a coffee house, Rex said, "I'm five feet eight inches [tall], fair, with blonde, spiky hair." Since he looks like what people expect a white American to look like, Rex is perceived as such in his business and social life. Friends tease him that he is "the whitest Mexican in town." Unlike his father, he does not have to choose whether or not to hide his racial/ethnic background because it is not visible in either his phenotype or surname, two indicators people use to racially categorize others. Rex acknowledges that his appearance allows him to escape negative Mexican-oriented stereotypes and benefit from positive white American ones. So easily accepted into mainstream culture, he feels completely a part of the U.S. mainstream rather than feeling like an "outsider looking in" or existing in a "third-space" liminal position, as many third-generation Mexican Americans with intramarried parents felt.

Rex is culturally, economically, and structurally assimilated into the U.S. mainstream. He does not refer to any traditions that he grew up with that he wants to make sure to maintain in his own life or pass on to his future children: "We didn't really have any customs, we didn't really celebrate any Mexican holidays. I don't know too much about the Mexican side." The one value Rex treasures and wants to preserve is the emphasis on family, something he learned from both the Mexican and the Italian sides of his family. Rex desires to keep the Mexican and Italian values in part because he was not raised with more specific customs from which to choose what to retain or discard: "[My sister and I will] keep a family atmosphere . . . we'll keep a tighter-knit family. . . . I'd want my kids to be close with their grandparents, like my parents were with my grandparents."

Rex is living out an assimilationist, or thinned attachment, lifestyle. Noting only one core value he wants to retain—the value of family closeness that arguably exists in numerous cultures and that he credits both sides of his family with providing him—Rex is not even remotely symbolically ethnic. He does not participate in any Mexican cultural organizations or engage in Mexican-oriented holiday festivities or daily practices. He belongs to an Italian club but does not engage in any Mexican cultural activities and has few Mexican friends.

A natural consequence of having a thinned attachment to his Mexican heritage, Rex is noncommittal about the prospect of marrying someone with a Mexican background. He notes that intramarriage, as well as intermarriage, have positive aspects: "[With intramarriage] you have better understanding about a person. But then again, I wouldn't mind learning a different side, [from someone with] a different type of upbringing." Rex is in favor of cultural diversity, even though he lacks a long list of traditions he maintains, noting that making time to do interviews such as the one he consented to do with me is one way he acknowledges and represents his Mexican background. He is part of mainstream U.S. culture yet is also a proponent of multiculturalism: "I know the U.S. is a melting pot, but there's also a lot of cultural diversity here and I think we should know our backgrounds, rather than just kind of get in mainstream America and work and make money." While upward socioeconomic mobility is a large component of the American Dream—as lived out by his family—Rex advocates "know[ing] our backgrounds," although this decree is qualitatively different from practicing an ethnic culture on an everyday basis. Due to his phenotype, his surname, and his father's assimilationist ideology, Rex is enacting thinned attachment toward his Mexican culture and is not engaged in "symbolic ethnicity" (Gans 1979).

Of the three intermarried families, the Contreras family is the one that in some ways is most complicated because Renata, the third generation, is seamlessly bilingual and bicultural and yet despite this cultural maintenance declares that she will not marry a Latino man. Milo Contreras is a 59-year-old second-generation Mexican American who intermarried with a European-descent American woman. Their 25-year-old daughter, Renata, exemplifies a conflictual relationship to Mexican culture in that she admires some aspects while simultaneously wanting to distance herself from the patriarchal gender norms she has witnessed.

Despite his out-marriage with a non-Hispanic white woman, Milo wishes to see his two daughters marry people who hail from a similar background. When I inquired about his own marital choice, he immediately directed his answer toward the fact that he chose to marry someone outside of his ethnic group. Milo explained,

[I've heard] everything from "race traitor" to "Mr. White Wannabe" to "Oreo" to whatever. The fact of the matter is that as an impartial employer would defend his hiring practices, "I just found the best candidate I could find." [His voice gets deep and entertaining and he chuckles.] It's not that

I had any aversion to marrying a Chicana, but I never really came across one that I was that attracted to or that I could see in the long run matching. Whereas with my wife I could see a connection at a lot of different levels. And then her own acceptance of me as a Mexican and my family as Mexican—never a sour look or a sour face. In fact the opposite: totally embracing the culture. . . . It's not that I consciously looked for a white person—either ethnicity would have been fine had it matched on all the points that I needed to match.

Milo quickly points to the way other people view his exogamy—labeling him as a race traitor, as a white wannabe, or as someone who is dark on the outside and white on the inside. Milo did not explicitly intend to marry a white woman, but he just happened to find one who "matched" him on the levels he found important.

Milo discusses the cultural intermixing that he observes when he considers himself and his siblings in comparison with their children, at least some of whom are offspring of Mexican American and non-Hispanic white partnerships. Milo remarks,

My brothers and sisters all pretty much feel the way I do: we all speak Spanish and we all have tamales and traditions at Christmas. But our children, because of the mixing with another culture, have to . . . blend it and accommodate it. Because you can't say, "Well, my father's Mexican and, gee, what a rich and beautiful culture that is, that's what I'm going to be." Because then there is a sense of betrayal or self-denial or self-hate by not saying, "I'm *gringa* [white] too! What's wrong with that?" It's not necessarily diluted. Maybe it's enriched by having one foot in one culture and one in the other.

Milo preemptively defends against the critique that the offspring of mixed marriages are "diluting" or weakening Mexican culture or white culture. Instead, he advances the perspective that the two cultures are "enriched" by their merging.

Milo, like most second-generation parents, desired to pass on Spanish to his children. However, in contrast to most other parents of his generation, he succeeded in this objective in part because he and his wife employed a Spanish-speaking nanny whom they referred to as Tía Carlotta. While she is not a blood relative, all family members referred to the nanny as "Tía," meaning "Aunt," a semantic move that suggests her close relationship to the family.

Milo discusses the importance of Tía Carlotta in the upbringing of his two girls and the maintenance of the Spanish language (a language in which he is fluent and his Anglo wife is not):

[My daughters] had the sitter, Tía Carlotta, who spoke Spanish to them all day long as two-year-olds. They spoke Spanish and saw all the soap operas in Spanish and knew all the characters. I, obviously, favored all of that and I spoke Spanish with them when they were growing up. And even now, on the phone when they call, we'll speak Spanish. They get stuck occasionally and they're not as [fluent] as they once were, but . . . they do make an effort to speak. I think they take a certain pride in being able to do that. Because sometimes they're with their friends and they're with me on the phone and they're speaking Spanish. I think that they derive some kind of pride in being able to have that.

Clearly, having Tía Carlotta in the girls' lives in their youth reinforced Spanish and other Mexican customs and promoted the intake of "mediated resources" (Macias 2006) such as Mexican soap operas. Living in an area with a high concentration of immigrants ensures that later-generation Mexican Americans have "abundant access to the ethnic raw materials—ethnically linked symbols and practices—that make for a more salient experience of ethnicity" (Jiménez 2010: 251).

In addition to employing a Mexican nanny, Milo believes that it was living near an extended Mexican family, as the Ponce family did, that tipped the scales in favor of his children growing up with an abundance of Mexican culture. Milo responds to the question of how he thinks his two daughters have handled being raised in a bicultural home:

I think that because of the extended family on my side—versus my wife was an only child and her father and mother were divorced early on— there were cousins they grew up with and played with and so there was kind of an unfair advantage from the Mexican side. But they move well in the Anglo world also.

As we will see, Milo's daughter, Renata, agrees with this assessment that having a large family was a vital resource in her youth that reinforced Mexican values, practices, and traditions. As Thomas Macias (2006) argues, "unmediated resources," namely, direct relationships and interactions with Mexican Americans, perpetuate Mexican ethnicity among later-generation Mexican

Americans. Conservative and liberal scholars alike argue that ongoing immigration from Mexico creates a particular social context for the perpetuation of Mexican ethnicity, particularly in the American Southwest, which is proximate to Mexico and where there is a concentrated Mexican-origin community (Huntington 2004a and 2004b; Jiménez 2010; Montejano 1987). In addition to "unmediated resources," which are relationships with people, "mediated resources," such as Spanish-language television programming or commercial consumption of food and ornaments that do not require direct interaction with Mexican Americans, allow for culture to be uprooted from its origins in local communities and interpersonal relations (Macias 2006: 27). Yet, as in the Contreras family, "it is . . . the unmediated, relational connection to the Mexican American community that endows . . . mediated experiences with ethnic meaning" (Macias 2006: 43). Thus, the "imagining" (Anderson 1991) of a Mexican community is facilitated by interactions with Mexican American people and buttressed by commercially available products.

Contrary to the prediction that intermarriage thins ethnic identification and commitments, Milo states that his affiliation to Mexican culture has "gotten strong over the years" since his marriage with a non-Hispanic white woman. Milo is dedicated to racial representation and visibility even while he is married to a non-Hispanic white woman. For example, when he is a guest speaker at his daughters' high school "career day," he asks to speak to two classes, one filled with Spanish speakers and the other comprised of English speakers. He makes this request in order to ensure not only that Mexican-origin students have a positive role model but also that white students see that a Mexican man can be a successful white-collar professional. Milo did not explain the reasons behind his strengthened devotion to his Mexican background after his marriage, yet clearly his intermarriage did not diminish his racial awareness. Because of the unlikelihood of Milo's *increased* concern with racial minority representation after his intermarriage, one can reasonably suspect that his activism grew out of a tacit fear that his ethnicity would become attenuated due to a bicultural family life. Milo is inconclusive as he advises his daughters on marriage: "I would prefer somebody [for my girls] close in culture. That could be Anglo, that could be Mexican. Obviously the most important thing is that the individual feel comfortable with that person. Life is hard enough without having dirty looks from racists. That's mainly my concern." Ostensibly, this is a vote for intramarriage with someone who is Anglo or Mexican (or both) and, while pleased with the biculturalism in his own marital home, Milo seems to be suggesting that marrying someone outside of the white or Latino racial/ethnic groups is less desirable.

As we observed in the Montes/Rosenberg family in the chapter devoted to "thinned attachment," gender roles and expectations can influence major life decisions, including whom to marry. We see that Renata Contreras, like Tamara and Jillian Rosenberg, consciously veers away from marrying a Mexican man for fear of being locked into rigid, traditional female gender roles. Milo portrays his gendered position in the home as patriarchal:

> There is a real *macho* element where I am the provider, I am the *chingón* [manly man], I'm the one that's gonna bring home the bacon, I'm the one that's gonna protect the house, I'm the one that knows how to fire the guns and train the dogs. . . . And I'm the one that can be out on the streets and still come back, dust myself off, and I'm nice and safe and sound and still the protector. . . . Even though it seems so patriarchal it, in fact, is quite matriarchal. Mothers really run the roost. They run the household and they are less tolerant as would seem on the outside. They have . . . a lot of power and authority in our culture. . . . Being a man means recognizing those [long-standing] dynamics. I suppose that I've asserted myself in a *macho* sense to the extent that I could get away with [chuckles], while recognizing that the one that holds the family together is really the mom.

Milo acknowledges male authority yet also defers to the authority of mothers, the glue that unites families. From Renata's standpoint, however, her father's patriarchal authority is not something she wishes to emulate in her own marital life.

Renata suspects that she will not marry someone of Mexican heritage. In fact, she was dating and discussing marriage with an Indian man at the time of the interview. Renata considers her dating and marriage desires:

> I haven't ever sought out someone of similar background. I've thought it might be interesting to meet someone who is half-Mexican just like me, but the kind of people that I'm attracted to are always dark-haired and have a little color to them. Not just blonde pasty guys. I think it'd be cool to marry someone who has the same background as me, because then we could tell our kids, "This is what you do when you have your first communion, or this is what you do when you have your *quinceñera*, or this is how you make a *piñata*, or little lingo. . . ." Having similar experiences growing up, that'd be kinda neat. But I don't think it's that important. I think whomever you are compatible with is the most important part. I never wanted a full Mexican though, because of my dad's influence. That's

not as important a factor—similar ethnic background—as having the same values or financial security, emotional security, similar education backgrounds, similar interests and personalities.

Renata is wistful about her ethnic background where marriage is concerned. She likes the idea of cultural similarity but she is not limiting her dating options as a result. She specifies what she is trying to avoid by not dating Mexicans:

> The Latin stereotype—even the Italians or French—you just have the image of the noncommitted kind of guy, more domineering or the "well, my dad did that so it's okay; that's the way we are." Mostly that *machismo* attitude that I just hate. I just feel like it's still there and it's part of our culture, but I don't want to go there . . . that's why I stay away from them. Even if my own dad is saying, "I don't want you to marry a Mexican. . . ."

Similar to the second- and third-generation women of the Rosenberg family, Renata is actively distancing herself from undesirable cultural attributes by dating outside of her ethnic group. She does not explain how she interpreted her father's advice not to marry a Mexican (nor did Milo confess to this advice giving during his interview), yet she was emphatic about wanting to out-marry.

Renata wants to avoid the stereotypical domineering or *macho* Mexican man by simply not marrying a Mexican. Interestingly, all third-generation Mexican American men I interviewed complained that *machismo* has had its heyday and must be extinguished. Mexican male authority has been so harshly criticized by women for so long that Mexican-origin women—like Renata—retreat from coethnic relationships in order to ensure they do not get entrapped. However, the distressing irony of this wholesale withdrawal from coethnic romantic relationships is that these women who are resisting patriarchy by refusing to date Mexican-origin men are not allowing for the possibility of cultural change. Notably, because Renata voluntarily isolates herself from relationships with Mexican men, she not only shields herself from the *macho* characteristics she wants to avoid, but she also cheats herself of the opportunity to meet Latino men who defy her negative expectations. In the same way that interethnic contact and friendships destabilize negative group stereotypes (McDermott 2006; Perry 2002), giving Latino men an opportunity to defy negative expectations could reveal or make way for cultural shifts. But, by retreating from Mexican relationships, self-protective later-generation Mexican American women like Renata and Jillian are complicit in perpetuating a static notion of culture and gender ideologies even as they fight against the "macho Mexican male" stereotype.[6]

Despite Renata's inclination to marry a non-Mexican, she said that she would like to give her children a background in Mexican culture and that she would like to ensure they learn Spanish. These aspirations are likely reactions to a probable loss of Mexican heritage in her offspring if she were to out-marry. Remembering that she is half-Mexican and half-Caucasian, she does not have reason to fear loss of her European-descent background because it is omnipresent in the mainstream U.S. culture. Acutely conscious of the influence of increasing generational distance from Mexico, growing assimilation over time, and her probable out-marriage, Renata desires to maintain Mexican culture and the Spanish language in the next generation. Renata contemplates how she could structure her children's lives so they can be immersed in Mexican culture despite having only one half-Mexican parent:

> When my mom went back to work [my parents] got Tía Carlotta for us. She was a Mexican immigrant and only spoke in Spanish, so I want to do that for my kids too. I want to speak in Spanish to them when they are little and have my mom and dad around a lot too and impart their experiences and their culture that way. I think I want to have a babysitter, like a Tía Carlotta, so that they can see this person that they love and they respect and who is totally Mexican and who will make sure that they only speak in Spanish and that they watch the *novelas* [soap operas] with her. I want them to get a good understanding of the world through a Tía Carlotta's eyes. It's very hard for her to get along. . . . I want them to understand how it feels to be walking around from her perspective. It's not just, "Oh, anybody can go buy anything they want and have it easy." You have to appreciate that other people are still struggling. . . .

Renata is sensitive to the intersection of race, class, gender, and nationality that shaped the life of her beloved babysitter. She seeks to impart this same understanding and empathy to her children by following in her parents' footsteps and employing a Latino/a immigrant babysitter. At this unmarried stage in her life, Renata is pondering hypothetical situations and is not taking a partner's preferences into account. So, the degree to which this branching toward cultural maintenance will occur is debatable. Keeping in mind that Renata is structurally assimilated like her third-generation Mexican American peers I interviewed, unlike those her same generation, she is substantively involved in her ethnicity. This engagement with her ethnicity is not wholesale preservationist, however, as she deliberately distances herself from patriarchal aspects she finds troubling and oppressive. As she chooses to claim some cultural features and shed others, Renata is substantially rather than merely symbolically attached to her ethnicity.

Primary relationships with Mexican-origin people and intramarriage are expected to maintain or increase a Mexican ethnic identity, whereas being in a racially mixed environment and intermarrying are predicted to loosen ethnic ties. However, recent research on Latino intermarriage challenges the assumption that out-marriage to whites equals cultural or political whitening (O'Brien 2008). Cross-racial intimacy, achieved either by being mixed-race or partnering with a non-Hispanic white, can lead to a racially progressive stance. A racial progressive is someone who approves of racial intermarriage, supports affirmative action, and acknowledges the reality of discrimination rather than espousing a "color-blind" ideology (Bonilla-Silva 2003; O'Brien 2008: 164). Latino intermarriage with non-Hispanic whites resulting in racial progressivism is *counter* to assimilation theory's whitening thesis, which predicts intermarriage will be an indicator of assimilation. Inverting this prediction, rather than minimizing attention to race, intermarried Latino respondents are acutely aware of race and racism because they compare their own racialized experiences with those of more privileged experiences of whites in their families (O'Brien 2008).

Since cross-racial intimacy can function either to diminish or to elevate the importance of ethnicity, the racial *ideology* of influential family members is consequential for racial identity formation. The Ponce family was committed, in philosophy and practice, to maintaining Mexican ways of life whereas the Schultz family was far more noncommittal (and, in fact, in the second generation purposely passed as non-Hispanic white). The Contreras family offers an insight into how gender influences the flow of cultural attachments. Bear in mind, however, that the influence of gender is complicated and does not determine whether one prefers to in- or out-marry. We have thus far seen cases of women specifically wanting to marry both within and outside of their ethnic group for cultural reasons. Renata Contreras wishes to out-marry in order to avoid the male dominance displayed by her father, yet she also wishes to retain Spanish and cultural practices. Structurally assimilated and mixed race, Renata lives an ethnically conscious life as she selectively retains and discards Mexican cultural elements. Reyna Madrigal, in contrast, desires to in-marry in order to facilitate her ethnic renewal. She desires to acquire through her husband and his family the Mexican culture and traditions she grew up without and pass them on to her children.

Men were disproportionately represented in the intermarriage category. In addition to exogamy, ideology can lead people in different directions. There was also a distinct difference in the ways men and women who intermarried talked about the process. Women wanted to flee patriarchy whereas men spoke about attraction and finding the best fit. "Best fit" is an enigmatic and malleable concept, and it is noteworthy that the three men intermarried with non-Hispanic white ethnics, such that one can argue they are "marrying up" racially and gaining a status advantage. As predicted by classic assimilation theorists, these second-generation Mexican American men are structurally assimilated, middle-class, and in predominantly white or racially heterogeneous social environments, all of which increases the probability of out-marriage (Gordon 1964). Women based their decisions to out-marry on not wanting to risk entrapment with a patriarchal marital partner. The ideologies one uses to consolidate a stance toward one's Mexican heritage also guides marital choice. Marriage decisions, in turn, affect the assimilation pathway one travels and become significant contributors to the racial/ethnic claims, beliefs, and cultural practices of the next generation.

Marriage as a "Bump" in Assimilation Processes

Marriage both shapes and is shaped by assimilation processes. Marriage marks a major potential turning point for cultural revitalization or diminution. In my sample, it is most common that women marry a coethnic, which consolidates their racial identity as Mexican American. Mirroring broader demographic trends of increasing intermarriage with each generation, the intermarriage rate among Mexican Americans "is so slow so that even by the fourth generation, nearly two-thirds are still married to other Hispanics" (Telles and Ortiz 2009: 265). For women interviewees, intramarriage with a Mexican-origin man becomes a driving force in women connecting with their Mexican cultural lineage, even if it was a previously absent or minimal part of their lives. In-marriage relationships clearly affect cultural transmission "down" the generational ladder as parents (in particular, mothers) raise children. Cultural learning and revitalization can move "up" generations as well as "down": in-marriage can cause members of an older generation to learn more about their ethnic identity as well.

If intramarriage is a means to (re)learn cultural knowledge, intermarriage presents an opportunity to diminish one's connection to Mexican people and culture. Exogamy offers an opportunity to speed the process of assimilation. Through marriage with an out-group member—in particular, a non-Hispanic white, which was the tendency among my respondents—Mexican Americans adopt more American cultural habits and associate more with racially mixed or predominantly Anglo crowds. Specifically, women viewed intermarriage as an escape route out of a patriarchal system of gender relations that they felt typified the Mexican-origin community. Men, alternatively, out-married with white ethnics and did so with the logic that they could still practice their Mexican culture if they cared to do so. Thus, ideology becomes an important piece of the gender and marriage puzzle in terms of who chooses to retain versus discard their native cultural trappings.

Marriage is highly influential in terms of how a family routes itself either toward or away from Mexican or American culture. The dynamics that marriage set in motion have potentially major consequences for multiple generations: the marital partners, the successive generation (children), and the prior generation (parents). In this way, marriage can be viewed as a "bump" in the loosely defined term "bumpy-line" assimilation.

Recall that Herbert Gans (1992a: 44) argued to "replace what has often been described as straight line theory with *bumpy* line theory, the bumps representing various kinds of adaptations to changing circumstances—and with the line having no predictable end." The incorporation trajectories of three-generation Mexican American families is accurately described as "bumpy" in that there are unpredictable departures, swerves, and then resurgences of commitments to both adopted and native cultures. Importantly, the "[bumpy] line having no predictable end" allows for a vast diversity of both processes and outcomes for any immigrant ethnic group, ranging from "thinned attachment" to "cultural maintenance." This open-endedness acknowledges that some strata of an immigrant group—be they distinguished by race, class, gender, human capital, skin color, etc.—may have trajectories or end points quite different from others.[7]

Children of intermarried couples tend to intermarry, identify less with Mexican origin, and are more likely to call themselves "American" (Telles and Ortiz 2009). My data on the third generation add to these findings that physical appearance, particularly skin tone, Hispanic-sounding names, and gender play important roles in whether Mexican Americans are perceived and treated as non-Hispanic white or are racialized as non-white (Vasquez 2010). Later-generation Mexican Americans who bear light complexions similar to those of non-Hispanic whites are awarded the (white) privilege of voluntarily claiming their ethnicity or quietly "passing" as non-Hispanic white. Due to volitional identity changes that range from adopting pan-Latino categories or embracing mainstream identities, Mexican-origin people may cease to call themselves Mexican, Hispanic, or Latino, instead becoming "Anglos with Mexican ancestry." This "loss" of members of the Mexican community due to identity changes "makes it impossible to measure the gains of this group; [uncounted gains becoming] 'unmeasured progress'" (Alba 2006: 293). If the most successful echelon of Mexican Americans are likely to intermarry or otherwise cease to identify themselves or their offspring as Hispanic, human-capital gains across generations may be understated (Grogger and Trejo 2002: 7–8). Thus, as we consider the consequences of intermarriage, it is important to note the potential "disappearance" of those who achieve upward mobility, intermarry, or, as children of intermarriages are multiracial, become "part Hispanics" (Lee and Edmonston 2006) and potentially blend into the fabric of American society.

Integration over three generations is a "bumpy" process in that while there is intergenerational progress in terms of structural assimilation, there is also a spectrum of ways in which Mexican Americans can choose to engage Mexican culture. Marriage choices—specifically, whether one marries endogamously or exogamously—have distinct consequences for the possibilities of either continued assimilation with the American mainstream or a turn toward cultural resurgence. As Telles and Ortiz (2009 284) note, both modern assimilation theory and segmented assimilation theory "exaggerate the consistency and uniformity in direction to which assimilation occurs across a wide range of social dimensions." Pursuing the critique that "assimilation, or the lack of it, can occur at quite distinct paces and even in an opposite direction" (Telles and Ortiz 2009: 284), this chapter demonstrates that marriage (including marital partner, families-in-law, ideologies, and gender) represents a "bump" that exists along the road of assimilation that can speed, stall, or redirect the flow of integration.

Part II

5

Whiter Is Better

Discrimination in Everyday Life

Eyes [can be] really clouded by lenses that are named racism.
—Pierre-Mecatl, 29-year old male interviewee

We should turn around and show we're not what they think!
—Beatrice, sixty-year-old female interviewee

Ruben and Adele Mendoza are a married second-generation couple who are both light skinned and have a Hispanic surname. They tell me a powerful tale about how their Spanish-sounding name—Mendoza as a "giveaway" last name—restricted their access to housing when they were newlyweds:

ADELE: We were looking for a place to live and we went apartment hunting. There was a small little cottage . . . we went to go look at—[it was] just perfect, what we had wanted. So we told the guy [property manager], "Would you give a chance to go home and get the money and we'll be back in an hour? And then we'll come back and give you the deposit and the rent." He was all, "Oh, yeah, yeah, fine." They had a formal book and so I put our names down on the register—"put you down so I'll know when you come back." When we came back they said, "Sorry, it's already been rented." And they slammed the door.
RUBEN: We asked a couple of our friends to go and check out the apartment for us: "Oh yeah, it's still vacant."
ADELE: I mean, "Ruben Mendoza." That is very obvious, who we are. [I]t's a dead giveaway. . . . What is the problem? Just because he thought we were white—because we were white!!—but once we put the name down we are all of a sudden these evil people.

The United States has a long history of housing segregation (Conley 1999; Massey and Denton 1993; Oliver and Shapiro 1995), and even now U.S. cities remain highly segregated. After being refused at the door by the property manager, the Mendozas confirmed the continued vacancy of the cottage and could not come up with an alternative explanation for having been refused besides the fact that they had written their last name, the "dead giveaway," down on the register.

Discriminatory practices such as this demarcate racial groups by establishing racial boundaries that exclude racial minorities from educational, workplace, or social arenas on the basis of their assumed inferiority. Discrimination erects boundaries to access at the entryway of valuable resources (school, housing, employment, church, commercial zones, social groups), making the sustainability or permeability of racial boundaries a significant question. "Discrimination" is defined here as "attitudes, overgeneralized beliefs, and actions that are mobilized to cement superior group position relative to other groups." Discrimination arises when individuals or groups are denied equality of *treatment*, as opposed to prejudice, which is an "*attitude* of favor or disfavor . . . and . . . related to an overgeneralized (and therefore erroneous) *belief*" (Allport 1979: 13). Discrimination is particularly deleterious in its capacity to instantiate a vision of the world, for "social divisions become principles of division, organizing the image of the social world" (Bourdieu 1984: 471). As people segregate themselves from "others" by way of discriminatory practices, they devise reproducible social categories and ways of life, such as segregated neighborhoods, as we saw in the opening vignette.

This chapter addresses the following questions: What are the sites and forms of the discrimination Mexican Americans face? Which types of discrimination are common across generations and which are distinctive? How do respondents react to discrimination? In what ways is discrimination challenged, resisted, or internalized? What are the generational differences in perception of discrimination and coping mechanisms?

Common Discrimination Experiences across Generations

Members of all three generations were targeted for discrimination on the basis of specific nonpersonal features such as name, skin color, and physical appearance. All three generations were subjected to extra degrees of surveillance in public spaces, whether by shop employees in retail stores or by police officers in municipal zones.

Color-Coded and Labeled: The Impact of Skin Color and Names

Discrimination does not affect all Mexican Americans equally. In a society where "the constitution of racism through . . . economies of color" (Harris 2009: 1) is prevalent, skin color plays a crucial role in the way people are categorized and treated. As one interviewee quipped, "White is right; you were born wrong." Interviewees informed me that they learned at a young age that "lighter is better," and thus they tried to "wash off" their darkness or use facial medications to lighten their skin color. Skin color holds the possibility of "passing," of being perceived and treated as an uncontested part of the white majority. While debate continues as to whether Mexican Americans are a race or an ethnic group—and if an ethnic group, whether they fall under white or nonwhite racial categories—privileges attendant with whiteness makes skin color a critical physical feature. Some Mexican Americans "pass"[1] as white, either intentionally or unintentionally.[2] Light skin color offers an "ethnic option" (Waters 1990) of claiming whiteness. Conversely, some Mexican Americans of light skin color find themselves having to continuously assert their group membership or else it will go unrecognized.

The advantage of being light-skinned lies in being the beneficiary of "white privilege," or at the very least obviating negative stereotypes to which darker-skinned individual are more quickly and more often subjected.[3] Evelyn Morelos draws a tight link among skin color, beauty, and snap judgments:

> I'll tell you about prejudice. It's not who you are and where you come from, it's how fair your skin is. You notice how if you're fair and pretty, if you're attractive, I don't care what you are. It's terrible, but that's the way it is. . . . I really feel that if you're really dark-skinned, people judge you. Right then and there.

Tyler Mendoza explains how his light complexion was an advantage when it came to avoiding police stops and obtaining employment. When I asked him the intentionally broad question, "When you look in the mirror, what do you see?" Tyler immediately honed in on the importance of his skin color to his social identity, as well as his gender and race:

> TYLER: [I'm] a man. A light-skinned man . . . Chicano/Latino man that has not earned the privilege but has received privilege because of my light eyes and my light skin.

JMV: And how does that receiving but not earning privilege work?

TYLER: [Friends of mine] get profiled by police and I don't. . . . For instance, I'll go to a party when I was really, really, really, really young and people would just wave their hand and okay, I can come in but the people behind you have to check to see who they are. Of course, they were darker than me. . . . [I] sometimes know that I've received a job over someone because of what I look like.

Tyler accurately discerned that he "has not earned the privilege but has received privilege," and he sees how unfairly rewards are distributed when he compares his experience with that of his darker-skinned peers. He noted that someone "paid the price" and rather than be riddled with guilt at receiving this unrequested advantage, he said he is committed "to making sure that door always stays open for someone behind [him]." Like Tyler, a number of light-skinned respondents claimed that they had escaped racism because they are assumed to be unquestionably white; a subset of those individuals remarked on being an insider-outsider positioned to hear derogatory comments made against Mexicans because the speaker wrongly correlated skin tone with ethnicity. A study on skin color revealed that light-skinned Mexican Americans "have a significantly warmer affect toward Anglo-Americans than do Mexican Americans of darker skin colors," sentiments that probably reflect experiences with Anglo-Americans that were colored by physical appearance (Murguia and Forman 2003: 75).

Both skin color and last name mark not only who gets perceived as Mexican American and who does not but also who is more likely to self-identify as Mexican American. As Mary Waters (1990) notes with regard to middle-class white ethnics in the United States, people often prioritize their last name in identification choice. Demonstrating the dominance of male lineage, 60 to 77 percent of her respondents expressed preference for their father's as opposed to their mother's ancestry (Waters 1990: 33).[4] Both formal name and phenotype are markers of ethnic background and can be criteria upon which others judge the allocation of scarce resources. Contemporary research has found that names that signal a racial minority status can work against a job applicant in obtaining a job interview (Bertrand and Mullainathan 2004). Understanding that names can be a disadvantage prompted one interviewee to change her Hispanic last name to a non-Spanish-sounding surname in order to avoid stereotypes.

Samantha Diaz is well aware of the potential pitfalls of her ethnic-sounding last name and her physical appearance. A third-generation woman, she has medium-olive skin, has black hair, and is short of average height. She attended a majority-white elementary school where she "thought that she was white," and it was in high school when she learned that others categorized her as Mexican. In answer to whether she felt her physical appearance had helped her or barred her from gaining entrance to any social or occupational arena, Samantha said,

> I don't know if it's reality, but I feel like it's restricted me. I got the feeling that I'm jinxing myself or something, but when I tell people my last name, I wonder what reaction they're going to have. Because "Diaz" is very Mexican. . . . When I'm talking to people or interviewing for things [jobs] . . . it's like I'm back in high school again and I have to pretend I'm white again. . . . The sad thing, in high school too, I wanted to be a lighter color. I actually put Clearasil on my face to get it a lighter skin tone. I thought that was pretty profound. . . . When interviewing, I know I probably could have gotten something higher, but I'm intimidated.

Here, Samantha packs in commentary about ethnic names, skin color, and internalized inferiority. While she never pointed out discrimination she faced directly, Samantha has perceived enough discrimination in the world that she knows the payoff there is to being perceived and treated as white, hence the attempts to lighten her skin tone. Samantha's surname and skin color have amounted to a mild psychological handicap and cause her to feel intimidated in job interviews and at work. She fears that her physical appearance and her ethnic-sounding name will saddle her with negative stereotypes by her potential employers. To overcome this, she is resolved to "prove" her worth through a combination of "walking on eggshells" and "working hard." However, discrimination and negative stereotypes insidiously converted into a sense of inferiority and discouraged her from competing for promotions ("I know I probably could have gotten something higher, but I'm intimidated."). Racism can reduce feelings of self-worth and heighten self-doubt (McDermott 2006; Menchaca 1995). Racism does not have to be actively deployed in order to be effective—its ripple effects run far and wide beyond the point of initial impact.

The "Shopowner Tailgate"

Being closely supervised or "tailgated" when shopping in retail stores was a common method of discrimination across all three generations. The obvious suspicion on the part of the store representative is that the Mexican

American intends not to purchase items but to steal them. A form of subtle harassment, the "shopowner tailgate" is not deployed even-handedly toward whites and minorities alike but is geared toward surveilling racial-minority customers. Elena, an attractive, olive-skinned professional woman who is forty-eight years old, explicitly states how shopkeepers link race and class when calculating which customers to watch with extra rigor:

> I have enough money that if I want to buy a three hundred dollar blouse I can buy one. . . . I've seen other people in the store that look not even as dressed as well as I was dressed and *they're* not followed around, but I am. So I think there's still a stereotype-thing that's going on with [people thinking] Latinos or Mexican people are thieves or "they-can't-afford-to-be-here-why-are-they-even-here?" kind of thing.

The "shopowner tailgate" can be a matter of a distrustful store clerk keeping an overly watchful eye on customers or it can mean a retailer calling Immigration and Naturalization Services and having customers deported. The responses to this discrimination can range from the self-censorship of "walking on eggshells" to social action undertaken in response to a real or vicarious experience of discrimination.

Racial Profiling and "Cross Discrimination"

Negative stereotypes play into the way police forces patrol minority and/or low-income communities. While these communities tend to have higher rates of incarceration, this is partly due to increased police presence in these areas as well as to the structural constraints that impoverish them in the first place. The "epidemiological" approach to policing—police forces targeting their surveillance in areas inhabited by black and Latino populations—insures the higher probability of these youths being stopped by officers of the law, perpetuating a vicious cycle (Brown 2003: 150). Harry Torres, the son of Mexican immigrants who was born in the United States, shows how race and immigration status can become intertwined in the eyes of the Immigration and Naturalization Services, commonly referred to as "La Migra":

> JMV: When did you first realize there was something in the world called "race," whether or not the concept was named at the time?
> HARRY: Very, very, very early. Before grade school we [he and his siblings] used to get stopped by *La Migra* [border patrol] all the time going to

work. They'd make us go back and get our papers. They wouldn't arrest us
   or nothing, but they'd make us go back and get our papers and we had to
   go back and show it to them. Right here in Watsonville.

Here, "Mexican" and "immigrant" become one and the same as Harry and
his siblings, all young United States citizens, are spotted as possible undocumented workers.

   If "Mexican" doesn't equate to "immigrant" in the eyes of police—
who are frequently acting on prevalent stereotypes, but with an authority
unmatched by laypersons—"Mexican" often equates to the assumption of
"poor," as demonstrated in the "shopowner tailgate." Being labeled as poor
has a totally different meaning if the accuser is a layperson as opposed to a
policeperson who has the power to pull over, detain, interrogate, and arrest
the accused.

   What if Mexican Americans, deliberately or not, try to prevent being perceived as Mexican American? Will the act of dissembling be effective protection against being racially profiled as Mexican American? While the answer
requires more study and probably breaks down according to specific features
of the situation, the experience of Pierre-Mecatl Ramirez, a third-generation
man, indicates that the answer is "no." Pierre-Mecatl tells me how he feels he
was racially profiled even though he was not "performing race" in stereotypical ways:

> I went to a little park in downtown Sacramento, a nice little spot I like.
> I was looking up at the sky, just being mopey [after a breakup with a
> girlfriend]. This cop comes up to me, just out of the blue, harassing me,
> asking me these questions about this piece of graffiti next to me that I
> haven't even seen. . . . This cop is talking to me about this piece of graf-
> fiti. . . . When I was a teenager, I affiliated with the Gothic subculture, so
> I was dressed in a velvet blazer and a bowler and this guy's talking to me
> about this graffiti. "Well this is Mexican graffiti." He's looking around for
> my pen. . . . I caught that he was basically saying, "This is Mexican gang
> graffiti and your last name is Ramirez." He had my I.D. I was like, "Is
> anything you're doing legal?" He gave me back my license and told me
> to get the fuck out of there. . . . If you can't tell I'm not a gang member,
> based on what I'm wearing, what kind of training do you actually have?
> I'm wearing velvet. No *cholos* wear velvet. I mean, maybe I have a low-
> rider car, but. . . . His eyes were really clouded by lenses that are named
> racism. [Laughs.]

Even when Pierre-Mecatl was not dressed in a typical *cholo* outfit—which serves to further demonstrate the diversity of ways one can "be" Mexican American—he was still pegged as Mexican American (complete with a negative stereotype of criminality) by the policeman. Social psychologist Erving Goffman envisioned social status or group association as something *performed*. Goffman articulated this "culture as practice" idea: "A status, a position, a social place is not a material thing, to be possessed and then displayed; it is a pattern of appropriate conduct, coherent, embellished, and well articulated" (Goffman 1959). Goffman argues that humans interact by way of "impression management" and that everyone, as a social actor, is always attempting to "define" situations, or gain some control over them. While Goffman was theorizing social interactions, it is interesting to contemplate how his theory might translate to social categories such as sex, race, age, or nationality. Dynamics of power are always at play in processes of hailing, interpellation, or applying social categories such as sex and race (Butler 1993; Butler 1995; Butler 1999). It is interesting, then, that even while Pierre-Mecatl performed a version of whiteness (Goth), a police officer reassigned a racial label to him. This refusal of the officer to acquiesce to Pierre-Mecatl's racial performance does not invalidate it, but it does demonstrate the complexity of race as a category that is not wholly projected from within or ascribed from without but is created in a dynamic process and varies according to social context (Okamura 1981).

While many respondents complained of negative stereotyping and racial profiling upon being perceived as Mexican American, others issued grievances after being discriminated against *as a different minority*. Joe Feagin notes the problem of "cross-discrimination" (Feagin 1991: 111)—that is, the way an ethnic or racial minority person may suffer from discrimination aimed at a different minority group by a person who is unable to distinguish one group from the other. This happened to a third-generation Mexican American adolescent male, Tom Acevedo. Tom is a slim young man who is dark skinned and has black hair and dark brown eyes. He is sometimes mistaken for an Arab, the most upsetting instance having been when, some months after the September 11th terrorist attacks, he was stopped by a police officer as he walked home from school. He recounted the incident that occurred when he was thirteen years old:

> TOM: I got stopped because I was carrying a suitcase with my trumpet in it. I kinda looked like I was Arab—the cop said so. He pulled me over . . . and questioned me. . . . And this is after September 11th, too, so they got a little more suspicious about that.

JMV: What did you think was going on there? How did you react in that situation?

TOM: I believe he thought I had a bomb in my hands. [Laughs.] But I told him that, "Nah." I asked him if he wanted to see what was in the box. He's like, "Yeah." So, I opened up the suitcase . . . and I showed him the trumpet. Under it is where I keep all my oil and stuff and [I] let him look under there. . . . He's like, "Okay, I see." I told him, "I'm not a terrorist or anything, sir, so don't take me for that."

JMV: How did you respond to that internally?

TOM: That kind of freaked me out, because you know, most of my friends they do kind of look Arab but they are actually Mexican. It just freaked me out. He might think I actually have a gun and he might not trust [me]. He might take me to jail. . . . It would frighten me sometimes because *I didn't want to get arrested for being Mexican.* [Laughs.] [my emphasis]

As this incident illustrates, people of color can fall victim to misdirected racism or racial profiling. Tom attributed being targeted by the police as a consequence of looking Arab in combination with heightened efforts after September 11th to rein in terrorist activity. As with Tom, Middle Easterners also fall prey to the "Muslim/terrorist" misplaced stereotype (Marvasti and McKinney 2004; O'Brien 2008: 156). Tom's comment that his friends "kind of look Arab but they are actually Mexican" emphasizes the socially constructed quality of race. Since racial distinctions are not a biological reality, they gain their force through the meanings people give them and the way people deploy them. Tom himself sees physical characteristics overlapping between Arabs and Mexicans, and he has been a victim of police mistaking which side of this blurry line he is on. His reaction to this racial profiling is to be fearful of the police force, frightened of possible police overreactions and of being unjustly incarcerated. He realizes that he was (wrongfully) racially profiled as an Arab rather than as a Mexican American, but these technicalities are moot when one is being interrogated by an officer of the law.[5]

Variable Discrimination Experiences across Generations

Most first-generation Mexican immigrants denied that they had experienced discrimination. Only one of eight immigrant interviewees claims to have been discriminated against. All immigrants lived most of their adult lives in ethnic enclaves among fellow Mexican-origin people, this coethnic community insulating them from interracial interactions and limiting their vulnerability to racist encounters. Both generation and historical moment condition perception of discrimination and willingness to label it as such.

Participants in the civil rights movement developed a heightened consciousness about racism, making these second-generation individuals quicker to point out disparities than the elder generation. This period effect conditions the perception of racism among members of the second generation. Beyond historical movements, some types of discrimination are specific to generation, such as discrimination around home ownership and spatial mobility, both of which occur more frequently in the second and third generation. The phenomena of home ownership and residential mobility are evidence of economic upward mobility, a trend occurring in the latter generations that places them in new social contexts and exposes them to new forms of prejudice.

The Civil Rights Movement

Perception of discrimination is influenced by generation in the United States (see also Rivadeneyra 2006; Roth 2008; Waters 1999). Activism during the civil rights movement in general, and the Chicano Movement[6] in particular, is one bond that some members of the second generation share, an experience that continues to influence their sociopolitical perspective. Many second-generation Mexican Americans in my sample were directly involved in the Chicano Movement, the goal of which was to advance the "right of the Mexican American people to justice, equality and self-determination" (Murguia 1975: 93). Those who were not activists were aware of the movement and its social agenda. Indeed, those who were social activists in the sixties reported to me their unwavering ethnic title of "Chicano/a," over and above other options like "Mexican American," "Mexican," or "Latino/a," because of the political implications of self-determination that the term "Chicano/a" implies. One man explained his rationale for maintaining his title "Chicano" decades after the movement: "It's political. It's a thing where there's no difference between you guys and us guys. In those days [1968–1972], Chicano was one that was more politically active . . . we would work with the *huelga* [strike] and we picketed and we went to march to Sacramento a couple times. . . ." Scholars have long noted the importance of self-determination in recouping a marginalized identity (Carmichael and Hamilton 1992; Collins 1991; Fanon 1963; Fanon 1967). In keeping with the spirit of self-determination, activists from the Chicano Movement retained the politically forceful and self-devised ethnic label "Chicano/a" and oftentimes taught their children the importance of this label as well as the agenda of social justice and representation that it embodies. Chicano activists, who strategically used iconography originating in the Mexican Revolution, promoted a politics of cultural maintenance during the movement. Their goals regarding equal access to opportunities, especially in education, were consistent with those of the civil rights movement, yet were encoded with Mexican-origin imagery that placed paramount importance on cultural maintenance and ethnic dignity.

A goal of the Chicano Movement was to move Chicanos (Mexican Americans born in the United States) from the periphery to the center of the United States collective consciousness. Mexican Americans had long felt treated as second-class citizens, and part of the agenda of the Chicano Movement was to uncover the ways in which Mexican Americans were systematically denied equal access to opportunity and resources. Since the outlawing of Jim Crow segregation that was prevalent throughout the U.S. southern states, discrimination against blacks and browns alike was forced to go underground. In practical terms, this spelled the disappearance of "white" and "colored" signs above bathrooms and water fountains and their replacement with "structured racism" or "color-blind racism." As Barlow (2003: 31) explains, "Unlike the racisms of previous epochs, such as the system of state power called Jim Crow racism, white privileges in the 1950s and 1960s became structured into the patterns of interaction in society so deeply that the overt defense of racial privileges became unnecessary."

While overt interpersonal racism still exists, racism after the 1960s became more covert and structured into society. Activists in the Chicano Movement possessed a heightened awareness of racial inequalities and an understanding of how racism came to be embedded in institutions. The social consciousness cultivated during the Chicano Movement stayed with those second-generation Mexican American participants and groomed them to be quick to discern institutional discrimination. Former activists tended to pass on their knowledge and consciousness to their children, thereby creating a third generation of Mexican Americans who were primed to decry social inequities based on race. Believing in civic participation as a means of representation, some Chicano Movement activists started organizations dedicated to Mexican American causes while others opted to work within already established organizations and be advocates for Mexican Americans from within those preexisting associations.

Rafael Treviño, who established a parent and child wellness health care program in Santa Barbara, credits the Chicano Movement for his career motivation. As other civil rights activists testify, the Chicano Movement helped unveil racism as not just interpersonal but also institutional. As a

Latino outreach worker in the health services in the 1960s, Rafael began to see that Latinos were not utilizing the system because they were "alienated"; there were no Latinos in the system and few recruitment efforts targeting the Latino community. Rafael reflects on his awareness of institutionalized racism that burgeoned during the Chicano Movement:

> It wasn't the kind of racism that says, "Hey, you have a darker skin than I do so you're inferior to me." Which is what I always thought racism was. But then I began to see that there is this institutionalized racism. This very subtle racism where they're not going to come out and tell you that they don't like you because you're not white. But they're going to let you know in a different way and it's up to you to find out what that way is because it's very hidden.

As did others advocating self-determination before him, Rafael concluded that to set up a health care organization devoted to a Latino clientele would be the best way to fulfill the needs of that underserved population (it now serves non-Latinos as well). Rafael explains how uncovering institutionalized racism was the catalyst for creating a Latino health organization:

> RAFAEL: [People ask me,] "Why do your people need to have a different approach to using services? Why do we have to go through all this outreach and all this hoopla to get people to use our services? Why don't they just use it?" Well, that's because this individual assumes that everybody gets the same type of education, had the same type of upbringing and background that they do.
>
> JMV: What was your strategy?
>
> RAFAEL: . . . [Malcolm X's] idea was to become independent. Start your own farms, start your own restaurants, start your own banks, start your own everything. That's where we came up with the idea of starting our own nonprofit organization. So that's why we formed this organization—on the basis that we would become independent. That we would become our own employer, we would employ our own people, we would employ our own advocates.

The answer to institutional racism, for Rafael, was to construct an independent organization serving Latino needs, in the spirit of self-determination.

Other second-generation Mexican Americans whose consciousness was raised by the Chicano Movement worked within already established institutions in order to achieve visibility. Raymond Talavera, a businessman and community leader in Santa Barbara, is frustrated by society's "judging a book by its cover" mentality, which discounts Mexican Americans in the professional world and society at large. He attempts to make change by working from within white-dominated organizations and institutions. Raymond counters marginalization by becoming active in civic organizations.

> You knock your head against the system long enough you learn . . . that the system ain't really gonna change, you just gotta get in it and deal from within. . . . I noticed when I became a board member at the college, there is a big difference sitting on this end of the table as opposed to sitting in the audience. You are now *influencing* decisions that are made that affect the people out there. . . . More than anything else, you can influence a vote as a voting member at the table. If we are not at the table then forget it. We can yell and scream and march as long as we want, and yeah you get some immediate impact and stuff, but in the long haul we have to be *at the table*, part of the table, part of the council, part of the district board, part of the this board, part of that board. It does make a difference. A lot of times issues do come up where you have a say, you have a vote, but you can also influence your fellow board members by making the argument as to why you should vote this way and not that way. So, yeah, a lot of times you win, you lose, but you are in the game, you aren't in the stands. You are actually playing the game.

Raymond sees "the system" as flawed and wants to work to correct it by becoming politically engaged and enacting changes from inside civic organizations.

Chicano activists Rafael and Raymond represent two primary reactions to having one's consciousness raised during the civil rights movement. One can argue that activists and sympathizers of the Chicano Movement promoted a politics of cultural maintenance. Paradoxically, while this "politics of protest" (Montejano 1999) combats the outdated notion of Anglo conformity, political engagement—including protest—is indicative of some degree of political assimilation into the dominant culture on the part of the participants. In the very attempt to enact cultural maintenance, these Mexican American advocates are politically assimilating. This tension of working within an established American political system to attain cultural maintenance ends underscores the fact that "Mexican American" is by definition an American identity.

Upward Mobility: Home Ownership, College Education, and Occupational Integration

While the immigrant generation generally experiences some economic success through hard work, it is usually the second generation that secures occupations with good compensation packages, gains a financial foothold, and is able to buy a house. This places the second generation in a new occupational arena, income bracket, and neighborhood. Home ownership has long been considered the gateway to the middle class, yet Mexican American prospective buyers have confronted numerous barriers to entry due to discrimination in rental, sales, and financing of housing (Orfield and Lee 2007).

Home ownership is an asset that has historically been boasted disproportionately by whites. Even today, U.S. cities remain highly segregated for blacks and whites, less so for Latinos (Massey and Denton 1993). A number of my homeowner respondents reported that their new neighbors were either disgruntled by their move into the neighborhood or openly questioned the legality of their source of income. Yolanda Segura and her family live in a large Victorian home atop a hill in Hayward, with a view of the San Mateo Bridge and the San Francisco Bay. Yolanda mentions how they were the first non-European descent white family to move into the exclusive neighborhood:

> [W]hen we moved here to this house, I think some of the neighbors kind of looked at us like, "Who are these people?!" And I remember my husband used to say, "Oh, I'm sure they think we're drug lords." Because how could people like us afford a place like this? . . . There is certainly that feeling of "how did you guys get to where you're at?" But, they don't know us and they didn't know what we had to go through at first to get to this point. So I think just in general there is this assumption that Latinos are not usually successful.

In that same vein, Guillermo Ramirez, second generation like Yolanda, spoke of his neighbors' incredulity over his purchase of his two-story Mexican colonial house in San Jose. The neighbors wanted to know how he could afford to live in the upper-class neighborhood. He quipped to the neighborhood go-between: "You just tell them, I pay my mortgage payment just like they pay theirs."

Second-generation Mexican Americans confront these questions of class and legitimacy in a way their parents did not because the first generation had different financial resources and objectives. In fact, as the second generation realizes the importance of home ownership in solidifying middle-class status, they impress upon their children the significance of buying a home for themselves. All three generations view home ownership as a keystone of middle-class success.

Another marker of upward mobility is achieving higher education, which, in turn, often leads to occupational integration. In both mainstream educational and job markets, the environment tends to be racially heterogeneous, thus exposing Mexican Americans to non-coethnic peers and coworkers. More likely to live in non-Mexican majority communities than their predecessors, second- and third-generation Mexican Americans are prone to have educational and work experiences that take them outside of California and into contexts where they are both an ethnic minority and a numerical minority. Irrespective of generation in the United States, social context bears on the formation of racial identity. Immigrant generations often follow social networks or established immigration routes that lead them to settle in ethnic enclaves or communities with a high proportion of residents of the same ethnic group. While immigrant social networks are not always beneficial for newcomers (Menjivar 2000) and may lead to labor exploitation (Lin 1998), a homogeneous community may have a protective effect for its residents. If immigrants are surrounded by people in similar social positions vis-à-vis immigration status and race, they may be less likely to experience discrimination. This could be one factor influencing the immigrant respondents to declare that they had never experienced racial discrimination. The second and third generations who resided in majority white environments were frequently in a numerical minority position, navigating the advantages and disadvantages of that social placement. These later generations had to determine how they fit into and related to their virtually all-white environment, or "white habitus" (Bonilla-Silva 2003).

Homogenous social contexts limit subjection to incidents of public discrimination. If people live in neighborhoods with a majority Mexican American population, they are less likely to experience discrimination because they live in a pocket of coethnics who share many commonalities and literally "look like" them. In particular, when adolescents move from their home context to a college campus, they often encounter racial diversity and the option to take ethnic studies classes. Exposure to people of various racial/ethnic backgrounds, experience of everyday racism in a mixed environment, and the opportunity to learn about one's heritage in a "legitimate" setting like a college classroom can all prompt a shift in one's racial self-understanding (Kibria 2002; Twine 1997; Vasquez 2005). In studies of second-generation

Chinese and Korean Americans (Kibria 2002), second-generation Vietnamese (Thai 1999), and biracial African American women (Twine 1997), scholars found that ethnic studies classes, ethnic politics, heightened racial consciousness, coethnic friendships, and race-based student organizations made race salient in new and critical ways for racial-minority college students. College campuses are fertile sites for "ethnic recovery" or "ethnic discovery" (Thai 1999: 66).

In keeping with the notion that social context—in particular the college experience—matters for racial self-understandings and identity shifts, Reyna Madrigal, a third-generation woman who grew up in a predominantly Mexican area of Whittier remarked,

REYNA: When I took Chicano studies, that is when I realized, "Wow, I'm Mexican."

JMV: Really?

REYNA: Yeah, I think because living here there was . . . probably 80 percent Mexicans that went to my high school so I never thought about other races and I didn't think I was [an] underrepresented group. I didn't know about discrimination because I didn't face any living here. There was Mexican markets, Mexican products. When I went to Cal-State Fullerton, Orange County, then it was like a big culture clash. . . . There's not that many people here that look [like] me.

Reyna did not confront racial/ethnic difference until she moved out of her majority-Mexican hometown and into a more racially diverse environment. Not only had racial homogeneity buffered her from discrimination; enrolling in a Chicano Studies class increased her knowledge of her background and prompted her understanding of herself as Mexican. The downside of living among a large number of Mexican Americans is intragroup tension, as some volley for status as more "authentic" than others, a topic that is covered in chapter 7.

Elena Vargas, a 48-year-old second-generation Mexican American woman, lives in the Napa region and works as a health care professional. Elena, who experienced the 1960s civil rights era as a young teenager, is well versed in the language of identity politics and race relations. She was able to achieve a higher occupational standing than her immigrant mother due to her higher educational level and her bilingual skills. The discrimination she experiences is not overt and confrontational but is nonetheless insidious. The discrimination she encounters takes the form of professional invisibility, where people do not seem to see, hear, or take her seri-ously on the job. Elena's white colleagues render invisible her voice, her skills, and even the money she controls. Elena has attained a middle-class occupation and income, and yet equality with her white peers is elusive. She complains of how difficult it is to have her professional voice heard, how she feels it is overridden or neglected on the job. Elena illustrates her point:

> I'm working with a lot of other health agencies and a lot of times . . . I won-der, I really wonder, is it that people don't really listen because I'm Latina, or is it because there's another issue? What would the other issue be? . . . I just had another person in my office go to one of these meetings and I said, "Tell me if you see this going on: I'll say something, even real positive things like 'I have a thousand dollars that I want to spend on an obesity program and I hear you all saying that you have some projects that you want to do. Well, let me help you.' Then somebody else will go, 'Well, I really don't know . . . we need to get some money.'" [Laughs.]

Indeed, Elena's coworker witnessed this dynamic at the meeting: "Yeah! I saw that. You would say something and they wouldn't hear it until somebody else said it." Elena attributes this professional invisibility to her race:

> *I'm* thinking 'cause they're white. . . . It's not like I'm new. I've been in the community for twenty-five years, I've been on Nutrition Council for twenty of those years, so what is it? Is it the Good Ol' Girls System still—just like there's a Good Ol' Guys System? Why are they not listening? Am I being too aggressive? Am I not being aggressive enough? Is it because I do not have a master's degree behind me—it could be education?

Elena goes through a self-questioning process in order to see if the lack of respect she faces in meetings could be a result of something else, a taxing process of "careful evaluation" (Feagin 1991: 103) found among middle-class blacks.

Due to upward mobility, later-generation Mexican Americans are mov-ing into new physical and social spaces. As Mexican Americans earn middle-class status, buy homes, get college educations, and move up the occupational ranks, they move into new social contexts, which leaves them vulnerable to newfangled forms of discrimination such as profes-sional invisibility.

Resistances to Discrimination across Generations

Resistances—referring to attitudes, belief systems, and practices that intentionally undercut racist ideologies—are always potentially transformative. They are aimed at challenging modes of thought and behavior in order to create alternate ideological and behavioral paradigms. Since discrimination is aimed at a victim, it is important to examine the reactions of those victims and see their agency rather than exclusively their oppression. To omit the responses to discrimination is to perpetuate an unequal power dynamic. Documenting resistances converts Mexican Americans who might wrongfully be assumed to be passive victims into "significant agents of social production and change" (Menchaca 1995: viii).

Generation in the United States plays an important role in the way Mexican Americans perceive and respond to discrimination. Each generation patterns unique ways of responding to discrimination that reflect its own distinctive relationship to the United States: first-generation immigrants from Mexico, no matter their tenure in the United States, opt to avoid uneasy situations whereas second- and third-generation Mexican Americans are inclined to struggle for social equity. This generational difference results from a myriad of factors, including the sense of permanence, post–civil rights era awareness, heightened education, and English-language ability that later U.S.-born generations tend to possess.

Two generation-specific influences contribute to my respondents' sociopolitical consciousness: first is their generation in the United States, and second is their historical frame of reference, that is, the historical periods through which they have lived or social movements in which they have been active that helped shape their awareness. Reactions to discrimination in the second and third generations are predicated upon a belief in permanent residence and citizenship (Flores and Benmayor 1997; Sanchez 1993), whereas the immigrant generation relies on a what John Ogbu calls a "dual frame of reference" (Ogbu 1990; Ogbu 1994). This dual frame of reference includes an "immigrant ideology" that perceives America as the "land of opportunity" (Cheng and Espiritu 1989: 528). Because of this immigrant perspective, the first generation is disinclined to criticize their adopted country. The second and third generations possess a post–civil rights language and assertiveness that is due to their historical frame of reference. This finding is especially true for those second-generation Mexican Americans who participated in the Chicano Movement, as well as their children. This is in line with Karl Mannheim's theorization of generations, that is, that their similarity of temporal location makes generations subject to common dominant social, intellectual, and political circumstances (Mannheim 1936). Mannheim defines generations as sharing a "particular kind of identity of location, embracing related 'age groups' embedded in a historical-social process" (292). Mannheim further specifies various kinds of bonds between generations, allowing for an affinity between group members based on social location, political leanings, and geographical proximity that produce a particular consciousness. Third-generation Mexican Americans are confident about their identity as American citizens, leading them to quickly stand up for their rights when they have been infringed upon.

Conflict Avoidance

Conflict avoidance is the way first-generation immigrants sought to distance themselves from discriminatory situations instead of fighting back. While this stratagem does not technically qualify as resistance, in that it is not aimed at changing perceptions, behaviors, or institutions, it was a common reaction among the first generation.

Ramona Vargas, a first-generation, 77-year-old widow who has spent the last fifty-two years in the United States, is the mother of Elena. She and her late husband worked hard in low-paying jobs (she in a cannery, a packing house, and housekeeping) in order to achieve, and then cling to, their middle-class status. Ramona, who struck me as a mild and gentle woman, told me how she felt discriminated against in church because no one would sit near her and her husband:

> Where we used to go to church we noticed that some American [white] people, if the bench was empty—it was just us—they see us there and they just look for another place to sit down. You notice all those things. . . . It was just my husband and me. We sit there and the whole bench was empty: just the two of us in one end and they just see us there and just keep going and look for other places [to sit]. Even if it was *crowded*, still they wouldn't sit there.

Ramona was clearly still agitated by these social slights, which whittled away at her self-confidence. She explained that she and her husband decided to stop going to church because they felt unwanted there. The church ended up hiring a "Spanish priest": "They have an American one [priest] and a Mexican one [priest]. Now I just go to the Mexican service, that's much better." She solved the dilemma of how to continue her churchgoing without enduring social slights by self-segregating and attending the Spanish/Mexican mass. Ramona conceded to the informal system of "social apartness," wherein "Anglo Americans determine the proper times and places" for inter-ethnic contact (Menchaca 1995: 172), by retreating to the "Mexican [church] service." As evidenced by her increasingly reclusive tendencies, Ramona's transgression of the rules of "social apartness" in her community makes her feel debased and socially inferior.

Ramona is firm in her philosophy of equality, as she utilized religious language to adamantly inform me, "God made me and made them so there shouldn't be any difference!" Still, her own convictions of equality do not match up with the social reality she experiences. So, when push comes to shove in racial matches, she declines being a contestant and leaves the situation. On a few occasions she attended a senior center where a similar situation of racial avoidance and discomfort ensued, prompting her to duck out of senior center activities: "They weren't friendly at all. You expect me to come over here? So I just stopped going. No, I'd feel worse if I come over here and see those faces [she turns up her face and looks away]. I'd rather stay home." Ramona makes the rational choice to remove herself from potentially damaging situations, a tendency that over time has grown into a more generalized distaste for public outings.

Ideological Resistances: "It's Your Problem," Logic, and Ignorance

Ideological resistances are rooted in a fundamental belief in human equality. One way to undercut discrimination is to attribute the problem or pathology of discrimination to the perpetrator rather than the victim. Logic plays a key role in disarming acts of prejudice. Beatrice Madrigal, a sixty-year-old, second-generation Mexican American woman, works as a campus monitor at an elementary school in Los Angeles. She displays a very "it's your problem" attitude when it comes to discrimination and "doesn't let it bother her." As a schoolyard monitor, she tries to be a mentor to the young kids who are often battling on the playground with race talk. She adheres to the principle that "we're all the same" and says to children, to illustrate her point, "you peel off your skin—but, don't do it!—and I'll peel off mine and you'll see that we're both the same underneath." Beatrice argues against racism by dismantling biological claims to racial difference.

Beatrice continues to use logic to crumble racist thought as she touches on racial epithets and name calling:

Even though they say "dirty Mexicans" or "you bean eater," it doesn't bother me. I say, "Think what you like! I eat beans, yes!" . . . I'm a Mexican and there's nothing I can do about it and I accept it and if they don't like it, well then that's their problem. But it doesn't hurt me. I think at one time, growing up, that word "bean eater" did bother me, but to me it was *just a word*.

They do that at school too [where she works]. They say "bean eater." I say, "Why? That's just a word." I tell the little girl, "Don't you eat beans?" She goes, "Yeah." "Well then we are bean-eaters, right?" She goes, "Yes." I kind of joke with them because I don't want them to take offense at "bean eater."

Logic is Beatrice's armor against racism. She uses logic to defuse racial insults, trying to show the elementary schoolchildren she supervises that racism is the problem of the aggressor. She tries to take the sting out of politicized words such as "bean eater" by showing that on a basic level, words are "just words" and if a "bean eater" really just refers to someone who eats beans then such statements of fact should not be injurious.

Beatrice, like a sizeable number of other respondents, doesn't take interpersonal discrimination seriously. She credits her mother and father with instilling her with an "oh, who cares?" attitude. This attitude stems from contentment with her own life, a stance she has concertedly tried to inculcate in her children. Beatrice informs me,

When I hear that, "Oh, you Mexican!" I think, "Who cares? I don't care what you think. I like being a Mexican." . . . I am who I am and their name calling isn't going to change it. "You got the problem, you deal with it because I don't have no problem with who I am." I always tell the kids, "Look what I'm saying. Do I have a problem with it? No. Is it going to bother me? No. I am not going to go over there and cry. . . ." You have to do the same thing. I pass that on to them.

Beatrice vacillates between unraveling the discriminatory act with logic, as she does for schoolchildren at her work, and writing the aggressor of discrimination off as "ignorant" and therefore "not caring" and not letting the action bother her.[7] Beatrice's notion of "who cares?" is echoed by Moises Ramos, a third-generation male: "I just worry about myself and make the best and be the best that I can be. Kind of like 'I don't give a fuck' kind of attitude. . . . But just the attitude of 'who cares what others think of me' and that's not going to stop me from doing what I need to do to achieve my goals that I need to achieve." In these excerpts, a calculated insouciance and fortitude are levied as disarming devices for racism.

Similarly, Milo, a 59-year-old second-generation male, recalls dating a Swedish woman in high school whose father was a racist. Milo felt "that little sting" when he was told by his girlfriend's mother that it would be best if he weren't there when the father got home. Milo remarks how the racist father of his girlfriend was "ignorant," yet he quickly follows up that "it's your problem"–type response with a justification for why he should be treated with respect. A lawyer in Ventura, Milo explains,

> I was okay with it because I just felt the guy was ignorant. He was a blue-collar welder who didn't know better. I had no need for his approval. I'm sure I'm not what he's used to. I'm sure he never went to what is now my office and met with a brown face that is his lawyer who is going to save his ass, who happened to be a Mexican. I'm sure he'd never experienced that. Had he ever experienced that then maybe he wouldn't have felt that way.

Milo sees racist beliefs as ignorant and uninformed, thus preventing him from feeling belittled in any significant way. Viewing racist ideology as ignorant is defensive armor against discrimination, yet even so, Milo follows up these assertions with the idea that he deserves to be respected due to having proven himself in his occupation as a lawyer. Even after writing racist beliefs off as "ignorance" and rejecting a need for "approval," he moves to show himself as an exception ("I'm sure I'm not what he's used to.") because of his success in a vocation that could potentially put the former girlfriend's father's legal fate in his hands. By highlighting his vocational capabilities, Milo rationalizes his positive self-image even beyond refuting racism as a folly of ignorance.

The third generation followed the second generation's lead of deflecting racism by repositioning the pathology of discrimination with its producer rather than its receiver. While the immigrant generation was overwhelmingly reluctant to recount instances of discrimination, their descendents were firmly rooted in the United States and succeeded the civil rights movement, giving them the confidence and voice needed to call out discrimination as illogical, unfair, and a deficiency on the part of the aggressor.

Racial Pride as Protection

Many Mexican Americans expressed racial pride, most often in the second and third generations. Pride acts as a preventative defense mechanism against nefarious consequences of discrimination. In particular, interviewees mentioned this need for pride as a tenet taught to them by their parents. Feagin and Sikes (1994) notes the role parents play in socializing their children regarding racism. When racial pride is relayed from parents to children, pride is intended to augment self-esteem and ward off the potentially damaging consequences of discrimination.

While two older immigrants claim to be very "patriotic" toward Mexico, on the whole, the immigrant generation is less inclined to be proud of their Mexican heritage than later generations. Remembering the reasons they left Mexico, immigrants are grateful for their new position in the United States, poised to take advantage of relative opportunity. Given their "dual frame of reference," immigrants, were appreciative of being in the so-called land of opportunity and looked forward to a relative upward adjustment of their lifestyle (Hochschild 1995). Indeed, a couple of first-generation immigrants denied ever being discriminated against—even when their children claimed that they had indeed suffered racist treatment. Again, this points to generational awareness of racism as well as a readiness to critique one's country of residence.

The second generation possessed a kind of "double consciousness" (Du Bois 1903) with regard to their racial background. They were cognizant of their families' feeling about their race (be it pride, indifference, or embarrassment), as well as society's feeling toward their race (largely disparaging). Navigating those various modes of sentiment can be tricky. The majority of second-generation Mexican Americans expressed pride in their background, saying it was either instilled by their parents or acquired in compensation for a personal experience of devaluation. Fractures within generations require explanation. Mannheim makes a distinction between an "actual generation," that is, youth experiencing the same concrete historical problems, and the more substantial bond of a "generation unit," groups within the same actual generation that have "an identity of responses, a certain affinity in the way in which all move with and are formed by their common experiences" (Mannheim 1936: 306). An actual generation can therefore boast a number of differentiated, polar forms of generation units that display antagonistic intellectual and social responses to identical environmental stimuli.

Mannheim's theory clarifies how second- and third-generation Mexican Americans can be alternately proud and embarrassed. Racial pride is often attributed to parental teachings, some of which are laced with a staunchness about the underbelly of racism and an encouragement for preparedness and fortitude. A common motivation for pride is expressed here:

> My mother . . . said to me, "Look, you're Latino—or, you're Mexican—and you should be proud of it. No one is any better than you, just like you are not any better than anyone else. You are equal to everyone. And you just have to stand by your ground." And that made me understand that if I was going to be confronted with racism there was nothing I had to be ashamed about, just to be strong, that's all.

The philosophy of equality is always advanced in statements of pride. The emphasis on equality is utilized to elevate people who occupy a mid-to-low position on the racial hierarchy. People are intensely aware of the reality of the racial hierarchy and sometimes use humor in order to raise their group position both in their own mind and in the mind of their interlocutor. Lance Morelos takes his mother's teaching one step further by using humor to call into question the extant racial hierarchy:

> My mom used to say, ". . . Nobody is better than anybody else. And you remember that." I used to say, "Mexican? Oh, the upper echelon?" I used to say that all the time when I was in high school and college. "Mexican? Oh, the upper echelon?" And it used to kind of off-set people. Because if people saw that you were proud of your heritage, they'd let you alone.

By problematizing the placement of Mexican Americans as somewhere other than the "upper echelon" of the racial hierarchy, Lance points out the cunning presence and divisive power of the racial hierarchy.

Not all members of the second and third generations are stalwart in their racial pride. Some, like third-generation Amalia Ruiz, were embarrassed. Unflattering self-perceptions are also passed down from one generation to the next:

> [I think that my grandparents and my dad] thought of themselves as second-class citizens because we were Mexican. . . . I think they internalized some of the discrimination that they experienced, as older generation Mexicans. So they never taught me to be proud to be a Mexican. . . . On a more conscious level I got from them that it's kind of shameful to be Mexican. I hate to say that.

Abashed and lacking racial strongholds, Amalia doesn't have the familial or societal resources to develop racial pride.

The possession of racial pride sometimes converts into active representation in civic organizations. On the other hand, racial insecurity leads to blending in with mainstream culture to the greatest degree possible. While pride was more prevalent than embarrassment, fractures exist within the second and third generations, demonstrating that orientation to racial heritage is not overdetermined by generation.

Behavioral Resistances: Proving Oneself through Overachievement

Behavioral resistances are practices and conduct that people employ as strategies to combat discrimination. In contrast to ideological resistances, which are based in thought, attitudes, and perspectives—specifically, fortifying one's own belief system or challenging other people's sets of beliefs—behavioral resistances are grounded in action. These two primary modes of resistance are not mutually exclusive but can be enacted simultaneously or in succession.

Racial and ethnic minorities encounter and then respond to both interpersonal and institutional discrimination, much of which is perpetuated by stereotypes. Negative stereotypes are an overlooked form of discrimination; they set up negative expectations that function as both a roadmap and a roadblock for individuals against whom they are directed. Negative stereotypes saddle their targets with the burden of puzzling through the situation and sometimes internalizing this maltreatment, lowering their sense of self-worth or heightening their sense of social insecurity. Sometimes negative stereotypes lead to lowered expectations for the performance of Mexican Americans, while at other times they lead to avoidance of Mexican Americans in social, community, or professional arenas. This social avoidance or professional invisibility is discrimination, a move toward exclusion, self-segregation, and marginalization of the "othered" group.

People often approach Mexican Americans with preconceived ideas about who they are, where they come from, and where they are headed that are based on negative stereotypes. These negative stereotypes are leveraged after a cursory assessment of a person's physical characteristics. For men, a typical assumption is that they are violent criminals or gang members. Ricardo Torres remarked on how his facial scars and moustache get him typecast as a gang-banger: "I think when people look at me they see my scars and the moustache or whatnot. A lot of times people get the impression that I'm a gangster or a *cholo* or something like that. That really bothers me because that is just totally what I'm not about."

Moises Ramos, a 28-year-old, third-generation male whose "dad was a drug addict and . . . mom was his number one customer" grew up in an environment where his "family, everybody, thought [he] was going to be a loser, a screw up." Moises overcame enormous family obstacles to lead a clean life and become a high school career counselor. He experiences the common reaction of needing to "prove himself": "I've got to still prove myself because people are still always going to have this doubt about me. So the more I prove myself the better that I feel about myself." Succeeding against others' doubts boosts his self-confidence, but certainly he suffers an uphill-battle burden of having to prove his self-worth rather than having it already assumed. He needs to "prove himself" not just because of his family background but also because of his racial background, the element visible to outsiders:

> People automatically judge you as being something you're not just because of the way you look. . . . For instance, I was in a bar celebrating one of my friend's birthdays. This lady saw me and she said out loud, "Oh, he's mean looking." I was thrown by it. For some reason I just smiled. She was like, "Oh my God, he has a dimple," or something like that. So we started talking and she asked what I did and I told her. "Oh my God, I never would have guessed." I was like, "Obviously you shouldn't judge a book by its cover." She had this image of us—Mexicans—in Santa Maria, that's where she's from, bald and mean and involved in gangs and stuff like that.

When confronted interpersonally with stereotypes, Moises engages in behavioral resistance by opening a dialogue in order to disprove and disarm the stereotype cast on him.

The idea of having to "prove oneself" was an undercurrent of many interviews. Tyler Mendoza and Milo Contreras felt the need to "prove themselves" against negative stereotypes and low expectations. Both men felt pressure to overturn the negative expectation of academic underachievement. Tyler, a third-generation man from Vacaville, refers to his parents' stress on education and his own need to disprove the expectation of educational failure:

> My parents always pushed school, school, school, school. So I had to do better in school. . . . You know, C's were not that good, you get A's and B's. C's meant that you could do better. So, they always pushed from day one

that I had to do better in school. I knew I had to try harder. I had to try harder and prove that I wasn't one of those dumb lazy Mexicans or the ones that are going to drop out and get somebody pregnant. . . .

Tyler's parents encourage him to behave in ways that will positively distinguish him from aggregate, pessimistic images of Mexican Americans that shadow him. Tyler comments further on the image of "dirty Mexican" that his parents were determined to guarantee he avoided by devoting extra attention to his cleanliness:

[T]hese are things we have to go up against: we're not as smart . . . we're not clean . . . we don't know how to act. . . . [I]n the sixth grade, I loved playing tether ball. I was pretty good at it and I wanted to wear a shirt that I wore yesterday. It was clean. And she said, "No, you can't wear that shirt twice because people will think that you're a dirty Mexican so you can't wear that twice. You never wear a shirt two days in a row. You always wash your shirt. You never do that." And that is when it struck me. Okay, I got to be cleaner. I got to be cleaner.

The strain of Mexican-inferiority ideology that spurred "germ theories" proliferated after the Mexican-American War. During this period in the mid-1800s, widespread low wages confined Mexican laborers to poverty; the housing they could afford or that employers provided was very substandard (often "renovated" animal living quarters), heightening the risk of disease. "Germ theories" held that "dirty Mexicans" were unhealthy and unhygienic, therefore deserving to be quarantined. The derogatory term "dirty Mexican" was a quadruple entendre: (1) a synonym for dark skin color and inferiority, (2) a reference to agricultural laborers who work the earth, (3) a descriptor for someone who is unhygienic, and (4) a metaphor for low status in the class structure (Montejano 1987: 227).

Milo Contreras, the second-generation Mexican American lawyer introduced earlier, proved himself against negative expectations by attaining a law degree and becoming a successful lawyer. His long narrative delves into a number of themes already touched upon, such as intra-Mexican stereotypes, proclaiming another's "ignorance" as a protective device, and overachievement as a primary way of capsizing stereotypes. Milo reflects on two formative experiences, starting with a coworker from his youth who was also Mexican American:

MILO: I remember an experience with this guy named Sidney who was a track star at the high school. . . . He worked at the store [I worked at] and so when I came in at thirteen he was about nineteen. . . . He was a meat cutter at the store. I eventually became a meat cutter and ran the register and pretty much did everything. And so he asked me, "Hey, what do you want to do when you grow up, man?" I said, "I wanna be a lawyer." "Baaaaah!" He almost rolled on the ground laughing. "You guy!" He was just cracking up. Well, he was one of my first invites to the University of California–Los Angeles Law School graduation. And I still have the tie that he gave me as a graduation present. Yeah, so that sort of changed his mind about stereotypes, even among our own people.

JMV: I imagine that was a proud moment to send off that invitation.

MILO: Sure, sure. And he was very proud, too. He could see how wrong one can be in our perceptions. . . .

Sidney, himself a Mexican American, outright laughed at Milo's dream of becoming a lawyer. Sidney had not only internalized a low expectation for his ethnic group but had also become an enforcer of such under-par achievement, as evidenced by his boisterous laughter at Milo's future hopes. Fortunately for both of them, Milo used the negative expectation as a benchmark to surpass. Notably, Milo shared news of his law degree with Sidney so that they could be proud both of his individual achievement and of how that success enfeebles the stereotype that had encroached upon them both years earlier.

Milo and I continued our conversation where we had left off:

JMV: Did you ever get the sense that you had to overcome those stereotypes?

MILO: I always felt that I was going to "get back at them." When I graduated [from] law school, I had recruitment letters from the navy, the air force, the army, the Marine Corps to go into the J.A.G. Corps, which is . . . the legal branch of the services. It's the Judge Advocate General Corps, which is military lawyers, and you go in as a captain. I thought to myself, "Gee that's tempting, only because all of these racist rednecks that I came across will now have to salute this short Mexican." [Laughs.] I had that sense, I don't know, revenge or whatever. . . . You say, "This stereotype you had is now a captain you salute!" when you see them. That's a lot more effective and more satisfying then just getting angry.

As noted briefly earlier, negative expectations can be converted into motivation for achievement. While Milo did not go into the J.A.G. Corps, he did become an established lawyer, still "proving" himself through his occupation and "getting back at them." Conducting his life according to the old adage that "living well is the best revenge," Milo verifies his self-worth and the worth of his ethnic group. Milo's law degree and legal profession symbolize his triumph over negative expectations and stereotypes and, even if he never has a chance to encounter the "racist rednecks" from his army days, these credentials empower his sense of equality.

Samantha Diaz, the 25-year-old legal secretary in Santa Barbara introduced earlier, explained how she feels as though her Mexican American background is a hindrance, a penalty she must "make up for" or "prove herself" against through her actions. As Third World feminist scholars, in particular, have noted, being a racial or ethnic minority *plus* being a woman makes one a "double minority" (Acevedo 2001; Collins 1986; Collins 1991; Segura 1995) or "multiply oppressed" (King 1988; Segura 1986). Minority women have two minority positions to account for (make sense of, make up for, battle from, etc.) as they navigate the social world and try to achieve equal treatment in gender and race relations, plus equal opportunity and remuneration in the work force. As is true for Chicanas in white-collar jobs more generally (Segura 1992), Samantha finds herself in a double bind because of being a Mexican American woman and feels she must "prove herself":

> I feel like I always have to prove something because I'm Mexican. I feel like people look down on me. . . . I don't know if that's racial, I don't know if that's self-esteem, but maybe sometimes they go hand in hand. . . . I tend to think people look down on me because I'm Mexican. I've convinced myself that I will never be as successful as someone who is white, who possibly has the same qualifications as me, but they will go more places than I can. And maybe too because I am a woman, too. I'm Mexican and a woman.

She is unable to attribute this feeling of people looking down on her to being Mexican or being a woman, probably because both of those social positions are currently undervalued in United States society. She points out that the inferiority that springs from being looked down upon might be due either to race or to low self-esteem, but she acknowledges that those concepts might "go hand in hand," race informing how high or low one's self-esteem can be.

Samantha's heritage plays a significant role on the job: "I think I put a lot of stress on myself with my job. Because I know that I'm Mexican and I know that I have to prove twice as much as a white coworker because I'm Mexican." For her, this translates to dressing well and being "on her toes" at work and being extra professional. She distinctly feels that she must be more professional than her white coworkers in order to make up for a racial penalty.

Asserting Demands for Equality

A second chief way that second- and third-generation Mexican Americans behaviorally resist discrimination is to make verbal demands for equality. Demanding equality attacks discrimination at its core principle of enforcing dominant and subordinate group relations. Discrimination is a matter of group position, not a set of feelings: "the locus of race prejudice is not in the area of individual feeling but in the definition of the respective positions of the racial groups" (Blumer 1958: 5). A group-status perspective finds that prejudice and discrimination are leveraged in order to secure a group-status position (Bobo and Tuan 2006). Since discrimination is centrally about preservation of group (superior) status through enforcement of exclusion and marginalization, asserting equality aims at the main objective in order to rectify the inequity.

For example, rather than "walk on eggshells" in response to the "shop-owner tailgate," some people engaged in practices that directly confronted and resisted discrimination in retail spaces. Cordelia Fuentes, a 55-year-old, second-generation Mexican American from San Diego, experienced "rebound racism" (Frankenberg 1993) as she felt herself vicariously betrayed by a retailer who mistreated Mexican-looking customers. She informs me,

> There was some discrimination here [San Diego] that got me very upset. A JCPenney's suspected that a Mexican family was stealing and so instead of calling the police they called Immigration [INS]. And they got deported. So that made me really angry. So I don't dare go into that store.

This incident fits with the alarmist "Latino threat narrative," which posits that Latinos are disproportionately "illegal aliens," have negative influences on society, and will ultimately not become part of the nation (Chavez 2008). Law and law enforcement—here depicted as the Immigration and

Naturalization Service[8]—are instrumental in the definition of legality and illegality, inclusion and exclusion. While we have no information on whether or not the Mexican family in JCPenney's was authorized or not, the "Latino threat narrative" remains operative here in that the Mexican family was deemed undesirable and drastic action to maintain "social apartness" (Menchaca 1995) was taken. People from Latin America are many times more likely to be deported to their home countries than Asians (Golash-Boza 2009), often for nonviolent, minor infractions such as petty theft, showing the importance of race, skin tone, and stereotypes (of criminality and model minority status, for example) in the way America conceives of itself. Further, citizenship status has not always provided equal legal protection for all, as the federal government has forcibly deported Mexican American citizens along with immigrants during economic downturns (Gutiérrez 1995; Massey, Durand, and Malone 2002). Even while Cordelia did not personally witness the discrimination she recounted, she felt the act was wrong and protested it through boycotting JCPenney's.

Cordelia's daughter, Marisol, reacted similarly to retail-related discrimination by verbally demanding equal treatment. Marisol recounted a time when she was fourteen years old and shopping at a "knick-knack" store with her mother. She was trying on barrettes when she overheard the store clerk telling her mother that she was not allowed to put on the hair accessories. Marisol interpreted this incident as overtly about race:

> [The store clerk told my mother that] you're not allowed to put those [barrettes] in your hair when a couple of minutes before there was a white lady and her white daughter there trying on the same things and nobody told them anything. [M]y mom was like, "Well, why? Why aren't we allowed to? If you guys didn't want [customers to touch items], then there should be a sign out here."
>
> . . . I guess in a way she [the store clerk] was calling [us] dirty or something. My mom told her that we washed our hair . . . and I just got really, really upset. . . . I got really mad and I was like, "Where's your manager?" . . . The manager was the same way . . . saying, "Well, you're really not allowed to do that." Like these people over here? [Marisol points to other patrons, a white mother and daughter.] I pointed them out. . . . You let them put things in their hair. She said, "Well, they weren't allowed to." And I was like, "But you didn't tell them anything." That's the difference. "Well, if you really didn't want people to do that, then you need to put a sign out because that's not right."

Marisol and her mother confronted the shopkeepers, asking for equal treatment on a par with the treatment granted other customers. The repeated emphasis on proper signage is central because a sign is universal and does not discriminate. A sign that indicates what is "off limits" would broadcast this line to all shop patrons, rather than allowing these lines to be drawn at the whim and will of store clerks. Here, the actions of white customers are condoned while those same actions undertaken by Marisol are rebuked. This excerpt rings with echoes of discrimination from earlier eras that decried Mexicans, Mexican Americans, and other minorities as "dirty" or "unclean" (Montejano 1987; Montejano 1999; Sanchez 1993). Clearly, vestiges of earlier forms of discrimination persist. Interestingly, Marisol related this story not in answer to a question about discrimination but in answer to a question about the first time she realized there was a concept in the world called "race." As was true for the majority of my respondents, it is extremely telling that she selected a tale of discrimination to demonstrate her knowledge of the reality of "race" in the world. Even if "race" has been debunked as a biological truth, it undoubtedly carries much social weight.

While it is impossible to determine what motivated the shopkeeper to prohibit Marisol from trying on the barrettes, Marisol is convinced that the reason was her Mexican heritage. This argument is supported by her interpretation of the natural experiment that presented itself—the store clerk did not rebuke a white customer for the same behavior. One point to note is that this racial discrimination seems to be class inflected in that Marisol and her mother are offended by the implication that they are unclean, hygiene being harder to adhere to if one is, as the saying goes, "dirt poor." Speaking to the intersection of race, class, and gender, Omi and Winant (1994: 68) write, "race, class, and gender . . . constitute 'regions' of hegemony. . . . It is crucial to emphasize that race, class, and gender . . . overlap, intersect, and fuse with each other in countless ways." Marisol and her mother are standing in the middle of an intersection of multiple categories. Teasing out class-based from race-based discrimination is an impossible task as I rely on only the recounting of the victim and I do not have access to the thoughts behind the storekeeper's action. While an action may (correctly) be decried as racial discrimination, we must keep in mind that racial discrimination is informed by historical and contemporary class and gender power differentials.

Behavioral resistances to discrimination are action-based challenges to inequality. Striving to out-perform expectations and demanding equality are two ways that Mexican Americans oppose discrimination.

Discrimination as a Means of Racialization

The kinds of discrimination that middle-class Mexican Americans encounter elucidate the interpersonal and structural injustices with which they contend. As with antiblack discrimination, "color stigma" (Feagin 1991: 114) is crucial to the way Mexican Americans are treated in public realms. As in the case of blacks, Mexican Americans regularly contend with two aspects of "additive discrimination": "(1) the cumulative character of an individual's experiences with discrimination; and (2) the group's accumulated historical experiences as perceived by the individual" (Feagin 1991: 114). Contrary to the reasonable expectation that racial minorities are more accepted (that is, acceptable) once they have climbed up the ranks of the socioeconomic ladder, the narratives of middle-class Mexican Americans suggest that discrimination relays the message that the welcome mat is not always rolled out. If discrimination is a means of racialization and if middle-class status cannot neutralize discrimination, a situation of "racialization despite assimilation" exists. Class advantage does not entirely shield Mexican Americans from discrimination or racialization. Piercing through the optimism of the American Dream, these experiences show that achieving upward mobility does not always "make up for" racial/ethnic disadvantage among middle-class Mexican Americans.

Sites of discrimination that are consistent through generation include retail spaces and other public venues. Who gets targeted for discrimination is based on specific factors such as name (Hispanic or non-Hispanic) and physical features. The phenomena of the shopowner tailgate, racial profiling, and cross-discrimination by police are ubiquitous in all three generations. Some sites of discrimination are specific to generation, such as the second and third generation experiencing more challenges in the areas of home ownership, residential mobility, and occupational advancement.

Responses to discrimination are generationally patterned. Victims' reactions to acts of discrimination are also worthy of scrutiny, for reactions reveal how individuals consolidate their group identity. The dominant group attempts to secure its group position by acts of discrimination (Blumer 1958), yet the targeted group's reactions are vital to their ability to recoup a dignified sense of identity. Each generation develops a stylized manner of responding to discrimination that both creates and reflects its own distinct relationship to the United States.

While all three generations experienced discrimination, they perceived and reacted to it differently. The first-generation Mexican immigrants, living among coethnics, were less likely to be exposed to discrimination on a regular basis than their descendents. When they did experience discrimination, this injustice was overshadowed by the immense sense of gratitude to the United States for a chance at a better life than they had had in Mexico, and they were thus loathe to criticize. As O'Brien (2008) argues, Latinos, as part of the "racial middle," may minimize the impact of discrimination in their lives in order to continue to believe in and espouse the American Dream. O'Brien (2008: 159) found that Latinos, already seen as un-American or foreign, chose a survival strategy concerning their everyday racism:

> [O]ne can control the extent to which he or she is further deemed un-American by adapting one's worldview to champion the American dream rather than appear to be criticizing it by "dwelling" on racial discrimination. Thus, while respondents may appear to be engaging in passive denial, they may indeed be actively practicing a resistance strategy by which they refuse to be further deemed un-American.

For foreign-born immigrants, this compunction over critiquing the United States, the land to which they electively migrated, is compounded.

In contrast, the second and third generations engage in social activism on the basis of the set of rights and privileges accorded to them as U.S.-born citizens and a well-honed ideology of permanence and belonging. Women spent mental energy and emotional resources pondering whether their unequal treatment was due to their gender or their race, illuminating how the intersectionality of identity makes for complex questions.

The immigrant generation's caution in critiquing the United States was in part due to its "dual frame of reference" (Ogbu 1990; Ogbu 1994) and gratitude for having a chance at a better life in the United States. In contrast, the two succeeding generations felt a sense of permanence (Sanchez 1993) and were therefore emboldened to argue for their "cultural citizenship" (Flores and Benmayor 1997). These later generations are inclined to struggle for social equity due to their generation in the United States and their historical frame of reference: they are confident as American citizens and they possess a post–civil rights movement assertiveness and race rhetoric. While all three generations were subjected to discrimination, the first generation either was disinclined to acknowledge it or adopted the coping strategy of avoidance, whereas the second and third generations had the propensity to resist using both ideological and behavioral strategies.

People in thinned attachment and cultural maintenance categories handle discriminatory experiences slightly differently. Recall that these are not simple binaries but two ends of a range of orientations. Cultural maintenance individuals, by definition more attuned to their ethnic heritage and history of racial oppression, were inclined to contest and protest discrimination. Culturally attached second-generation Mexican Americans, many of whom were involved in the Chicano Movement, were especially primed to engage in politics of protest where they discerned inequality. Those on a cultural maintenance trajectory were sensitive to issues of subjugation and inequity, making them prone to detect and defend against discrimination.

Alternatively, while some people on a thinned attachment course spoke up in the face of discrimination, showing variation within these ideal type categories, most were less vigorous in their protests against racial/ethnic discrimination. Many thinned attachment people explained how they would carefully calculate whether or not to directly verbally confront racist behavior. This quandary was usually decided according to whether the perpetrator was someone who mattered to the individual; if the perpetrator was a friend or a peer, the respondent deemed it "worth it" to challenge and correct him or her. On the whole, thinned attachment people had milder reactions to discrimination than did cultural maintenance people. This difference is due in part to the fact that thinned attachment people were comparatively less concerned with safeguarding their ethnic heritage in their everyday lives, wearing their culture more lightly, making them less obvious targets. Additionally, by virtue of being less emotionally tied to their heritage, thinned attachment individuals' reactions were less emotionally charged and defensive in nature.

Regardless of their citizenship status, time of arrival, assimilationist or preservationist tendencies, "Latinos are simultaneously subjected to processes of whitening and racialization" (Davila 2008: 12) as a nonwhite racial category. Racialization is enforced through consistent prejudice and discrimination. Alternatively, when Latinos are "whitened," they are allowed to "pass" as non-Hispanic white and awarded a "flexible ethnicity," which will be discussed in chapter 7.

Racialization of Latinos—as non-Hispanic white, Hispanic/Latino, or non-Hispanic black (Golash-Boza and Darity Jr. 2008: 901)—is yet another "bump" in the road of assimilation that can orient individuals to different assimilation trajectories. Given that discrimination (and therefore racialization) occurs despite marked assimilation, Mexican Americans as a group remain unequal to non-Hispanic whites. As with middle-class blacks, racial discrimination in public places is an ongoing and major problem (Feagin 1991; Feagin and Sikes 1994). While public opinion holds that racial discrimination has decreased dramatically in the post–civil rights era, it continues to be a sizeable hurdle for blacks. In fact, the public policy shift in focus toward the "underclass" (Wilson 1987) has eclipsed attention from the issue of racial discrimination (Feagin 1991; Pattillo-McCoy 1999). As we have seen, the experiences of Mexican Americans, as a population beyond the black-white dichotomy, testifies that racial discrimination is an ongoing and sizeable social problem. Yet, relative to blacks, Latinos experience a more porous boundary to whiteness. Hispanic newcomers in the rural South "perceive the social distance separating themselves from whites as more permeable than that separating themselves from blacks and are engaging in distancing strategies that may reinforce this distinction" (Marrow 2009: 1053).

Racial/ethnic identity choices Latinos make on the U.S. Census reflect the processes of racialization and discrimination analyzed in this chapter. Nearly half the population of Latinos in the United States see themselves as a separate racial category that is captured by neither the "white," "black," "Native American," or "Asian" options. In the 2000 Census, 42 percent of Hispanics preferred "some other race," while 48 percent selected "white," 4 percent selected "black," and 1 percent selected "American Indian" (Gómez 2007: 153). Of those who checked "some other race," 97 percent were Latinos (Lee and Bean 2004: 224). Referring to Mexican-origin people specifically, 50 percent of Mexican Americans picked the "white" racial category in Census 2000 whereas 47 percent selected "some other race" (Gómez 2007: 157). This breakdown of identity choices supports the experiences of my interviewees. Those who undergo racialization as nonwhite are probably inclined to mark "some other race" because they feel excluded from mainstream society. In contrast, those who are socially "whitened" and feel relatively included in dominant society—particularly those with a non-Hispanic white parent, light skin color, and/or anglicized names—are probably predisposed to select "white" as their racial category.

As in this chapter, we see in the following chapter that historical period bears on the type of treatment Mexican Americans receive in social spaces, namely, schools. As with public interactions, educational systems and families transmit messages about racial meanings. The next chapter takes the specific social space of schools to show how racial significance is taught, learned, and reshaped through a diametrical process that toggles between schools and home life.

Fit to Be Good Cooks and Good Mechanics

Racialization in Schools

Through *policies* which are explicitly or implicitly racial, state institutions organize and enforce the racial politics of everyday life.

—Michael Omi and Howard Winant,
Racial Formation in the United States

School systems are simultaneously racialized and racializing. Educational institutions possess tremendous capacity to reproduce the power structure and racial hierarchy of society. Family, as another social institution, mediates the racializing effects of the educational system. The family is a critical site of racial identity development as it is a locale where intergenerational biography-based teaching occurs and strategies of action and resistance are formed. Within both schools and families, students respond to racializing messages and renegotiate their racial self-understanding. School experiences are conditioned by historical context, gender, and parental influences as parents use their own schooling experience as fodder for the intergenerational transfer of knowledge and ideologies to their children.

This chapter asks, What influence do educational systems have on immigrants' and citizens' racial identity formation? What role do families play in amplifying or mitigating the process of racialization? From a long-term perspective, what are the cumulative effects of racialization across family generations? This chapter examines how second- and third-generation Mexican Americans experience their social identity within the educational system and how parents' experiences with their own schooling shape their parenting styles.

First-Realization-of-Race Stories Crosscut Generations

Schools are a chief locale of socialization outside of the family and, as such, are places where much teaching and learning about social life and national culture takes place. The two generations educated in the United States apprehend the importance of race for the first time at school. Children first realize race in school and then come to identify with it, along a number of major axes of difference such as phenotype, formal name, language, and food. Recognizing skin-color variations often consolidates a conception of race, as with second-generation Rafael Treviño: "Somebody pointed out to me [in elementary school in the 1950s] that I was a little darker than they were. . . . I went home and I was washing my hands and I was trying to wash the darkness out. It was just a split moment, just realizing, 'Hey, this isn't gonna come off.'" Realizing the disadvantage that skin color carries (Pager and Quillian 2005) led some respondents to try to "cleanse" themselves of this liability by earnestly washing or using skin-bleaching agents. Third-generation Daniel Zagada speaks simply of being in a racially heterogeneous setting and of how "seeing" different skin colors and physical features is tantamount to seeing race: "I went to a school that was very diverse so we had lots of blacks and Filipino, white, Asians. So pretty early on, you can't miss that. I mean, you see it."

A person's first and last name is also an axis of difference that distinguishes groups according to Spanish and non-Spanish origin. Timothy, whose given name is "Timoteo," tells me how his grade school teacher anglicized his name to make it easier to pronounce and linguistically increased his Americanness (Murguia and Forman 2003). In this case, Timothy's teacher muted his foreignness as she used her school-sanctioned authority to acculturate him:

> TIMOTHY: My name is "Timoteo." When I was in fourth grade my teacher, Miss Green—she was from England—she changed my name to "Timothy." And I've always had it since. Except for my family, to my family I'm "Timoteo."
>
> JMV: How is it your fourth grade teacher renamed you?
>
> TIMOTHY: You know, people thought teachers were pretty smart, they knew what they were doing. [Laughs.]

Timothy noted that "everybody got their names changed" in the forties and fifties. To have one's name anglicized by a school authority whom you are taught to respect inculcates the sense that one's new name is better, imputing deficiency to one's original name. Moreover, a teacher changing—or correcting—students' names serves to transport them figuratively from their family's country of origin and into the United States via the road of cultural acceptability. Language marks cultural crossings, so for teachers to rename students is for them to erase a native culture and superimpose a U.S.-centered national culture.[1]

Part of the acculturation process of migrants to the United States, especially across generations, involves the acquisition of English. The educational system is pivotal in teaching English to immigrants and their families. Schools not only teach classes in language and other substantive areas, but they also teach cultural, national, and racial lessons. Albert Schultz, a child of immigrants, remarks, "When I was in school I couldn't speak English. My first language was Spanish and I remember practicing 'Pledge Allegiance to the Flag.' [Those were] probably the first words in English that I learned how to speak." Other interviewees recalled being punished for speaking Spanish, being warned not to speak Spanish in order to avoid having their mouths taped shut, and, most disturbingly, being placed in a class for the mentally retarded. Nearly all of my second-generation interviewees complained that schools decried Spanish speaking as a deficiency rather than a linguistic advantage. In the 1990s, the tide slowly turned such that some of these same second-generation interviewees found that Spanish speaking abilities were finally seen as a benefit in the work force. That said, some schools steered third-generation interviewees away from Spanish, including Tony Lopez, who refers to the mid-1970s:

> [In] probably kindergarten or first grade, I remember a teacher telling me not to talk Spanish. "We don't speak Spanish here, we speak American." "American" as opposed to "English." When I was in grade school—and it wasn't that long ago—it was not proper to speak Spanish. So, I didn't speak Spanish in school. Whereas now it is so widely accepted and promoted. I do a lot of things for the Spanish community. It is very much promoted now. "Oh, do you speak Spanish? Good, we want that. We want people to speak their native tongues." Whereas when I was in kindergarten I was told by a teacher, "We speak American here."

Cultural teaching comes in the form of language requirements enforced in the classroom. Being American means speaking American . . . that is, English.

Much like language, food does a lot of culture work. Cuisine serves as a cultural marker and is similarly difficult to hide in a school environment that is filled with policing eyes and ears. American identity, in this case, is measured by the contents of one's lunch bag. As Rafael Treviño quipped, "The American Dream was an Anglo family, a white Anglo family. We knew [we were] eating burritos and somebody else was [having] peanut butter sandwiches. There's a difference and you understand that." Noting that Mexican food has recently become fashionable (Davis 2000), he continues, "Now burritos and taquitos and enchiladas, everybody loves them. When I was a kid, you couldn't show 'em. They would make fun of you." Pressure to conform and desire to fit in is what makes some of this school-age surveillance so poignant.

Schools highlight the salience of race. School classrooms (Lucas 1999; Oakes 2005; Weis and Fine 2005) and social spaces (Tatum 1997) are often segregated by race. Race, racial scripts, and racial inequality are reproduced in day-to-day life in schools (Lewis 2003). Furthermore, school authorities frequently (if unwittingly) judge and treat racial minorities according to prevalent racial stereotypes and, by impressing them, re-create those stereotypes (Ferguson 2000). In interacting with students according to their understandings of race and class, teachers and administrators maintain discourses and systems of inequality (Morris 2005). For the Mexican-origin population specifically, education has been called the "linchpin" that consolidates and perpetuates intergenerational disadvantage (Telles and Ortiz 2009).

Whether the axis of difference is phenotype, formal name, language, or food, youth in school comprehend the overarching lesson being taught: in order to be socially accepted in peer circles, within the school at large, or in the nation as a whole, one must minimize the cultural and linguistic distance between oneself and the larger American mainstream. Schools, and the actors within them, inform students, in one way or another, that they were not just individuals but *racialized* individuals.

A Common Ideology: Education as Key to the "American Dream"

Schools are a primary site of socialization outside of the family. They are locales where much teaching and learning about social life and national culture take place (Tobin, Wu, and Davidson 1989). Schools across the globe are concerned "that young children be *taught to identify* with something larger than themselves and their families" (204, emphasis added).

Yet, families also have formative power. Axes of social division intersect in families, forcing families to devise strategies of action and teach their children accordingly (Lareau 2003). Families are key in reinforcing particular aspects of

TABLE 6.1
Educational Attainment By Generation

	Jr. High or Less	High School	GED	Some College	College	Master's	Doctoral Degree	Total
Gen1	8	0	0	0	0	0	0	8
Gen2	1	2	1	12	6	5	3	30
Gen3	0	5*	1	6***	12*	4*	1*	29
Total	9	7	2	18	18	9	4	67

 * Gen3 is the youngest age group, so educational attainment not completed.
 ** All five Gen3 noted here were currently attending high school, on track to graduate, and envisioning continuing on with higher education at a city college, college, or university.
*** Three of the six Gen3 in this cell were attending college at the time of the interview.

identity, such as race, religion, or gender (Cohen and Eisen 2000). They also mold educational aspirations (although the link between aspirations and outcomes is unclear) (Kao 1998; MacLeod 2004). Families and "fictive kin" can also be a wellspring of survival strategies and interdependent support (Stack 1974). This chapter argues that racial identities are constructed in interaction between two primary socializing institutions: families and schools.

The predominant family ideology about education espoused by the twenty-nine families I interviewed is rooted in the American Dream. Families perceive education as a means to attain this dream (namely, financial gain, upward mobility, and overall success). All of the families interviewed followed a pathway of upward mobility through the three generations. The educational attainment of virtually all families rose in each succeeding generation. Table 6.1 profiles the educational achievement of all three generations in my respondent pool. As will be detailed below, the dominance of the American Dream ideology varies by gender, generation, and class status.

This claim of intergenerational educational progress needs some contextualization. First, recall that this book is based on a relatively small sample of interview respondents with the objective of capturing the complexity and nuance involved in racialized life experience and is not designed to make sweeping generalizations about broad educational trends. Second, the families in my sample had all achieved middle-class status by the third, if not second, generation. This class advantage is not to be understated, as financial resources can be converted into other resources such as living in middle-class neighborhoods with reputable schools and the ability to send children to private schools, such as Catholic schools, which have a beneficial effect on Mexican American schoolchildren (Telles and Ortiz 2009: 134). In this way, class status may be a precursor to educational advancement.

Studies assessing educational progress (or lack thereof) among Mexican-origin students have found that the Mexican American second generation outpaces the immigrant generation in educational gains but that this achievement flattens in third and later generations (Telles and Ortiz 2009: 133). Another study using nationwide survey data from 2000 found that "second generation [Mexican American] educational attainment exceeded immigrant educational attainment by more than three years, while [the] third or later hardly exceeded [the] second generation at all" (Perlmann 2005: 62). There is agreement that the second generation rapidly overtakes the educational outcomes of the immigrant generation, yet there is some disagreement about whether third and later generations sink or continue to slowly rise relative to the second generation. All in all, we see that my findings regarding education are distinctive in showing continuing education gains with each of the three generations, a result probably influenced by the families' middle-class status and consistent with status attainment theory, which holds that parents' education and income are the best predictors of children's educational outcomes (Telles and Ortiz 2009: 133).

The American Dream equates education with career options and financial rewards. Guillermo Ramirez, a second-generation man from Sacramento, links together all three generations of his family as he discusses how his parents, and in turn he, came to recognize education as a lynchpin of the American Dream. Mexican American families desired to obtain the American Dream not only for their own aggrandizement but also to prove their worth to mainstream culture. As with all of my immigrant-generation respondents, Guillermo's parents had less than junior high school educations from Mexico. Yet, they saw the value of education:

> My parents—I don't know how it happened—but my parents somehow became aware of the value of education. They were always telling us, "I'll help you as much as I can." I had that support. . . . Many times [for] the second generation it was: "You're old enough to go to work and help the family." And it wasn't that [for me]. . . . I don't think [my parents] finished *primaria* [grade school] . . . in Mexico. . . . My grandmother was very instrumental in me going to law school because she would just tell me, *"Sea abogado."* ["Be a lawyer."] I'd say, "What's *'abogado,'* mama?" She'd tell me, "Lawyer."

Guillermo indeed got his law degree and established his own law firm. In addition to being a proponent of education at the community level (he formed an association in the sixties to raise money for scholarships for Mexican American students), he espoused the value of schooling to his two sons. He spoke of the unified vision he and his wife shared: "We've always inculcated [that] it was not *whether* they were going to get a college education— they were going to get a college education. . . . People with an education get better jobs, earn more."

Lance Morelos, a third-generation man, spoke about how his parents worked hard, sacrificed, and selected a residence according to the quality of the school district. Lance spoke about how his parents enacted their family ideology about the importance of education in both word and deeds:

> [My dad's] whole key in life was to get us educations. My mom, since I was in high school, would say, "I don't care if you get a degree in underwater basket weaving, get a degree." So we always lived in a very good area, which was predominantly a white area, in the smallest house, because they had the better schools. And they knew that. And so there would be nine of us in a three-bedroom house. For a lot of years until my dad really started to prosper. The goal was "education, education, education." We all went to Catholic school. My parents were in debt most of their life because of it. [Laughs.] . . . My dad was store manager . . . and he was the only one driving a VW bug when [his coworkers] were all driving Cadillacs and Mercedes.

Lance stressed how getting a degree had unlocked the door to career choice and higher pay:

> At [my aerospace engineering job] I got paid more than [others] did just because I had a piece of paper. . . . There were greater opportunities if you had a college degree. They weren't any smarter than me, I wasn't any smarter than them, but I had the opportunity and the piece of paper. [Before,] I couldn't get a job because I didn't have a piece of paper. . . . Like my mom said, "It doesn't matter if it's underwater basket-weaving, ping-pong, P.E., political science, just get a piece of paper." I saw it, I lived it.

Lance's degree propelled his occupational and financial upward mobility.

As with middle-class blacks (Pattillo-McCoy 1999: 66), second-generation Mexican American parents in my sample with college degrees raised children with the expectation that they will obtain college degrees, which they tend to do. In addition to guidance and financial support, parental goals of educational achievement are also important to children's ambition (Portes and Rumbaut 2001: 219). In this way, a college degree often begets a college degree and in turn opens up occupational and monetary opportunity and points the way to the American Dream.

First Generation: Mexican Immigrant Parents' Parenting Strategies
"Do As the Americans Do"

The American Dream ideology was sometimes accompanied by an assimilationist perspective. Ruben and Adele Mendoza, both second-generation Mexican Americans living in Vacaville, were taught to "do as the Americans do." This meant an increase in their educational aspirations and a decrease in their contact with Mexican relatives and their grasp on Mexican tradition. Ruben explains that his parents "wanted us to get our education here and do as the Americans do. Now I'm sad and kick myself in the rear for not going with them to Mexico and meet lots of uncles and so forth. . . . As far as holding onto the Mexican traditions, I don't think we ever thought about that." Ruben's wife, Adele, concurs with his assessment: "I don't think [traditions] were pushed onto us. I think once we came and were here it was pretty much you live where you are at and follow what is here. [We spoke Spanish at home yet my mom] didn't teach us reading or writing in Spanish, so when we went to school we would learn English and so it was easier for us to pick up." In her youth, the educational expectation for daughters was far less than for sons. Adele remarks, "We didn't have [child labor] laws back then. We were always working the fields as far as I can remember. . . . Back then it was 'girls didn't go to school, college, just get married and then the man does all the work.'"

Immigrant parents sometimes saw more immediate use in having their children work at home or in jobs rather than in schools. Since class informs race, it is important to examine how lower-class status in immigrant families' beginnings condition their educational aspirations. In poorer families (as all but one family was at the first generation), there is a tension between work and school, with work obligations impeding school success (Zhou et al. 2008). Discouraging education in favor of work "detoured" some youth from obtaining a college degree, foreclosing high-paying career options. Recall Tamara Rosenberg from chapter 2, who was deemed "the black sheep" for bucking family expectations and earning a college degree.

While the ideology of education as a tool for socioeconomic upward mobility is salient for immigrants and their families, it was not evenly endorsed across genders. Immigrant parents did not necessarily express enthusiasm for their daughters' education because of gender ideologies of the time and lingering attachments to a traditional gendered division of labor. Interestingly, as discussed later, school systems in the 1950s-1960s were more supportive of second-generation Mexican American girls than boys. In this way, the institutions of family and school provided diametrically opposed supports and pressures for the Mexican American second generation based on gender.

"Get a Job; School Is Just Recess"

The emphasis on education as a way to attain the American Dream varied not only by gender but also by class position. Families with substantially lower class origins did not subscribe wholesale to the notion of education as a pathway to the American Dream, in part due to their lack of knowledge about educational opportunities following high school. The lower a family's class status, the more likely they are to push the next generation out into the job market for immediate remuneration rather than delaying earning income due to schooling. Some parents' experience with labor-market discrimination and restricted occupational opportunity lowered their hopes for their children. Albert Schultz, a second-generation man who recalls his first English words as those in the "Pledge Allegiance to the Flag," spoke of how culture conditioned his parents' expectations: "One of the traditions they had at that time was that all Mexicans should be *zapateros* [shoesmiths] or *carpinteros* [carpenters] or *mecánicos* [mechanics] for automobiles, so it was hard for them to understand why I was going to college. For them, going to school was just recess." Second-generation individuals were intermediate between the immigrants who had grade school educations and the third generation, for whom college degrees became the norm. Sometimes the second generation pushed for educational credentials that were outside of their parents' ability to financially support or emotionally understand. Ruby Castillo, who speaks of her own biography as well as that of her son, Dillon, captures her family's three-generation educational trajectory:

> Education was not a big part of our family. Mom had third-, fourth-grade education and dad had the same. . . . So in the family [education] was

never really pushed, stressed, but I felt that I needed to pursue a higher education so I pushed myself. . . . Get an education. I saw that as a pathway to get out of poverty. . . . In my kids' generation, unfortunately, they don't know any struggles. I had to struggle if I wanted to get ahead, I had to take it upon myself to get educated and to get out and to work to buy my own clothes, etc., etc. And I say that unfortunately, because I don't see their inner passion. And for example, the son at University of California, Santa Barbara, [is] so used to having everything . . . taken care of from food, roof over the head, etc., to knowing that somehow we will be paying for [his] education. Where I felt I had to pay for my own education or find the money. So when I saw his [application] essay, there was nothing about a struggle. [It was], "I want to be God, I want to be president," that type of essay.

While Ruby had to seek out educational opportunities and funding sources, part of the downside of achieving comfortable middle-class standing may be her children's loss of some character-building passion and zest. While a consequence of her children's more coddled lifestyle may be the undesirable attribute of entitlement, her college degree granted her knowledge to coach her children through the college process and financially assist them.

"Girls Don't Need to Get an Education"

The Mexican immigrants in my sample arrived in the United States with little grade school education; some of the women wanted more education but were prohibited by their patriarchal husbands. This was the case with Ramona Vargas, an immigrant whose husband first came with the Bracero Program[2] in 1944 and who eventually got legal papers through her husband's employment. She worked in a packing house, canneries, and then for ten years in housekeeping in a hospital. Her husband worked in the fields as well as in hospital maintenance. I asked how she adjusted after her move from Mexico to the United States, and she complained about the educational cap that her husband enforced and the occupational and income ceiling this imposed:

I didn't know anything when I came here. Nothing. . . . He never agreed for me to go to school. I wanted to go to school to learn but he didn't agree with that. So, okay. We were going to get the lowest-paying jobs around because we had no education, so no good jobs.

I later explicitly asked about how she felt her gender affected the way in which she could navigate her life. She was unequivocal in her response:

> I wish I would be a man instead of a woman. [Laughs.] . . . I couldn't do things on my own, I couldn't make my own decision or anything like that. . . . It [gender] makes a lot of difference in life, because to me I wanted to go to school and have a little bit of education. I went to school in Mexico but not enough to get a good job here. I wanted to be a dressmaker and I wanted to go take classes at the junior college. I couldn't do that because my husband didn't want me to. To go to school? Nope. So I just worked and come home and raise kids and that's about it. I didn't learn anything and now I regret that because I could have found a job part-time like a receptionist or something where you sit and don't have to be moving so much or lifting heavy things. To file in hospitals or something, to learn to be a nurse or something. . . . But I couldn't do it. But I started to go to those classes for sewing and I made three things. I made a skirt, I made an apron, and I made a dress. That's it. Then I had to stop. Because I was having a lot of problems at home.

Ramona's husband's patriarchal ideals stunted her educational aspirations and thereby capped her occupational mobility as well as limited her sense of satisfaction and self-realization. Left to her own devices, Ramona would have pursued more education. Interestingly, her job objectives (and even the three items she made in sewing class) still fall into the gender-coded labor category of "pink collar" jobs, most likely a reflection of her time. While not all husbands in the first generation were as patriarchal as Ramona's mate, husbands sought to demonstrate their masculinity by being the primary (if not only) breadwinner for the family. This gendered ideology affected not just the education of wives but that of daughters as well. This tendency for men to prove masculine value by economically providing for the family is most prevalent in the first generation. These immigrant men imported cultural ideals from Mexico and were conditioned by the norms of the early to middle 1900s when traditional gender roles and separate spheres were dominant in both Mexico and the United States. As Hondagneu-Sotelo (1994) points out, it takes families years—if not a whole generation—to adjust to the more egalitarian gender roles in the United States. Plus, at the time of the first generation's arrival in the 1940s and 1950s, the United States boasted its own version of traditional gender scripts.

Second-Generation Mexican Americans: The Bridge Generation

Brown v. Board of Education, 347 U.S. 483 (1954), held that racial segregation in public schools violates the Fourteenth Amendment's guarantee of equal protection of the laws. This decision overruled the 1896 decision in *Plessy v. Ferguson* that upheld state-imposed racial segregation based on the separate-but-equal doctrine (that separate facilities for blacks and whites was permissible under the Fourteenth Amendment so long as they were equal). The *Brown* decision concluded that separate is inherently unequal.

Desperately unequal school buildings typify the pre-1954 *Brown v. Board of Education* era. Some of the second-generation respondents who are now in their early to middle sixties were school age in the 1950s, around the time of the *Brown v. Board of Education* decision. Perhaps contrary to popular belief, Jim Crow–style racism reached beyond blacks in the South and affected the Mexican Americans in the Southwest as well (Montejano 1987). Timothy Ponce describes these separate and unequal conditions in the late 1950s and early 1960s:

> There was a Mexican high school and there was the other one. We always knew that. It was just different being in a different place. It wasn't all Mexican, but that's where all the Mexicans went. We lived in the barrio in the north side [of San Jose] and . . . of course, for the new areas south of the city, there was a new high school for them. That was a pretty fancy high school and then we went to the old one. . . . That's just the way things are. . . . There wasn't much you could do, it just happened all the time. I always wondered, "What the hell's going on?"

Timothy sensed that this disparity was unjust and that he was denied opportunities available to others. He notes that he "never went to a college prep program" even though he was a "pretty smart kid." His response to these unequal school conditions was to persevere, although his response was rare among his peers, many of whom dropped out of school altogether. Timothy eventually earned his master's degree and became a junior high school principal.

Marcel Ruiz, living in Goleta, California, three hundred miles south of Timothy Ponce and three years his senior, experienced a similar separate and unequal school setting. Marcel found that "all the Mexicans" were in one smaller building and "the white daughters of the landowners would be in the big building." Marcel's narrative suggests the psychological repercussions of educational segregation. Marcel discusses his experience with a kindergarten and first grade English immersion program, after which he was integrated into the big school:

JMV: How did that integration work?
MARCEL: Well, I don't think it worked very well because . . . when I got to the big school I felt that I was always behind. I . . . wasn't quite up to the rest of the white, um, classmates so there was a lot of struggle in learning in the transition . . . When we got through the . . . integration, uh, I . . . began to feel again that low self-esteem that . . . I wasn't very smart. . . . They gave us some I.Q. test . . . and I didn't even understand the questions so I must [have] scored very low. So they would put us in bonehead reading class and mostly the Latinos are in the bonehead reading class and . . . we always seemed to be a little behind and I didn't do very well in school as I recall.

Marcel struggled with thinking he had a low I.Q. because he was tested before being English proficient, leading him to conclude that he was not smart. As it turns out, Marcel, at sixty-five years old, is a well-established fashion designer who reported the highest household income of all my respondents, at four hundred thousand dollars or above.

There is a gender difference in this rule of unequal distribution of school staff attention and encouragement. Tamara Rosenberg reported institutional support from her high school. She is an exception to the argument above that second-generation Mexican Americans fell outside school counselors' net of guidance and care. In Tamara's case, a school counselor informed her of her college potential and helped to fill the knowledge gap she lacked:

I was incredibly lucky, because I had never thought of going to college and it wasn't a vocabulary that was in our family. It was the high school counselor who called me. And I really thought that I was in trouble, because I had gotten kicked out of [two high schools previously]. I had an attitude. And so when I got called in, I really thought it was because I was in trouble. And then the counselor just called [me in] individually and asked [me], "What plans do you have for when you graduate?" And it was—"I don't know, I hadn't thought about it." And the counselor said, "Well, what kind of interests do you have? What do you think you might want to do? Have you ever thought of college?" And I said, "No." And I said, "Well, I can interior design." And she said, "Well, what about being an architect?" "Yeah, I guess so. Maybe." She pulled me out of all of my classes and put me in the college track. She said, "You know, it won't hurt you—if you don't go, you don't go. But if you want to, then at least you have that choice." I got on that track because of this woman just doing her job.

Thus, there are exceptions to the claim that the educations of second-generation Mexican Americans were universally marked by overt Jim Crow discrimination and outright school-sanctioned neglect and disempowerment. This gender variation shows how overt discrimination was unevenly employed even while it remained the dominant protocol of the era.

The Parenting Strategies of the Second Generation

The second generation employs three main parenting styles, all of which partially reflect parents' own experience at home and school in their youth. Middle-class parents display a "concerted cultivation" logic of child rearing (Lareau 2003). In "concerted cultivation," parents actively "develop" their children, often by utilizing parent-child conversations. To the extent that a majority of my respondent families are middle-class by the third generation, the three parenting styles elaborated here fall within the rubric of "concerted cultivation" (Lareau 2003). The first parenting style is one of "wholehearted encouragement." By adulthood, most second-generation Mexican Americans I interviewed had risen to middle-class status or above and were in a position to encourage their children (the third generation) in education. Second-generation Mexican Americans who achieved middle-class status as a consequence of educational degrees were vocal in encouraging their children to see education as a key to success. The second parenting style regarding education is "healthy skepticism." While generally supportive of educational goals for their children, a number of second-generation Mexican Americans, on the basis of their own experiences, felt skeptical about the payoff of the school system. Second-generation Mexican Americans whose progress was stymied by the discriminatory inner workings of the educational system were supportive of their children's education but were watchful and involved in order to ensure fair treatment of their children. The third parenting style is "pointed encouragement," which was developed in reaction to the gender difference in childrearing practices wherein parents encouraged boys' education more than that of girls.

Wholehearted Encouragement

Milo Contreras, who served in the U.S. Army and earned a law degree after being injured in combat, instilled in his daughter Renata that education is a tool for mobility. Injured in service, Milo received a stipend for school expenses from the G.I. Bill, as well as "'rehabilitation,' which is something like worker's compensation . . . where they retrain you back into the workforce." The Veteran's Administration paid for his retraining as a lawyer, since he could no longer perform the duties of his old job. Now a successful lawyer who earned his way into the middle class after a youth of poverty, Milo considers his family's progression, from his parents to his children:

MILO: The second generation looks for education. I think the first generation could see the value of it and was very encouraging as far as obtaining an education. . . . [For most of my siblings] . . . there has always been some progression to a better economic situation than agricultural work, which is the bottom of the scale.

JMV: For your children, what kind of trajectory do you think they're on?

MILO: I hope they become professionals just because that offers a lot of independence. And mobility. . . . With a profession you call your own shots.

Education is a key to upward mobility. Milo's family went from agricultural labor in the first generation to a law degree in the next generation to at least a bachelor's degree in the third generation. Milo's daughter, Renata, learned the importance of education from her father. Milo self-consciously impressed his daughter with this value through stories of his hard-won education. Renata remarks, "The importance of education . . . came from both parents but more from my dad, just 'cause he'd been through having nothing and putting himself through school and law school. He always really, really valued [education] and thought that can bring you *so* many opportunities, more than anything else." Education propelled Milo out of the agricultural fields, out of wartime operations, and into a profession where he earns a middle-class living and is his own boss.

Healthy Skepticism

A number of second-generation Mexican Americans who encountered obstacles to achieving educational goals were skeptical of the payoff of the school system for their children. While they were generally supportive of educational goals for their children, a dose of pragmatism deriving from experience kept some parents from unqualified encouragement of a system that had treated them unequally a generation earlier.

Marcus Lopez, at fifty-seven years old, experienced the overt segregation of the 1950s and early 1960s and this seeped into his children's perspectives on school. Marcus's high school counselor actively discouraged him from honors classes and steered him into remedial and vocational classes solely because of his Mexican descent. As school authorities, counselors and administrators embodied the institutional power that enforced the overt racial/ethnic segregation. Marcus reviews his high school years:

> My old [high school] counselor . . . told me I'd be nothing, that I should take nothing but shop class because that was all I was good for. That was all my people were good for: to be mechanics or cooks. . . . That was one of my worst experiences because I was doing well in school and I wanted to get into honors classes. But when I went to see my counselor to ask him why I couldn't get harder classes, or more classes besides three periods of study hall and a shop class, I was told *by my counselor*: "Take shop classes because your kind of people are good cooks and good mechanics."

Marcus did not finish high school but served in the U.S. Marine Corps, during which time he completed his GED and took some college courses. After completion of his military service, he visited his former high school and confronted that same school counselor:

> I looked him straight in the eye and I said, "I want my diploma and I want it dated 1964." . . . He just looked at me and he says, "Well, I hope you learned to be a mechanic when you were in the service." [I said,] "No, I was an instructor. I *taught* guerilla warfare. And hopefully I helped some of the guys come back from Vietnam."

Marcus's reaction to his high school counselor's disdain and racism was to achieve exactly *what he had been told he couldn't*. He succeeded both *in spite of* and *because of* the counselor's negative expectation. He took pleasure in showing off his status as a U.S. military instructor to precisely the person who was both a practical and symbolic obstacle. He petitioned the school board for a diploma, which he won. On a wider scale, his racially centered hardships spurred him to agitate for social change by becoming active in the Brown Berets, a militant Chicano group born in the 1960s.

Low expectations of Mexican Americans' achievement are often disastrously successful at squelching ambition. In a fraction of cases, however, these sub-par expectations can be converted into a motivating force. While Marcus's is a success story against a system that was set against him, the material, psychological, and emotional hardship he endured in order to succeed should not be minimized. It is a substantial burden for minorities to straddle the line between being sensitive to "additive forms of discrimination" (both individual and group histories) and being paranoid as they assess present situations and calculate responses (Feagin 1991).

Marcus shared his story with his children and warned of the pitfalls of the school system while also upholding the value of education. My interview with Marcus was book-ended by platitudes about education. Marcus told me that when he was counseling his high-school-age son about career and education plans after high school graduation, he put it flatly: "You can work at McDonald's, but why not *own* McDonald's?" Marcus believes that "education is power, pure power." Marcus achieved his GED while in the U.S. Marine Corps and also received his high school degree upon petition. Marcus put aside his skepticism about the meritocracy of the school system as he instructed his children about the value of education. Above all, Marcus claims, "Mostly what I taught [my children] is that you have to work hard, it's not free. It's not served to you." This ethic of working hard is born from experience: one must combat stereotypes, prove oneself, and transcend barriers through determination. As a consequence, Marcus drove his children hard to succeed.

Tony, Marcus's son, learned the lessons his father taught him. Tony did not just learn the didactic principles his father self-consciously tried to pass on but also the lessons that were transmitted through his tales of difficulties and blocked opportunities in high school. Tony dropped out of high school in tenth grade, barely able to read or write, in part because of the skepticism he picked up from his father about the unfairness of the system. However, Tony heard not only his father's complaints about education but also the value of determination and hard work. Tony joined the military at age twenty without a high school diploma. Through working hard on the job he achieved rank quickly and earned his GED, like his father.

Second-generation parents were regularly confronted with negative stereotypes in school. They naturally suspected that their offspring would be up against similar unflattering preconceived notions. Fully aware of the stereotypes they encountered, these parents were very realistic in the goals of social decorum, good grades, and propriety they established for their children. Two illustrations from the second-generation cohort make this point, including Tina Acevedo, who offers instruction to her children: "Hold your head up high, be on honor roll. Show people what you're made of. The stereotype that we're all dropping out of school or not showing up, that doesn't fit this family. That's not tolerated. We have a standard that we follow." In the same vein, Tyler Mendoza refers to his parents' motivation for him to rebut society's low expectations:

My parents always pushed school, school, school, school. So I had to do better in school. . . . C's were not that good, you get A's and B's. C's meant that you could do better. So, they always pushed from day one that I had to do better in school. I knew I had to try harder. . . . I had to try harder and prove that I wasn't one of those dumb lazy Mexicans or the ones that are going to drop out and get somebody pregnant. . . .

This realistic encouragement for school reflects a sizeable portion of the second generation's orientation toward the school system and their children. Taking their own lived experience into account, they are diffident about offering "wholehearted encouragement." Yet, they desire the best for their children and are aware that an education unlocks doors of opportunity. Also wanting to shield their offspring from social slights, they proffer pragmatic advice or biographical narratives that both caution and fortify their children.

Pointed Encouragement

In immigrant families supportive of education, male children were often offered the opportunity and resources for school in preference to female children. In part as a consequence of lack of encouragement in their youth, second-generation mothers developed a strategy of "pointed encouragement" when parenting their own children. Yolanda Segura recalls how her father ridiculed her desire to go to college:

I never finished my college education and part of that was because of opportunity and environment. . . . When I started to go to college right after high school, my dad sort of ridiculed it and was you know, "What do you need that for? . . . You don't need that." And not having good study habits or really not knowing how to survive in college and not having the right people to guide me was what deterred me the most.

In particular, Yolanda remembers how her experience was influenced both by race and gender. She connects the way her parents digested societal assumptions about Mexican immigrants and their families and how this influenced her gendered upbringing as a "Mexican girl":

There was always the people out there that just made assumptions about your skin color and your country; . . . that we weren't smart enough. . . . Certainly some of those [assumptions] were internalized by my parents bringing us up because there was this sense of you had to be humble and . . . being a Mexican girl . . . that you had your place in life.

Yolanda grew up in a traditional home and also describes her marital home as "very traditional"; she is the full-time mother of three girls, and her husband, a high-level executive of a large public relations firm, is the sole income earner. She wanted an education, though she never finished her college degree, and her husband, with two master's degrees and an upward occupational trajectory, further convinced her of the value of education. Fueled by her husband's conviction as well as her own, she was committed to encouraging her three female children in their academic lives.

Remembering how her father discouraged her educational dreams, Yolanda crafted a parenting style reflecting the way she *would have liked to be* supported. Yolanda refers to her experience with her parents as she draws a distinction between that parent-child relationship and the relationship she is trying to foster with her children:

Back to my own kids is that I didn't want them to feel that way [ridiculed, unsupported] at all. . . . From Day One I always told them "when you finish college" as opposed to "when you finish high school." Whereas in my own family it was "when you finish high school."

Yolanda is active in the Parent-Teacher Association at her children's schools and helps to organize extracurricular events like talent shows, yet another way she demonstrates her commitment to her children's educational agenda. Yolanda's hope is that, by changing the treatment of her children from the way she was treated as a child, she can modify her daughters' experience and improve their educational outcomes.[3]

Experiences outside of school also influence parental ideologies concerning education. For example, Beatrice Madrigal instructed her daughter, Reyna, to get a college education in order to earn economic independence. Beatrice did not base this instruction on her own educational experience, but on the connection she draws between her limited education and her difficulty supporting herself after her divorce from her husband. What came across most clearly in Beatrice's interview was not her sense of race or ethnicity but her sense of strength as a woman. Beatrice separated from her husband when she learned he had another family outside the marriage. As Reyna watched her mother learn to be strong, independent, and assertive, Reyna said that she learned by example and took those lessons to heart.

REYNA: [My mom] . . . taught us to be responsible people. . . . When she broke up with my father—I might have been like twelve—she started teaching us how to be really independent and not to rely on anyone. And to take care of yourself and . . . I think that is why I went off to college.

JMV: Really?

REYNA: Yeah, because she was a stay-at-home and when my dad left she had to go to work because my dad didn't give her any help or support. . . . That is what she has taught us: "Well, you need to work to take care of yourself. You have needs and you support yourself." And then she had said, "You should go out to college." And, you know, she started talking about "so you don't have to rely on a man," and then she had started talking about what had happened to her.

So, the lesson that passed between the generations of Madrigal women is not about race or ethnicity but about gender. Lessons of gender, as well as of race, can involve teachings about how education is a pathway toward independence, emotional as well as economic.

Third-Generation Mexican Americans: The Youth

Discrimination is dynamic: forms of discrimination are contextual and refract political, economic, and cultural arrangements. In the post–civil rights era, discrimination became embedded in institutional practices and the fabric of everyday life. "Institutional discrimination" holds civic and social institutions responsible for discriminatory practices that are structured into organizations and reproduce inequality. Modern-day forms of racism and discrimination are qualitatively different than before the civil rights era. While overall racial segregation, in particular between white and Hispanic children, persists in many school districts (Saporito and Sohoni 2006), state-mandated racial segregation has been replaced by covert forms of discrimination. In the educational experiences of third-generation Mexican Americans in the mid-1970s and later, this means that separate school buildings or outright school administration disregard have been replaced by school tracking systems, low expectations for minority performance based on negative stereotypes, and classroom curriculum that devalues non–European American "subjugated knowledges" (Collins 1991).

Third-generation Mexican Americans complained of being (nearly) trapped in tracking systems. Those who escaped were those whose parents rigorously oversaw their schooling and engaged the school administration when necessary. Regardless of region in California, a sizeable portion of third-generation Mexican American students reported a severe tracking system in place in their schools. Seventeen-year-old Andrew Rosenberg captures the role of race in school tracking systems. Andrew refers to the racialized sorting patterns behind student placement in high school classrooms:

"Oh, he's Mexican—put him in that class." It's really kind of how it is. It's really bad. I don't think it's that intentional. But if you're Mexican and you walk into a class of all white people, it's like—oh, this is the GATE [Gifted and Talented Education] class. I don't belong here. When really a lot of those Mexicans who are in the normal classes should be in the GATE classes. And some of the people who are in GATE classes shouldn't be at all . . . most of them are just cheating their way through. So a lot of people don't even deserve to be in it. But I think the counselors feel too afraid to put a white kid in a normal class, because the parents would probably get mad or the kid would be like—what am I doing in this class? So I think a lot of people just automatically get put in these classes. They say—oh, you need to keep a "B" grade or whatever to stay in GATE classes. But a lot of people are failing these classes, but they still get put back in there anyway.

While the practice may not be "intentional," the school persists in internally segregating the classrooms, giving whites access to advanced classes and systematically denying them to minorities.

Hector Avila was funneled into a racialized tracking system that Andrew Rosenberg was able to avoid. Hector offers an extreme example: he was tracked into an English as a Second Language (ESL) classroom when he was already fluent in English and Spanish. Because ESL classrooms focus on acquiring English language skills, Hector's educational progress was stunted because he was placed in a classroom that was well below his aptitude. I asked if he felt any key events shaped his sense of racial or ethnic identity, to which Hector responded,

I can remember one thing that made me upset. . . . See, I was born in the United States and I spoke perfect English and I also spoke Spanish. So I probably spoke better Spanish when I was younger, but I also spoke very good English, as well. . . . [W]hen I moved to Serra Vista [Arizona][4] . . . [the school] automatically put me in ESL. Even though I spoke perfect English. I don't think my parents, at the time, really paid attention or understood what that was. So, instead of going to regular English class, I got behind in English because they were putting me in ESL. . . . And then the teacher wasn't smart enough to say, "Hey, this kid speaks English and Spanish. . . ." They just put me there with these Mexican kids . . . who didn't speak any English. This . . . was through all of second grade. . . . I struggled a little bit with English classes [later] because I think I got a little behind. Now, I look back at it and I go, "That really pissed me off that they did that. What the hell is their problem?"

As a second grader, Hector didn't figure out that he had been misplaced in the ESL classroom. He thought, "Wow, I get pulled out of class for an hour to go to this place where there's all these other Mexican kids and I had fun talking to them. And I spoke to them in Spanish." Because he was fluent in Spanish and English he would get all the answers to the lessons, leading to boredom. One repercussion of not being challenged in the classroom was that he started to act out and thus got pinpointed as possibly having Attention Deficit Disorder [ADD]:

I became a little bit disruptive in elementary school because I don't think I was being challenged because I was . . . put in this [ESL] class. . . . They were like, "We think he had ADD because he's not doing well in English." But yet in all the other class, like math, it was real easy for me. . . . Then they did some more tests and they were like, "Oh, we're sorry, we're wrong."

Once Hector was correctly placed in appropriate-level classrooms, he did well, earning straight A's in middle school.

Relationships with school administrators mirror the racialized tracking system: whites and Asians get the majority of positive attention while Latinos and blacks often are not able to foster this same rapport and instead are disregarded or receive negative attention.[5] Veronica Guzman tells me about how she and her dark-skinned brother have a markedly different relationship with their high school vice principal than does their light-skinned, dark-blonde-haired sister:

My sister, she's light skinned, she looks American, but she's a Mexican American. The vice principal thought she was white. They [the administration] didn't know that my brother and sister and I were related. And they would send information for her in English and for my brother they would send it in Spanish. She's blonde and according to them she's a *güera* [white woman] and he's *Mexicano*, Mexican. The vice principal treated her differently because she was a blonde, she was a *güera*. When they found out she was Hispanic, she was a Mexican, it wasn't the same anymore.

This starkly different treatment for siblings of the same family powerfully reinforced Veronica's sense of racial identity. Veronica's response was to distrust the administration. While she called in her mother to speak to the principal on her behalf, after which relations improved, a lesson she learned from school was the salience of race—or even the appearance of race—in obtaining school resources and support.

Classroom curriculum is another way in which the educational institution determines which races and cultures are "legitimate" and deserve scholastic attention. In so doing, schools reinstantiate the disequilibria of societal power dynamics. The sociology of culture and education literatures have, since the 1970s, discussed the power politics that operate behind decisions about what kinds of content merit inclusion into disciplinary canons (Bourdieu and Passeron 1977; Bourdieu and Passeron 1979). Classroom curriculum is not neutral but political. National curricula and canonized scholarship represents a *"selective tradition . . .* some group's vision of legitimate knowledge [that] is produced out of the cultural, political, and economic conflicts, tensions, and compromises that organize and disorganize a people" (Apple 1996: 22). Rather than remaining entrenched in white-supremacist, masculinist, and imperialist ideologies of old, schools can positively transform future social and race relations by changing classroom pedagogy and traditional epistemologies. bell hooks calls for "excitement" in the classroom, which is a condition for, as well as a byproduct of, Paolo Freire's "concientization," or critical awareness and engagement (Freire 1970; hooks 1994). hooks envisions a feminist and racially conscious classroom wherein students are critical and active and knowledge is stripped of its dominant-class politics.

The multicultural education project of the 1970s developed in response to America's changing demographics and a growing need for schools and curriculum to incorporate students of color. Race is a matter of both social structure and cultural representation (Winant 2000). Since schools make decisions on how racial groups are represented both structurally (faculty and student body composition) and academically (course content and course offerings), they are fertile loci for (re)teaching and (re)learning about race.

Third-generation Mexican Americans voiced dismay over not seeing their experience reflected in official school curricula. My respondents echoed the sentiments of education theorist Henry Giroux, who decries the omissions of "master narratives and hegemonic discourses that make up the official curriculum" and demands integration of "the self-representations of subordinated groups as they might appear in 'forgotten' histories, texts, memories, experiences, and community narratives" (Giroux 1992). Araceli Treviño offers her story of frustration in high school with seeing the history of Latinos and women excised from her world history class:

> I remember going to our [world history] text book and . . . going through the section in there where they talk about Mexican Americans and César Chávez and farm workers' struggle and in that same chapter there was . . . lesbians and gays, [women's rights,] and Puerto Ricans, different ethnicities in this one chapter. . . . Whatever the minority stuff was, [it] was all [in] this one lump sum chapter. And I was so excited. . . . "Okay, let's learn!" . . . We get to it and [the teacher] goes, "we're skipping this chapter. We're going to the Reagan years." I was like, "What!" I was so bummed. I was so bummed and I asked him, "Why? Why do we have to skip this chapter?" And he said that the Reagan years are more important. And I said, "To whom?" And we got into a little conversation and I remember going home crying, crying to my parents about how I was so mad that he felt the Reagan years were so important than this one little section. . . . It was maybe three or four pages on Latin America. . . . I remember it being such a huge issue and . . . we had a meeting with the principal. So he ended up teaching that next. And it ended up being in the final but I remember it was such a stir and I was so hurt. I just remember being so hurt about [how] he could say that it wasn't important. . . . And how [he] could say that is not important considering that there is a lot of Mexican American kids in that school. . . .

In the end, Araceli won her appeal to the high school principal and the teacher apologized for saying that the world history chapter on women, gays and lesbians, and racial minorities was not significant. Araceli actively challenged her teacher and the curriculum arrangement at large because she found that a master narrative that excludes minorities of various kinds was overtaking her own history. The consequences of her observation and resistance empowered her sense of racial and ethnic identity and emboldened her sense of entitlement to "subjugated knowledge" (Collins 1991).

To be included in classroom curriculum is to be deemed legitimate and valuable. Most of my respondents who directly discussed multicultural education were proponents of it. As education systems determine how to handle questions of race in classroom curriculum and pedagogy, and classroom and structural diversity, they are endowing race and racial categories with varying significances and levels of power.

Affirmative Action: Pushing the Door Ajar

Affirmative action policies were drafted in the 1960s and 1970s to improve underrepresented minorities' access to education and employment. Thus far this chapter has detailed the historically coded ways in which the school system has made Mexican Americans keenly aware of their racial identity and status as marginal to the dominant, white society. The Telles and Ortiz (2009: 271) study that includes Mexican Americans of various socioeconomic statuses found that by 2000, third-generation Mexican Americans "were about 30 percent as likely as non-Hispanics to have completed college." In my smaller sample, however, where middle-class status may bias in favor of school quality and graduation rates, affirmative action policies seem to have benefited the third generation. Affirmative action policies opened doors to education and jobs that might otherwise have remained closed. Some third-generation Mexican Americans enthusiastically "checked the box" while others were reluctant to do so. Considering one's ethnic claim in a situation with pecuniary consequences was often a struggle, and the responses to this quandary varied widely (Jiménez 2004). For those who claimed minority status, receiving affirmative action benefits only reinforced their identity as ethnic Americans (particularly for those of mixed ethnicity).

Respondents who claimed that they were beneficiaries of affirmative action policies asserted that these policies "opened the door" to higher education. They were all quick to declare that they were indeed qualified for admission. In their view, affirmative action encouraged admissions committees to consider their applications more holistically, taking their (sometimes multiple) disadvantages more seriously than they would do without such a policy in place. As Cristina Talavera expresses, "Affirmative action . . . opened the door. While I had good grades, I was also working in high school. . . . It just really opened the door so that I could show what I had to show." Cristina, like many college-bound minority students of the late 1990s and the new millennium, felt a backlash after the passage of California's Proposition 209 in November 1996, effectively halting affirmative action policies in public institutions, including the University of California. Cristina notes, "When I went to go apply for law school—which was the first year that it was revoked—I felt it really worked against me. I mean, I could sit there and scream in my essay all I wanted . . . but at the same time I felt like the door wasn't even open for anyone to hear me speak." No one can say whether Cristina would have gotten into law school under affirmative action, but it has been well publicized that the University of California's law school admissions of minority students plummeted after the passage of Proposition 209. Far from making the issue of race disappear, in Cristina's case at least, the repeal of affirmative action heightened her sense of ethnic disadvantage.

Tony Lopez, working for a sheriff's department as a community liaison, made the point in chapter 3 that given the influx of Latinos from Mexico and other Latin American countries, his ethnic background and bilingual abilities were in demand. He remarked that his "race has kicked open doors [and that he] gets things done." Akin to Cristina Talavera's notion of "show[ing] what I had to show" once inside, Tony's "willing[ness] to work hard" legitimates his occupational placement. By saying that he works hard, Tony sends the message that affirmative action opens doors to those who are industrious and deserving. Lance Morelos, who spoke regarding business entrepreneurship, defended affirmative action from misconceptions: "There is no free lunch. It's not 'if you're female or a minority here's a check.' People don't realize that; that's not the way it is." These discursive moves head off the conservative critique that affirmative action goes to the "undeserving poor" and the underclass whose problems are bred from cultural pathologies rather than macro-structural issues (Steele 1990; Thernstrom and Thernstrom 1997).

For Jillian Rosenberg, the question of "whether or not to check the box" on college and medical school applications threw her into ethnic identity pandemonium because she has a European-descent parent. Affirmative action programs operate on the beliefs that to be a racial/ethnic or gender minority is to be historically, if not currently, oppressed and that diversity is an asset in workplaces and schools. Some people, such as Jillian, do mental and emotional contortions in order to figure out what it means to be a minority (or half a racial/ethnic minority) and to have achieved middle-class socioeconomic standing. When I met her, Jillian was attending Yale University and considering applying to medical school. When applying to Yale, she had marked that she was a racial/ethnic minority yet felt unsure as to whether she was exploiting her background, and at the time of my interview she was facing a similar predicament regarding medical school applications:

> I definitely had a struggle with how I feel about affirmative action type stuff, because I know that when I'm applying to med school being Mexican is going to help me in. I know that it helped me get into Yale. I know there were a lot of really good things that I did and I deserve to be there, but I know that it [being Mexican] played a part. . . . I felt like I was exploiting it. . . . So, it's just hard.

On the whole, respondents who received affirmative action benefits were grateful. Their tacit understanding is that while they encountered both institutional and public discrimination, race relations in the United States improved slightly from that which their parents experienced. While this chapter has demonstrated the ways in which both institutional mechanisms and historical context shape racial formation and integration into dominant society, state policies such as affirmative action help ameliorate racial inequality. With the passage of Proposition 209 in California in 1996, however, state-enforced affirmative action in public institutions was dismantled. Since "inequality is not fated by nature . . . [but] is a social construction, a result of historical acts," the good news is that intentional policies can be *changed* to produce more equitable outcomes (Fischer et al. 1996: 7). As the state and nation struggle with how to repair historical and contemporary racial power imbalances and injustices, it is important to think about the ways in which the state and other institutions have a formative hand in both creating and, alternatively, eradicating racial inequalities.

Assimilated and Racialized

While thinned attachment and cultural maintenance families' levels of commitment to Mexican culture vary, they are indistinguishable in their levels of academic achievement. A difference between thinned attachment and cultural maintenance families was the tendency for thinned attachment families to be more pacifist and accommodationist than their more culturally identified counterparts. This is due to the stress that a thinned attachment orientation placed on acculturating to and succeeding in mainstream institutions. By definition, those on a thinned attachment trajectory were more likely to check their ethnicity at the school's front door and try to succeed by the established rules. There were notable exceptions, however, where thinned attachment individuals and families took defensive action that contradicted their normally accommodating stance. In situations risking or damaging a family member's academic achievement, thinned attachment families changed their cooperative stance. Threats to educational attainment pushed most respondents, regardless of attachment to heritage, to adopt direct, confrontational action, such as meeting with school officials and challenging students' mismatched academic placement, unfair treatment, or the curriculum.

As we saw in the prior chapter on discrimination, cultural maintenance families were generally more assertive, combative, and interventionist than thinned attachment families. This self-confident and forceful quality was mediated by generation. The first-generation immigrants were relatively uninvolved as overseers of their American-born children's education because of their unfamiliarity with and insecurity about navigating the educational system. The second-generation Mexican American parents, by contrast, were educated in the United States and well versed in racialized and racializing educational systems. Cultural maintenance parents were especially predisposed to take on their children's educational plights with attention and vigor since living proudly as an ethnic minority in a nation with predominantly white leadership was a chief goal.

A commonality beyond academic achievement that cross-cuts thinned attachment and cultural maintenance designation, generation, and gender is the experience of racialization despite assimilation. Despite English proficiency, adoption of dominant cultural norms, ability to effectively navigate mainstream institutions, and even impressive educational achievements in later generations, many Mexican-origin individuals are racialized as non-white and treated as inferior.

Institutions shape a host of life outcomes, including immigrants' incorporation into a community (Bloemraad 2006; Menjivar 2000; Reitz 1998) and notions of civic participation and national identity (Bellah 1986; Wedeen 1999). Immigrant groups' incorporation trajectories depend in part on the interplay among context, "structures of opportunity" (institutions, cultural beliefs, and social networks) (Alba and Nee 2003: 14), and purposive action by immigrants and their descendants. Since "every state institution is a racial institution" (Omi and Winant 1994: 83), examining the interplay between structures (schools) and agency (families and individuals) is crucial in understanding how these social influences bear on racial self-understandings and the assimilation process. The way Mexican American students are treated in schools and the way families handle their children's experiences of schooling is another "bump" in the nonlinear process of incorporation into U.S. society. Schools, among other social arenas, play a major role in constructing race, endowing it with meaning and creating differential treatment and inequality based on racial divisions.

Schools are a racializing agent for all three generations, marking, categorizing, and treating their Mexican-origin pupils differently in various sociohistorical milieus. Yet, students and their families are not mere social sponges. Families play a profoundly important role in shaping students' racial identity formation, resistance strategies, and educational trajectories. Family ideologies reflect parents' own experiences in their educational and family systems. In this way, as parents call upon their own experiences in school, gender ideologies and parenting tactics interact with the processes of racial identity formation and incorporation into U.S. institutions. However, as Pattillo-McCoy (1999: 115) notes in her study of middle-class black youth, "Without minimizing the importance of individual agency, . . . context exists above and beyond individual and family circumstances. Choices are made within the limits of what options are presented to these young people." For the Mexican American families in this book, this signals the importance of understanding the influence of generation and historical timing on the structure of educational systems as well as the ways in which families can serve as a buffer for their children.

Although education was consistently seen as key to achieving the American Dream, changing sociopolitical environments meant that the racial messages conveyed by institutions and families shifted accordingly. The immigrant generation advocated the ideology of education leading to upward mobility but with a gender bias. The education of the second generation was marked by overt Jim Crow–style segregation, while the third generation was typified by a more covert institutional discrimination. While these ideologies are not clearly defined by time period and probably coexisted, the primary distinction between the two eras is the degree of intensity of segregation and prejudice. Second-generation Mexican Americans attended school in unequal buildings and were oftentimes barred from access to "white" schools or advanced classes. This second-rate treatment made second-generation Mexican American students view their race as a social identity feature to be managed—to pass, to downplay, to assert, to subvert. This recognition of the salience of race in schools played into the teaching strategies they developed once they became parents.

In contrast to the overt discrimination typical of the 1950s and 1960s, third-generation Mexican Americans, educated in the 1970s and 1990s, had school experiences that were marked by covert discrimination. School tracking systems racially/ethnically segregated students in classrooms (though the school student body might be racially diverse) and classroom curricula valued mainstream American cultural knowledge, ignoring minority forms of knowledge. While the form of discrimination varied with the historical period, the lesson that race is an important aspect of one's social identity remained constant.

Racial identity formation does not work exactly the same way for females and males, as families and schools bore different expectations for youth according to their gender. Immigrants were inclined to exclude women (wives and daughters) based on patriarchal expectations. Immigrant parents placed more emphasis on boys' education, yet these young males faced more barriers from schools. The second-generation females' experience in schools moderated the effect of lack of familial support: despite overt segregation, school officials were more disposed to mentor and advance female students than male students. Combining these experiences from home and school results in particular parenting strategies used to coach the third generation. Three parenting styles evolved, with "pointed encouragement" reflecting female parents' desire to furnish direct encouragement to their children (especially daughters) on the basis of what they would have liked to receive in their own youth.

Educational outcomes,[6] while not central to the analysis presented here, deserve some attention. Educational attainment, which in part reflects changing sociopolitical milieus as well as shifting parenting styles, has risen in each successive generation in my sample. Among my interviewees, college degrees have at least doubled from the second to the third generation (with no college degrees in the first generation). The third generation is on track to meet or exceed their parents' educational levels. While this chapter has focused less on scholastic achievement than the racialized and racializing components of both school and home lives, the middle-class Mexican Americans whom I interviewed showed intergenerational progress in education gains.

This academic success of my second- and third-generation middle-class Mexican American interviewees needs to be contextualized within broader trends of educational outcomes. While there is nationwide intergenerational progress in that the Mexican American second generation experiences higher levels of educational (and occupational) attainment compared to their parents, they "still trail well behind the mean of the American population" (Zhou et al. 2008: 41). Latinos lag behind non-Latinos in education and in other socioeconomic characteristics (Chapa and De La Rosa 2004). While "Mexican Americans experience dramatic gains in education and earnings between the first and second generations" (Grogger and Trejo 2002: viii), schooling achievement is "modest" (ibid.) or "remains flat in following generations" (Telles and Ortiz 2009: 133). Beyond this trend of noticeable—followed by limited—educational assimilation, racialization in school compounds disadvantage. "Racialization through schooling seems to help cement their low status in American society" (Telles and Ortiz 2009: 133). One reason why my small sample may have achieved educational success is their class advantage, in that most families achieved middle-class status in the second generation.

Finally, it is interesting to consider how social forces that impinge upon the third generation steer this generation's racial self-concept and may inform their future parenting strategies. The third generation's experience of family support for education and struggles in school over institutional discrimination, multicultural curricula, and affirmative action have undoubtedly forced them to deliberate about the salience of race in the United States. We turn next to the third generation, where I investigate the various social spheres that influence this generation's racial and ethnic self-perceptions.

As Much Hamburger as Taco

Third-Generation Mexican Americans

> A notable and intriguing feature of race is its ubiquity, its pres-
> ence in both the smallest and the largest features of social rela-
> tionships, institutions, and identities.
> —Howard Winant, "Race and Race Theory"

Nearly seven million people are third-plus generation Mexican Americans (Macias 2006: 6), yet there is great *diversity* and *fluidity* within this group regarding the way they classify themselves. This chapter analyzes how the contradictory forces of "flexible ethnicity" and "racialization" influence the way third-generation Mexican Americans identify. "Flexible ethnicity" refers to the ability to deftly and effectively navigate different racial terrains and be considered an "insider" in more than one racial or ethnic group. "Racialization," by contrast, refers to the process of distancing and oppressing people perceived as nonwhite. In this case, other people's expectations and enforcement of difference create or reproduce social distance and unequal power dynamics. Regardless of whether Mexican Americans experience their racial/ethnic identity to be more "flexible" or "racialized," they often encounter challenges to their racial "authenticity."

This chapter is organized in four sections. First, I examine the diversity of racial/ethnic claims third-generation Mexican Americans make. Second, I develop the concept of "flexible ethnicity." Third, I analyze the process of racialization. Finally, I discuss the issue of racial authenticity and the dynamism of culture, especially with regard to gender.

Variety of Racial and Ethnic Labels

The scholarly literature is undecided about whether to categorize Latinos as a race or an ethnicity. As discussed in chapter 1, whether Latinos have been recognized as a race or ethnic group on the U.S. Census has changed over the decades. Scholars remain divided as to how to classify and discuss this group. Regarding Latinos/Hispanics, scholarly opinions range; this group has been classified as a race (Flores-Gonzales 1999), an ethnic group (as the U.S. Census did in 1980, 1990, and 2000), a "pan-ethnic minority group" (Portes and Rumbaut 2001), or even a combination race/ethnicity where no line is drawn (Lee and Bean 2004; Ochoa 2004). Opinion is equally divided about how to classify Mexican Americans. Some scholars regard Mexican Americans as a race (Acuna 2000; Gómez 2007), as did the U.S. Census in 1930 (but never before and never since). Others consider Mexican Americans an ethnic group (Chavez 1992; Jiménez 2004; Macias 2006; Skerry 1993; Smith 2003). Others take a political-historical perspective to argue that Mexican Americans are both a distinct ethnic population *and* a "socially supposed race" when "subjected to policies of discrimination or control" (Montejano 1987: 4–5). Yet other scholars straddle the race or ethnicity question by theorizing Mexican Americans as a "racialized ethnic group" (Golash-Boza 2006; Telles and Ortiz 2009).

In addition to the scholarship being divided on how to classify Latinos and Mexican Americans, there is also much indecision within the group itself (Oboler 1995). This ambivalence is clear in the way my third-generation Mexican American respondents' racially/ethnically identify. Respondents offered a range of answers from "Chicano," "Hispanic," "Latino," "Mexican," and "Mexican American" to detailed ratios of their heritage, such as "half-Mexican, half-Italian" or "Mexican/Polish/Swedish/Russian/Jewish." Third-generation Mexican Americans identify in a wide variety of ways, often using multiple labels and shifting them according to social context.

Marisol Fuentes ruled out several possible choices before deciding upon "Mexican American" as the most fitting identifier. For her, this process began (and continues) through informal personal interactions. One day in high school the issue of racial self-titles was a topic of discussion:

[My teacher] gave us a list of all these different terms, like "Hispanic," "Latino," "Chicano," "Mexican American," "Mexican" . . . all those words and little definitions [of] what they meant. I remember seeing "Mexican American": it said something like being born in the United States but still like having Mexican traditions but being more Americanized. I was like, "Okay, I guess that's me." Because the other terms were like "Chicano," people who were involved in the sixties and I'm like, "No." Then "Mexicans," people who are from Mexico, and I would say, "Okay, that's not me." "Latino"—I don't know what the heck it said—Latin American or something. I'm like, "No." "Hispanic," I don't know what it said for Hispanic. The only thing that I found [myself] closest to was Mexican American. That makes sense because . . . I'm Mexican culturally and ethnic-wise. . . . [Yet] I felt like Americanized. . . . A lot of credit . . . towards being American was my dad . . . being in Vietnam. [He served] this country and I feel like I have to give some kind of credit to being American because even though he didn't go voluntarily, he was still drafted. I feel like it's my responsibility in a way to say that I am American because my dad went to fight an American war. I think that has to do with why I started calling myself "Mexican American" and where the "American" came from. Because the "Mexican" I totally knew.

Marisol evaluates the range of identity options to determine the label that makes the most sense to her. She finds that "Mexican American" suits her because it is a middle ground between Mexican and American and honors both identities.

Third-generation Mexican Americans in my sample, who are too young to have been participants in the Chicano Movement but whose parents were alive at the time, had divergent opinions on whether or not they liked the term "Chicano/a." Those in favor of the term thought of it as an empowering self-definition that implied value and dignity. Those who did not like the term considered it low-class or outdated. Caitlyn Benavidas understands "Chicano/a" to be a political label that refers to someone of Mexican descent born in the United States:

I definitely consider myself completely culturally Mexican but Chicano is because I was born here. I . . . politically identify as Chicano and Chicana, like my parents did in politics. My own meaning [of Chicano/a] is mostly being that I was born in the United States and that I have ancestors from the Southwest on both sides of my family. Also just the politicalness behind it—having parents that were part of the [Chicano] Movement.

As one might expect, the children of Chicano Movement activists were more inclined to claim a "Chicano" identity than children of nonactivists. Carmina Dos Santos's parents were active in the Chicano Movement, using their home for Chicano artist and activist meetings:

My parents were always Chicanos. They were active during the Chicano Movement. . . . They are Chicano activists so they raised us [my brother and I] with a strong sense of larger community purpose as connected to

our ethnicity. . . . "Chicana" for me means identity with a larger political purpose. I don't know if I'm into the Chicano militancy but I think
that there is room for holding on to some sort of legacy of the Movement
and by claiming that identity I'm in a way committing to continuing that
legacy of social activism.

While children of Chicano Movement activists often claimed "Chicano,"
many others who are children of nonactivists found that the Chicano label
accurately portrayed their ideals of self-representation and anticolonialism.
Tyler Mendoza explains his understanding of the various labels that could
apply to him:

"Mexicanos" were always people that just got here. But I always grew up
knowing that we have these labels: we're called "Hispanic," "Latino," "Mexican American," "Mexicano." [Of] all these terms, "Chicano" is the only
one that people wanted to be called and fought, struggled, and got beat
down to be called. And not only to be called that but have the rights that
go with that like everybody else. . . . "Chicano" is a political term. I like
that term more than all the other ones first because there was a struggle,
there was a Movement. . . . "Latinos," well, there is something that needs to
encompass all of us globally and that is the word that I like best. "Latino"
is something that I would choose to encompass all of us, but "Chicano"
would be first thing.

Other respondents disliked the term "Chicano." Gabriel Ponce dislikes
"Chicano" because he associates it with racial or ethnic separatism. As a man
of Mexican heritage born in the United States, Gabriel resists separatism and
hopes to find a way to assimilate more smoothly:

I don't like "Chicano," I don't like that word. Because I feel like . . . you're
really separating yourself when you're Chicano. . . . I was born in the
United States, so for me I'm Mexican born in the United States . . . just
a Mexican guy. I'm not a Chicano. I went to a couple of the United Farm
Worker marches when I was a baby, but I'm not a Chicano. My parents
took us. So, yeah, I don't really like it. It's real separatist.

Indeed, the racial politics of the Chicano Movement were premised on
rejecting the previous generation's assimilationist orientation. The Chicano
Movement disclaimed whiteness and sought to define Chicanos as mem-

bers of a "brown race," converting "non-white status into a badge of pride" (Haney Lopez 2003: 2). Interesting, however, was Gabriel's claim that "I'm Mexican born in the United States . . . just a Mexican guy" because while he declares the United States as his country of birth, his claim of being "a Mexican guy" positions him *outside* of the label "American," which he does not mention (Murguia and Forman 2003).

Social context is relevant to the way people amplify or downplay their ethnicity. "Situational ethnicity" suggests that actors subjectively evaluate the behavioral options available within a particular objective setting (Okamura 1981). Many third-generation Mexican Americans' racial self-titles change depending on social context. Carmina Dos Santos reflects,

> [At college] in Boston I met a lot of Dominicanos and Puerto Ricanos . . . so I sort of claimed the title "Latina" to be more inclusive. . . . I mean, I think I always switch between "Chicana" and "Latina" and it depends on context. "Chicana" for me means identity with a larger political purpose. "Mexican American" is appropriate when I don't have the energy to explain and I assume that people wouldn't understand. I have a hard time with "Hispanic" [because it is a government label and] it doesn't fit who I think I am.

For Carmina, her racial self-title depends on social context. Her response is typical of many third-generation Mexican Americans in that "Chicano/a" is associated with politics, "Latino/a" is seen as embracing other Latin American people, and "Mexican American" is an easy self-title because people in California are familiar with the term. Reyna Madrigal comments similarly:

> REYNA: I say I'm "Chicana." That is what I identify myself with because I was born here [United States] and from the classes that I have taken I understand that is the correct terminology for myself. Actually, I say I am "Mexican." But if I'm at the University [where I work in a Chicano Studies Center], I say I'm "Chicana." I think it depends who I am . . . with because sometimes you get some people that don't understand "Chicana" and you have to explain to them and they think it's derogatory. And there are people like my mom's generation who are like, "Why do you call yourself that? You rebel, you *chola* gang member." . . . Among my husband's family [who live in Mexico, I say] I'm "Mexican" so they understand that I am from a Mexican descent. I don't call myself "Latina." If people will say, "Oh, you're Latina," I'll just say, "Okay."

JMV: Why do you not care for "Latina"?

REYNA: [Latino/a refers to] people from Latin America—probably people from South and Central America . . . and I'm not from there.

Reyna illustrates a couple of interesting points. First, she is more apt to call herself "Chicana" in a social environment wherein people have the same definition of the label—one of political resistance rather than low-class or gang-member status. Second, she finds "Latina" ill-fitting because she is not from a Latin American country (conceived of as Central and South American). Other respondents disagree with her precise geography-based use of the word "Latino/a" and see it as a term ready-made for political alliances among people from Latin American countries, broadly conceived.

Mary Waters (1990) found that people often give priority to their surname when making racial-identification decisions. People also frequently reduce their racial or ethnic background to the largest segment, producing "selective forgetting and simplification" (Waters 1990: 25). However, Waters did not consider the pivotal role of geography in people's identification choices. According to my respondents, proximity to the country of heritage and the demographics of one's surrounding area affect identification. California's proximity to Mexico and the immigration streams flowing northward make "Mexican" or "Mexican American" an easily understood label.

Dillon Castillo is half-Mexican, one-quarter Puerto Rican, and one-quarter Nicaraguan, but refers to himself as "Mexican American" because it is a simple answer and "easier" than explaining where Puerto Rico and Nicaragua are located. While this ethnic title eclipses some of Dillon's other heritages, he is comfortable with it because it is honest and a label that people in California are likely to grasp. Dillon outlined his logic:

I mostly just say I'm "Mexican" because the people I talk to, they wouldn't understand if I said "Latino" and I'd have to explain Nicaragua and Puerto Rico and Mexican. So usually I just say "Mexican American." I don't like using "Hispanic" because my mom says it's a white guy's name for the Latinos. Usually I just say I'm "Mexican American" so it's easy for people. I like one-word answers. I say, "Mexican American" and they'll be like, "Okay, fine." If I say "Latino," then I have to go "Nicaragua"—most people don't know where that is—then "Puerto Rico," then "Mexican."

While Dillon simplifies his racial title, he acknowledges that "Mexican" or "Mexican American" does not entirely capture his background.

Racial categorizations further the myths of race as rooted in biology and of "racial purity." Racial classification systems force multiracial individuals to self-classify into rigid systems that, furthermore, allow for rank ordering of races. Davina Segura resists being defined by "a box":

> You don't want to be confined by a box. . . . Because I am Mexican, Puerto Rican, American . . . sometimes I have to check the "other" box [or] put them both. . . . When it says "please circle only one," I hate that because people aren't one box.

Third-generation Mexican American respondents exercise discretion as they make racial identification choices. To some extent there is some "flexibility" to the racial claims they can make; yet I argue that these are limited options within a situation of constraint.

"Flexible Ethnicity" and Living in Two Worlds: The Privilege and Predicament of Being "White-xican"

Gloria Anzaldúa (1987) theorizes "*mestiza* consciousness," that is, the consciousness and social location of racially mixed people (especially Native American Indian and European ancestries). Anzaldúa (1987: 79) refers to *mestiza* women as she writes,

> The new *mestiza* copes by developing a tolerance for contradictions, a tolerance for ambiguity. She learns to be an Indian in Mexican culture, to be Mexican from an Anglo point of view. She learns to juggle cultures. She has a plural personality, she operates in a pluralistic mode. . . . Not only does she sustain contradictions, she turns the ambivalence into something else.

According to Anzaldúa, mixed-race people "juggle cultures" and have "plural personalities." This nimble and pluralistic identity holds true for my third-generation Mexican American respondents.

Third-generation Mexican Americans live "between" Mexican and American social worlds; yet, they also live "in" one or both social spheres. This "in between-ness" is due in part to later-generation Mexican Americans' life experiences and the way others perceive and treat them, as well as their physical appearance. Racial liminality is a complicated position: it requires people to do work constructing their identities. For some this leads to crises, while for others it leads to opportunities. These processes are dynamic, are based on social context, and are reshaped over the lifespan.

Some third-generation Mexican Americans display a "flexible ethnicity." "Flexible ethnicity" is the ability to navigate two different social worlds— mainstream U.S. culture and a Mexican-oriented community. Extending the concept of "situational ethnicity," which holds that context matters in the way a person amplifies or downplays his or her ethnicity (Okamura 1981; Root 1996), I maintain that situational constraints limit the reception of one's potential responses. "Flexible ethnicity" differs from "situational ethnicity" in acknowledging that while people may background or foreground certain identity features in different contexts, there is not a 100 percent correspondence between the way people *want* to be perceived and the way they *are* perceived. "Flexible ethnicity" recognizes that although actors may assert racial/ethnic identities, intended audience may not accept these claims. While flexible ethnicity may be purely "symbolic" (Gans 1979) for some, the terrain of flexible ethnicity is larger in that some people do substantively and meaningfully engage in their Mexican culture. Due to U.S. citizenship, "cultural toolkits" (Swidler 1986), and skill sets that mark the third generation as undeniably American, the majority of this generation is able to play out flexibly their racial background, amplifying or downplaying their heritage. Yet, the volitional aspect of "flexible ethnicity" is limited by the way others perceive, treat, and racially mark third-generation individuals. Julie Bettie's work (2003) with Mexican American and white high school girls in California underscores that phenotype and surname restrict one's agency and "ethnic options." Bettie argues that "one's race performance was *expected* to correspond to a perceived racial 'essence,' marked by color and surname" (Bettie 2003: 85).

Several third-generation Mexican Americans commented on being "in between" Mexican and American social worlds. As Reyna Madrigal commented, "I have no identity. I'm in between. I don't fit here and I don't fit in either culture. So I'm looking for something." While some understood being "in between" as an advantage, for others it precipitated an "identity crisis."

Samantha Diaz exists in a liminal racial space, neither "Mexican Mexican" nor "American":

I see myself as Mexican, but a little more whitewashed. I'm part of the generation that is a little lost. Some people consider me not Mexican enough but I'm not American enough. So I'm really stuck in the middle. I don't categorize myself as Mexican Mexican or American. I'm in the middle.

Samantha considers how she can morph into different social contexts because of her flexible ethnicity and her biculturalism:

> When I'm around my Mexican friends, I'm Mexican. When I'm around people at work [Anglo-dominant law office], I'm less Mexican. Honestly, I slip into it when it's convenient. When I have to fit whoever I am around my personality changes.

While Samantha can "fit" a number of different social situations, the voluntary nature of personality or cultural shifts should not be overstated. Her ethnic scripts are limited due to a number of elements, including phenotype and cultural repertoires, two "bumps" in the path of assimilation that steer her course.

Renata Contreras, easily perceived as non-Hispanic white because of her blonde hair and pale skin passed on from her fair Caucasian mother, also makes calculated decisions about her racial claims depending on her social context:

> If it's like the Junior League or something like that I . . . probably would put "white" and ignore the Hispanic part. Because I just feel like the people there would judge me: "Oh, a Hispanic, how nice, what diversity" [sticky sweet and sing-song voice]. In high school I played tennis a lot and we'd go to the tennis club in Montecito [high-class neighborhood], I wouldn't highlight the Mexican part. Just because . . . I should be proud of it, but then again, you know how people judge and . . . I don't need that kind of judgment. I don't accentuate it if it's not necessary. In those situations, I'd probably just put "white." Then "white-slash-Mexican American" probably for job applications or [if] I feel like people really would have an open mind or encourage diversity, like a job application or a random survey. Just so I'm sure that they get a diverse perspective. I'm not just another Caucasian person.

Because of her light, European-looking physical characteristics, Renata is able to "pass" as non-Hispanic white. There are certainly limits to how much Renata can control the way others perceive her. Yet, when considering what racial background to write on forms or aspects of her background to highlight or downplay, Renata weighs the positive and negative consequences of claiming one or both parts of her half-white and half–Mexican American background.

Caitlyn Benavidas also discusses what it feels like to live between cultures:

> Definitely as a Chicana I don't feel like I'm part of mainstream culture. . . .
> Yeah, I'm born here and my family is from here but I don't identify myself
> as an American above anything else. A lot of it is I'm Chicana, my fam-
> ily is native to this land. We don't necessarily abide to the same kind of
> identity . . . we don't grasp being American as white Americans do or even
> immigrant groups do. . . . I feel educationally and language-wise I very
> much fit into mainstream culture and I'm very much a part of mainstream
> culture but . . . I don't identify myself with white America.

Caitlyn begins by saying that as a Chicana she is not part of mainstream culture. Then she goes on to delineate how she is a part of mainstream culture
in terms of education and language and yet she still stands apart. In essence,
Caitlyn is "in" mainstream culture yet she is not "of" mainstream culture. It is
unclear whether it is due to external racialization or an internal cultural maintenance sentiment that Caitlyn feels that "as a Chicana" she is set apart from
mainstream culture. She reflects on her struggle to delineate her identity:

> In high school I was . . . identifying with being Latina outside of school
> but still had a lot of white friends. . . . [I was] not really like them because I
> wasn't white. That was a struggle just . . . being different and not really fit-
> ting into one group completely. . . . It was a headache. You cry about stuff
> like, "Who am I and who am I supposed to be and what am I going to do
> with myself?"

Despite this identity struggle, Caitlyn sees benefits to navigating two social
worlds:

> I definitely think [my racial background] gave me insight to a lot of dif-
> ferent kind of groups of people. . . . I feel like it's definitely been positive
> because I kind of understand people and the way they think. . . . I know
> where they get their train of thought. I think it's cool to be able to jump
> from culture to culture.

Humans are social beings who crave cultural belonging. Caitlyn was unsettled by not knowing where she fit and yet she found some positive elements
in being in a diverse environment where she was at times seen as white and
at other times seen as Latina.

Carmina and Auscencio Dos Santos, both third generation and children of Chicano activist parents, found flexible ethnicity an advantage as well as a source of identity struggles. Carmina, who has light hair and skin and green eyes, tells me about the privilege of "passing" for non-Hispanic white:

> I guess it's an advantage. I have the privilege of blend[ing] in. . . . I think there are certain privileges to looking not stereotypically Mexican. Things I take for granted like not being followed in a store, not being labeled as somebody who doesn't have money, you know, all those sort of labels that I think people give to you. So in that sense, I think there are benefits.
>
> The other thing is that . . . because I am so light I see things and I hear things that other people say just assuming that I'm on their side. I've also had, "You're not that kind of Mexican. You're not like the rest of them." So, yeah, it gives you so many windows to look into.

Carmina does not experience the "shopowner tailgate" discussed in chapter 5 or the presumption that she is lower class because she does not look "stereotypically Mexican." She is accorded white privilege due to her pale features, yet this white "insider" status is a double-edged sword as it lets her in on conversations people have when they assume they are in all-white company.

Carmina Dos Santos's older brother, Auscencio, tells a similar story about living in a "third space" where he is both Mexican *and* American. Auscencio reflects on what it means to be Chicano and "in between":

> It's really weird: what does it mean to be Chicano? I mean, the basic principles are there: you're born here . . . you're first or second generation. You were raised with both—my dad would say, "I'm as much hamburger as I am taco." Hamburgers and hot dogs; tacos and burritos. You have both of those. It's being too white for Mexicanos and too Mexicano for the white people. So you're somewhere in between. You have your own dialect, your own foods.

Being "as much hamburger as taco," Auscencio figures himself in the middle of a cultural borderland. He is enacting a cultural maintenance lifestyle in that Mexican culture is instrumental and meaningful to him in his everyday life. Nonetheless, like all third-generation Mexican Americans I interviewed, he is also very much American by both birthright and way of life. Auscencio, who goes by Ceño among friends and family, reviews his bicultural, borderland status:

I think it's clear that I'm probably more Americanized than I think I would like to admit. I've got my Internet, got my . . . . Just my whole lifestyle is pretty American. But I do feel, at times . . . when I read history books or I see the horrible things that this country has done, I'm like, "Oh, man, I'm so glad I'm not 100 percent American." I don't feel I fit in anywhere. I'm like right in between—and it's okay. Especially here in California. We have our own type of world here. I think my attitude would be very different in somewhere like Nebraska. Or Montana. Your environment dictates who you are, and almost how you act. That's definitely how it is with me. So I guess it almost depends where I am too, because when I was living in El Paso, Texas, . . . I felt much more Mexicano there than I did American. Because I was "Ceño" and my friends were Julio and Oscar. I would go to the store and the woman would swipe my card and say, "Thank you, Mr. Dos Santos" [correct Spanish pronunciation]. I'd be like, "Yeah!" . . . There is something to be said for being completely accepted and understood. I have a really big spot in my heart for El Paso.

This rich passage touches on a number of important themes. First, Auscencio envisions his attachment to Mexico as a way to distance himself from the imperialist history of the United States. Second, he notes the importance of California as his social context: he is among many others who share his in-between status. Third, he describes the "situational ethnicity" (Okamura 1981) he felt when he was residing in a border town in Texas with a large Mexican population and his Mexican identity was endorsed and even reinforced.

Jillian and Andrew Rosenberg, met in chapter 2, also experienced "flexible ethnicity" and identity struggles due to their biculturalism and physical features that are not automatically read as of Mexican origin. Jillian has experienced two extremes of her Mexican identity. It was "dirty" and something to actively estrange herself from when she was younger: "I had really awful stereotypes of what Mexican people were like too, like all Mexican people are gardeners and maids. . . . It was always . . . the half of me that I had to hide. I was always so embarrassed of that; I was soiled in some way because I had Mexican blood in me." Now, in college on the East Coast, she is exoticized by her peers, who are enthusiastically looking for some "uniqueness" to mark them as "not just white." Jillian considers the "identity crisis" that her "flexible ethnicity" produced upon her move to Yale University and her changed social contexts:

It's actually really funny now because going to Yale, it's a total reversal. I'm having a completely new identity crisis. Because suddenly it's cool to be

Mexican, it's exotic, and "I'm of a different race, I'm not just a white kid" [her voice gets breathless and sexualized]. It's a really diverse campus and people definitely put a lot of emphasis on diversity. It's just so funny. Now all the white kids are like, "Oh my god, I wish I were half of something like you are, at least, to make me exotic." I'm like, I never thought of being Mexican as exotic. I always thought it was gross and dirty and lame and not exotic. "Oh, your eyes are so Mexican, they are so exotic and pretty." I'm just like, "What is this? What is happening there?" It's just really interesting seeing that. All of growing up I was trying hard to be white and I was too Mexican and it was bad and now it's like the other Mexican kids there think I'm not Mexican enough because I'm half-white.

Social context significantly bears on one's racialized experience. In her youth in Santa Barbara, California, Jillian was ashamed of her Mexican heritage because she felt it carried negative, lower-class connotations. She then moved to Yale, where she was racially exoticized; this exoticization, which had a sexual aspect to it, became just another way to "other" her and consider her different. While being referred to as an exotic beauty is ostensibly a compliment, these references create social distance that instantiates social divisions and builds dichotomous boundaries of you-me, self-other, normal-abnormal, normal-other.

Andrew Rosenberg also felt pulled between his two racial backgrounds: "I guess just my overall experience with growing up with two completely different backgrounds . . . it's kind of weird. . . . I guess I have always felt pulled between the two. So that was always kind of hard." Jillian's and Andrew's high school had racially segregated classes, as discussed in chapter 6. In addition to their bicultural background, one reason why Jillian and Andrew navigate white settings seamlessly is that they were placed in Advanced Placement classes with white students. Andrew experienced segregated classes: "That's just what I see in the school system: 'Oh, he's Mexican—put him in that class.' . . . It's really bad. . . . They are actually having problems with the high school. People are saying all the Mexicans are just getting put in the lower classes." As half-white and half-Mexican, Andrew struggled in school with his identity and the way he fit into a racially stratified white-and-brown environment:

I guess just my experience in school has been . . . kind of . . . hard. . . . I have been put mostly in GATE classes. . . . It was always "the white kids" and then "the Mexicans." And I was like—what am *I* supposed to do? You know? So it's . . . awkward. Because my skin is white. Especially in high school, you know? I hear so many people being like, "Oh, yeah, look at the beaner car." Or, "Oh, the stupid beaners." And I'm like—hey! I just don't really know what to do a lot. . . . I'm starting to see and hear stuff that I didn't think people really would say. . . . So for me, just growing up with two different backgrounds just has been awkward.

While Andrew is already perceived and treated as non-Hispanic white due to his skin tone, last name, and class status, he resists totally "passing" when his Mexican heritage is threatened. In contrast to "symbolic ethnicity" (Gans 1979), in which the stakes to claiming an ethnicity are minimal, Andrew enacts a sort of "sentimental ethnicity" as he defends his marginalized background when it is defamed. In fact, he proactively claims his Mexican background as a way to ward off demeaning aspersions that may be cast against his racial group:

I have always tried to let people know that I was Mexican. I don't really know why I've always done that. I guess maybe it was partly I was afraid they would start making fun of Mexicans and I didn't want to be in that situation. So a lot of times I joke around and be like, "Oh, whatever just because I'm Mexican?" And make jokes like that. . . . It's just . . . scary because you don't really know where you fit in.

Andrew problematizes "passing" and makes racializing conversations difficult for others. Andrew regrets not having many Mexican friends:

I have always regretted that I haven't had as many Mexican friends. I have hung out mostly with white people. And I think it's partly because of the classes that I got put into. It's just kind of . . . disappointing. I guess it's like I don't feel like completely Mexican, you know? I feel just kind of stuck in the middle. . . .

Playing soccer, a sport that draws a lot of participation from Mexicans, was a way for him to meet more Mexican students and "stay in touch with his Mexican side."

While flexible ethnicity carries with it emotional challenges of belonging to two cultures, it can be a source of delight as respondents are "insiders" in multiple communities. This dual insider existence renders both costs (social discomfort, identity crises, witnessing racism, vulnerability to stereotypes, issues of allegiance) and benefits (fitting into two or more cultures and communities, cultural translation, increased empathy, ethnic representation, ethnic cultural capital). This complex identity, flexible ethnicity, is a hallmark of many third-generation Mexican Americans' lives.

Racialization: Forced and Enforced Racial Identity

"All ethnicities are not equal, all are not symbolic, costless, and voluntary" (Waters 1990: 160). Herbert Gans (1979) put forth the notion of "symbolic ethnicity," the proposition that as acculturation takes place, the new manner of ethnic involvement will revolve around the use of ethnic symbols. This "ethnicity of last resort" will be more "expressive" than "instrumental" in its function in people's lives, more of a leisure activity or "nostalgic allegiance" than a regulatory mechanism (Gans 1979: 9). Gans predicted that symbolic ethnicity would be the dominant form of ethnicity for the third and later generations once they have become upwardly mobile, yet he was theorizing the experience of white European ethnic groups and conceded that his theory might be limited when applied to other racial groups due to dissimilar experiences with racism (Gans 1996: 453, 457).

Mary Waters (1990) also found that white ethnics in America attach symbolically to their ethnic background. White ethnics experience an ethnicity that is voluntary and essentially meaningless in the way it structures their lives, except for ways in which they choose to engage it (language, marital choice, family traditions, passing knowledge onto children). Later-generation white ethnics experience their ethnicity as an "ethnic option" rather than an ascribed characteristic. In contrast to people of European ancestry, racial and ethnic minorities often experience their racial and ethnic identity as not voluntary but imposed (Ochoa 2004).

The "symbolic ethnicity" or "ethnic option" that white ethnics enjoy—they may practice elements of their ethnicity with no detrimental effects—is evidence of white privilege. The experience of racial minorities in the United States is quite different. Various social and political components prohibit racial minorities' ability to experience their ethnic background as individual and voluntary. It is this critical difference between instrumental ethnicity and symbolic ethnicity to which we now turn.

Ongoing immigration from Mexico creates a particular social context for later-generation Mexican Americans in California to negotiate. In a majority minority state like California, intra-ethnic relations are also very influential. At times Mexican Americans sympathize and bond with Mexican immigrants, and at other times they distinguish and separate themselves from the newcomers (Gutiérrez 1995; Jiménez 2010; Ochoa 2004). A reason for the sense of connectedness is a similarity of place of origin and immigration and acculturation experiences. A motivation for maintaining social distance from the new arrivals is the threat that stereotypes against immigrants will adversely affect Mexican Americans born in the United States. Thomas Macias (2006: 8) writes, "ongoing immigration tends to create a heightened, if distorted, awareness of ethnicity among the population in general, such that prejudice and stereotypes against groups experiencing ongoing immigration are maintained over time." This collective awareness of Mexican immigration, coupled with the inability of mainstream society to notice differences between immigrants and natives, complicates the situation of Mexican Americans. In many respects, as Mexican immigrants are racialized, so too are Mexican Americans.

Discrimination is a primary way racialization—the enforcement of a nonwhite racial identity that is devalued and oppressed—is enacted. Perhaps it is easiest to see the process of racialization at work in situations when a Mexican American initially "passes" as non-Hispanic white and is later "outed" as Mexican American. The change in the way people are defined racially often leads to a corresponding change in treatment—loss of jobs, withholding of support or friendships, and withdrawing of resources. For example, recall from chapter 6 the experience of Veronica Guzman, whose blonde, light-skinned sister was treated preferentially by the high school vice principal until she was "discovered" to be Mexican American.

Caitlyn Benavidas similarly experienced racialization when she was "found out" to be Mexican American. While she feels she looks Mexican, Caitlyn often "passes" as non-Hispanic white or Persian. She becomes vulnerable to racialization at the moment when others reinterpret their misreading of her racial identity:

> I've had some . . . really uncomfortable situations with people thinking that I was not Mexican. . . . I was hired as a waitress by a Jordanian family and they hired me thinking I was Greek or Persian. I started speaking Spanish to the busboys once and they were like, "Why the hell are you speaking Spanish? You can't be Mexican." And basically went off on me about how they probably wouldn't have hired me if they had known I was [Mexican] and that my mom was too beautiful to be Mexican. . . . As flattering as it [is] to be able to float to different groups and for people to think that you might be something else, I start getting offended by it because that's actually who I am.

The process of racialization occurs here as Caitlyn's Jordanian boss made race-based assumptions about her character, competence, and desirability in the workplace. While some people might want to pass in order to accrue the benefits associated with whiteness, Caityln wishes she were darker so that she could avoid treatment based on a racial misperception:

> Sometimes I wished I looked maybe a bit more stereotypically Mexican because I don't like that people might treat me differently because they think I'm not. . . . I think a lot of people would rather be fairer skinned because of racism but I wished I was a little bit browner because people think I'm white.

Granted, Caitlyn says this having lived with a flexible ethnicity but, even so, she has clearly been subjected to racialization. Caitlyn dislikes being racially misunderstood because she is proud of her heritage and because she associates darker-skinned people with beauty. Wanting to be darker is a strategic move to avoid uncomfortable situations when people make racist remarks in her presence, taking for granted that she is "one of them."

Jillian Rosenberg also experiences a "magnified moment" of racialization as she reveals her Mexican heritage. In a situation with significant long-term ramifications, a college career counselor told Jillian Rosenberg that the program she was interested in was for minorities only. When she told him that indeed she is Mexican American, he retorted that she would have to "prove" that she is a "real Mexican" on the application. Jillian recounts the conversation:

> Another experience I had in college was that I went to speak with a pre-med advisor about my plans and mapping out my courses. He's known for being a really big jerk. People hate him because he tells it like it is and flat up tells you, "You're not going to get into med school," stuff like that. I asked the counselor about a minority program I heard about. "Oh, that's just for minorities."
>
> I said, "Oh, actually I am Mexican."
>
> "Oh, well, if you want to take advantage of that, on applications you are really going to have to prove that, I don't want to sound un-PC [politically correct] here or anything, but you are really going to have to prove that you are a real Mexican."
>
> I was like, "Excuse me?"
>
> "Well, I mean, are you part of any cultural organizations here?"

"No, I don't really agree with a lot of their purposes so I chose not to join them."

"Well, have you gone to cultural events or organized Latino heritage month?"

"No, like I said, I don't really agree with their purposes."

"Well, do you speak Spanish fluently?"

"Actually, it was my first language, but I lost it. I can understand it pretty well, but I don't really speak very well."

"Well, are you taking any Spanish classes at least?"

"No, it doesn't fit into my schedule."

"Well, you are really going to have do something here to prove that you are a real Mexican."

"I'm sorry, but organizing a cultural dinner does not prove that I am a real Mexican."

That's just who I am. It's just been difficult. Because it is who I am and I'm not going to be able to change that no matter what. I can't make myself more or less Mexican, but at the same time, there is this constant push and pull. . . . I feel like I have to prove it to people. How do I do that? Do I really need to do that? . . . Even though I've come to terms with it within myself, now it's like I have to bring everyone else to terms with it.

The college counselor's effort to racialize Jillian is notable: he challenges her authenticity while simultaneously commanding her to fit into a preconceived and static notion of Mexican American identity.

Racialization can involve assuming on the basis of racial stereotypes that someone has cultural knowledge. Respondents were often expected to have superior knowledge of Spanish due to their Mexican heritage. In their Spanish classes, both Amalia Ruiz and Gabriel Ponce were presumed to be conversant in the language:

AMALIA: I'm not [fluent in Spanish]. In high school . . . I got really pissed off because a teacher asked me a question in second-year Spanish. I just barely passed first-year Spanish. And I didn't know the answer. In front of the whole class he said, "You know, just because you speak Spanish at home doesn't mean that you don't have to study for this class." What?! I felt so angry and humiliated. First of all, I didn't know Spanish so I don't speak it at home! He assumed that I did. And he scolded me in front of the whole class. I legitimately didn't know the answer. And he thought . . . I was just . . . lazy. He thought I was just going to be a lazy Mexican, basically.

GABE: My Spanish teachers in high school were really hard on me because they knew my name was Spanish. I struggled a lot with that 'cause I was always the first guy called on.

Here teachers racialize students as they expect both negative stereotypes and linguistic abilities to be inherent within racial group members.

Another concept that emerged in respondents' narratives is what I call "complimentary othering," yet another form of racialization or racial alienation. Complimentary othering occurs when people consider certain Mexican Americans as "exceptions to the rule," the "rules" in question being racist assumptions of underachievement, intelligence, success, beauty, and so on. In this way, the speaker simultaneously downgrades a group of people on the basis of negative stereotypes while extolling the virtues of a single individual. This backhanded compliment does not consider the *variance* within any group of people. The implicit suggestion of complimentary othering is that the person being complimented does not serve as a positive example of the capabilities of the group but rather needs to be distinguished from the group in order to explain his or her "exceptionalism." "Othering" occurs here despite the individual-level compliment in that the complimented individual is ultimately demeaned on the group level.

Jillian Rosenberg, the Yale undergraduate, provides an example of how "complimentary othering" works:

I do think that people, when they find out that I'm Mexican, [think] that I'm an exception to the rule. I want to try really hard to be a good example and show people that Mexicans aren't just gardeners. I definitely feel like I get written off as, "Oh well, she's not like most Mexicans." . . . I feel like I get written off as an exception. Even if I do do something really great, it's like, "Oh, okay, well, she's not like the rest. Most Mexicans wouldn't be able to do something like that."

If perceived as a racial minority, one is in jeopardy of being saddled with negative stereotypes. Jillian, like many other college-going or college-educated third-generation Mexican Americans, is seen as an "exception to the rule" when she performs well. Complimentary othering is in part based on "ethnic lumping" (Ochoa 2004) wherein nonmembers of the ethnic group fail to differentiate between often economically disadvantaged newcomer Mexican immigrants and Mexican Americans who were born and raised in the United States. In the minds of many, "Mexican-origin" equates to "Mexican immigrant." This conflation obscures the acculturation, upward mobility, and structural integration of later-generation Mexican Americans. Like the model minority stereotype that singles out the successful and discounts racism (Chou and Feagin 2008; O'Brien 2008: 125), complimentary othering is a racist maneuver that lifts only an individual as it castigates the group. Complimentary othering is probably applicable to other subordinated social groups as well.

"Racial/ethnic lumping" often occurs in the wake of political movements (for example, California ballot initiatives such as Propositions 187,[1] 209, 227, and 54), when the effects of a racialized political environment are expanded from one racial/ethnic group to another (such as from Mexican immigrants to Mexican Americans, regardless of generation in the United States, or Latinos more generally) (Ochoa 2004: 143). Perhaps as a response to "racial/ethnic lumping," "linked fate" suggests that, for racial minority group members, "group interests [serve] as a useful proxy for self-interest" (Dawson 1994: 77). Especially with regard to political action and voting, "linked fate" explicitly links perceptions of self-interest to perceptions of racial group interests.

Racialization, complimentary othering, and ethnic lumping are all experiences of racialization despite assimilation. All third-generation interviewees were college graduates, in college, or in high school and on a college-bound track, showing their structural integration into a U.S. institution crucial for upward mobility. Even given this success, we see mainstream society erecting roadblocks to education, employment, and personal gain—from racist bosses and educators to prejudiced interpersonal interactions. Intergenerational advancement is not sufficient to entirely escape racialization, as contrary to the hopeful tenets of the American Dream as that reality is.

Battle for Authenticity: Identity Struggles in Contested Terrain

Intragroup tension occurs as Mexican Americans (and Mexican immigrants) vie for "authentic" status, a process one respondent referred to as the "super-Chicano" phenomenon. As Julie Bettie (2003: 48) found in her work on Mexican American and white youth, "class and racial/ethnic signifiers are melded together in such a way that 'authentic' black, and sometimes brown, identity is imagined as lower-class, urban, and often violent—and male as well." Central elements of Mexican-origin in-group struggles over authenticity include Spanish language fluency, cultural competency, skin color, class status, clothing, and behavior. These same traits that Mexican immigrants use to critique Mexican Americans for having "lost their culture" (Gutiérrez 1995) are markers that the majority population can use to single people out for racialization and subjugation. These yardsticks for authenticity constitute "bumps" in the assimilation process that can facilitate, pause, disrupt, or divert progression into mainstream society. Many features that are used for marking and judging as "us" or "them" operate beyond individual will and agency. "Us" can be both Mexican community members and dominant society members, showing that Mexican Americans are appraised by two different contingents. So, despite individual efforts at retaining Mexican cultural elements and/or becoming American, judgment occurs from dual constituencies that accept or reject the plea for membership.

Cultural Toolkit: Spanish Language Fluency

Spanish language competency is a litmus test of one's degree of association with Mexico (Ochoa 2004). Language is a marker of national boundaries, a type of "cognitive insulation" that nations build in order to cement their identities and demarcate their borders (Cerulo 1995). Fluency in legitimate, national language is a mark of social distinction, a form of capital (Bourdieu 1991: 55). Some Mexican immigrants fluent in Spanish—and not necessarily proficient in English—feel superiority over people of Mexican origin who speak English only. For Mexican Americans who do speak fluent Spanish, linguistic proficiency can be an asset in authenticity contests. Renata Contreras, a light-skinned third-generation woman with blonde hair, explains how her Spanish ability allows her to openly contradict other Mexicans' assumption that she is a *gringa,* or white girl. Renata describes this intra-ethnic prejudice and her reaction:

> From Mexican girls at school: *"Oh, mira, gringa!"* ["Oh, look, white girl!"] That gets me so mad. I would think, "I can speak better Spanish than you!" Maybe [not better than] someone straight from Mexico but a Mexican American. "Oh, *gringa.*" Just not very nice attitudes. . . . They don't even know. It would make me laugh and then it would make me mad. "Where do you get off?! I probably have more tie to the culture than you do. Just because I look a certain way or hang out with a certain group of people, you can't just assume."

As with all respondents who felt they had been unfairly judged by their appearance and were expected to fit a corresponding ethnic profile, Renata invokes the old axiom of "not judging a book by its cover." While Renata in a sense won this battle over authenticity, many other people lose this contest and must justify to themselves, if not others, that there is not one single way to be Mexican American.

This struggle was particularly difficult for third-generation Mexican Americans who lacked Spanish language fluency. Even while arguing that limited Spanish skills did not diminish their claims to heritage, these Mexican Americans still felt embarrassed and wounded by attacks from more recent immigrants who asserted that they were not Mexican because they could not speak the language. Samantha Diaz ruminates on Spanish as a barometer for Mexican "authenticity":

> After high school, when I was twenty-one, I went in to the high school and was a color guard instructor. Most of them were Mexican and fluently speaking Spanish. I thought I could connect with these girls and have something in common. And then, I'll never forget because two girls dropped out and I heard the reason they dropped out was because I wasn't Mexican enough. Uh-huh. I wasn't Mexican enough. I didn't speak Spanish and I was basically a different culture than them. It sticks in my mind [to] this day. *How can I not be Mexican enough?* But, it's probably my life story. I don't feel Mexican enough. But I'm not white. I'm just in the middle.

Samantha, like many others, exists in between two worlds and is not fully accepted in either: she is "not Mexican enough" but she is also "not white." While each person navigates his or her social context differently, pervasive battles over authenticity that Mexican-descent people must negotiate remain a reality.

Personal Traits: Phenotype and Name

While my dark-skinned respondents vociferously complained of the obstacles that their appearance presented, some of my light-skinned respondents noted that they had to fight for "authenticity" and acceptance. While being immediately recognized as Mexican has its hardships, so does being dismissed as not being Mexican. Dillon Castillo, a light-skinned, third-generation seventeen-year-old, tells me that he "feels stronger than he looks." He wishes he had a darker complexion so that his heritage would be questioned less often. Dillon's strategy in authenticity fights is to display cultural symbols and accessories that signal what his pale skin does not. Dillon answers my question on how he describes himself racially or ethnically:

I feel stronger than I look. I'm not very dark. So, most people wouldn't assume that I'm Latino. So it's difficult—when I say I am [Latino] to people [they say], "Oh yeah?" They look at me funny. But I have a lot of stuff. My car is kinda low-rider, I had a *zarape* [Mexican blanket] over my seat, I have *la Virgen de Guadalupe* [the Virgin of Guadalupe] on my window. I used to have a little Mexican flag in my room. I'm proud of it. But I don't really look like it, I guess. But I'm very proud.

Since skin color is often (mis)understood to equate with cultural allegiance, Dillon elects to do "cultural work" by displaying cultural symbols that he hopes will make up for his light skin color. If he lacks dark skin, he can at least have *"la Virgen"* in his window. Throughout the skin color spectrum, physical looks have zero correlation with one's sense of culture, identity, or allegiance to Mexico or the United States.

Carmina Dos Santos, a light-skinned woman with light brown hair and green eyes, illustrates how her unintended passing for European-descent white can work against her. People discount her attachment to her heritage because they cannot visually perceive her Mexican background.[2] In her words, "there are times when people just assume that I'm a sellout because of the color of my skin. . . . So in that sense I think it's a total disadvantage because I often have to prove myself to the community that I belong to." In contradistinction to Adele and Ruben Mendoza in chapter 5, who were denied housing on the basis of their Spanish surname, Carmina utilizes her Spanish surname in order to authenticate her race:

My freshman year in college . . . I went to a [Latino/a club] meeting in campus and was completely ignored. They just didn't say hello to me. . . . They were saying hello to everybody else and . . . I pretty much sort of snuck away. I was like, forget this, they're not paying attention to me. But the next quarter my dad was invited to come give a poetry reading and I sat in the front row and my dad introduced me and they said, "Well, how come you don't come to our meetings?" And I just looked at them and I said, "I did." I think [if] they don't know my name or they're not familiar with my parents I think I'm just ignored. . . . I think part of me has learned to not care. When it's to my advantage then I tend to bring my parents' names up. Not so much to use as a crutch but definitely if it works to my advantage.

Carmina's "Dos Santos" surname is often recognized as belonging to a family of Chicano activists and artists, which gains her status and authenticity cachet. Carmina had mixed feelings about pulling out the last-name card, but it is one way she can combat being misrecognized as non-Latina.

As a consequence of being a light-skinned, green-eyed Mexican American, Carmina would often respond to what she called "micro-aggressions" by retorting about the physical diversity of Mexican Americans. She described "micro-aggressions" as small-scale insults, often with regard to race or gender, that have an injurious and cumulative effect. She provides an example of a brief conversation she had with an anonymous man in an elevator:

> "You must be Italian."
> "No." I went through the whole thing and then I said, "Mexican."
> He said, "You don't look Mexican."
> And I said, "Really, what do we look like?"

She viewed this exchange as a micro-aggression for two reasons: first, she was incorrectly perceived, and second, her interlocutor had a narrow assumption of what Mexicans look like that rendered her invisible. Carmina makes herself visible by underscoring the physical diversity of Mexicans, broadening the physical definition of Mexican so that it can encompass her. Carmina concludes, "I work hard to hang on to the Mexican part because I think it would be so easy for me to pass." Renata Contreras, who is similarly light skinned and has blonde hair, finds that she could easily "ignore the Contreras" side of herself and "pass" as non-Hispanic white. Yet, she enjoys her ethnicity: "I don't want to be the same as everybody else, it's nice to have a little difference and spice."

Generation in the United States

Generation in the United States is another yardstick by which racial authenticity gets measured. In her study of the relationship between Mexican Americans and Mexican immigrants in southern California, Gilda Ochoa (2004) argues that these relationships fall along a "continuum of conflict and solidarity." My Mexican American respondents reported cultural struggles between themselves and Mexican immigrants. Clearly there are limits to the "flexibility" of ethnicity. Mexican immigrants often claim a superior status because they are more recent arrivals and they are more in tune with Mexican culture than Mexican Americans—who are sometimes derogatorily referred to as "whitewashed" or "*pochos*."

Although Jillian Rosenberg considers herself both Mexican and American, not everyone willingly grants her entrance into Mexican circles. These racial gatekeepers, often first-generation Mexican immigrant youth, use generation as a measure of a person's "authenticity":

> The other Mexican kids [at Yale] think I'm not Mexican enough because I'm half-white. I've had terrible, terrible interactions with other Mexican students where they find that I'm half-white and they just turn around and walk away. It was unbelievable.

One does not need to be half-Anglo to be treated as a Mexican outcast or imposter. Marisol Fuentes, both of whose parents are second-generation Mexican Americans, is subject to similar scrutiny by Mexican immigrant youth. Marisol, born and reared in San Diego, attended largely Latino schools and seldom experienced racial discrimination from whites. Yet Mexican nationals who crossed the border from Tijuana judged her as insufficiently Mexican and put her in a defensive position. Reflecting on her experience of racial strife in school, Marisol stressed the importance of recognizing the variation within the Latino community. She describes the difference between the Mexican nationals who come from Tijuana, Mexico, and third-generation Mexican Americans such as herself:

> In community college we had a lot of people come from across the border to come to school. It wasn't until then that I realized the difference between Mexicans on the U.S. side of the border and the Mexicans on the other side of the border. It was just very different. And it was then when people started telling me, "You're not really Mexican. You don't speak Spanish as well as we do and you don't dress the way we do and you don't talk the way we do and you don't go to the same places and you've never been to Tijuana. . . . We live there, we know what Mexico is like."

This highly personal critique has affected Marisol's identification choices:

> It was just very recently that I decided that I'm Mexican American. . . . In high school . . . I would say, "I'm Mexican." It wasn't until community college that I was confronted with those things like, "You're not Mexican." So I didn't know what to call myself. I'm like, "I'm Mexican," and they're like, "No, no you're not."

The social context of San Diego, a border city that is a hub for both immigration and transmigration, is key to Marisol's identification quandaries.

San Diego is a social context wherein Mexican immigrants and third-generation Mexican Americans exist side by side. This close proximity can yield intra-ethnic conflicts regarding both racial "authenticity" and racial self-titles.

Generational differences (i.e., Mexican nationals as compared to third-generation Mexican Americans) actually subsume and stand in for a number of other differences, such as language and socioeconomic status. As discussed above, language is a significant social divider. Marisol considered the differences that "generation" embraces:

> I think just language. Language is a big thing. Not knowing perfect Spanish the way they [Mexican nationals] do was always a big put back on me. . . . I was more ashamed of speaking Spanish around them because I didn't know it as well as they did. . . . I felt kind of ashamed that I didn't know Spanish—like I was suppose to know it because I was Mexican and in order to be truly Mexican you had to know Spanish.

Not just language but also socioeconomic status is confounded with generation:

> I don't know where they [Mexican nationals] get their money. . . . I don't think their families have money. . . . Other people that I've met do come from the lower [class] of Tijuana, Mexico, and that is why they are coming to school in the United States because they know the education is better.

Marisol sees a parallel between generation in the United States, Spanish language ability, and class status. While her third-generation status has afforded her advantages such as education, English fluency, and middle-class status, it also comes with detractors such as limited Spanish ability that weaken her claim to so-called authentic Mexican identity.

A similarity in generational status can minimize cultural, linguistic, and class arguments. Some respondents felt that fewer authenticity battles occur when they are among other third-generation Mexican Americans. Auscencio Dos Santos commented about the cultural comfort he feels when he is in the company of other Mexican Americans: "There is something to be said for being completely accepted and understood." Similarly, Ricardo Torres feels most comfortable around other third-generation Mexican Americans. Ricardo explicitly highlights generation in the United States as a key indicator of what facilitates a cultural comfort zone:

RICARDO: Ever since I was little I've been mostly around first-generation Mexicans. I was raised with those kids. . . . Those were the guys that I ran with . . . but there was always a distance, I can't lie. I had a lot of third-generation friends and the third-generation Mexicans were always my best friends. Those were the guys I closely identified with; I went to their houses and their parents were like mine. I really value those friends, when I come to look at it.

JMV: In what ways were your friends' parents like your parents? What made that special?

RICARDO: Because they were Mexican and they felt comfortable speaking English and at the same time we'd be eating *frijoles* [beans], tortillas, all that stuff. There's just kind of a camaraderie, I guess, between more assimilated Chicanos, just because there is not as many. It's like a minority within a minority.

Ricardo feels "camaraderie" with other third-generation "more assimilated Chicanos" who speak English and eat beans and tortillas. In short, those third-generation Mexican Americans occupy a similar space on an assimilation and nationality spectrum as he. While there are "battles of authenticity" that occur among groups of Mexican-origin people—around issues like Spanish fluency or generation in the United States—there is a cultural comfort zone shared by similarly situated Mexican Americans. Little cultural translation is necessary within third-generation Mexican American social networks.

Notions of racial "authenticity," struggled over by Mexican-origin people along axes of language fluency, phenotype, and generation, *essentialize* what it means to be Mexican American. Third-generation Mexican Americans overwhelmingly argue that there is a wide variety of ways to "be" Mexican American or "enact" that hybrid identity. Mexican nationals often confront Mexican Americans about the validity of their racial identity, suggesting that there are discrete ways to measure and judge this very subjective concept. In response, third-generation Mexican Americans either puzzle over how to "prove" their Mexican culture or, conversely, eschew the challenge to prove themselves and underscore the diversity of Mexican Americans.

Despite the fact that Mexican American identity can be enacted in many ways, select characteristics are reified as essential components of a racial identity. While these measures of authenticity get attention, no particular set of traits can be enshrined as the racial standard. First, race is a social construction, making boundaries both arbitrary and somewhat permeable. Second, racial intermarriage in the United States (more so for Latinos and Asians with whites than for blacks with whites) (Feliciano 2001; Qian and Cobas 2004) blurs these racial boundaries. This racial blurring continues with the multiracial children of intermarriages. Third, culture itself is dynamic rather than static; ethnic culture can embrace an array of meanings and practices. The variety of ways available to live out a racial identity belies the essentialist notion that some physical, behavioral, or attitudinal elements are necessary to cause a person to be considered a true or authentic member of a racial group.

Dynamism of Culture: Changing Ideas of Masculinity

Culture is neither monolithic nor static. Currently, third-generation Mexican Americans are debating machismo (patriarchy) and gender norms. While antimachismo sentiments and actions are widely embraced, some remnants of gender traditionalism persist. A post–1970s feminist movement re-reading of gender roles is producing a progressive but incomplete gender revolution. The first step in recognizing social change is to acknowledge the cultural diversity within any social group. The second step is to acknowledge the effect that historical era, social movements, and circumstances have on cultural content.

Gender is one culturally shaped social identity that is adapting to a post–feminist movement United States. Shifts in gender that rupture traditional breadwinner/homemaker gender roles, or "gender flexibility," can occur due to contracted labor markets and economic pressures (Sherman 2009). Mexican migration to the United States has also been found to facilitate change in traditional Mexican gender norms due to the United States' relatively more egalitarian gender system (Hondagneu-Sotelo 1994; Smith 2006b). However, it is not just the economically stressed or the migrants who expressed changing views on gender. Financially stable third-generation men and women spoke about their desires and attempts to change patriarchy and rigid gender roles.

A negative consequence of intragroup "battles for authenticity" is that they reify and freeze particular versions and visions of racial identity. Race, class, and cultural repertoire become fused, producing a static notion of the meaning and content of Mexican American identity. Mexican nationals, Mexican Americans, and European-descent Americans engage in this reductionist thinking. While the tendency to essentialize Mexican identity is widespread, there are ways in which Mexican American culture is changing.

Third-generation Mexican Americans possess more progressive gender norms than do their predecessors. Attitudes and actions, including childrearing techniques, motor this shift toward gender egalitarianism. Twenty-eight-year-old Araceli Treviño reflects on raising her two young boys: "I definitely want to push the family aspect and that family is first. . . . You can be making all the money in the world but if I'm not seeing my kids, it's pointless." Attached to this "family first" value is also a desire to change the traditional family model by raising boys who have a sensitive side and are not macho. Araceli explains her antimacho parenting style:

> It's tough as a single mom trying to raise your kids strong but at the same time I don't want them to have the whole macho mentality. And so, it's hard because you get so many people around saying that "you're so soft on them. They need to be strong. . . ." But I don't think there is anything wrong with having a boy that is really sensitive. I get frowned upon from so many Mexican guys that I hang out with. "He's going to be a sissy or he's going to be gay." And I'm like, "Just because he's sensitive or just because he doesn't want to tackle you doesn't necessarily mean gay." I want them to know that it's okay to own up to their feelings. It's okay to cry and it's okay to be sad. It's okay to express your feelings. . . . And a lot of the guys that I hang out with can't stand it. . . . It's very funny how ignorant people still are . . . they think if they hug a doll they're going to turn out to be a girl. You kind of look at them and say, "Gosh, that's so old."

Araceli was raised in a home where there were different rules for boys and girls—her brothers could go out to parties but she was allowed to cry. She is trying to equalize both opportunities and "feeling rules" (Hochschild 2003) by her androgynous childrearing techniques.

Marisol Fuentes, like Araceli Treviño, is doing her part to drive the dynamism of culture and transcend narrow, static versions of Mexican American gender identities. Marisol considers how she would educate her children to embrace egalitarian gender roles:

MARISOL: There are some traditions that I would probably break with my own children that I went through. Like . . . the whole patriarchal issue . . . like worshiping the man, I guess. I'm totally not going to do that.

JMV: How do you see that enacted in your family?

MARISOL: Just seeing how controlling my dad is, especially to my mom. Just seeing her cry. . . . She just takes it and she cries and my dad can be an asshole and . . . I don't want that kind of thing. I don't want my kids to be afraid of their father—because I was afraid of my dad for a long time. I want somebody who cannot be afraid to show their emotions. . . . If I do have sons, I'm hoping to teach them that it's okay to show emotions.

We see here again that parenting is a primary avenue through which to change ideologies and practices—in this case, gender dynamics—through time and family generations. While Marisol does not yet have children, she is using her parents' relationship and childrearing styles as a model to actively revise when she becomes a parent.

Gender and age influenced who criticized machismo. Women of all generations I interviewed were outspoken about the need to update and equalize traditional gender norms. While older men did not critique the patriarchal family system that benefited them, younger men often did. Seventeen-year-old Manny Medina disliked the way his paternal grandfather treated his grandmother and witnessed his father change that pattern in his relations with his wife and children. Manny hopes for the eradication of machismo and spoke eloquently about the equality of the sexes:

My parents taught me not to use gender as criteria when judging people or just in the world. In Oakland, too, all my teachers have educated me this way. . . . Females are equal counterparts and in no way should you . . . think that they are inferior to you and less capable.

Another seventeen-year-old, Andrew Rosenberg, remarked, "I don't really agree with—especially in the older generations—the power that most of the males have." Rick Torres, twenty-one, commented, "I don't like *machistas*. I just don't like tyrants, basically. A lot of men push their weight around a lot. They think that they could run the household. . . . That's a stereotype, but that is something that exists."

Auscencio Dos Santos has first-hand experience with a macho father whose hard-handed parenting serves as a negative model to be overturned in the next generation. Auscencio was raised by a father who was "wonderful" in many respects but whose disciplinary tactics he will not repeat:

A lot of times after my dad would hit me he'd be like, "You know, my dad would have given it to me ten times worse. You're lucky. You got off easy." "Yeah, whatever." But it certainly gave me an idea of how I don't want to raise my children. . . . Violence doesn't get you anywhere. It really, really doesn't. I can see once in a while parents kind of losing it and giving a child a swat. But I think when you are actually angry enough to hold your child down and hit him with something while they're going nuts, you have to be really angry and almost out of control. I don't have that in me. . . . So, I'm hoping to reverse that angry Mexican father trend. It really doesn't have to be that way. . . . I think people respond better to talking.

Again, the third generation's parents serve as a model to either uphold or update as the next generation determines its own parenting strategies.

While an antimacho and antipatriarchal attitude was predominant among the third generation, it was not a unanimous sentiment. While most third-generation women railed against macho Mexican-origin men, some carefully distinguished between domineering and chivalrous qualities. Some women used their natal families as positive examples of how a gendered division of labor in the household was functional, as long as both the husband and wife respected the work of the other. Respect, in addition to men "helping out" in the home, may be the key distinctions between these "transitional" gender roles (Hochschild 1989) and "traditional" gender roles of separate spheres. Caitlyn Benavidas reflects on how her parents worked out a transitional division of labor that was mutually beneficial and respectful:

> For people outside of our culture they see the gender roles as being offensive sometimes. Because my mom still, as much of a feminist that she is, she still serves the men in our family first for dinner. She still cleans up after her sons; everything about her is very nurturing. . . . I identify that as being Mexican because that is what I see in my own family. . . . My dad's not sexist—that's just how things go in our family. . . . Coming from outside people have this perception of machismo . . . but it works in our family. . . . I'm sure I'll be guilty of it myself. I'll be cleaning up after my kids. . . . Moms clean and cook, moms put you to bed and I think that might be something that is carried down from a lot of generations of women in our culture. . . .
>
> My dad's definitely very much of a feminist man. He's very progressive and definitely doesn't have the machismo issues, but at the same time he allows my mom to serve him. He helps around the house, he cooks and cleans, he gardens. He does a lot of everything. They are definitely pretty equal but at the same time because of the way that he grew up with his mom making dinner and setting it out for the men in the family, he doesn't mind if my mom does that. He definitely helps her out and he definitely

appreciates her, but to him it's not weird to have a woman serving the man and being the wife and the mom. But they share duties. When I was born my mom worked and my dad stayed home with me a lot so he definitely sees both sides. We call him a feminist.

Caitlyn calls both her mother and father "feminists." This politicized language of gender equality marks the difference between earlier eras of male dominance and female subservience. Caitlyn is cautious about destabilizing gender roles, yet her parents' gendered behavior and division of labor are far more egalitarian than the heavy-handed machismo and patriarchy argued against by others. When one analyzes the views of the third generation on gender and machismo, it is important to notice that *changes in gender have already been occurring.* Gender roles and norms are relatively elastic through generations, meaning the definitions of "machismo" or "patriarchy" change with time and generations. A traditionally gendered division of labor is losing ground in the minds and lives of the third generation as the majority favors an equalization of power dynamics between the sexes.

Later-Generation Mexican American Ethnicity

This chapter shows how the popular and scholarly understanding of Mexican Americans as a distinct racialized group *and* an assimilating ethnic group are both right. The experience of flexible ethnicity shows not only that the intensity of ethnicity wanes and becomes more "symbolic" by the third generation but also that racialization prevents the ethnicity of the third generation from being more "expressive" than "instrumental." This finding limits the generalizability of scholarship on white ethnic immigrants. Mexican Americans have indeed encountered racism that has undermined their acceptance in mainstream U.S. society. We cannot underestimate the costs of non-European ethnicity. While European immigrants faced challenges to integration, these hardships usually abated or disappeared by the third generation. In the case of Mexican Americans, there remains a relatively high degree of racialization that continues for generations after their immigration (Telles and Ortiz 2009). These third-generation Mexican Americans are assimilated in numerous important ways (education, class, language, culture), yet when Mexican American identity is racialized and demeaned, U.S. nativity and cultural fluency do not always equate to first-class citizenship. Ethnicity remains a real issue—not merely a symbolic one—into the third generation.

Another complication of Mexican American ethnicity among the third generation is its inherent hybridity. As we saw in the section on racial and ethnic self-labels, people actively contemplated what "American" meant in comparison to "Mexican." Even while interviewees themselves drew boundaries around these identities and sometimes reduced them to essentialized core elements, it is important to recognize the heterogeneity, hybridity, and interpenetration of American and Mexican identities. Part of the conundrum respondents faced as they puzzled over self-referential titles—"Mexican," "American," "Mexican American," "Chicano," "Latino," "Hispanic," and others—was the false dichotomy they established of "American" *in contrast to* "Mexican."

Far from existing as distinct opposites, the cultural spheres of the United States and Mexico are deeply interconnected. In areas of the United States with sizeable Latino presence, this translates to a two-way process of cultural change, a course contrary to the earlier straight-line assimilation forecast of Anglo conformity wherein minority cultures are subsumed under the dominant mainstream culture. As an example of the borders of "American" and "Mexican" being permeable rather than unchanging, consider that salsa is now a more popular condiment than ketchup in the United States (Chavez 2008: 179). An active hybridity that creates a third culture amalgamation means that to be American, with or without Latino ancestry, is to be influenced by Latino culture and to be a Latino in the United States is to also be undeniably American. Mike Davis (2000: 23) envisions this symbiotic cultural exchange and malleability as resulting in "a balanced rise of 'Latinos *agringados*' and 'Gringos *hispanizados.*'"

Even while the meaning of being Mexican in the United States has transmogrified over the generations, many third-generation Mexican Americans find their ethnicity to be more than "symbolic" because it is an influential part of their identity. Some respondents found their "two world" perspective to be an advantage of being biethnic and bicultural. Others, however, were beset with identity crises that were neither positive nor voluntary. Rather than permit Mexican heritage to become background and "symbolic," society racializes people it can identify as of Mexican origin. This imposed ethnicity has very real consequences for these individuals' self-esteem, self-perceptions, and educational and career opportunities. These third-generation Mexican Americans who are middle-class and structurally integrated into U.S. occupations, institutions, and mainstream culture live at a racial identification and ethnic culture "crossroads" (Anzaldúa 1987: 195).

The difference between thinned attachment and cultural maintenance individuals is primarily the strength with which they held on to their Mexican culture. Ethnic titles ran the gamut of "Chicano/a," "Latino/a," "Mexi-can," "Mexican American," and fractional identities where respondents wrote in "Mexican and _____." The one notable difference between the thinned attachment and cultural maintenance categories was that the most frequent fill-in response among cultural maintenance individuals (seven out of eighteen) was "Chicano/a," whereas no one in the thinned attachment group used this label.

All third-generation interviewees possessed a post–civil rights movement language of multiculturalism and equal opportunity. Varying relationships to ethnic culture resulted in different levels of perceptions of social injustices and types of reactions; cultural maintenance individuals were sensitized to racial issues and more likely to take corrective measures. Orientation to one's ethnic heritage also affects one's relationship to mainstream culture: people who were thinly attached had a more relaxed and calm connection to mainstream culture because they felt associated with it, whereas those who were resolutely bonded with their ethnic culture were more suspicious of mainstream culture and wary of power dynamics. People on a cultural maintenance pathway were concerned about minority representation in social spaces and institutions such as their schools and workplaces, as well as about overall race relations in the United States. Anxiety over power politics and equal representation was not the exclusive domain of highly identified Mexican Americans, however, but rather was a point of concern for most third-generation respondents who were reared in a time that (at least overtly) heralded the benefits of multiculturalism, especially in the majority minority state of California. Additionally, most parents had tales of unequal treatment with which their children were familiar, so a sense of family legacy of inequality or blocked opportunity made most third-generation Mexican Americans attentive to American race relations. Given that thinned attachment and cultural maintenance are ideal types, these endpoints embrace the myriad perspectives, ways of life, and integration possibilities that people can possess and enact.

Later-generation Mexican Americans exist in a double bind. They do not necessarily seamlessly fit into the U.S. mainstream, yet they also do not necessarily find camaraderie among other Mexican-origin groups. Static and dichotomous visions of "American" and "Mexican" have only hindered race relations and integration processes. As Gilda Ochoa (2004: 223) notes, "historical and contemporary factors . . . have fostered narrow, binary, and static conceptualizations of Americanness and Mexicanness." Rather than acknowledge the vast intragroup heterogeneity of Mexican Americans, some people insist on being "'self-appointed gatekeepers' who exclude those individuals who do not possess some socially constructed benchmark of Mexicanness, such as fluency in the Spanish language" (Barrera 1991: 83). Instead of building walls based on the sufficiency or deficiency of one's "cultural toolkit" (Swidler 1986)—such as Spanish language ability—we need to recognize the variety within the Mexican American population.

Some third-generation individuals had phenotypic features that did get recognized as "Latino." Others perceive them as racially ambiguous and difficult to classify. In this way, third-generation Mexican Americans can traverse multiple racial terrains with equal dexterity. While racial ascriptions remain key in defining (and defending) racial boundaries, some third-generation Mexican Americans who are either part European descent or have lighter skin and hair color find it easier to "pass," or be considered non-Hispanic white.

While flexible ethnicity affords individuals room to negotiate their racial identity, this is not an agent-centered process or state of being. Flexible ethnicity posits that a variety of ethnic scripts is available to actors within a situation of institutional and cultural constraint. Flexible ethnicity allows for a number of forms of racial identification. They include passing as European-descent white, being "Mexican American, light on the 'Mexican,'" an "American with some spice," "Mexican American yet I wish I was darker," and "American by birth, Mexican by culture." By the U.S.-born third generation, racial descriptors ran the gamut of "American" options, from "with some spice" or "Mexican by culture," to emphasize ethnic distinction, to "light on the 'Mexican,'" to reduce dissimilarity from American mainstream. As the third generation develops into its own racial generation, bifurcated as it is, it is crafting its own set of racialized identities. These racial identities respond to impinging institutional messages, cultural framings, family teachings, and the sociopolitical milieu. As the third generation lives out, or even expands, its flexible ethnicity, it paves the way for revised race relations in the United States. Yet acceptance by the mainstream is forestalled by continuing racialization that is based on phenotype, name, class, and essentialized (and assumed) cultural behaviors. For U.S.-born Americans of Mexican descent, facing an enforced and subjugated racial status that prohibits a first-class identity is especially challenging because they are not recognized as the Americans that they truly are.

Conclusion

Racialization despite Assimilation

This book has addressed the question of Mexican immigrants' and their descendants' integration into U.S. society. One more glimpse into respondents' lives reinforces the point that racial/ethnic identity is a fluid process that is highly contingent upon context and that assimilation pathways are not straightforward but open to voluntary personal switchbacks and vicissitudes driven by external social forces.

Both second-generation Mexican Americans, Lee and Evelyn Morelos reared their son Lance in a primarily middle-class, white Los Angeles suburb. Lance picked up cues about race and class from his neighborhood, in which he "fit." His young mind concluded that to be middle class is to be non-Hispanic white and, conversely, to be working class is to be of Mexican descent. Lee explains how Lance didn't realize that he was Mexican-origin in his youth:

> I always loved the green grass. We lived in Los Angeles and this time of year [summer] the green grass dies. So you have to thatch it and put rye and then rye comes up and you have green grass through the winter. [My two sons] were eleven and twelve, and they were working like crazy. Lance comes up to me and says, "Dad, why are we doing all this?!" "I want green grass," I says. "Why don't you hire a couple of Mexicans to do it?" I said to them, "I have. And guess what? I don't have to pay 'em." They didn't even realize they were Mexican! They didn't realize they were Mexican. That's how they were brought up because I was brought up that way. So right there and then I said to myself, "Oh my goodness!" Here we had a beautiful home that was on two acres, a pool, orchards in the back, the whole thing, all surrounded by a community that didn't have minorities. And they didn't go to minority schools, so how the hell were they to know they were Mexican or not?! I never thought of it!

By Lee and Evelyn's own admission, they wanted to raise their children in financially secure neighborhoods with high-performing schools—which translated for them to white, middle-class suburbs. Lee did not want to "forget" his heritage, but he was careful not to "overemphasize" it at home. Lee lays out his philosophy: "I really feel that if you overdo the heritage thing it's not good. You're living here and you should become an American. Don't forget your heritage, enjoy your heritage, but don't overemphasize it."

Despite this youthful lack of awareness of his Mexican heritage, Lance grew up to portray himself as extremely self-confident and active with regard to his Mexican American background and the Hispanic community. I connected with Lance through a Hispanic chamber of commerce and we met for the interview at his family-owned restaurant in Walnut Creek. Lance, who has olive-colored skin and dark, slightly wavy hair, arrived for the interview in a shiny black Mercedes and dressed in business casual clothes. Even before we settled into the interview, Lance let off steam about a break-in to the restaurant catering van. "This is the second time a break-in has happened in two months—they break the window and steal the windshield wipers. I don't even keep anything of value in the van. Today I come in and on the front windshield there is scrawled writing: 'Go back to Mexico, Beaner.'" It was quite a coincidence that on the day I intended to interview Lance about the role of race in his life, the opening scene of his business day was a break-in and racist vandalism.

This vignette illustrates the "bumpy" nature of racial identity and awareness. As a child Lance was utterly ignorant of his Mexican American identity, influenced by his non-Hispanic white neighborhood environment, his observations and overgeneralizations about which racial groups have middle-class versus working-class status, and his father's teachings about walking the balance beam of remembering one's heritage without overemphasizing it. Thirty years later, Lance not only identifies as Mexican American but is identified as such by others and is the target of vehement racist vandalism that wrongly presumes that Lance is foreign born. Lance's bumpy road of assimilation moves from nonrecognition to high identification, in part on the basis of his physical appearance and name, which signal to others his Latino identity. Lee's position on ethnic identity is somewhat contradictory: he promoted "becom[ing] an American" and did not push ethnic awareness on his children, yet was surprised and dismayed by their lack of ethnic consciousness in their youth. Lee treats Mexican American identity as a symbolic ethnicity in this narrative, yet his son's experience testifies that Mexican ethnicity is not optional and recreational but rather imposed and sometimes costly.

Two generations of businessmen, the Morelos father and son pair is clearly well integrated into the U.S. economy and occupational structure. Considering their different eras of upbringing and work life, it is perhaps *because* of his successful structural integration that Lee wears his ethnicity lightly and Lance, whose academic and work life succeeded the civil rights movement, feels empowered to wear his ethnicity with dignity (Jiménez 2010; Macias 2006). In sum, we see here how class, historical context, physical appearance, name, and parental teaching all play into the way identity is consolidated. We also observe how these elements become more or less salient during one's lifetime, and how these social forces can channel racial and ethnic identity in different directions, such as from thinned attachment to cultural maintenance.

Given the steady increase of racial and ethnic minority populations in the United States, the standard of a middle-class, white American mainstream is changing. While some meet this changing demographic profile with grave concern over the "browning" of America, we need to address this issue using life stories and experiences rather than ideological positions. This study of middle-class, multigenerational Mexican American families has showed increasing American identification over time, even as "American" is an increasingly hybridized term. It has also demonstrated that Mexican-origin families can be educationally, financially, and occupationally successful *and* either loosely or strongly adhere to their ethnic heritage. Given the significant influence of gender, skin color/physical characteristics, and name, this study calls into question the utility of discussing topics like race, immigration, and assimilation without considering these essential elements.

The question of whether Mexican Americans are a race or an ethnic group is not resolved by middle-class status; experience of Mexican heritage as imposed versus optional depends on gender and personal attributes such as phenotype and name. "Thinned attachment" results from both personal choice and one's social and institutional surroundings. Gender, family teachings, marriage, phenotype, and religion can all contribute to thinned attachment. Even in thinned attachment, ethnic identity persists, however "distilled" it may be, and can be (re)ignited by oneself or others. Gender, family teachings, marriage, phenotype, religion, as well as the civil rights movement and era of multiculturalism make possible the cultural maintenance trajectory. Multicultural ideology, which gained support following the civil rights era, "helps lift the stigma placed on Mexican ethnicity, making it a desirable and even a rewarding aspect of identity for Mexican Americans" (Jiménez 2010: 103). Marriage with other Mexican Americans was the most common family form, which led to cultural maintenance, whereas the less common occurrence of marriage with a non-Hispanic white led to thinned attachment. Gender, patriarchy, and interest in ethnic culture all played a strong part in family formation. Women were motivated in one of two ways (that are in tension with one another): some avoided partnerships with Latino males for fear that they would be oppressive, whereas others felt a gendered responsibility for maintaining ethnic culture in the home and viewed the cultural similarity they shared with Latino men as a virtue.

While family teachings tend to flow "down" the generational ladder from older to younger generations, the reverse can also be true as a younger person who is sparked to reignite a cultural connection can pass this knowledge and excitement to older generations. Discrimination, which is a means of racialization that even middle-class status cannot neutralize, affects all three generations of Mexican-origin families and is deployed on the basis of skin color, physical characteristics, and name. Historical moment contextualizes each of the three generations, influencing each generation's reaction to discrimination, which ranges from avoidance among the immigrants to attitudinal/ideological and behavioral resistance strategies among the U.S.-born generations. While schools are both racialized and racializing, historical context, gender, and parental ideologies and actions mediate their impact. The middle-class families boasted educational gains over the three generations, yet in this process, the U.S.-born generations educated in the United States were subjected to the predominant racialized and racializing practices of their time. The second generation experienced a Jim Crow style of education that was largely separate and unequal— boys were funneled into remedial classes or out of school entirely—whereas the third generation was subjected to educational tracking and institutional racism, which were only partially destabilized as a result of affirmation action. The Mexican American third generation demonstrates a variety of social experiences, ranging from flexible ethnicity to racialization. This youngest generation displays norms of masculinity that are broadening to embrace emotional sensitivity and gender equality. Mexican American identity is not yet symbolic but carries emotional and practical costs that prevent it from being merely another colorful ancestry that is seamlessly woven in the tapestry of U.S. society.

Understanding the Bumps in the Road of Assimilation

Multigenerational families are a powerful unit of analysis in that they reflect historical moments, reveal family dynamics, and refract racialized and gendered discourses and identities. First, I analyzed generations "horizontally," as I considered all first-, second-, or third-generation respondents, respectively. "Generation styles" (Mannheim 1936) develop out of sociopolitical contexts that bear marks of an era and are imprinted upon human lives and identities (Cohen and Eisen 2000; Takahashi 1997). "Each generation . . . has a memory bank of images and code words" (Gillespie 1995: 12), causing each generation to respond to the same phenomena in a patterned fashion. Generations are embedded within particular historical eras, and these periods exhibit dominant racial paradigms and attendant "common sense" understandings about race (Frankenberg 1993; Haney López 1996; Omi and Winant 1994). For instance, the power of phenotype, gender, and name to shape life experience and influence identity claims was consistent in all three generations. The political climate changed in each generation, however, moving from ideologies of Americanization in the immigrant generation to Jim Crow and the civil rights movement in the second generation, and finally to affirmative action and multiculturalism in the third generation. Tracing life experiences across family generations sheds light on the formative power that intergenerational family communication, institutions, historical movements, and micro-interactions all have on racial/ethnic identities and incorporation patterns.

Second, I analyzed interviewees' narratives "vertically," as I considered grandparent-parent-child links, paying special attention to generation within families. My research design specified both generation-in-a-family and nation-of-birth such that family generations map perfectly onto generation-since-immigration (Telles and Ortiz 2009). (The first-generation immigrants were all grandparents, and the second and third generations were immigrants' U.S.-born children and grandchildren, respectively.) Intergenerational family memory, as shaped by historical period and life experiences, significantly influences the ways in which Mexican immigrants and their descendents incorporate into U.S. society. The experiences and memories of one family generation often become the memories and struggles of the next generation. Parents pass more than genes and didactic lessons on to their children. Through personal narratives, parents convey who they are, what they have been through, how they struggled, what they achieved, and what their dreams have been. These lessons, directly or indirectly relayed, are formative for children. These intergenerational lessons, often about gender issues, racial strife, and struggle for class mobility, are socializing stories. Just as knowledge about ancestors is a primary factor influencing racial/ethnic ancestry choice (Waters 1990: 36), so too is intergenerational transfer of knowledge formative for people's larger sense of identity and orientation to their community and nation.

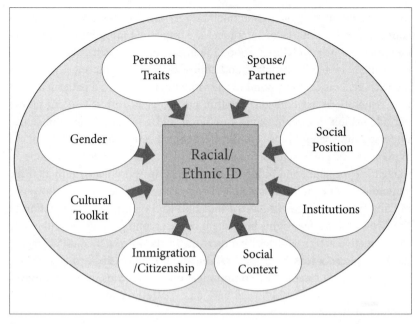

Figure 8.1

My study extends current scholarship on Mexican Americans, immigration, assimilation, and identity formation by interviewing not just the Mexican immigrants but also their children and grandchildren born in the United States. In comparison with my methodology, which focuses on race, ethnicity, family, and generation, other studies on Latinos typically concentrate on only two generations (which are most often disembedded from family units), study a single generation or cohort, or use the community as a site of investigation. I refine assimilation and segmented assimilation theory by highlighting the experiential level of immigrants' incorporation and demonstrating that incorporation is a "bumpy" process. Several factors drive incorporation patterns and contribute to the way immigrant families conceive of their racial/ethnic identity (see figure 8.1). According to my interviewees' life stories, the following elements are of primary importance.

- Spouse/Partner
- Personal traits (phenotype and name)
- Gender
- Social position (class position, status position)

Of secondary importance are the following social traits and institutions.

- Cultural toolkit (i.e., English language ability, Spanish language ability, American traditions/cultural fluency, Mexican traditions/cultural fluency)
- Social context (geography, demographic context)
- Institutions (e.g., church, school, work)
- Immigration/Citizenship status (whether one is an immigrant or U.S. citizen)

To be sure, the dimensions of legality/illegality have profound effects on life chances and outcomes (De Genova 2005; Gonzalez 2008; Zhou et al. 2008). Citizenship is not prominent here because it was not central to my analysis; the first-generation immigrants I interviewed either were documented workers or were naturalized U.S. citizens by the time of the interview. Two other elements that provide the larger context in which life unfolds, as illustrated in figure 8.2, include the following.

- Family members' ideology, practices, and teachings
- Historical period

While the elements pictured here may be considered "inputs," variability occurs as factors align differently for people and as they negotiate—resist, challenge, partially accept—these influences, making their life, incorporation, and racial/ethnic identity formation a dynamic process.

Figure 8.2 illustrates the way I conceive of the transmission of knowledge across generations. Note that each "wheel of racial identity formation" pictured above is duplicated for each of the three generations: grandparent, parent, and child. The generations are linked by a porous two-way arrow of "ideologies, practices, and teachings," showing how parents and children, as well as grandparents and grandchildren, are connected. The arrow is dashed rather than solid to indicate that there is slippage between the "ideologies, practices, and teachings" that are taught and the lessons learned. The arrow connecting the family generations (first to second, second to third, and first to third) has two tails on it, showing that "ideologies, practices, and teachings" can flow both "down" the generational ladder (from parents to children and grandchildren) and "up" (from children to parents and grandparents), as seen in the Madrigal family in chapter 4. The arrow at the bottom labeled "historical time" indicates that all of these racial-identity-creation and intergenerational-transmission processes are embedded within historical periods.

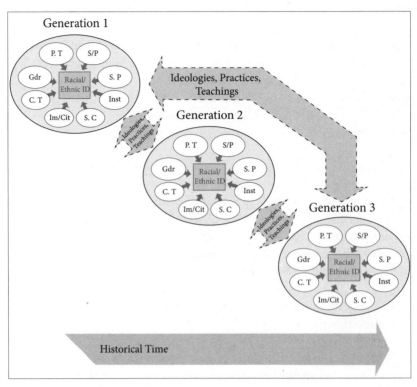

Figure 8.2

Over three generations, families can express thinned attachment, in which racial/ethnic background is not central, or can live out cultural maintenance, in which Mexican-oriented traditions and communities are integral to everyday life and identity. Historical context shapes the experiences of each generation, which, in turn, affects both junior and senior generations in the family. Racism is historically dependent, having "changed over time, taking on different forms and serving different purposes in each time period" (Lipsitz 2006: 4). This historically dependent experience with race creates the "interpretive backdrop" (Vasquez 2005) against which both antiracist and identity-making strategies are crafted. The grandparents, parents, and children in this book tell us that intergenerational family memories, communication, and practices are foundational to one's racial identity formation in that they provide a template to be stylized, a void to be filled, or grievances to be rectified. These families demonstrate that race, ethnicity, identity, and culture are not meaningless abstractions but are significant concepts that are created through the institutions of family and society, and in conjunction with historical social movements.

Given that this book focused on families who were middle class by the third generation, this evidence suggests that Mexican Americans *can* be upwardly mobile and structurally assimilate. While some people are accepted more readily (largely due to phenotype, education, or income level) (Telles and Ortiz 2009), a contingent of second- and third-generation Mexican Americans remains racialized despite assimilation. My findings are that integration in language, education, income, occupation, and civic participation occur over generations and yet Mexican-origin people may live out their ethnic heritage by choosing either to loosen or to tighten their grip on Mexican culture. Considering the diversity of cultural orientations and identity constructions, a "multi-directional cross-cultural acculturation" (Moya 2000: 88) seems to be occurring wherein white, middle-class American values are no longer the singular pinnacle of achievement.

The Immigration Debate Revisited: Revising Assimilation Theory

A portrait of Mexican Americans as a racialized and disadvantaged group (Acuna 2000; Almaguer 1994; Portes and Rumbaut 2001; Telles and Ortiz 2009) coexists with an image of Mexican Americans as an assimilating ethnic group (Alba 2006; Alba and Nee 2003; Perlmann 2005; Skerry 1993; Smith 2003; Smith 2006a). Federal and state policies, such as affirmative action, suggest a racial status for Mexican Americans, as do scholars who find persistent subordination and disadvantage (Acuna 2000; Almaguer 1994; Gómez 2007; Ortiz 1996; Telles and Ortiz 2009). On the other hand, political elites, analysts, and scholars have contended that Mexican Americans are just like other immigrant ethnic groups. Some add the caveat that since Mexican immigrants tend to arrive with little education and wealth—their starting gate is set further back—they may take an extra generation or two to catch up to the assimilated outcome of the European immigrants who arrived at the beginning of the twentieth century. Making sense of those dual perspectives is challenging because they appear to be polar opposites, yet in reality, both ring true. As we have seen, at least among families who achieve middle-class status, a segment of that constituency remains racialized as nonwhite while another portion—those who bear physical resemblance to white ethnics, do not have Hispanic first and last names, and display American cultural behaviors—is less often, if ever, reminded of their outsider status. Thus, the process of racialization as nonwhite versus the process of social whitening is not uniform, even among the middle class (Vasquez 2010).

Nativist rhetoric turns a blind eye to the multiple ways in which Mexican Americans are integrating into, contributing to, and are undeniably a (native-born) portion of the population. Fearful racist, classist, and xenophobic contingents view Latinos as "separatists" and a multiethnic society as inherently "fragile" and "combustible." This vision harkens back to the era of the Anglo-conformity brand of straight-line assimilation that required "forsaking old loyalties . . . [and] melt[ing] away ethnic differences" (Schlesinger 1998: 17). Those who believe that the Latino presence in the United States is undermining American culture are quick to forget that the United States is a nation of immigrants—aside from Native American nations, that is. Those who romanticize a golden era of Anglo unity and dominance overlook the centuries-long presence Mexicans had in southwestern territories now under the U.S. flag, as well as erase the contributions of Latinos to "American" culture. Obscured by the ideological rhetoric surrounding immigration is the fact that the "demand for Latino immigrant labor in the United States has become *structural* in character" (Cornelius 2002: 167). Latinos and other racial minorities tend to be scapegoated as eroding a coherent, common American culture (Gitlin 1995; Huntington 2004a; Huntington 2004b; Schlesinger 1998), when U.S. culture is in fact a nonmonolithic, regional, highly hybridized conglomeration. Those who speak of the bygone golden age of American identity are glamorizing a fictional consensual identity and continuing the invisibility of racial minorities (and women) whose existence is subordinated by an exclusionary master narrative. Rather than viewing multiculturalism as the splintering or "disuniting" of America (Gitlin 1995; Huntington 2004a; Huntington 2004b; Schlesinger 1998), Americans need to recast their understanding of the meaning of "American" and embrace those who exist on its territory, participate in its various institutions, and co-create its culture and future.

One problem with the classic assimilation perspective is that it "tends to de-emphasize the kinds of power differentials that have historically been so crucial in structuring . . . inequality, placing a group's attempts at becoming like the majority group at center stage to the neglect of the structural barriers that might prevent it from doing so" (O'Brien 2008: 14). In this way, the supposed success or failure of immigrant groups' integration has been placed on the groups themselves, without regard for the context into which they were received. We have seen how strong an impact racializing institutions, racial discourses, and interpersonal prejudices have on individuals' access to precious resources, sense of self-identity, and sense of group position or worth. The onus is not merely upon immigrant groups but upon American society to admit newcomers to the national community and change the outdated image of an Anglo-Saxon Protestant nation so as to accurately reflect the existing racial, ethnic, and national-origin diversity.

My research supports "new" assimilation theory's argument that assimilation is an incremental process, propelled by both quotidian and key decisions and experiences (Alba 2006). When a generational approach is taken (i.e., controlling for birth cohort and generation simultaneously), the picture becomes clear that linguistic, educational, occupational, and income (in terms of wages) assimilation is occurring (Alba 2006; Perlmann 2005; Smith 2003; Smith 2006a). Richard Alba (2006) argues that "it is the diversity within groups of patterns of incorporation into American society that needs recognition today," and this book shows that diversity of incorporation. One can be both assimilated in terms of education, occupation, language, culture, *and* be highly or minimally affiliated with Mexican-origin culture and identity.

The older straight-line assimilation theory is unrealistically linear, proposing a strict step-wise process. Straight-line assimilation theory assumes that assimilation would "inevitably end with the eventual total disappearance of all traces of ethnicity after several native born generations" (Gans 1992a: 44). Herbert Gans (1992a: 44) instead argued in favor of a "*bumpy line*" theory, the bumps representing various kinds of adaptations to changing circumstances—and with the line having no predictable end." My empirical work confirms and extends Gans's bumpy-line assimilation theory. There is more than one destination for immigrant ethnic groups, and there are multiple paths by which to get there. Families travel various routes that are not always straightforward in order to reach their middle-class and structurally integrated status; some desired Anglo-conformity from the point of immigration, others held on to notions of cultural pluralism that were supported by the civil rights era, and still others made decisions in one generation that they revisited and renegotiated in the next.

Several social forces, as detailed above, are the "bumps" that influence the speed, direction, and forks in the road of both assimilation and racial identity formation. This list of factors—topped by spouse/partner, personal traits such as phenotype and name, gender, and social position—steer the direction of cultural assimilation and racial identification. Notably, the cultural destination is not predetermined in bumpy-line assimilation, allowing for structural assimilation that is complemented by thinned attachment, cultural maintenance, or an in-between status. Bumpy-line assimilation implies that assimilation is a condition that is dynamic and in flux as opposed to an end point. Considering incorporation patterns and racial/ethnic identity as a bumpy process allows for trajectories that are charted and recharted throughout one's life course and open to development over multiple family generations.

As segmented assimilation propounds, race is central to integration possibilities. My data clarify that race works *in tandem with* other elements that influence incorporation processes and racial identity formation. Contrary to segmented assimilation's prediction about the Mexican-origin population at large, there is at least a segment of this ethnic group that is not downwardly assimilated into an already stigmatized subgroup. Since I studied families that had managed to enter the middle class, I did not study the marginalized subpopulation that segmented assimilation theory describes (Portes and Rumbaut 2001; Rumbaut and Portes 2001). While my sample was structurally assimilated into the U.S. mainstream, they were not necessarily assimilated in terms of identification, marriage, and culture. These findings problematize assimilationist notions that suggest an eventual, necessary, and desirable outcome of wholesale integration. "Bumpy-line" assimilation—where the points detailed in the "wheel of racial identity formation" drive integration trajectories—holds that the process of assimilation is highly uneven, susceptible to turns, reversals, accelerations, and decelerations (Gans 1992a).

The family history narratives that I gathered for this book support elements of the various theories of assimilation listed above as well as develops them. The multigenerational family life histories support "new" assimilation theory by showing clearly that integration occurs gradually and over successive generations. Also supported is the insight from segmented assimilation theory that race, along with human capital and neighborhood context, is critical to incorporation. Beyond this agreement, my data illustrate that prior studies have underestimated the critical nature of gender, phenotype, and name, and have overlooked the branches and reversals that can occur over both lifetimes and family generations.

The findings concerning gender and gender ideologies (which, in turn, affect mate selection) suggest that assimilation theory to date has undervalued the crucial role that gender plays in social integration and racial identity formation. Many women spoke fervently about their desire either to grow closer to or to detach from their Mexican heritage; in the case of women who were retreating from Mexican culture, this language was often code for patriarchal gender relations. In both cases, gender and gender ideologies motivated marital choices, family dynamics, and childrearing practices that shaped the gender and racial identities of both parent *and* child generations.

Middle-class, multigenerational Mexican American families can be simultaneously structurally assimilated and yet range from thick to thin Mexican cultural attachment. Their degree of affiliation can change over their lifetime, and one individual's experience can permanently alter the trajectory of other family members, older or younger, by virtue of communication, sharing, and teaching that crosscut family generations. There is a spectrum of possible reactions that follow upward mobility, from "some people of Mexican origin . . . [who] minimiz[e] social distance between themselves and majority whites [to] others [who] . . . although participating in the larger American society . . . maintain a cultural pluralistic point of view and choose . . . biculturalism" (Murguia and Forman 2003: 70). Among the middle-class Mexican American population in Los Angeles, orientations to the American mainstream range from straight-line assimilation to incorporation into a "minority middle-class culture" (but not downward assimilation) (Vallejo and Lee 2009). The processes of upward mobility and structural integration in the United States do not entail the disposal of a minority culture. An immigrant ethnic group enacting an array of cultural incorporation options (thin to thick ethnicity) proves that lingering sending-country cultural attachments do not undermine structural assimilation.

Regardless of degree of Mexican cultural attachment, these middle-class, multigenerational families are undoubtedly structurally incorporated—a finding at odds with assimilation theory's precept that native culture must be jettisoned in order for one to be integrated. Structural incorporation does not necessitate abandonment of an ethnic culture and wholesale adoption of American culture. My findings also conflict with segmented assimilation theory's prediction that the Mexican-origin population would most likely undergo downward assimilation. While that may be true for some, that pessimistic picture does not capture the variety of class and ethnic experiences of Mexican American families. That said, seamless incorporation into the American mainstream is not a foregone conclusion for Mexican Americans of all phenotypes, names, genders, and cultural behaviors. Indeed, barriers to integration persist, including institutional and interpersonal discrimination that racializes those perceived as Mexican Americans *despite their assimilation*.

Upwardly mobile Mexican Americans who are perceived as racially "other," despite their success in mainstream institutions, face the constraint of racialization. Mexican Americans are restricted by the way others perceive, treat, and racialize them. Regardless of how Mexican Americans may choose to identify, outsider perspectives that classify them as nonwhite or "off-white"[1] (Gómez 2007) severely limit the possibilities of being liberated from racializing interference. Some scholars promote curtailing racial identity politics in order to foster assimilation (Skerry 1993), yet this option is not solely up to Mexican Americans but is partially dependent on the way the U.S. mainstream reacts to and treats this population. The lives of Mexican Americans, and Latinos at large, are structured by the racializing experiences they undergo in public spheres. Honoring the potency of human agency, these racializing experiences can be at least partially offset by the racial lessons taught within families, individual resistances, and collective social movements.

These findings suggest that race-based policies such as affirmative action remain necessary measures to counteract historical and contemporary exclusionary mechanisms. Scholars have argued that "inequality [is the] . . . socially constructed and changeable consequence of Americans' political choices" (Fischer et al. 1996: 7). Intentional policies and reward structures can be changed to produce more equitable outcomes (Fischer et al. 1996). If the state has historically deprived U.S.-born Mexican Americans of actionable citizenship rights and continues to deprive Mexican immigrants of fair working conditions and living wages, the state should be responsible for devising a remedy. While some politicians, journalists, and scholars call for the eradication of race-conscious policies (such as affirmative action), race has historically shaped state policy (Oliver and Shapiro 1995), and race-conscious policies are necessary to counteract the ways in which racial discrimination continues to disadvantage racial minorities.

The literature on immigration recognizes that federal and state aid to immigrants facilitates their settlement in the United States (Garcia 1996; Reitz 1998; Zhou and Bankston 1998; Pedraza 2007). While having the education and skills that match the needs of the labor market is key to successful adjustment to a host country (Steinberg 2001), federal and state immigration policy that grants work visas with a path to citizenship would be the first step to incorporating Mexican immigrant laborers who build lives in the United States. If the government can support the inclusion of Mexican laborers— rather than perpetuate their alienation—the force of one racializing agent will be curbed.

The middle-class composition of my respondent pool offers a natural extension for future research in that incorporation patterns and racial identity formation probably vary by class. My sample of middle-class families is clearly marked by an upwardly mobile class experience. Other families remain in the lower class, so comparing middle-class families with lower-class families would be an important extension. A class comparison could better determine who achieves upward mobility, how this is accomplished, and how class affects incorporation patterns and racial identity.

In the future, scholars could continue to carry out research on other racial or ethnic populations to discover to what extent my findings regarding middle-class Mexican Americans are relevant to other groups. Empirically testing the robustness of my theoretical contributions by studying other populations would test the limits of the generalizability of my study and uncover the theoretical insights that are applicable to other groups. Another important line of future inquiry would be a regional comparison. California has a particular history and demographic mix, especially as it relates to the Chicano Movement and past and continuing Mexican immigration. A comparison with other regions, such as southwestern and midwestern states with sizeable Mexican American populations and/or immigration flows, would be fruitful. The topics of immigration and Mexican Americans are brimming on the national consciousness and are particularly prominent on the minds of Californians. In the last several years, newspaper headlines about Mexican immigration, Mexican guest worker programs, Border Fence Bills, and Minutemen militias have been abundant. In the four months following the May Day 2006 national rally that called for immigrants' labor rights, a path to citizenship for undocumented immigrants, living wages, decriminalization of immigrants, and demilitarization of the U.S.-Mexico border, coverage in the *Los Angeles Times* was plentiful. Various headlines read, "The Protests of Allegiance," "A Real Fence for a Real Problem," "How L.A. Kept Out a Million Migrants," "Those Are Dollars, Not Pesos—Keep Them Here," "Can-do Spirit Fuels Immigrants," "Get Out, but Leave the Quesadilla," "Governor [Schwarzenegger] Refuses Bush Request for Border Troops," "One More Embrace, Then Slam the Door," and "Borders without Visas." An interstate or regional comparison would illuminate the ways in which my findings are specific to California and underscore the conclusions that are transposable to other locales.

Mexican-origin families are undergoing an assimilation pattern that is bumpy in that trajectories are uneven, non-stepwise, and subject to both volitional and structural accelerations, stalls, and turns. Physical appearance, gender, and name affect reception and treatment in America's institutions and social circles. Family units use biographical narratives, teaching strategies, and defensive techniques, in particular around the axes of race and gender, to organize social identity and fend off racializing treatment outside the home. In a context where race remains eminently important, the prospect of Mexican Americans' racial/ethnic identity entering a "twilight" (Alba 1985), as it did for white ethnics, is dubious. Due in part to continuing Mexican immigration that allows for the public to view and treat the Mexican-origin population as "a permanent immigrant group" (Jiménez 2010: 259), as well as due to the way the United States rewards its members using a color-coded schema where whiteness is superior and nonwhiteness or "off-whiteness" (Gómez 2007) is devalued, racial and ethnic heritage will continue to mark Mexican Americans to the degree it is perceived. Despite claims to the contrary, the United States remains a racially conscious, hierarchical environment. As debates about the importance of race and structures of privilege and oppression carry on, the U.S. racial hierarchy continues to dole out high rewards and pernicious costs across generations.

Methodological Appendix

A Note on Sociological Reflexivity
and "Situated Interviews"

The Question of Reciprocity

I am always concerned with the question of reciprocity. When people agree to do interviews with me, I get a couple of hours of their time and a piece of their story that I fashion into a publishable work product. What do my respondents get? They get to spend time with someone who cares to hear their story but who will not have an ongoing reciprocal relationship with them. Robert Weiss (1994) suggests that people are eager to talk about themselves, that they get satisfaction from having an eager audience, and that they may experience some relief or gratification by reflecting on their lives (Weiss 1994: 122). True to Weiss's assessment, interviewees told me that they benefited from and appreciated an interviewer with a sympathetic ear who provides an atmosphere for self-reflection.

In the interview situation, I provide my respondents an opportunity to talk about themselves in an unselfish way. I believe there is a self-building or revising function to the self-telling that occurs in the interview. Interviews are a free space in which people are afforded the time and encouragement to reflect on their lives. While some respondents found the interview difficult to the extent that it brought up sensitive topics, most ended their encounter with me with an expression of neutral or positive emotion. Interviewee Albert Schultz seemed to appreciate reflecting on his own life with an interested listener. While an interview situation and a therapy session have very different goals (and listeners with very different professional training), they both hinge on atmospheres of active listening. Albert Schultz observed, "Wow, this is like therapy. I haven't been this open with anyone besides my close friends in a long time." I took that to be a compliment toward the atmosphere of trust and confidence that I try to foster in the interviewer-interviewee interaction.

Manny Medina reflected on his interview experience with me this way: "I really don't think of this stuff all that much so it was a good chance to think about new things." Manny finished the interview with a renewed appreciation of his parents' support and contribution to his life. While I was not pushing any perspective (either assimilationist or pluralistic), Manny's deliberation during the course of the interview about what it means to be an American with Mexican heritage led him to consider how to strike a balance that suits him and his ideals. He commented at the end, "Wow, you've really got me thinking that when I go to college I really should start or join a club that is with and for Latinos. Just to keep it up. But definitely not to overdo it and have it be to the exclusion of my American identity." It is this quality of thoughtfulness that I hope my respondents engage in and find productive as a consequence of our brief time together.

I hope this study benefits the public and provides a way for people (not just members of the group studied) to better understand themselves and each other. Regarding the issue of my reciprocity with high schools for their assistance in my recruitment process, I was asked by a vice principal of one of the high schools to give a speech at the MEChA (Latino student organization) graduation awards ceremony, which I accepted. In a few cases, parents of teenagers asked for my input on their children's college options. Seen as an educational resource, I was asked for advice on the application process, school selection, and financial aid. Throughout the research and writing process, I desired to give back to my respondents and the community because there would be no book without their participation. I sent all interviewees a personalized thank-you card within a week of the interview.

Mirroring or Fueling an Interest in Family

It is interesting that—as many of my respondents have indicated—my research asks questions that interviewees themselves enjoy pondering. Either they have mused on these questions beforehand or my investigation prompts a new quest for them. One woman who was too geographically distant to take part in the study wrote over email, "It's interesting that your e-mail was forwarded to me . . . as I was recently thinking of my family (parent, aunts & uncles) who have passed away and who have taken our family history to their graves. I have been hoping that me and my generation of cousins asked enough questions and know our history."

Similarly, interviewee Michael Jimenez phoned me after the interview to say that he wanted to use my family-based interview project as an opportunity to open up his family history. He wished to gain more knowledge about his family and ethnic roots. As much interest as he expressed in his family history during the interview, he lacked detailed family stories. It is unclear whether my questions made him realize his deficiency of familial knowledge or whether he craved a more in-depth family history before my interview with him. Regardless, *he saw a way to use the interview with me as a tool for accomplishing his own goals.* I felt cheered by this because the question of reciprocity always looms for me; it is easier to see what my interviewees provide me than the other way around. While I walk away with a tape-recorded narrative that I will eventually craft into a publishable piece of scholarship, my respondents have shared two hours and a part of their life story with me, and the benefit to them is less obvious. Perhaps my interviewees experience some emotional or psychological relief by talking to me—but there is the alternative possibility of the interview dredging up buried and best-forgotten histories. Further, I am trained as a sociologist, not a psychologist or a social worker, and so my ability to aid my interviewees is severely limited. Given these concerns and constraints, I was always heartened to hear that my interviewees could see ways to use their interviews with me for their own personal goals and benefit. I would certainly be glad to be seen as a vehicle for family communication and memory transmission.

Assertions of Solidarity

In response to my email advertisements, many people chose to express solidarity with me and my work. While I drafted the email content in English, some people responded in Spanish for a flare of camaraderie (even though they would have no way of knowing my level of Spanish knowledge). A typical email reads, "I would be honored to help you with your data & would enjoy contributing to such a much needed body of knowledge. Please let me know how I can help an Hermana [sister] out!!!! Paz [peace], [Signed]." A couple of things are noteworthy here. First is the claim that my research area is a "needed body of knowledge," which I think prompted a number of volunteers. Potential interviewees see themselves as interesting, important, and understudied. Second is the imagined sisterhood/brotherhood indicated by the writer's use of "*hermana.*" I am certain that I benefited from a sense of "imagined community" (Anderson 1991). Insofar as potential respondents envision me as part of a community to which they belong (especially if they view it as marginalized, understudied, or threatened) they are more inclined to "help a [sister] out." Third is the code switching into Spanish. This intermingling of Spanish words into a primarily English text further buttresses the idea of an imagined community, one that is braced by language. Other sign-offs at the ends of emails offering interest or assistance included, "Siempre para nuestra gente . . . " [Always for our people.] and "Buena suerte y adelante mujer!" [Good luck and keep going, woman!]. I received many "congratulations" for conducting my research, people often thanking me for doing the work that I am doing because they believe it to be necessary.

Recruitment

"I'm a Researcher, Not a Telemarketer"

When calling families that had been referred to me as possible interview subjects, I generally tried to introduce myself quickly before I was mistaken for a telemarketer. Indeed, as I introduced myself over the phone to the husband of a woman I had been trying to reach, I explained that a member in a community organization referred me to her and that I was a researcher affiliated with the University of California–Berkeley. The husband chuckled and said, "In other words, you are not a telemarketer."

This presumption was not unusual. When I worked with the Montes/Rosenberg family highlighted in chapter 2, Tamara and Jillian needed to cajole Maria into doing the interview. Maria's family reported her to be a very "strong" woman but "shy," and probably not prone to think that her narrative was of "use" to a social science researcher. It no doubt helped that I conducted interviews with her other family members first and that they were able to report neutral or positive experiences with me to her. They assured her that I would not ask embarrassingly personal questions—or that if I did she could skip them—and that it was an "easy" conversation with a young woman doing a "school project." She—like other initially reluctant older interviewees—warmed up to the idea of assisting me in my education.

At the end of the interview with Maria, which had gone smoothly, Maria's fifty-something-year-old niece came into the house for a visit. Maria had earlier invited me to speak to the niece about whether she and her family might participate in my project. Maria introduced me and I explained that we had just finished an interview for a project I was doing and asked if she would consider doing the same. She immediately and curtly said, "No." I said "thanks anyway" and dropped the subject. Then Maria interjected that "she had been afraid I would ask lots of personal questions, but I didn't, it was just about her, her opinions, her stories and history." "Plus," she added with emphasis, "it's for a big school project she's doing, so I wanted to help out."

The niece's icy tone and demeanor melted and she said, "Oh, sorry about that, that was just my automatic reaction. I thought you were a reporter or something, so I slipped into my mode I get into with telemarketers where you just say 'no' off the bat." She softened after Maria backed up my request with her own positive experience—Maria said she "enjoyed talking to me." The niece ultimately still declined, this time saying that she didn't think her mother would like to participate. The emphasis on people "helping me with my education" was unexpectedly important in securing interviewees. It was also useful to do an interview with a younger-generation respondent first and have them report their experience to the older generation so they could make an informed decision about whether or not to participate.

Well-Intentioned High School Administrators Using Stereotypes

In my attempts to gain access to high school students, I was most struck by the mental short-circuiting that would happen even among well-intentioned administrators: when I asked about third-generation Mexican American students, they routinely routed me to English as a Second Language classes. In several over-the-phone attempts to get directed to the appropriate administrator at a high school in the Bay Area, school employees would consistently route my call in the direction of English as a Second Language/ Limited English Proficient, Spanish for Spanish Speakers, bilingual liaisons, immigrant family coordinators, or bilingual education teachers. I explained each time that I was looking for "third-generation Mexican American students"—meaning that grandparent(s) rather than parent(s) emigrated from Mexico. Despite my specificity, I was routinely funneled to a population that was too close to the immigrant generation (1.5 or second) to be useful for this project. Revealing stereotypes in action, administrators easily translated "third-generation Mexican American students" into "immigrants," "children of immigrants," or "Spanish speaking."

Familism in Hispanic Chambers of Commerce

I was warmly received by most of the Hispanic chambers of commerce that I contacted for recruitment purposes. I attended the mixers to which I was invited, connecting with my initial contact, and then was informally introduced to his/her friends and associates. The introduction flow was much like a game of dominoes: as one person would get excited about my project, he or she would introduce me to someone else they thought might be able to directly or indirectly help me. Certainly, I did not get a 100 percent response rate from the Hispanic chambers of commerce I contacted, but those who did respond were enthusiastic. When I remarked on this openness and enthusiasm about my project, someone in the crowd to whom I was talking at a mixer remarked, "Of course! Because, after all, the Hispanic chamber of commerce is all about community." I definitely had not considered this angle as a benefit to my recruitment tactic with the chambers. Because they are voluntary organizations built around racial and ethnic solidarity and common purpose, my own part-Latina identity and my Latino topic facilitated a bond with the people involved with the Hispanic chambers of commerce that allowed me to be quickly embraced. In my late twenties at the time, I was associating with chamber members who were between forty-five and sixty-five years old, so they perhaps slipped into a paternal (most mixer attendees were men) or mentor role with me. This paternalistic/mentor role was facilitated by the fact that I was (or felt like I was) in a subservient position as I asked for their help, advice, and social connections. To this point, at least one person cooed over me and my project, referring to me as "*mija*" (a Spanish endearment meaning literally "my daughter" and loosely "darling").

Interview Format

Triangulation among Three Generations

One of the strengths of interviewing several people from different generations in the same family was the way I could parse out similarities and differences among the narratives. This way, I achieved an understanding of both common experiences within the family and points of departure. For instance, in the Vargas family, I interviewed the first- and second-generation women who were very strongly identified as Mexican and immersed in the Mexican community. To my surprise, the third-generation descendant had virtually nothing to report in the way of family stories or events that highlighted her Mexican identity. Her mother made it sound as though they "lived and breathed" Mexican culture and yet the third-generation woman came up blank when I asked questions about Mexican cultural practices. Here, the third-generation interview contradicted the assessments of the earlier two generations. I treat all interviewee narratives as explaining their social worlds the way they see and experience them. Therefore, perspective—in this case generational perspective—matters. The differences between generations were stark in this example; yet that is valuable data that is a benefit of conducting interviews with multiple family members about the same topic. This is a lesson of the maxim in qualitative methodology that different people in the same family may have vastly different experiences within and regarding the same family.

Balancing Active Listening and My Interview Schedule

Several years ago in a methods class, Arlie Hochschild commented, "Sometimes the interviewer's questions are interruptions." In the course of an interview, I would juggle peering down periodically at my interview schedule while at the same time listening to the interviewee's narrative for thematic leads to follow. As I became comfortable with interviewing and my interview schedule became seared into my memory, I realized that I was conversationally delivering my questions. I was playing the game of mentally checking off the questions the interviewee had answered while still keeping an ear open for attention-grabbing pieces of narrative to curiously follow. As Jewel, a pop musical artist, remarked in an interview with a radio disk jockey, "I dislike it when I am in interviews with people and they are looking down at their papers for the next question rather than listening to what I am saying."[1] Hearing this comment from a much-interviewed popular culture star, I thought about how minimizing my reliance on an interview schedule could ease an interviewee's concern over not being heard. By practicing active listening, and periodically rather than constantly referring to a list of questions or topics, interviewers acknowledge their interviewees. Attention to the flow of the interview and following leads when they appear allows the interviewee to talk in a guided, semi-organic fashion. The interviewer continues to steer the conversation to address points of interest yet the interview moves forward with attention to how the narrative naturally develops.

My task as a social science researcher is to look beyond what meets the eye of the naïve observer. This penetration entails figuring out how interviewees conceive of themselves and experience their place within the world. To do this, some interviewees required a stream of questions to guide their narrative, while others took more assertive control in telling their story. While the latter style required fewer prompts from me, I would occasionally use questions as guideposts to keep the conversation on topic. Due to the unfolding of the interview process that is built on a rapport with the interviewee that encourages his/her participation as well as the interviewer's active listening skills, each interview takes on its own shape. Even with an interview schedule, some questions were covered in depth while others were briefly touched on. Depending on interviewer-interviewee dynamic and rapport, an interviewee's life history, and personal style, the interview takes on its own form. Beginning with the same recipe, each interview is unique. Given these flexible contingencies plus a life story and perspective that can be told from myriad angles at any time, I believe that all interviews are the result of an interviewee's story that is told *in interaction with* the interviewer.

On Being a "Gendered" Interviewer: Interviewee Surveillance

True to Simone de Beauvoir's revolutionary statement, "One is not born, but rather becomes a woman" (Beauvoir 1978), I found that I was not just an interviewer but a woman interviewer. Of course, I was not just a woman interviewer but an unmarried, American-born, educated, middle-class, mixed-ethnicity (European mix and Mexican), light-skinned, dark-haired, Spanish-surnamed, heterosexual, and young interviewer. The social location of all interviewers bears on the interview dynamic, so this is not new. What is of interest to me here is the ways in which I was constituted as a "woman" in the context of some interviews.

My unmarried status was jarring to a few older-generation respondents who expected a 28-year-old woman like myself to be married. This is probably due to their youthful experience of seeing marriages occur at a relatively early age, in combination with their racialized expectation that a Mexican American woman should be married by thirty. This is illustrated in my interview with 84-year-old, first-generation immigrant Juan Ramos. To my surprise, as I was packing up to leave during the "wind down" after-interview conversation, Juan asked if I was married. He sounded shocked when I stated, "No." He came back with, "What?! No?! But you are so pretty!" He is of an older generation, and yet he was stunned that I upset his expectation that a woman in her late twenties would/should be married. In making sense of me, he had to reconfigure—if briefly—his notion of gender in the world around him. I, on the other hand, was momentarily gendered as he stereotyped me as a woman who should be married.

An interview with second-generation Lee Morelos echoed this theme of a respondent surveilling my marital status and policing my gender. Unlike Juan, Lee was not shocked by my unmarried status, because he is a businessman used to seeing women delay marriage for the sake of education or a profession. Lee took on a paternalistic voice as he offered up his gender-making advice. Lee asked near the end of the interview, "Have you ever been married?" I said, "No." He replied, "Wow, well, I'd have thought that someone should have snatched you up by now." I smiled slightly, knowing it was a compliment. Lee's wife was easy with the exchange and as they both walked me outside they asked me more questions about my experience and background. In the context of a discussion of marriage, Lee boisterously laughed and said, "What you need is a big Anglo man!" He slapped my back and said, "Oh, I'm just kidding." Just then his wife was chiming in loudly, "No, she just needs a good man. That's what counts, she wants a good man." Lee continued, "Well, in my day, people got married young. In my children's day they got married in their mid to late twenties. Now it seems like if a woman wants a career she puts off having a husband and having children. What has been your experience? Are you putting marriage off till after school or have you not found the right man yet?" After I provided a brief answer, Lee offered some unsolicited counsel:

> If I can offer you some advice: stay choosy. You also don't want to marry someone who is not as educated as you. You don't want him to always have that sense of insecurity with you. So you shouldn't marry a farmhand—not that they're not good people—but he wouldn't be able to understand you and you are going to need that. So don't marry down, if you can help it. You want someone who is at your level and can be there with you and understand you. Plus you just don't want to put that insecurity in someone and have that be an issue, have that always be there and have him feel like he's not enough for you.

I nodded, listening. He followed up, "So it's good to be choosy, but don't be too choosy!"

Lee was enforcing gender roles through his well-intentioned paternalistic advice. He cautioned me against being overeducated in comparison to a future spouse, lest I intimidate him. I should not partner with someone below my educational station because I might emasculate him. If a man is not the "head of the house"—or perhaps one of two nearly equal heads of household—in terms of breadwinning and education level, then an unhappy union would ensue. In this gendering process, I was told to stay within certain gender bounds for the good of my future relationship. I claim this is part of a gendering process, for I certainly cannot imagine him telling a *man* not be more educated than his future female partner—this would be *expected* and there would be no alarm over a highly educated man making his wife insecure about her lesser level of educational attainment. In the spirit of looking out for me, Lee finally advised me to strike a balance between being "choosy" but not "too choosy," for assertiveness on the marriage market has been traditionally less the business of women than of men.

Apart from marital expectations and advice that were cast in my direction, another way in which I "became" a woman was through the act of interviewing itself. Listening has long been considered a particularly feminine virtue. While "equality feminism"[2] sociologists have long battled the socially constructed quality of such sex-typed traits, it is still popularly held that women are "better" at listening than men. As a female interviewer, I sometimes fell victim to this sex-typed role of listener. While I actively engaged the interviewee with questions, I still spoke less often and was thus the more passive of the interlocutors. Understanding listening as a traditional female trait—one that perhaps men select as they search for heterosexual partners—sheds an interesting light on an exchange I had with Moises Ramos (Juan Ramos's grandson) at the end of my interview with him. I interviewed Moises first and we arranged that I would return on another day to the home that he shared with his grandfather, Juan, for an interview with the older man.

At the end of our interview, Moises looked up at me and started chuckling. I asked why and he said, "Well, I was going to ask you when I can see you again." He bowed and shook his head in mild embarrassment. Shrugging his shoulders he added, "I don't know, that's just what you say to a woman." I don't know if this question was meant to refer to the fact that I would be returning to interview his grandfather or whether he in fact wanted to see me in a social situation. He had laughed self-effacingly at his impulse but what I found interesting was the impulse itself. If listening is coded as feminine and I, as a female interviewer, engage this behavior as professional conduct, then the confusion of professional versus personal is fascinating. This dynamic of the man being revealing and the woman being in the position of the "empathetic listener" mimics traditional gender scripts of an "active" man and a "passive" woman. Further, traditional gender roles would expect the woman to be emotionally sensitive, to elicit emotion and sharing from the man, and to respond sympathetically to him. Such gendered expectations are relevant here, as in the professional capacity of interviewer I end up fitting in the role of an empathetic female with whom males can discuss emotional topics. My inquisitiveness and responsiveness could have fostered the illusion of a nonprofessional relationship. Additionally, the content of the interviews themselves was of a personal nature. This furthered the conceit of the interview situation bordering on a gender-typed social situation.

Insider Dilemma

Patricia Zavella, a Chicana feminist sociologist, instructs, "we [researchers] should realize that we are almost always simultaneous insiders and outsiders" (Zavella 1993). She points out that studying one's own population (be it race, class, gender, etc.) and being an "insider" carries advantages and disadvantages. On the one hand, it can facilitate access to that population. On the other hand, it can amplify feelings of responsibility to the population that exceeds the researcher's abilities or resources.

I have wondered if my subject matter impelled highly positively identified Mexican Americans to participate in my research project. For example, activists in the Chicano Movement of the 1960s may be inclined to agree to participate in my study because they believe that their involvement may further the cause of Chicano representation. I can be seen as furthering this cause in two ways: (1) through academic work that raises consciousness about Chicano history and presence; and (2) as an educator who is Mexican American herself and concerned with representing her bicultural background. Speaking to this point, interviewees would periodically refer to me as a "good example of a successful Latino/a." For example, Tina Acevedo made it clear she was interested in helping out because she thought my book was worthwhile and because she is always in support of "*nuestra gente*" (our people). There is a way in which my insider status (at least by Mexican heritage, if not gender in this case as well) helps me gain access to respondents. Some respondents saw my work as important and, above that, appreciated "one of us" doing something to understand "our" culture. While this is somewhat reductionist—because I am not only of Mexican descent but of European heritage as well, a woman, educated, middle class, and so on—being an "insider" lets me pass the first test of authenticity and prompts acquiescence to the interview. While I cannot guess at the myriad motivations respondents had for participating in my research, I suspect that my being an "insider" on some axes of social position facilitated participation.

Appendix A

Respondent Demographic
Information (Pseudonyms)

Income Breakdown Key		
	Household:	*Individual:*
Lower	UNDER $25,000	UNDER $20,000
Middle	$25,000–$90,000	$20,000–$60,000
Upper Middle	$90,000–$120,000	$60,000–$80,000
High	$120,000+	$80,000+

Abbreviations Key:
    NR=Not Reported
    Convo=Conversational
    Less C=Less Than Conversational

Respondent Demographic Information (Pseudonyms)

Name	Generation	Age	Sex	Education	Occupation	SES Category	English	Spanish	Years in CA
Tina Acevedo	2nd	45	F	College	Registered Nurse	High	Fluent	Convo	All
Tom Acevedo	3rd	17	M	High School	High School Student	High	Fluent	Less C	All
Rosa Avila	1st	87	F	Jr. High or Less	Nurse	NR	None	Fluent	None (AZ)
Alfonzo Avila	2nd	45	M	Some College	Cosmetologist	Upper Middle	Fluent	Fluent	6 of 45
Hector Avila	3rd	23	M	Some College	Student/Security Guard	Upper Middle	Fluent	Convo	2 of 23
Benjamin Benavidas	2nd	56	M	Master's	TV Producer/Director	Upper Middle	Fluent	Fluent	All
Caitlyn Benavidas	3rd	24	F	College	University Administrat-or	Upper Middle	Fluent	Convo	All
Ruby Castillo	2nd	46	F	College	Production Company Owner	High	Fluent	Fluent	All
Dillon Castillo	3rd	17	M	High School	High School Student	High	Fluent	Fluent	All
Ishmael (Milo) Contreras	2nd	59	M	Doctoral Degree	Lawyer	Middle	Fluent	Fluent	All
Renata Contreras	3rd	25	F	College	Legal Assistant	Middle	Fluent	Convo	All
Sergio Diaz	2nd	47	M	High School	Mechanic/Auto shop owner	Middle	Fluent	Less C	All
Samantha Diaz	3rd	25	F	College	Civil Litigation Clerk	High	Fluent	Less C	All
Luna Dos Santos	2nd	59	F	Master's	University Administrat-or	Middle	Fluent	Fluent	All
Carmina Dos Santos	3rd	28	M	College	Student/ Social worker	Lower	Fluent	Convo	26 of 28
Auscencio (Ceño) Dos Santos	3rd	30	F	Master's	Graduate Student	Middle	Fluent	Convo	All
Cordelia Fuentes	2nd	55	F	Master's	Licensed Clinical Social Worker	High	Fluent	Convo	All
Marisol Fuentes	3rd	21	F	Some College	Student (college)	Middle	Fluent	Convo	All
Constantina Guzman	1st	82	F	Jr. High or Less	Flower Nursery/ House-cleaner	Middle	None	Fluent	43 of 82
Gloria Guzman	2nd	47	F	Jr. High or Less	Receptionist	Middle	Fluent	Fluent	43 of 47
Veronica Guzman	3rd	19	F	High School	Student	Middle	Fluent	Fluent	All
Monica Hernandez	2nd	38	F	Some College	City Parks & Recreation	Middle	Fluent	Convo	All

Name	Generation	Age	Sex	Education	Occupation	SES Category	English	Spanish	Years in CA
Ruth Jimenez	2nd	64	F	Some College	Retired (Secretary)	Middle	Fluent	Convo	50 of 64
Michael Jimenez	3rd	38	M	College	Architect	High	Fluent	Less C	37 of 38
Juan Lopez	1st	84	M	Jr. High or Less	Farmer & Maintenance	Lower	Fluent	Fluent	83 of 84
Marcus Lopez	2nd	57	M	College	Retired (manufacturing supervisor)	High	Fluent	Less C	All
Antonio Lopez	3rd	35	M	GED	Police Officer	Middle	Fluent	Convo	28 of 35
Beatrice Madrigal	2nd	60	F	Some College	Campus Monitor	Lower	English	Convo	All
Reyna Madrigal	3rd	35	F	College	Educator	Middle	Fluent	Less C	All
Celia Medina	2nd	52	F	Some College	Business Owner	Middle	Fluent	Fluent	All
Manny Medina	3rd	17	M	High School	Student	Middle	Fluent	Convo	All
Adele Mendoza	2nd	62	F	Some College	Health Assistant	Upper Middle	Fluent	Fluent	All
Ruben Mendoza	2nd	65	M	High School	Retired	Upper Middle	Fluent	Convo	All
Tyler Mendoza	3rd	41	M	Master's	Counselor	NR	Fluent	Convo	All
Maria Montes	1st	65	F	Jr. High/Less	Retired (packing house; small business owner)	NR	Fluent	Fluent	61 of 65
Lee Morelos	2nd	66	M	Some College	Business Executive	Upper Middle	Fluent	Convo	All
Lance Morelos	3rd	45	M	College	Restaurant Owner	Upper Middle	Fluent	Less C	All
Timothy Ponce	2nd	62	M	Master's	High School Principal	High	Fluent	Fluent	55 of 62
Gabriel Ponce	3rd	36	M	College	Sales	High	Fluent	Less C	All
Guillermo Ramirez	2nd	73	M	Doctoral Degree	Attorney	High	Fluent	Fluent	All
Pierre-Mecatl Ramirez	3rd	29	M	Master's	Law Student/Legal Advocate	Upper Middle	Fluent	Less C	All
Juan Ramos	1st	84	M	Jr. High or Less	Agriculture & Construction	Middle	None	Fluent	55 of 84
Moises Ramos	3rd	28	M	Master's	Counselor	Middle	Fluent	Convo	All
Tamara Rosenberg	2nd	47	F	College	Architect	High	Fluent	Fluent	All
Jillian Rosenberg	3rd	17	M	High School	Student	High	Fluent	Less C	All

Name	Generation	Age	Sex	Education	Occupation	SES Category	English	Spanish	Years in CA
Andrew Rosenberg	3rd	20	F	Some College	Student	High	Fluent	Less C	All
Marcel Ruiz	2nd	65	M	Some College	Architect	High	Fluent	Fluent	All
Amalia Ruiz	3rd	34	F	College	Architect	High	Fluent	Less C	All
Albert Schultz	2nd	65	M	Master's	School administrator	High	Fluent	Fluent	60 of 65
Rex Schultz	3rd	32	M	College	Auctioneer/ Auto Dealer	NR	Fluent	Less C	21 of 32
Yolanda Segura	2nd	48	F	Some College	Housewife	High	Fluent	Fluent	All
Davina Segura	3rd	22	F	College	Teacher	High	Fluent	Convo	All
Raymond Talavera	2nd	51	M	College	Sales	Upper Middle	Fluent	Fluent	All
Cristina Talavera	3rd	30	F	College	Chef	Middle	Fluent	Fluent	All
Mercedes Torres	1st	88	F	Jr. High or Less	Retired (Cannery)	Middle	None	Fluent	66 of 88
Juana Torres	2nd	64	M	Some College	Wastewater Collections	Upper Middle	Fluent	Fluent	All
Harry Torres	2nd	65	F	Some College	Retired	Middle	Fluent	Fluent	All
Ricardo (Rick) Torres	3rd	21	M	Some College	Student	Lower	Fluent	Convo	All
Rafael Treviño	2nd	59	M	Some College	Community Health Organization	Upper Middle	Fluent	Convo	All
Araceli Treviño	3rd	28	F	Some College	Community Health Organization	Middle	Fluent	Convo	All
Ramona Vargas	1st	77	F	Jr. High or Less	Cannery, Packing house, Housekeeping	Lower	Convo	Fluent	52 of 77
Elena Vargas	2nd	48	F	GED	Nutrition Educator	High	Fluent	Convo	All
Erica Vargas	3rd	31	F	Some College	Operations Manager	Middle	Fluent	Less C	All
Norma Vasconcelos	1st	65	F	Jr. High or Less	Restaurant Owner	NR	Less	Fluent	43 of 65
Gustavo Vasconcelos	2nd/3rd	47	M	College	Restaurant Owner	Middle	Fluent	Fluent	All
Paul Zagada	2nd	62	M	Doctoral Degree	Governmental Affairs Consultant	High	Fluent	Convo	All
Daniel Zagada	3rd	28	M	Doctoral Degree	Law student	Lower	Fluent	Less C	25 of 28

Notes

PREFACE

1. Some Mexican-origin Santa Barbarans are miffed at Fiesta being named "Old Spanish Days," as they feel this highlights the role of the Spanish conquistadors/colonizers and obscures the more indigenous aspects of the town's heritage.

2. Factfinder.census.gov accessed on Aug. 24, 2009.

CHAPTER 1

1. Four California propositions are noteworthy. (1) California Proposition 187, a 1994 ballot initiative billed as the "Save Our State" initiative, was designed to deny illegal immigrants social services, health care, and public education. It passed with 59 percent of the vote but was overturned by a federal court. (2) California Proposition 209 (1996) proposed to amend the state constitution to prohibit public institutions from taking race, sex, or ethnicity into account in hiring or admittance decisions. Supported by then University of California Regent Ward Connerly and opposed by pro–affirmative action groups, it was voted into law with 54 percent of the vote. The U.S. district court blocked enforcement of the measure and the ruling has subsequently been overturned. (3) California Proposition 227, "English Language in Public Schools," passed with 61 percent of the vote in 1998. Supporters believed that

English immersion is the best way to teach English to limited-English-proficient (often immigrant) children. Opponents believed that English-only detracts from necessary bilingual education and is an authoritarian measure that undervalues cultural diversity. (4) California Proposition 54, the "Racial Privacy Initiative," was on a 2003 special election ballot. It failed to pass with 63.9 percent against the measure. Had it passed, Proposition 54 would have prevented the state of California from using racial classifications in most of its business. Supporters of the measure said it was the first step towards a "color-blind" society, while opponents argued that it would make it more difficult for the state to provide services and identify and correct racial disparities.

2. The 1882 Chinese Exclusion Act, the Exclusion of Japanese and Koreans in 1907, and the Immigration Act of 1917 (All Asia Barred Zone) top the list of restrictionist acts during this era.

3. The Office of Management and Budget (OMB) determines federal standards for the reporting of "racial" and "ethnic" statistics. The OMB Directive 15 of 1977 described four races (i.e., American Indian or Alaskan Native, Asian or Pacific Islander, Black, and White) and two ethnic backgrounds (of Hispanic origin and not of Hispanic origin). Under this definition, Hispanics are an ethnic group of any race (American Anthropological Association 1997).

4. I use the terms "white," "non-Hispanic white," "Anglo," and "European-descent" interchangeably.

5. This is not to obscure the fact that Europe was not perceived as a single point of origin during the "Great Migration." European immigrants (especially of Southern and Eastern European origin) underwent a period of questioned assimilability, during which time some white ethnic groups distanced themselves from blacks and Native Americans in order to claim whiteness and attendant status privileges (Ignatiev 1995; Jacobson 1998; Roediger 1999).

6. As a brief comparison with U.S. blacks, audit studies show that blacks and Latinos both experience labor market discrimination (Bertrand and Mullainathan 2004; Cross et al. 1990; Turner, Fix, and Struyk 1991) as well as discrimination in housing (Oakland 2004; Yinger 1995). Despite these similarities, experiences of blacks and Latinos differ in important ways. Latinos are much more likely than blacks to intermarry with whites, a key sign of assimilation (Bean and Stevens 2003; Kalmijn 1998). Latinos are also more likely than blacks to experience residential integration upon achieving upward mobility (Emerson, Yancey, and Chai 2001).

7. Studies on families tend to focus on the nuclear family unit (two generations) (see Conley 2005; Hochschild 1997; Kibria 1993; Lareau 2003; Pattillo-McCoy 1999; Rubin 1994; Sherman 2009; Valdes 1996), usually in combination with another institution of interest, such as work, school, or community. One study that spans five family generation is conducted by a researcher who is also a family member (Chávez 2007).

8. Generation in the United States was a central influence in respondents' choice of racial/ethnic identification designations. First-generation immigrants claimed "Mexican" because of their nativity. Second-

generation members most often called themselves "Mexican American," some simply stated "Mexican," and a portion asserted "Chicano" if they were involved in the Chicano Movement. Members of the third generation either referred to themselves as "Mexican American," "Latino/a," or "Chicano/a" if a parent was active in the Chicano Movement, or detailed a specific, fractional answer such as "Mexican/Polish/Swedish/Russian/Jewish." The only regional variation was a higher likelihood of claiming "Chicano/a" among those who lived in southern California.

9. I use "Latino" and "Hispanic" as synonyms.

10. Asian suboptions include "Asian Indian," "Chinese," "Filipino," "Japanese," "Vietnamese," "Korean," "Other Asian (fill in box)," "Native Hawaiian," "Guamanian or Chamorro," "Samoan," "Other Pacific Islander (fill in box)."

11. Spanish/Hispanic/Latino suboptions include "Mexican/Mexican American/Chicano," "Puerto Rican," "Cuban," "Other Spanish/Hispanic/Latino."

12. Http://pewhispanic.org/ accessed on May 11, 2009.

13. New York follows second with nearly half (1.5 million) the legal permanent resident population that is hosted by California.

14. See John Ogbu (1990) for a discussion on "voluntary" and "involuntary" immigrants.

15. Mexican migration followed the "slow increase, spike, decrease" trend of national migration patterns through the 1990s to 2005. The spike of total immigration inflow (from all nations) was in 1999–2000 at 1.5 million. Since 2000, immigration from international origins has slowed to the rate of the mid-1990s (1.1 million in 2003). Mexican migration has held relatively steady at about one-third of the overall flow (Passel and Suro 2005: 6–7).

16. I set the minimum age for participation at seventeen. While I did not establish an age maximum, potential respondents were less inclined to participate as their age increased.

17. American Community Survey 2005–2007 Estimates. Factfinder.census.gov accessed on July 14, 2009.

18. Given that I was interviewing multiple members of a family, and not all families lived in close proximity to one another, I traveled outside of these regions to conduct some interviews.

19. In two cases, due to geographical distance, I conducted phone interviews.

20. This data comes from the 2004 American Community Survey located at http://factfinder.census.gov/home/saff/main.html?_lang=en accessed Feb. 18, 2008. My household income question was fixed-choice, one option of which was forty-five to sixty thousand dollars. I included the respondents who selected this option in the middle-class category.

21. See appendix A for a list of interviewees and some demographic information.

22. For studies of Mexican Americans that include lower- and working-class strata, see Barajas 2009; Bettie 2003; Chavez 1992; De Genova 2005; Dohan 2003; Grebler, Moore, and Guzman 1970; Griswold del Castillo 1984; Jiménez 2010; Murray 1997; Smith 2006b; Telles and Ortiz 2009; Vigil 1988.

23. I had a Spanish interview schedule and consent forms with me for those who preferred to speak with me in Spanish.

24. I used an inductive, grounded theory approach to analyzing the data (Glaser and Strauss 1967; Lofland and Lofland 1995; Strauss 1987). I utilized ATLAS.ti, a qualitative data analysis software program that allows researchers to code sections of interview material based on keywords and themes. Working with the data inductively, I analyzed the verbatim transcripts and coded emergent themes represented in my respondents' accounts. Coding categories

were not mutually exclusive; hence, any passage could be coded as more than one theme. To ensure measurement validity, I asked several differently worded questions targeting the same topic, and then assessed the agreement or disagreement among respondents' answers. I coded all of the interview material myself, eliminating the concern of intercoder reliability. I built my arguments from the coded interview data.

CHAPTER 2

1. I chose to showcase this family as an "ideal type" because they most clearly demonstrate the analytic category of "thinned attachment." There are ways in which this family is not typical, but given that each family has particularities, the commonalities between the Montes/Rosenberg family and other thinned attachment families far outweighed their differences. Two primary differences between this family and others in its analytic category are (1) that the second generation intermarried with a Jew (While three second-generation individuals married non-Hispanic whites, twenty-six married Mexican Americans or Latinos.); and (2) that the interviewees from this family discussed here are all female, inadvertently providing some gendered material that may not emerge from mixed-sex family lines. Note that I interviewed two third-generation members of the family (one male and one female). I utilize data from the female's interview here and I use data from both the female's and the male's interviews in chapter 7.

2. See tables 3.1, 3.2, and 3.3 in chapter 3.

3. Mexican American writer Sandra Cisneros wrote a short story entitled "Never Marry a Mexican." The first lines read, "Never marry a Mexican, my ma said once and always. She said this because of my father. She said this though she was Mexican too" (Cisneros 1992: 68).

4. In contrast to the Montes/Rosenberg family, other thinned attachment families demonstrate the pattern of feeling ashamed of their Mexican background until they achieve a middle- or upper-class standing. Drawing from a different family narrative, these families dodge (or deny) their Mexican identity until socioeconomic success is achieved, at which point it can be reclaimed and shame can be converted into pride. Two sociological principles are at work here. First is the fear that one's race will be a social, economic, or occupational handicap and so denial seems necessary. The second is the notion that success can "buy" racial pride and esteem, both for oneself and in the eyes of one's peers. This is akin to the idea that "money whitens," except that in this scenario of "buying" racial pride, socioeconomic advancement does not assume acceptance into white networks.

5. For an ethnographic account of the way seeing (or not seeing) structural barriers to educational, occupational, and financial success leads to different explanations for minority groups' failure or stymied progress in these arenas, see Bourgois 2002; MacLeod 2004.

6. For critiques of this conservative approach, see Fischer et al. 1996, and Brown 2003.

7. Unlike her younger siblings, she does not practice her father's religion (Judaism).

8. Gender plays a significant role in the racial identity development and cultural attachments or aversions in the three generations of females in the Montes/Rosenberg family depicted here. Jillian's brother, Andrew, desired to change the traditional gender ideologies that oppressed the female members of his extended family. Nonetheless, as a male, he held a less oppositional stance toward being half-Mexican than his sister. Gender is inextricably bound to racial experiences, as scholars have long pointed out (Bettie 2003; Collins 1991; King 1988; Segura 1995).

9. The range for second-generation Mexican Americans in my sample was from "junior high or less" to "doctoral degree."

10. All first-generation immigrants married Mexican nationals or, in one case, a Mexican American.

11. My sample is limited by a lack of class heterogeneity. The experiences of families that do not experience upward economic mobility but are poor and working class by the third generation in the United States most likely have decidedly different incorporation patterns and racial identity formulations than those presented here.

CHAPTER 3

1. See also Waters 1999; Zhou and Bankston 1998.

2. Several factors were used in assigning families to one pattern versus the other, so no one factor "determines" whether someone falls into one category or the other. I used Spanish language ability, Catholic observance, importance of Mexican traditions to daily life, and strength of family memory to assist in categorizing individuals and families as either "thinned attachment" or "cultural maintenance."

3. While Juan arrived in the United States as a young child in the early 1920s, most first-generation immigrants in my sample arrived between the late 1930s and the early 1960s.

4. Marcus, Juan's son, believes that his father did in fact face discrimination but that he either did not recognize the discrimination or it did not matter because he was so grateful to live a better life in the United States than he would have lived in Mexico.

5. His first wife (Antonio's mother) and his second wife are both Mexican American.

6. The Brown Berets were the militant vanguard of the Chicano Movement. The Brown Berets claimed a brown (nonwhite) identity, their pledge reading, "I wear the Brown Beret because it signifies my dignity and pride in the color of my skin and race." They protested injustices (especially police brutality) through mass mobilization and militant street action, declaring they would fight for Mexicans "by all means necessary." By 1970, the Brown Berets had over sixty chapters throughout the Southwest (Haney Lopez 2003: 18–19, 178). See also Muñoz (2007).

7. Many third-generation respondents spoke about positive experiences they had with multicultural education, but since Tony Lopez did not attend college, he had less educational experience to comment on.

8. The Spanish Conquest lasted through the 1780s, during which time the Spanish Franciscan missions under Father Junipero Serra in present-day California were constructed.

9. One drawback of my sampling strategy is that I interviewed only one side of every family. In Tony's case, I interviewed his paternal line because they fit my project's ethnic and generational profile, yet it was his maternal line that was more influential in his formative years. It is noteworthy that *both* of Tony's parents are of Mexican descent (his mother having immigrated as a child) and that his Mexican grandparents were very involved in his upbringing. This generational proximity to Mexico and close-knit relationship to his Mexican grandparents predisposed him to a cultural maintenance lifestyle.

10. This "ethnic conversion" arose in other families who similarly attempted to claim a higher or more "respectable" status in the racial hierarchy.

11. While Tony says he has not experienced discrimination, his father disagrees: "He's experienced it, 'cause he's told me. I think his experience with racism has been more professional. I don't think racism nowadays is where they call you 'wetback.'"

12. Coethnics frequently used Spanish knowledge to determine who qualified as an "authentic" or "true" Mexican American (Vasquez and Wetzel 2009).

13. While retaining Catholicism was highly valued by others, Tony emphasized this less.

14. The feminist movement was occurring at roughly the same time. While the feminist movement does not figure in the narratives of this three-generation male family, it was influential in the feminist consciousness of the second and third generations. Second- and third-generation respondents used the rhetoric of equality stemming from this movement (if implicitly) to justify their belief in gender equality and call for the dismantling of patriarchy and machismo.

15. See García (1997) for Chicana feminist narratives that describe the Chicano Movement as male dominated, with women as supporting actors who strove to carve out a niche for themselves and their needs.

16. Traits shared between cultural maintenance and thinned attachment at the third generation include citizenship, English monolingualism to English/Spanish bilingualism, middle-class status, and a college education (or trajectory toward it).

CHAPTER 4

1. I use "intermarriage," "out-marriage," and "exogamy" as synonyms. Similarly, I use "intramarriage," "in-marriage," and "endogamy" interchangeably.

2. For the purposes of this chapter, I consider "intramarriage" to include marriage with a Mexican-origin person or someone with Latin American heritage. One could argue that only marriage with another Mexican-origin person would

qualify as intramarriage, yet the quantity and kind of similar racial/ethnic and cultural experiences that my respondents claim that their Latino/a spouses shared gives me confidence in this designation.

3. My respondent pool does not include anyone who intermarried with someone of Asian, African, or Native American descent.

4. Rudy is technically a "1.5 generation" immigrant (he was born abroad and his migration occurred at an early age) (Portes and Rumbaut 2001: 24).

5. Most of the third generation was unmarried at the time of the interview, making future marriage tendencies an open question.

6. Chapter 7 addresses the way gender norms are changing through the generations.

7. Consider, for example, the variegation among the four waves of Cuban refugees that began in 1959 following the Cuban Revolution. The first two waves were largely wealthy, white, and educated/skilled whereas the latter two were poorer, darker, and less educated/skilled. Cuban success is largely based on the business entrepreneurship and socioeconomic advancement of the first two major waves of Cuban immigrants (Newby and Dowling 2007: 348).

CHAPTER 5

1. I write "pass" here with the understanding that Mexican Americans occupy an ambiguous and sometimes contradictory racial and ethnic position. According to modern-day racial categories, Mexican Americans are an ethnic group of any race. This contemporary understanding of the way Mexican Americans are mapped racially and ethnically can be used to substantiate claims of belonging to the white race, making the notion of "passing" as white both nonsensical and potentially inflammatory.

2. Some scholars consider this kind of "passing" as "taking the racial bribe," meaning that minorities sell out their political allegiance in favor of accepting racial benefits of whiteness (Guinier and Torres 2002).

3. The privilege of whiteness is not universal across classes. McDermott (2006) finds that skin-color privilege is limited among working-class whites.

4. My work is in agreement with Waters in that people often identify with their surname, especially if others use it to label them. Physical appearance also pushes identification. Some interviewees were content to be perceived as European-descent white and offered no correction when this happened.

5. A number of third-generation Mexican American U.S. citizens reported being stopped and vigorously interrogated at the U.S.-Mexico border by U.S. Immigration and Naturalization Services officials who presumed they were Mexican nationals.

6. The Chicano Movement (late 1960s to early 1970s) arose within the context of widespread social mobilization, spearheaded principally by the black struggle for civil rights. The thrust of the Chicano Movement was to agitate for equal citizenship and civil rights not only on paper but also in legal and everyday practice. Chicanos imported lessons on anticolonial protest tactics and organizing strategies from the Black Power movement, as well as, to a lesser extent, campus radicalism and student strikes from the Free Speech Movement occurring at the University of California–Berkeley (Haney Lopez 2003; Muñoz 2007).

7. This response of targets of discrimination decrying racists as "ignorant" was found in another study on Asians and Latinos (O'Brien 2008).

8. INS has been renamed under the Department of Homeland Security as "Immigration and Customs Enforcement."

CHAPTER 6

1. While Timothy found the idea of reverting to his given name in adulthood "kinda strange," another interviewee did exactly that in order to reclaim Mexican roots that had been jettisoned at the hand of a schoolteacher.

2. The Bracero Program was a guest worker program created in 1942 by the U.S. federal government in order to fill labor shortages brought on by World War II. The Bracero Program was terminated in 1964 although the tide had already turned against Mexican labor with the passage of the 1954 Operation Wetback program that called for Immigration and Naturalization Services sweeps of suspected illegal aliens. During this program, one million Mexican nationals (including some U.S. citizens of Mexican descent) were deported (Gutiérrez 1995; Montejano 1987).

3. Second-generation Mexican American women employ "pointed encouragement" not just for their daughters but also for their sons.

4. Hector Avila is the one interviewee who spent the majority of his primary and secondary education in a state other than California.

5. While this is a generalization and does not explain instances of school support, this phenomenon has been documented elsewhere (Davidson 1996; Ferguson 2000).

6. See table 6.1.

CHAPTER 7

1. For a critical analysis of the way Proposition 187 was designed to create legal divisions between "worthy" and "unworthy" immigrants, see Jacobson (2008).

2. In the words of Chicana poet and novelist Sandra Cisneros,

> There are green-eyed Mexicans. The rich blond Mexicans. The Mexicans with faces of Arab sheiks. The Jewish Mexicans. The big-footed-as-a-German Mexicans. The leftover-French Mexicans. The *chaparrito* compact Mexicans. The Tarahumara tall-as-desert-saguaro Mexicans. The Mediterranean Mexicans. The Mexicans with Tunisian eyebrows. The *negrito* Mexicans of double coasts. The Chinese Mexicans. The curly-haired, freckled-faced, red-headed Mexicans. The jaguar-lipped Mexicans. The wide-as-a-Tula-tree Zapotec Mexicans. The Lebanese Mexicans. (Cisneros 2002: 353)

CHAPTER 8

1. Gomez (2007: 4, 83–84) defines "off-white" status as the "*legal* construction of Mexicans as racially 'white' alongside the *social* construction of Mexicans as non-white and as racially inferior."

METHODOLOGICAL APPENDIX

1. Radio interview with musical artist Jewel conducted by Alice 97.3 FM on March 15, 2005.

2. "Equality feminism" is contrasted with "difference feminism" here.

Bibliography

Acevedo, Luz del Alba. 2001. *Telling to Live: Latina Feminist Testimonios*. Durham, NC: Duke University Press.

Acuna, Rodolfo. 2000. *Occupied America: A History of Chicanos*. New York: Longman.

Alba, Richard D. 1985. *Italian Americans: Into the twilight of Ethnicity*. Englewood Cliffs, NJ: Prentice-Hall.

———. 2006. "Mexican Americans and the American Dream." *Perspectives on Politics* 4: 289–96.

Alba, Richard D., and Victor Nee. 2003. *Remaking the American Mainstream: Assimilation and Contemporary Immigration*. Cambridge, MA: Harvard University Press.

Allport, Gordon W. 1979. *The Nature of Prejudice*. Cambridge, MA: Perseus Books.

Almaguer, Tomas. 1994. *Racial Fault Lines*. Berkeley: University of California Press.

American Anthropological Association. 1997. "Response to OMB Directive 15." Www.aaanet.org/gvt/ombdraft.htm.

Anderson, Benedict R. 1991. *Imagined Communities: Reflections on the Origin and Spread of Nationalism*. London: Verso.

Anderson, Margaret L., and Patricia Hill Collins. 2007. "Why Race, Class, and Gender Still Matter." Pp. 1–16 in *Race, Class, and Gender*, vol. 6, edited by M. L. Anderson and P. H. Collins. Belmont, CA: Wadsworth.

Anzaldúa, Gloria. 1987. *Borderlands/ La Frontera: The New Mestiza*. San Francisco: Spinsters/Aunt Lute.

Apple, Michael W. 1996. *Cultural Politics and Education*. New York: Teachers College Press.

Astin, Alexander W. 1993. "How Are Students Affected by Multiculturalism?" *Change* 25: 44.

Barajas, Manuel. 2009. *The Xaripu Community across Borders: Labor, Migration, Community, and Family*. Notre Dame, IN: University of Notre Dame Press.

Barajas, Manuel, and Elvia Ramirez. 2007. "Beyond Home-Host Dichotomies: A Comparative Examination of Gender Relations in a Transnational Mexican Community." *Sociological Perspectives* 50: 367–92.

Barlow, Andrew L. 2003. *Between Fear and Hope: Globalization and Race in the United States*. Lanham, MD: Rowman & Littlefield.

Barrera, Martha. 1991. "Cafe con Leche." Pp. 80–83 in *Chicana Lesbians: The Girls Our Mothers Warned Us About*, edited by C. Trujillo. Berkeley, CA: Third Woman Press.

Bean, Frank D., and Gillian Stevens. 2003. *America's Newcomers and the Dynamics of Diversity*. New York: Russell Sage Foundation.

Bean, Frank D., and Marta Tienda. 1987. *The Hispanic Population of the United States*. New York: Russel Sage Foundation.

Beauvoir, Simone de. 1978. *The Second Sex*. New York: Knopf.

Bellah, Robert Neelly. 1986. *Habits of the Heart: Individualism and Commitment in American Life*. New York: Harper & Row.

Bertrand, Marianne, and Sendhil Mullaina-than. 2004. "Are Emily and Greg More Employable Than Lakisha and Jamal? A Field Experiment on Labor Market Discrimination." *American Economic Review* 94: 991–1013.

Bettie, Julie. 2003. *Women without Class: Girls, Race, and Identity.* Berkeley: University of California Press.

Blauner, Bob. 1989. *Black Lives, White Lives: Three Decades of Race Relations in America.* Berkeley: University of California Press.

———. 2001. *Still the Big News: Racial Oppression in America.* Philadelphia: Temple University Press.

Bloemraad, Irene. 2006. *Becoming a Citizen: Incorporating Immigrants and Refugees in the United States and Canada.* Berkeley: University of California Press.

Blumer, Herbert. 1958. "Race Prejudice as a Sense of Group Position." *Pacific Sociological Review* 1: 3–7.

Bobo, Lawrence D., and Mia Tuan. 2006. *Prejudice in Politics: Group Position, Public Opinion, and the Wisconsin Treaty Rights Dispute.* Cambridge, MA: Harvard University Press.

Bonilla-Silva, Eduardo. 2003. *Racism without Racists: Color-Blind Racism and the Persistence of Racial Inequality in the United States.* Lanham, MD: Rowman & Littlefield.

———. 2004. "From Bi-racial to Tri-racial: Towards a New System of Racial Stratification in the USA." *Ethnic and Racial Studies* 27: 931–50.

Bourdieu, Pierre. 1984. *Distinction.* Translated by R. Nice. Cambridge, MA: Harvard University Press.

———. 1991. *Language and Symbolic Power,* edited by J. B. Thompson. Cambridge, MA: Harvard University Press.

Bourdieu, Pierre, and Jean-Claude Pas-seron. 1977. *Reproduction in Education, Society, and Culture,* vol. 5. Translated by R. Nice. Beverly Hills, CA: Sage.

———. 1979. *The Inheritors.* Translated by R. Nice. Chicago: University of Chicago Press.

Bourgois, Philippe. 2002. *In Search of Respect: Selling Crack in El Barrio.* Cambridge: Cambridge University Press.

Brown, Michael K. 2003. *Whitewashing Race: The Myth of a Color-Blind Society.* Berkeley: University of California Press.

Breuer, Josef, and Sigmund Freud. 1966. *Freud & Breuer: Studies on Hysteria.* New York: Avon Books.

Briggs, Jean. L. 1992. "Mazes of Meaning: How a Child and a Culture Create Each Other." *New Directions for Child and Adolescent Development* 1992, no. 58: 25–49.

Buriel, Raymond. 1987. "Ethnic Labeling and Identity among Mexican Americans." Pp. 134–52 in *Children's Ethnic Socialization: Pluralism and Development,* edited by J. S. Phinney and M. J. Rotheram. Beverly Hills, CA: Sage.

Butler, Judith. 1993. *Bodies That Matter: On the Discursive Limits of "Sex."* New York: Routledge.

———. 1995. "Subjection, Resistance, Resignification: Between Feud and Foucault." Pp. 229–50 in *The Identity in Question,* edited by J. Rajchman. New York: Routledge.

———. 1999. *Gender Trouble: Feminism and the Subversion of Identity.* New York: Routledge.

Carmichael, Stokely, and Charles V. Hamilton. 1992. *Black Power: The Politics of Liberation in America.* New York: Vintage Books.

Cerulo, Karen. 1995. *Identity Designs.* New Brunswick, NJ: Rutgers University Press.

Chapa, Jorge, and Belinda De La Rosa. 2004. "Latino Population Growth, Socioeconomic and Demographic Characteristics, and Implications for Educational Attainment." *Education and Urban Society* 36: 130–49.

Chávez, Christina. 2007. *Five Generations of a Mexican American Family in Los Angeles*. Lanham, MD: Rowman & Littlefield.

Chavez, Leo R. 2008. *The Latino Threat: Constructing Immigrants, Citizens, and the Nation*. Palo Alto, CA: Stanford University Press.

Chavez, Linda. 1992. *Out of the Barrio: Toward a New Politics of Hispanic Assimilation*. New York: Basic Books.

Cheng, Lucie, and Yen Espiritu. 1989. "Korean Businesses in Black and Hispanic Neighborhoods: A Study of Intergroup Relations." *Sociological Perspectives* 32: 521–34.

Chou, Rosalind, and Joe R. Feagin. 2008. *The Myth of the Model Minority: Asian Americans Facing Racism*. Boulder, CO: Paradigm Publishers.

Cisneros, Sandra. 1992. *Woman Hollering Creek and Other Stories*. New York: Vintage Books.

———. 2002. *Caramelo, o, Puro cuento*. New York: Knopf.

Cohen, Steven Martin, and Arnold M. Eisen. 2000. *The Jew Within: Self, Family, and Community in America*. Bloomington: Indiana University Press.

Collins, Patricia Hill. 1986. "Learning from the Outsider Within." *Social Problems* 33: 14–32.

———. 1991. *Black Feminist Thought*, vol. 2. New York: Routledge.

———. 2004. *Black Sexual Politics: African Americans, Gender, and the New Racism*. New York: Routledge.

Conley, Dalton. 1999. *Being Black, Living in the Red: Race, Wealth, and Social Policy in America*. Berkeley: University of California Press.

———. 2005. *The Pecking Order: A Bold New Look at How Family and Society Determine Who We Become*. New York: Vintage Books.

Cooley, Charles Horton. 1998. *On Self and Social Organization*. Chicago: University of Chicago Press.

Cornelius, Wayne A. 2002. "Ambivalent Reception: Mass Public Responses to the 'New' Latino Immigration to the United States." Pp. 165–84 in *Latinos: Remaking America*, edited by M. Suárez-Orozco and M. Paez. Berkeley: University of California Press.

Cornell, Stephen E., and Douglass Hartmann. 1998. *Ethnicity and Race: Making Identities in a Changing World*. Thousand Oaks, CA: Pine Forge Press.

Crenshaw, Kimberle, Neil Gotanda, Gary Peller, and Kendall Thomas. 1995. "Introduction." Pp. xiii-xxxii in *Critical Race Theory: The Key Writings That Formed the Movement*, edited by K. Crenshaw, N. Gotanda, G. Peller, and K. Thomas. New York: New Press.

Cross, Harry, Genevieve M. Kenney, Jane Mell, and Wendy Zimmermann. 1990. "Employer Hiring Practices: Differential Treatment of Hispanic and Anglo Job Seekers." Urban Institute Report, Washington, DC.

Davidson, Ann Locke. 1996. *Making and Molding Identity in Schools: Student Narratives on Race, Gender, and Academic Engagement*. Albany: State University of New York Press.

Davila, Arlene. 2008. *Latino Spin: Public Image and the Whitewashing of Race*. New York: New York University Press.

Davis, Mike. 2000. *Magical Urbanism: Latinos Reinvent the U.S. City*. New York: Verso.

Dawson, Michael C. 1994. *Behind the Mule: Race and Class in African-American Politics*. Princeton, NJ: Princeton University Press.

De Genova, Nicholas. 2005. *Working the Boundaries: Race, Space, and "Illegality" in Mexican Chicago*. Durham, NC: Duke University Press.

DeVault, Marjorie L. 1991. *Feeding the Family: The Social Organization of Caring as Gendered Work*. Chicago: University of Chicago Press.

Di Leonardo, Micaela. 1984. *The Varieties of Ethnic Experience*. Ithaca, NY: Cornell University Press.

Dohan, Daniel. 2003. *The Price of Poverty: Money, Work, and Culture in the Mexican-American Barrio*. Berkeley: University of California Press.

Du Bois, W. E. B. 1903. *The Souls of Black Folk*, edited by C. B. Johnson. New York: Simon & Schuster.

Duster, Troy. 2003. *Backdoor to Eugenics*. New York: Routledge.

Duster, Troy, et al. 1991. "Diversity Project." UC–Berkeley: Institute for the Study of Social Change, Berkeley, CA.

Edmonston, Barry, Sharon Lee, and Jeffrey Passel. 2003. "Recent Trends in Intermarriage and Immigration and Their Effects on the Future Racial Composition of the U.S. Population" Pp. 227–54 in *The New Race Question: How the Census Counts Multiracial Individuals*, edited by Joel Perlmann and Mary C. Waters. New York: Russell Sage Foundation.

Emerson, Michael, George Yancey, and Karen Chai. 2001. "Does Race Matter in Residential Segregation? Exploring the Preferences of White Americans." *American Sociological Review* 66: 922–35.

Erikson, Erik H. 1968. *Identity, Youth, and Crisis*. New York: Norton.

———. 1980. *Identity and the Life Cycle*. New York: Norton.

———. 1985. *Childhood and Society*. New York: Norton.

Fanon, Frantz. 1963. *The Wretched of the Earth*. New York: Grove.

———. 1967. *Black Skin, White Masks*. New York: Grove.

Feagin, Joe R. 1991. "The Continuing Significance of Race: Antiblack Discrimination in Public Places." *American Sociological Review* 56: 101–16.

Feagin, Joe R., and Jose Cobas. 2008. "Latinos/as and the White Racial Frame: The Procrustean Bed of Assimilation." *Sociological Inquiry* 78: 39–53.

Feagin, Joe R., and Melvin P. Sikes. 1994. *Living with Racism: The Black Middle-Class Experience*. Boston: Beacon.

Feliciano, Cynthia. 2001. "Assimilation or Enduring Racial Boundaries? Generational Differences in Intermarriage among Asians and Latinos in the United States." *Race and Society* 4: 27–45.

Ferguson, Ann Arnett. 2000. *Bad Boys: Public Schools in the Making of Black Masculinity*. Ann Arbor: University of Michigan Press.

Fischer, Claude, Michael Hout, Martin Sanchez Jankowski, Samuel Lucas, Ann Swidler, and Kim Voss. 1996. *Inequality by Design: Cracking the Bell Curve Myth*. Princeton, NJ: Princeton University Press.

Flores, William Vincent, and Rina Benmayor. 1997. *Latino Cultural Citizenship: Claiming Identity, Space, and Rights*. Boston: Beacon.

Flores-Gonzales, Nilda. 1999. "The Racialization of Latinos: The Meaning of Latino Identity for the Second Generation." *Latino Studies Journal* 10(3): 3–31.

Foley, Neil. 1997. *The White Scourge: Mexicans, Blacks, and Poor Whites in Texas Cotton Culture*. Berkeley: University of California Press.

Frankenberg, Ruth. 1993. *White Women, Race Matters: The Social Construction of Whiteness*. Minneapolis: University of Minnesota Press.

Fredrickson, George M. 1981. *White Supremacy: A Comparative Study in American and South African History*. New York: Oxford University Press.

Freire, Paolo. 1970. *Pedagogy of the Oppressed*. Translated by M. B. Ramos. New York: Continuum.

Freud, Sigmund. 1938. *The Basic Writings of Sigmund Freud*. New York: Modern Library.

——. 1961. *Civilization and Its Discontents*. New York: Norton.

Galvez, Alyshia. 2009. *Guadalupe in New York: Devotion and the Struggle for Citizenship Rights among Mexican Immigrants*. New York: New York University Press.

Gans, Herbert J. 1979. "Symbolic Ethnicity: The Future of Ethnic Groups in America." *Ethnic and Racial Studies* 2: 1–20.

——. 1992a. "Comment: Ethnic Invention and Acculturation: A Bumpy-Line Approach." *Journal of American Ethnic History* 12: 42–52.

——. 1992b. "Second-Generation Decline: Scenarios for the Economic and Ethnic Futures of the Post-1965 American Immigrants." *Ethnic and Racial Studies* 15: 173–92.

——. 1996. "Symbolic Ethnicity: The Future of Ethnic Groups and Cultures in America." Pp. 424–59 in *Theories of Ethnicity: A Classical Reader*, edited by W. Sollors. New York: New York University Press.

García, Alma M. 1997. *Chicana Feminist Thought: The Basic Historical Writings*. New York: Routledge.

Garcia, Maria Cristina. 1996. *Havana USA: Cuban Exiles and Cuban Americans in South Florida, 1959–1994*. Berkeley: University of California Press.

Gibson, Margaret. 1988. *Sikh Immigrants in an American High School*. Ithaca, NY: Cornell University Press.

Gillespie, Joanna Bowen. 1995. *Women Speak: Of God, Congregations, and Change*. Valley Forge, Pa.: Trinity Press International.

Gilroy, Paul. 1987. *"There Ain't No Black in the Union Jack": The Cultural Politics of Race and Nation*. London: Hutchinson.

——. 1993. *The Black Atlantic: Modernity and Double Consciousness*. Cambridge, MA: Harvard University Press.

Giroux, Henry A. 1992. *Border Crossings*. New York: Routledge.

Gitlin, Todd. 1995. *The Twilight of Common Dreams*. New York: Metropolitan Books.

Glaser, Barney G., and Anselm L. Strauss. 1967. *The Discovery of Grounded Theory: Strategies for Qualitative Research*. Hawthorne, NY: Aldine de Gruyter.

Goffman, Erving. 1959. *The Presentation of Self in Everyday Life*. Garden City, NY: Doubleday.

——. 1973. *The Presentation of Self in Everyday Life*. Woodstock, NY: Overlook Press.

Golash-Boza, Tanya. 2006. "Dropping the Hyphen? Becoming Latino(a)-American through Racialized Assimilation." *Social Forces* 85: 27–56.

——. 2009. "Immigration Raids in the U.S.: The Human Costs of This Scare Tactic." In *Latin American Studies Association XXVIII International Congress*. Rio de Janeiro.

Golash-Boza, Tanya, and William Darity Jr. 2008. "Latino Racial Choices: The Effects of Skin Colour and Discrimination on Latinos' and Latinas' Racial Self-Identifications." *Ethnic and Racial Studies* 31: 899–934.

Gómez, Laura E. 2007. *Manifest Destinies: The Making of the Mexican American Race*. New York: New York University Press.

Gonzalez, Roberto. 2008. "Born in the Shadows: The Uncertain Futures of the Children of Unauthorized Mexican Migrants." Dissertation, University of California–Irvine.

Gordon, Milton Myron. 1964. *Assimilation in American Life: The Role of Race, Religion, and National Origins*. New York: Oxford University Press.

Grebler, Leo, Joan W. Moore, and Ralph C. Guzman. 1970. *The Mexican-American People: The National Second Largest Minority*. New York: Free Press.

Griswold, Wendy. 1987. "The Fabrication of Meaning." *American Journal of Sociology* 92: 1077–1117.

Griswold del Castillo, Richard. 1984. *La Familia: Chicano Families in the Urban Southwest, 1848 to the Present*. Notre Dame, IN: University of Notre Dame Press.

Grogger, Jeffrey, and Stephen J. Trejo. 2002. "Falling Behind or Moving Up? The Intergenerational Progress of Mexican Americans." Public Policy Institute of California, San Francisco, CA.

Guinier, Lani, and Gerald Torres. 2002. *The Miner's Canary: Enlisting Race, Resisting Power, Transforming Democracy*. Cambridge, MA: Harvard University Press.

Gutiérrez, David. 1995. *Walls and Mirrors: Mexican Americans, Mexican Immigrants, and the Politics of Ethnicity*. Berkeley: University of California Press.

Hale, C. Jacob. 1998. "Consuming the Living, Dis(re)membering the Dead in the Butch/FtM Borderlands." *GLQ: A Journal of Lesbian and Gay Studies* 4: 311–48.

Hall, Stuart. 1996. "Introduction: Who Needs 'Identity'?" Pp. 1–17 in *Questions of Cultural Identity*, edited by Stuart Hall and Paul du Gay. Thousand Oaks, CA: Sage.

Hall, Stuart, David Morley, and Kuan-Hsing Chen. 1996. *Stuart Hall: Critical Dialogues in Cultural Studies*. London: Routledge.

Hamilton, Nora, and Norma Stoltz Chinchilla. 2001. *Seeking Community in a Global City: Guatemalans and Salvadorans in Los Angeles*. Philadelphia: Temple University Press.

Haney López, Ian. 1996. *White by Law: The Legal Construction of Race*. New York: New York University Press.

———. 2003. *Racism on Trial: The Chicano Fight for Justice*. Cambridge, MA: Belknap Press of Harvard University Press.

Harris, Angela. 2009. "Introduction: Economies of Color." Pp. 1–9 in *Shades of Difference: Why Skin Color Matters*, edited by E. Nakano Glenn. Palo Alto, CA: Stanford University Press.

Harris, Cheryl I. 1993. "Whiteness as Property." *Harvard Law Review* 106: 1707–91.

Heller, Celia Stopnicka. 1966. *Mexican American Youth: Forgotten Youth at the Crossroads*. New York: Random House.

Hochschild, Arlie Russell. 1983. *The Managed Heart: Commercialization of Human Feeling*. Berkeley: University of California Press.

———. 1989. *The Second Shift: Working Parents and the Revolution at Home*. New York: Viking.

———. 1997. *The Time Bind: When Work Becomes Home and Home Becomes Work*. New York: Metropolitan Books.

———. 2003. *The Commercialization of Intimate Life: Notes from Home and Work*. Berkeley: University of California Press.

Hochschild, Jennifer L. 1995. *Facing Up to the American Dream: Race, Class, and the Soul of the Nation*. Princeton, NJ: Princeton University Press.

Hondagneu-Sotelo, Pierrette. 1994. *Gendered Transitions: Mexican Experiences of Immigration*. Berkeley: University of California Press.

———. 2001. *Doméstica: Immigrant Workers Cleaning and Caring in the Shadows of Affluence*. Berkeley: University of California Press.

———. 2003. "Introduction." Pp. 3–19 in *Gender and U.S. Immigration*, edited by P. Hondagneu-Sotelo. Berkeley: University of California Press.

hooks, bell. 1994. *Teaching to Transgress*. New York: Routledge.

Huntington, Samuel P. 2004a. "The Hispanic Challenge." *Foreign Policy*. March/April.

———. 2004b. *Who Are We?* New York: Simon & Schuster.

Hurtado, Aida, and Carlos H. Arce. 1986. "Mexicans, Chicanos, Mexican Americans, or Pochos . . . Que somos? The Impact of Language and Nativity on Ethnic Labeling." *Aztlan* 17: 103–30.

Ignatiev, Noel. 1995. *How the Irish Became White*. New York: Routledge.

Inglehart, Ronald, and Pippa Norris. 2003. *Rising Tide: Gender Equality and Cultural Change around the World*. Cambridge: Cambridge University Press.

Jacobson, Matthew Frye. 1998. *Whiteness of a Different Color: European Immigrants and the Alchemy of Race*. Cambridge, MA: Harvard University Press.

Jacobson, Robin Dale. 2008. *The New Nativism: Proposition 187 and the Debate over Immigration*. Minneapolis: University of Minnesota Press.

Jiménez, Tomás R. 2004. "Negotiating Ethnic Boundaries." *Ethnicities* 4: 75–97.

———. 2008. "Mexican-Immigrant Replenishment and the Continuing Significance of Ethnicity and Race." *American Journal of Sociology* 113: 1527–67.

———. 2010. *Replenished Ethnicity: Mexican Americans, Immigration, and Identity*. Berkeley: University of California Press.

Jones-Correa, Michael. 1998. "Different Paths: Gender, Immigration, and Political Participation." *International Migration Review* 32: 326–49.

Kadi, Joanna. 1996. *Thinking Class: Sketches from a Cultural Worker*. Boston: South End Press.

Kalmijn, Matthijs. 1998. "Intermarriage and Homogamy: Causes, Patterns, Trends." *Annual Review of Sociology* 24: 395–421.

Kao, Grace. 1998. "Educational Aspirations of Minority Youth." *American Journal of Education* 3: 349–84.

Kao, Grace, and Marta Tienda. 1995. "Optimism and Achievement: The Educational Performance of Immigrant Youth." *Social Science Quarterly* 1: 1–19.

Kasinitz, Philip, John H. Mollenkopf, and Mary C. Waters. 2004. *Becoming New Yorkers: Ethnographies of the New Second Generation*. New York: Russell Sage.

Keefe, Susan E., and Amado M. Padilla. 1987. *Chicano Ethnicity*. Albuquerque: University of New Mexico Press.

Kelly, Mary, and Joane Nagel. 2002. "Ethnic Re-Identification: Lithuanian Americans and Native Americans." *Journal of Ethnic and Migration Studies* 28: 275–89.

Kibria, Nazli. 1993. *Family Tightrope: The Changing Lives of Vietnamese Americans*. Princeton, NJ: Princeton University Press.

———. 2002. *Becoming Asian American: Second-Generation Chinese and Korean American Identities*. Baltimore, MD: Johns Hopkins University Press.

King, Deborah. 1988. "Multiple Jeopardy, Multiple Consciousness." *Signs: Journal of Women in Culture and Society* 14: 42–72.

Kurien, Prema. 2003. "Gendered Ethnicity: Creating a Hindu Indian Identity in the United States." Pp. 151–73 in *Gender and U.S. Immigration*, edited by P. Hondagneu-Sotelo. Berkeley: University of California Press.

Lareau, Annette. 2002. "Invisible Inequality: Social Class and Childrearing in Black Families and White Families." *American Sociological Review* 67(5): 747–76.

———. 2003. *Unequal Childhoods: Class, Race, and Family Life*. Berkeley: University of California Press.

Lee, Jennifer, and Frank D. Bean. 2004. "America's Changing Color Lines: Immigration, Race/Ethnicity, and Multiracial Identification." *Annual Review of Sociology* 30: 221–42.

Lee, Sharon, and Barry Edmonston. 2006. "Hispanic Intermarriage, Identification, and U.S. Latino Population Change." *Social Science Quarterly* 87: 1263–79.

Levine, Lawrence W. 1988. *Highbrow/ Lowbrow: The Emergence of Cultural Hierarchy in America*. Cambridge, MA: Harvard University Press.

Lewin, Tamar. 2005. "Up from the Holler: Living in Two Worlds, at Home in Neither." Pp. 63–72 in *Class Matters*. New York: Times Books.

Lewis, Amanda E. 2003. *Race in the Schoolyard: Negotiating the Color Line in Classrooms and Communities*. New Brunswick, NJ: Rutgers University Press.

Lieberson, Stanley. 1980. *A Piece of the Pie: Blacks and White Immigrants since 1880*. Berkeley: University of California Press.

Lin, Jan. 1998. *Reconstructing Chinatown: Ethnic Enclave, Global Change*. Minneapolis: University of Minnesota Press.

Lipsitz, George. 2006. *The Possessive Investment in Whiteness: How White People Profit from Identity Politics*. Philadelphia: Temple University Press.

Lofland, John, and Lyn Lofland. 1995. *Analyzing Social Settings: A Guide to Qualitative Observation and Analysis*. Belmont, CA: Wadsworth.

Lopez, Nancy. 2003. "Disentangling Race-Gender Work Experiences: Second-Generation Caribbean Young Adults in New York City." Pp. 174–93 in *Gender and U.S. Immigration*, edited by P. Hondagneu-Sotelo. Berkeley: University of California Press.

Lucas, Samuel Roundfield. 1999. *Tracking Inequality: Stratification and Mobility in American High Schools*. New York: Teachers College Press.

Macias, Thomas. 2006. *Mestizo in America: Generations of Mexican Ethnicity in the Suburban Southwest*. Tucson: University of Arizona Press.

MacLeod, Jay. 2004. *Ain't No Makin' It: Aspirations and Attainment in a Low-Income Neighborhood*. Boulder, CO: Westview.

Maher, Frances A., and Mary Kay Thompson Tetreault. 1994. *The Feminist Classroom*. New York: Basic Books.

Mannheim, Karl. 1936. *Ideology and Utopia: An Introduction to the Sociology of Knowledge*. Translated by L. Wirth and E. Shils. New York: Harcourt Brace Jovanovich.

———. 1952. *Essays on the Sociology of Knowledge*. New York: Oxford University Press.

Marrow, Helen B. 2009. "New Immigrant Destinations and the American Colour Line." *Ethnic and Racial Studies* 32: 1037–57.

Marvasti, Amir B., and Karyn D. McKinney. 2004. *Middle Eastern Lives in America*. Lanham, MD: Rowman & Littlefield.

Massey, Douglas S., and Nancy A. Denton. 1993. *American Apartheid: Segregation and the Making of the Underclass*. Cambridge, MA: Harvard University Press.

Massey, Douglas S., Jorge Durand, and Nolan J. Malone. 2002. *Beyond Smoke and Mirrors: Mexican Immigration in an Era of Free Trade*. New York: Russell Sage Foundation.

Matute-Bianchi, Maria E. 1986. "Ethnic Identities and Patterns of School Success and Failure among Mexican-Descent and Japanese-American Students in a California High School: An Ethnographic Analysis." *American Journal of Education* 95: 233–55.

McAdam, Doug. 1988. *Freedom Summer*. New York: Oxford University Press.

McDermott, Monica. 2006. *Working-Class White: The Making and Unmaking of Race Relations*. Berkeley: University of California Press.

Mead, George Herbert. 1934. *Mind, Self, and Society: From the Standpoint of a Social Behaviorist*. Chicago: University of Chicago Press.

Menchaca, Martha. 1995. *The Mexican Outsiders: A Community History of Marginalization and Discrimination in California*. Austin: University of Texas Press.

Menjivar, Cecilia. 2000. *Fragmented Ties: Salvadoran Immigrant Networks in America*. Berkeley: University of California Press.

Millard, Ann V., and Jorge Chapa. 2004. *Apple Pie and Enchiladas: Latino Newcomers in the Rural Midwest*. Austin: University of Texas Press.

Mills, C. Wright. 1959. *The Sociological Imagination*. New York: Oxford University Press.

Montejano, David. 1987. *Anglos and Mexicans in the Making of Texas, 1836–1986*. Austin: University of Texas Press.

———. 1999. *Chicano Politics and Society in the Late Twentieth Century*. Austin: University of Texas Press.

Moraga, Cherríe, and Gloria Anzaldúa. 1983. *This Bridge Called My Back: Writings by Radical Women of Color*. New York: Kitchen Table Women of Color Press.

Morris, Edward W. 2005. "From 'Middle Class' to 'Trailer Trash': Teachers' Perceptions of White Students in a Predominantly Minority School." *Sociology of Education* 78: 99–121.

Moya, Paula. 2000. "Cultural Particularity versus Universal Humanity: The Value of Being *Asimilao*." In *Hispanics/Latinos in the United States*, edited by J. J. E. Gracia and P. De Greiff. New York: Routledge.

Muñoz, Carlos. 2007. *Youth, Identity, Power: The Chicano Movement*. London: Verso.

Murguia, Edward. 1975. *Assimilation, Colonialism, and the Mexican American People*. Austin: Center for Mexican American Studies, University of Texas at Austin.

———. 1982. *Chicano Intermarriage: A Theoretical and Empirical Study*. San Antonio, TX: Trinity University Press.

Murguia, Edward, and Tyrone Forman. 2003. "Shades of Whiteness: The Mexican American Experience in Relation to Anglos and Blacks." Pp. 63–79 in *White Out: The Continuing Significance of Racism*, edited by A. Doane and E. Bonilla-Silva. New York: Routledge.

Murray, Ixta Maya. 1997. *Locas*. New York: Grove.

Nagel, Joane. 1996. *American Indian Ethnic Renewal: Red Power and the Resurgence of Identity and Culture*. New York: Oxford University Press.

Newby, C. Alison, and Julie Dowling. 2007. "Black and Hispanic: The Racial Identification of Afro-Cuban Immigrants in the Southwest." *Sociological Perspectives* 50: 343–66.

Nieto, Sonia. 1999. "Multiculturalism, Social Justice, and Critical Teaching." In *Education Is Politics: Critical Teaching across Differences, K-12*, edited by I. S. C. Pari. Portsmouth, NH: Boynton/Cook.

Norris, Pippa, and Ronald Inglehart. 2001. "Women and Democracy: Cultural Obstacles to Equal Representation." *Journal of Democracy* 12: 126–40.

Oakes, Jeannie. 2005. *Keeping Track: How Schools Structure Inequality*. New Haven, CT: Yale University Press.

Oakland, Sentinel Fair Housing of. 2004. "Alameda Rental Audit." Sentinel Fair Housing of Oakland, Alameda, CA.

Obasagie, Osagie. 2009. "Playing the Gene Card? A Report on Race and Human Biotechnology." Center for Genetics and Society, Oakland, CA.

Oboler, Suzanne. 1995. *Ethnic Labels, Latino Lives: Identity and the Politics of (Re) presentation in the United States*. Minneapolis: University of Minnesota Press.

O'Brien, Eileen. 2008. *The Racial Middle: Latinos and Asian Americans Living beyond the Racial Divide*. New York: New York University Press.

Ochoa, Gilda. 2004. *Becoming Neighbors in a Mexican American Community: Power, Conflict, and Solidarity.* Austin: University of Texas Press.

Ogbu, John U. 1990. "Minority Status and Literacy in Comparative Perspective." *Daedalus* 119(2): 141–68.

———. 1994. "From Cultural Differences to Differences in Cultural Frame of Reference." In *Cross-Cultural Roots of Minority Child Development,* edited by P. Greenfield and R. C. Greenfield. Hillsdale, NJ: Erlbaum.

Ogbu, John U., and Signithia Fordham. 1986. "Black Students' School Success: Coping with the 'Burden of Acting White.'" *Urban Review* 18: 176–206.

Okamura, Jonathan Y. 1981. "Situational Ethnicity." *Ethnic and Racial Studies* 4: 452–65.

Oliver, Melvin L., and Thomas M. Shapiro. 1995. *Black Wealth/White Wealth: A New Perspective on Racial Inequality.* New York: Routledge.

Omi, Michael, and Howard Winant. 1994. *Racial Formation in the United States: From the 1960s to the 1990s.* New York: Routledge.

Orfield, Gary, and Chungmei Lee. 2007. "Historic Reversals, Accelerating Resegregation, and the Need for New Integration Strategies." Pp. 1–49. Los Angeles: University of California at Los Angeles Civil Rights Project/Proyecto Derechos Civiles.

Ortiz, Vilma. 1996. "The Mexican-Origin Population: Permanent Working Class or Emerging Middle Class?" Pp. 247–77 in *Ethnic Los Angeles,* edited by R. D. Waldinger and M. Bozorgmehr. New York: Russell Sage.

Pager, Devah, and Lincoln Quillian. 2005. "Walking the Talk? What Employers Say versus What They Do." *American Sociological Review* 70: 355–80.

Park, Robert Ezra, Ernest Burgess, and Roderick McKenzie. 1925. *The City.* Chicago: University of Chicago Press.

Passel, Jeffrey S., and Roberto Suro. 2005. "Rise, Peak, and Decline: Trends in U.S. Immigration, 1992–2004." Pew Hispanic Center, Washington, DC.

Pattillo-McCoy, Mary. 1999. *Black Picket Fences: Privilege and Peril among the Black Middle Class.* Chicago: University of Chicago Press.

Pedraza, Silvia. 1991. "Women and Migration: The Social Consequences of Gender." *Annual Review of Sociology* 17: 303–25.

———. 2007. *Political Disaffection in Cuba's Revolution and Exodus.* Cambridge: Cambridge University Press.

Perlmann, Joel. 2005. *Italians Then, Mexicans Now: Immigrant Origins and Second-Generation Progress, 1890 to 2000.* New York: Russell Sage Foundation.

Perry, Pamela. 2002. *Shades of White.* Durham, NC: Duke University Press.

Pew Hispanic Center. 2007a. "Changing Faiths: Latinos and the Transformation of American Religion." Washington, DC.

———. 2007b. "Statistical Portrait of the Foreign-Born Population in the United States." Washington, DC.

Portes, Alejandro, and Rubén G. Rumbaut. 1996. *Immigrant America: A Portrait.* Berkeley: University of California Press.

———. 2001. *Legacies: The Story of the Immigrant Second Generation.* Berkeley: University of California Press.

Portes, Alejandro, and Min Zhou. 1993. "The New Second Generation: Segmented Assimilation and Its Variants." *Annals of the American Academy* 74–96.

PPIC. 2002. Public Policy Institute of California, San Francisco.

Qian, Zhenchao, and José A. Cobas. 2004. "Latinos' Mate Selection: National Origin, Racial, and Nativity Differences." *Social Science Research* 33: 225–47.

Ragin, Charles C. 1987. *The Comparative Method: Moving beyond Qualitative and Quantitative Strategies.* Berkeley: University of California Press.

———. 1994. *Constructing Social Research: The Unity and Diversity of Method.* Thousand Oaks, CA: Pine Forge Press.

Reed, Deborah, Laura E. Hill, Christopher Jepsen, and Hans P. Johnson. 2005. "Educational Progress across Immigrant Generations in California." Public Policy Institute of California, San Francisco.

Reitz, Jeffery. 1998. *Warmth of the Welcome: The Social Causes of Economic Success for Immigrants in Different Nations and Cities.* Boulder, CO: Westview Press.

Rivadeneyra, Rocio. 2006. "Do You See What I See? Latino Adolescents' Perceptions of the Images on Television." *Journal of Adolescent Research* 21: 393–414.

Rodriguez, Clara E. 2000. *Changing Race: Latinos, the Census, and the History of Ethnicity in the United States.* New York: New York University Press.

Roediger, David R. 1999. *The Wages of Whiteness: Race and the Making of the American Working Class.* London: Verso.

Root, Maria P. P. 1996. "The Multiracial Experience: Racial Borders as a Significant Frontier in Race Relations." Pp. xiii–xxviii in *The Multiracial Experience: Racial Borders as the New Frontier,* edited by M. P. P. Root. Thousand Oaks, CA: Sage.

Rosenfeld, Michael. 2002. "Measures of Assimilation in the Marriage Market: Mexican Americans, 1970–1990." *Journal of Marriage and the Family* 64: 152–62.

———. 2009. *The Age of Independence: Interracial Unions, Same-Sex Unions, and the Changing American Family.* Cambridge, MA: Harvard University Press.

Roth, Wendy D. 2008. ""There Is No Racism Here": Understanding Latinos' Perceptions of Color Discrimination through Sending-Receiving Society Comparison." Pp. 205–34 in *Racism in the Twenty-first Century: An Empirical Analysis of Skin Color,* edited by R. Hall. New York: Springer Press.

Rubin, Lillian B. 1994. *Families on the Fault Line: America's Working Class Speaks about the Family, the Economy, Race, and Ethnicity.* New York: HarperCollins.

Ruddick, Sara. 1989. *Maternal Thinking.* New York: Ballantine.

Rumbaut, Rubén G., and Alejandro Portes. 2001. *Ethnicities: Children of Immigrants in America.* Berkeley: University of California Press.

Rytina, Nancy F. 2006. "Estimates of the Legal Permanent Resident Population and Population Eligible to Naturalize in 2004." Department of Homeland Security Office of Immigration Statistics.

Sanchez, George J. 1993. *Becoming Mexican American: Ethnicity, Culture, and Identity in Chicano Los Angeles, 1900–1945.* New York: Oxford University Press.

———. 1994. ""Go after the Women": Americanization and the Mexican Immigrant Woman, 1915–1929." Pp. 284–97 in *Unequal Sisters: A Multicultural Reader in U.S. Women's History,* edited by V. Ruiz and E. DuBois. New York: Routledge.

Sánchez-Jankowski, Martín. 1991. *Islands in the Street: Gangs and American Urban Society.* Berkeley: University of California Press.

Santa Ana, Otto. 2002. *Brown Tide Rising: Metaphors of Latinos in Contemporary American Public Discourse.* Austin: University of Texas Press.

Saporito, Salvatore, and Deenesh Sohoni. 2006. "Coloring outside the Lines: Racial Segregation in Public Schools and Their Attendance Boundaries." *Sociology of Education* 79: 81–105.

Schachtel, Ernst. 1959a. "The Development of Focal Attention and the Emergence of Reality." Pp. 251–78 in *Metamorphosis.* New York: Basic Books.

———. 1959b. "On Memory and Childhood Amnesia." Pp. 279–322 in *Metamorphosis*. New York: Basic Books.

Schoem, David, and Sylvia Hurtado (eds.). 2001. *Intergroup Dialogue*. Ann Arbor: University of Michigan Press.

Schoen, Robert, Verne E. Nelson, and Marion Collins. 1977. "Intermarriage Among Spanish Surnamed Californians, 1962–1974." *International Migration Review* 12: 359–369.

Schlesinger, Arthur M. Jr. 1998. *The Disuniting of America*. New York: Norton.

Schoen, Robert, Verne E. Nelson, and Marion Collins. 1977. "Intermarriage among Spanish-Surnamed Californians, 1962–1974." *International Migration Review* 12: 359–69.

Segura, Denise. 1986. "Chicanas and Triple Oppression in the Labor Market." Pp. 47–65 in *Chicana Voices: Intersections of Class, Race, and Gender*. Austin: Center for Mexican American Studies, University of Texas.

———. 1992. "Chicanas in White-Collar Jobs: 'You Have to Prove Yourself More.'" *Sociological Perspectives* 35: 163–82.

———. 1995. "Labor Market Stratification: The Chicana Experience." Pp. 111–46 in *Latina Issues: Fragments of Historia (Ella) (Herstory)*, edited by Antoinette S. López. New York: Garland.

Sherman, Jennifer. 2009. *Those Who Work, Those Who Don't: Poverty, Morality, and Family in Rural America*. Minneapolis: University of Minnesota Press.

Skerry, Peter. 1993. *Mexican Americans: The Ambivalent Minority*. New York: Free Press.

Smith, James P. 2003. "Assimilation across the Latino Generations." *American Economic Review* 93: 315–19.

Smith, Robert C. 2006a. "Immigrants and the Labor Market." *Journal of Labor Economics* 24: 203–33.

———. 2006b. *Mexican New York: The Transnational Lives of New Immigrants*. Berkeley: University of California Press.

Sohoni, Deenesh 2007. "Unsuitable Suitors: Anti-Miscegenation Laws, Naturalization Laws, and the Construction of Asian Identities." *Law & Society Review* 41: 587–618.

Solari, Cinzia. 2006. "Professionals and Saints: How Immigrant Careworkers Negotiate Gender Identities at Work." *Gender & Society* 20: 301–31.

Somers, Margaret R., and Gloria D. Gibson. 1994. Reclaiming the Epistemological 'Other': Narrative and the Social Constitution of Identity." Pp. 37–99 in *Social Theory and the Politics of Identity*, edited by Craig Calhoun. Cambridge, England: Blackwell.

Spencer, Steven J., Claude M. Steele, and Diane M. Quinn. 1999. "Stereotype Threat and Women's Math Performance." *Journal of Experimental Social Psychology* 35: 4–28

Sprague, Joey. 2005. *Feminist Methodologies for Critical Researchers: Bridging Differences*. Walnut Creek, CA: AltaMira.

Stack, Carol B. 1974. *All Our Kin: Strategies for Survival in a Black Community*. New York: Harper & Row.

Steele, Claude M., and Joshua Aronson. 1995. "Stereotype Threat and the Intellectual Test Performance of African Americans." *Journal of Personality and Social Psychology* 69: 797–811.

Steele, Claude M., Steven J. Spencer, and Joshua Aronson. 2002. "Contending with Group Image: The Psychology of Stereotype and Social Identity Threat." Pp. 379–440 in *Advances in Experimental Social Psychology*, edited by Mark P. Zanna. San Diego: Academic Press.

Steele, Shelby. 1990. *The Content of Our Character: A New Vision of Race in America*. New York: St. Martin's.

Steinberg, Stephen. 2001. *The Ethnic Myth: Race, Ethnicity, and Class in America*. Boston: Beacon.

Strauss, Anselm L. 1987. *Qualitative Analysis for Social Scientists*. Cambridge: Cambridge University Press.

Sudbury, Julia. 1998. *"Other Kinds of Dreams": Black Women's Organizations and the Politics of Transformation*. New York: Routledge.

Swidler, Ann. 1986. "Culture in Action: Symbols and Strategies." *American Sociological Review* 51: 273–386.

———. 2001. *Talk of Love: How Culture Matters*. Chicago: University of Chicago Press.

Takahashi, Jere. 1997. *Nisei/Sansei: Shifting Japanese American Identities and Politics*. Philadelphia: Temple University Press.

Tatum, Beverly Daniel. 1997. *"Why Are All the Black Kids Sitting Together in the Cafeteria?" A Psychologist Explains the Development of Racial Identity*. New York: Basic Books.

Telles, Edward, and Vilma Ortiz. 2009. *Generations of Exclusion: Mexican Americans, Assimilation, and Race*. New York: Russell Sage Foundation.

Thai, Hung. 1999. "'Splitting Things in Half Is So White'! Conceptions of Family Life and Friendship and the Formation of Ethnic Identity among Second Generation Vietnamese Americans." *Amerasia Journal* 25: 53–88.

Thernstrom, Stephan, and Abigail M. Thernstrom. 1997. *America in Black and White: One Nation, Indivisible*. New York: Simon & Schuster.

Thorne, Avril. 2000. "Personal Memory Telling and Personality Development." *Personality & Social Psychology Review* 4: 45–56.

Tobin, Joseph Jay, David Y. H. Wu, and Dana H. Davidson. 1989. *Preschool in Three Cultures: Japan, China, and the United States*. New Haven, CT: Yale University Press.

Turner, Margery Austin, Michael E. Fix, and Raymond J. Struyk. 1991. "Opportunities Denied, Opportunities Diminished: Racial Discrimination in Hiring." Urban Institute, Washington, DC.

Twine, France Winddance. 1997. "Brown-Skinned White Girls: Class, Culture, and the Construction of White Identity in Suburban Communities " Pp. 214–43 in *Displacing Whiteness: Essays in Social and Cultural Criticism*, edited by R. Frankenberg. Durham, NC: Duke University Press.

Valdes, Guadalupe. 1996. *Con Respeto: Bridging the Distances between Culturally Diverse Families and Schools*. New York: Columbia University Press.

Valdez, Zulema. 2006. "Segmented Assimilation among Mexicans in the Southwest." *Sociological Quarterly* 47: 397–424.

Valenzuela, Angela. 1999. *Subtractive Schooling: U.S.-Mexican Youth and the Politics of Caring*. Albany: State University of New York Press.

Vallejo, Jody Agius, and Jennifer Lee. 2009. "Brown Picket Fences: The Immigrant Narrative and 'Giving Back' among Mexican-Origin Middle Class." *Ethnicities* 9: 5–31.

Vasquez, Jessica M. 2005. "Ethnic Identity and Chicano Literature: How Ethnicity Affects Reading and Reading Affects Ethnic Consciousness." *Ethnic and Racial Studies* 28: 903–24.

———. 2010. "Blurred Borders for Some but Not 'Others': Racialization, Flexible Ethnicity, Gender, and Third-Generation Mexican American Identity." *Sociological Perspectives* 53: 45–71.

Vasquez, Jessica M., and Christopher Wetzel. 2009. "Tradition and the Invention of Racial Selves: Symbolic Boundaries, Collective Authenticity, and Contemporary Struggles for Racial Equality." *Ethnic and Racial Studies* 32: 1557–75.

Vigil, James Diego. 1988. *Barrio Gangs: Street Life and Identity in Southern California*. Austin: University of Texas Press.

Warren, Jonathan W., and France Winddance Twine. 1997. "White Americans,
the New Minority? Non-Blacks and
the Ever-Expanding Boundaries of
Whiteness." *Journal of Black Studies* 28:
200–218.

Waters, Mary C. 1990. *Ethnic Options:
Choosing Identities in America*. Berkeley:
University of California Press.

——. 1999. *Black Identities: West Indian
Immigrant Dreams and American Realities*. New York: Russell Sage Foundation.

Williams, L. Susan, Sandra Alvarez, and
Kevin Hauk. 2002. "My Name Is Not
Maria: Young Latinas Seeking Home
in the Heartland." *Social Problems* 49:
563–84.

Weber, Max. 1978. *Economy and Society: An
Outline of Interpretive Sociology*, edited
by G. Roth and C. Wittich. Berkeley:
University of California Press.

Wedeen, Lisa. 1999. *Ambiguities of Domination: Politics, Rhetoric, and Symbols in
Contemporary Syria*. Chicago: University
of Chicago Press.

Weis, Lois, and Michelle Fine. 2005.
"Beyond Silenced Voices: Class, Race,
and Gender in United States Schools."
Albany: State University of New York
Press.

Weiss, Robert. 1994. *Learning from Strang-
ers*. New York: Free Press.

West, Candace, and Sarah Fenstermaker.
1995. "Doing Difference." *Gender &
Society* 9: 8–37.

Wilson, William J. 1987. *The Truly Disadvantaged: The Inner City, the Underclass,
and Public Policy*. Chicago: University of
Chicago Press.

Winant, Howard. 2000. "Race and Race
Theory." *Annual Review of Sociology*
169–85.

Yamane, David. 2001. *Student Movements
for Multiculturalism*. Baltimore, MD:
Johns Hopkins University Press.

Yinger, John. 1995. *Closed Doors, Oppor-
tunities Lost: The Continuing Cost of
Housing Discrimination*. New York:
Russell Sage Foundation.

Yuval-Davis, Nira. 1997. *Gender and Nation*.
Thousand Oaks, CA: Sage.

Zavella, Patricia. 1993. "Feminist Insider
Dilemmas: Constructing Ethnic Identity
with 'Chicana' Informants." *Frontiers* 13:
53–76.

Zhou, Min, and Carl L. Bankston. 1998.
*Growing up American: How Viet-
namese Children Adapt to Life in the
United States*. New York: Russell Sage
Foundation.

Zhou, Min, Jennifer Lee, Jody Agius
Vallejo, Rosaura Tafoya-Estrada,
and Yang Sao Xiong. 2008. "Success
Attained, Deterred, and Denied:
Divergent Pathways to Social Mobility
in Los Angeles's New Second Generation." *Annals of the American Academy*
620: 37–61.

Zimmerman, Don. 1978. "Ethnomethodol-
ogy." *American Sociologist* 13: 6–15.

Index

1st generation Mexican Americans: age range of respondents, 26; citizenship, 235; definition, 23; discrimination, 135–136, 141, 144, 149, 159–160; "dual frame of reference," 144, 149, 160; educational aspirations, 170–173, 191–192; educational attainment, 60, 67, 167–168; girls' education, 172–173; gratitude toward United States, 67, 71–72, 85; intermarriage/exogamy, 73; intramarriage/endogamy, 65; marriages, 92, 264n10; parenting strategies, 170–173; racial pride, 149; residential patterns, 141; segmented assimilation theory, 10–11; self-definition, 262n8; Spanish language skills, 78; work ethic, 72

2nd generation Mexican Americans: activism, 43, 85, 136, 160, 161; age range of respondents, 26; Chicano Movement, 86–87; civil rights movement, 136; cultural citizenship, 72, 160; cultural maintenance, 86–87, 90; definition, 23; discrimination, 136, 140–141, 144, 148, 149–150, 156–158, 160; "double consciousness," 149; education, experiences of, 179, 191, 232; education, healthy skepticism toward, 177–180; education, pointed encouragement of, 180–182, 192, 267n3.ch6; education, wholehearted encouragement of, 176–177; educational aspirations, 171, 174–182, 191–192; educational attainment, 60, 167–168, 192, 264n9; English language acquisition, 41; gender equality, 265n14; higher education/college, 169–170; home ownership, 140–141; intermarriage/exogamy, 73, 79, 263n1; intramarriage/endogamy, 65; marriage, 92–93; parenting strategies, 176–182; perception of racism, 136; racial pride, 149–150; racialization despite assimilation, 237; residential patterns, 141; responses to racial slights and exclusions, 43; segmented assimilation theory, 10–11; self-definition, 262n8; Spanish language skills, 36, 78, 79, 165

3rd generation Mexican Americans, 194–228; activism, 160; affirmative action programs, 187; age range of respondents, 26; American way of life, 204–205; antimachismo sentiments, 118, 221–225; antipatriarchal sentiments, 81; assimilation, 47–48, 225; bumpy-line assimilation, 122; camaraderie among, 219–220; civil rights movement, 227; confidence about American citizenship, 145; cultural citizenship, 160; cultural maintenance, 80, 89; definition, 23; discrimination, 141, 144, 148, 149–150, 156–158, 160; double bind, 227–228; educational aspirations, 182–189, 191–192; educational attainment, 60, 167–168, 192; essentialization of racial identity, 220–221; flexible ethnicity, 200–208; gender dynamics/ideologies, 221–225; gender equality, 265n14; higher education/college, 187; identity crisis, 47–48, 226; inherent hybridity, 226; intermarriage/exogamy, 73; intramarriage/endogamy, 65; marriage patterns, 89, 266n5.ch4; Mexican cultural identification, 58; Mexican immigrants, 208–209, 217; multicultural education, 265n7; multiculturalism, 227, 233; ongoing immigration, 208–209; population, 194; racial authenticity contests, 213–225;

3rd generation Mexican Americans (*continued*): racial/ethnic identity, 193, 194–200, 226, 228, 262n8; racial in between-ness/liminality, 200–208; racial options, 7; racial pride, 149–151; racialization, 208–213, 225; racialization despite assimilation, 237; representation of Hispanic community, 80–81; residential patterns, 141; school experiences, 191; school tracking systems, 182–183, 232; skin color/phenotype, 58, 228; Spanish language skills, 36, 78–79, 215; symbolic ethnicity, 109, 207–208, 226; thinned attachment, 89; upward mobility, 47–48
4th generation Mexican Americans, intermarriage/exogamy and, 93

acculturation: Americanization programs (1915-1929), 66, 85; diverse possibilities of, 1, 2; English language acquisition, 41, 165; food, 165–166; Gans on, Herbert, 1, 2; human capital, 9; paradigms of (*see* cultural maintenance; thinned attachment); selective acculturation, 87–88; thinned attachment, 37. *See also* assimilability; assimilation
Acevedo, Tina (pseudonym), 179, 255, 258
Acevedo, Tom (pseudonym), 134–135, 258
activism: 2nd generation Mexican Americans, 43, 85, 136, 160, 161; 3rd generation Mexican Americans, 160
"additive discrimination," 159
affirmative action: 3rd generation Mexican Americans, 187; educational attainment, 187–189; employment opportunities, 79–80, 84, 86; necessity for, 242; Proposition 209 (California, 1996), 187–188
Alba, Richard, 239
American Community Survey (2007), 21
American Dream, 166–170; assimilationist perspective, 170; education, 166–170; educational attainment, 95; individualism, 41; Latinos, 160; Montes/Rosenberg family, 40; Morelos on, Lance, 169; Ramirez on, Guillermo, 168–169; Treviño on, Rafael, 166; work ethic, 40

Americanization programs (1915-1929), 66, 85
"Anglo" (the term), 262n4
antimachismo sentiments, 118, 221–225
antimiscegenation laws, 91
antipatriarchal sentiments, 81
Anzaldúa, Gloria, 200
appropriated memories, 4, 15
Arizona, Hispanic population, 20
assimilability: European immigrants, 262n5; Mexican immigrants, 2–3, 4, 6, 7, 21–22, 237
assimilation, 6–15, 237–244; 3rd generation Mexican Americans, 47–48, 225; accommodation without assimilation, 9; barriers to, 241–242; bumpy-line assimilation (*see* bumpy-line assimilation); cultural identification, 24; cultural maintenance, 65; disposal of minority culture, 241; downward assimilation, 6, 240–241; family memories, 233; gender, 240; identity crisis, 47–48; incorporation trajectories, 11; incremental/intergenerational nature, 10, 239; intermarriage/exogamy, 60, 91, 120, 121–122, 262n6; labor market needs, 242; Latino threat narrative, 3; linear direction, 10–11; marriage, 121; Mexican Americans, 231; "new" assimilation theory, 239–240; political assimilation, 139; race, 240; racial identity politics, 241–242; racial progressivism, 120; racial self-perception, 4; racialization, 7–8, 14–15, 159, 189–193; segmented assimilation (*see* segmented assimilation); socioeconomic advancement, 24; straight-line assimilation, 8–9, 62, 239; structural assimilation, 62–63, 87, 94; theories of, 8–11, 123, 237–244; thinned attachment, 65; upward mobility, 7
Avila, Alfonzo (pseudonym), 258
Avila, Hector (pseudonym), 183–184, 258, 267n4
Avila, Rosa (pseudonym), 258

Barlow, Andrew L., 137
Beauvoir, Simone de, 252
Benavidas family (pseudonym), 64, 66, 82–84
Benavidas, Benjamin (pseudonym), 83–84, 258

Benavidas, Caitlyn (pseudonym): affirmative action, 84; demographic information, 258; educational attainment, 84; employment opportunities, 84; gendered division of labor in the household, 224–225; passing as non-Hispanic white, 209–210; racial in between-ness/liminality, 203; racialization, 209–210; self-definition, 196

Benavidas, Melissa (pseudonym), 64

Bettie, Julie, 51, 201, 213

biculturalism: assimilationist orientation, 48; child rearing, 115; employment opportunities, 80, 85; marriage preferences, 113, 116

bilingualism, 66, 80, 85, 113

blacks, 161–162, 262n6

Blauner, Robert, 18

Bracero Program (1942–1964), 18, 67, 172, 267n2.ch2

Brown Berets: Lopez, Marcus, 68, 69, 72, 85, 86, 178; MEChA (Movimiento Estudiantil Chicano de Aztlán), 69; pledge, 265n6

Brown v. Board of Education, 174

"browning of America," 3, 16

bumpy-line assimilation, 232–237; 3rd generation Mexican Americans, 122; cultural destination, 239; cultural repertoires, 202; definition, 9–10; factors influencing, 239; Gans, Herbert, 92, 122, 239; incorporation trajectories, 239–240; Lopez family, 66; marriage, 28, 92, 121–123; Mexican Americans, 11; racial authenticity, yardsticks for, 214; racial/ethnic identity, 239–240; skin color/phenotype, 202

California: Hispanic population, 20, 21, 23, 24; Los Angeles County, 24; LPR (legal permanent residents) population, 21; Mexican immigrants, 243; Proposition 54 (2003), 261n1.ch1; Proposition 187 (1994), 261n1.ch1; Proposition 209 (1996), 187–188, 189, 261n1.ch1; Proposition 227 (1998), 261n1.ch1; propositions defining racial and ethnic boundaries, 2; San Diego, 218–219; San Francisco Bay Area, 24; Santa Barbara County, 24; Spanish Conquest, 265n8; statehood (1850), 18; undocumented immigrants, 21

Castillo, Dillon (pseudonym), 170, 199, 215–216, 258

Castillo, Ruby (pseudonym), 171–172, 258

Catholicism: conversion away from, 44; cultural maintenance, 65, 73, 83; distaste for, dwindling devotion to, 56, 59; divorce, 44; gender dynamics/ideologies, 52; gender equality, 52; Mexican culture, 44, 56, 59; Mexican identity, sense of, 59, 83

Chávez, César, 69, 84, 186

Chavez, Leo, 3

Chicana feminist narratives, 265n15

"Chicano/a" (the term), 136, 195, 196–199, 227

Chicano Movement, 68–75, 136–139; 2nd generation Mexican Americans, 86–87; Benavidas, Benjamin, 84; in Chicana feminist narratives, 265n15; children of activists, 197; goals, 136, 137, 255; influences on, 266n6.ch5; Lopez, Juan, 71; Lopez, Marcus, 66, 68, 69, 71, 86; as performance, 86; racial politics of, 197–198; as response to racial slights and exclusions, 43; self-identification of participants in, 262n8; social consciousness cultivated by, 137–139, 144–145, 161; spirit of self-determination, 136–137; Talavera, Raymond, 139; thrust of, 266n6.ch5; Treviño, Rafael, 137–138, 139. *See also* Brown Berets

Cisneros, Sandra, 263n3, 267n2.ch7

citizenship: 1st generation Mexican Americans, 235; Mexican Americans, 17, 18, 24; race, 2; racial/ethnic identity, 235

civil rights, race and, 2

civil rights movement: 2nd generation Mexican Americans, 136; 3rd generation Mexican Americans, 227; Benavidas family, 82–84; cultural maintenance, 65, 82, 89–90; Lopez family, 69–71; multicultural education, 70; multicultural ideology, 90, 231; race consciousness, 82–83; racial identity formation, 86, 90; racial pride, 69–70; thinned attachment, 82; upward mobility of Mexican Americans, 90

class. *See* social class

Colorado, Hispanic population, 20
complimentary othering, 212–213
Connecticut, Hispanic population, 20
Connerly, Ward, 261n1.ch1
Contreras family (pseudonym), 113–116; bicul-
    turalism, 115, 116; cultural maintenance,
    113; distancing from patriarchy, 107; gender
    influence on cultural attachments, 120;
    Mexican culture, 116; nanny Tia Carlotta,
    114–115; Spanish language skills, 115; whole-
    hearted encouragement of education, 177
Contreras, Milo (Ishmael) (pseudonym),
    113–117; demographic information, 258;
    friend Sidney, 154; ideological resistance
    to discrimination, 148; maintenance of
    Spanish language, 115; out-marriage with
    non-Hispanic white woman, 106, 113–114,
    116; patriarchal home, 117; proving
    oneself through overachievement, 152,
    153–155; racial awareness, 116; University
    of California Los Angeles Law School,
    154; wholehearted encouragement of
    education, 176–177
Contreras, Renata (pseudonym), 117–121; bicul-
    turalism and bilingualism, 113; demographic
    information, 258; father's wholehearted
    encouragement of education, 176, 177;
    machismo, experiences with, 118; marriage/
    dating preference for non-Hispanics, 113,
    117–119, 120–121; Mexican values, culture, 115,
    119–120, 120–121; movement from cultural
    maintenance to thinned attachment, 106;
    passing as non-Hispanic white, 202, 217;
    Spanish language skills, 214–215
Cortés, Hernan, 74
critical race theory, law and, 12–13
"cross discrimination," 134–135, 159
Cuban refugees, waves of, 266n7.ch4
cultural citizenship, 68, 72, 160
cultural forgetting, 74, 75
cultural identification, socioeconomic
    advancement and, 24
cultural maintenance, 64–90; 2nd genera-
    tion Mexican Americans, 86–87, 90; 3rd
    generation Mexican Americans, 80,
    89; acceptance by non-Hispanics, 81;

assimilation, 65; Benavidas family, 64, 66,
    82; categorization of families as, 264n2;
    Catholicism, 65, 73, 83; "Chicano/a" (the
    term), 227; civil rights movement, 65, 82,
    89–90; Contreras family, 113; definition,
    4, 64–65; differences between thinned
    attachment and, 88; discrimination,
    161; educational attainment, 189; factors
    influencing, 82, 83, 85, 88, 231–232;
    family memories, 65; gender dynamics/
    ideologies, 65; as "ideal type" incorpora-
    tion trajectories, 89; intermarriage/
    exogamy, 92; intramarriage/endogamy,
    65, 72, 79, 83; Lopez family, 66; marriage,
    91, 92, 231–232; ongoing immigration,
    116; political assimilation, 139; Ponce
    family, 107, 120; progressive ideals, 81;
    racial pride, 74; residence in an ethnic
    enclave, 83, 115–116; residential patterns,
    88–89; selective acculturation compared
    to, 88; skin color/phenotype, 58, 65;
    Spanish language skills, 78, 79; structural
    assimilation, 87; surnames identified
    with Latinos, 65; thinned attachment
    compared to, 62, 64–66, 87–90, 226–227,
    265n16; upward mobility, 61, 87, 94. See
    also ethnic re-identification/resurgence
cultural transmission: downward transmis-
    sion, 109, 121; intergenerational transfer
    of knowledge, 15, 233; intramarriage/
    endogamy, 121; model of, 235–246; ongo-
    ing immigration, 116; survival mode of
    parenting, 35–36; upward transmission,
    28, 102, 103; women, 75, 78

Davis, Mike, 226
deportation, 66–67, 71, 85, 90, 157
Diaz, Samantha (pseudonym): demographic
    information, 258; ethnic re-identification/
    resurgence, 104–105, 106; fiancé Roberto,
    104; internalized inferiority, 131; physical
    appearance, 130–131; proving oneself
    through overachievement, 155–156; racial
    in between-ness/liminality, 201–202;
    Spanish language skills and Mexican
    authenticity, 215; surname, 130–131

Diaz, Sergio (pseudonym), 258

discrimination, 127–162; 1st generation Mexican Americans, 135–136, 141, 144, 149, 159–160; 2nd generation Mexican Americans, 136, 140–141, 144, 148, 149–150, 156–158, 160; 3rd generation Mexican Americans, 141, 144, 148, 149–150, 156–158, 160; "additive discrimination," 159; avoidance strategies, 133–134, 144, 145–146 (*see also* passing as non-Hispanic white); behavioral resistance to, 151–156; blacks, 161–162; "cross discrimination," 134–135, 159; cultural maintenance, 161; definition, 128; demands for equality, 156–158; denying experiences of, 51, 67, 77, 135–136, 264n4.ch3, 265n11; distancing from blacks, 162; experiences across generations, common, 128–135; experiences across generations, variable, 135–143; generational responses to, 232; group status position, 156; home ownership, 136; housing segregation, 127–128, 262n6; ideological resistance to, 146–148; institutional discrimination, 182; labor markets, 262n6; Latino threat narrative, 156–157; by Latinos, 262n6; Mexican-inferiority ideology, 153; middle-class Mexican Americans, 27, 76–77; negative stereotypes, 151–153; overlap of class- and race-based, 158; passing as non-Hispanic white, 129, 266n1, 266n2; perception of, 136; post-civil rights era, 182; prejudice compared to, 128; professional invisibility, 142–143; proving oneself through overachievement, 151–156; racial/ethnic identity choices, 162; racial performance, 133–134; racial pride as protection against, 149–151; racial profiling, 132–133, 159; racialization, 161–162, 209; repositioning pathology with its producers, 148; residence in an ethnic enclave, 141; resistance across generations, 144–158; shopowner tailgating, 131–132, 156–158, 159; sites of, 159; skin color/phenotype, 128–131; social class, 26, 159; spatial mobility, 136; surnames, 127–128, 129–131; thinned attachment, 161; upward mobility, 140–143

distilled ethnicity, 46–47, 58

Dos Santos, Auscencio (Ceño) (pseudonym), 204–205, 219, 223–224, 258

Dos Santos, Carmina (pseudonym): demographic information, 258; "micro-aggressions" by, 217; passing as non-Hispanic white, 204, 216–217; self-definition, 196–197, 198

Dos Santos, Luna (pseudonym), 258

"double consciousness," 149

downward assimilation, 6, 240–241

downward mobility, 9

education: "acting white," 53; American Dream, 166–170; higher education/college (*see* higher education/college); Montes/Rosenberg family, 41–43; racial identity formation, 163; racialization in schools (*see* racialization in schools); realization of race, 164–166; socialization, 166

educational aspirations, 170–189; 1st generation Mexican Americans, 170–173, 191–192; 2nd generation Mexican Americans, 171, 174–182, 191–192; 3rd generation Mexican Americans, 182–189, 191–192; gender, 171, 172–173, 180–181; healthy skepticism toward education, 177–180; patriarchal ideals, 172–173; pointed encouragement of schooling, 180–182, 192, 267n3.ch6; wholehearted encouragement of, 176–177. *See also* racialization in schools

educational attainment, 166–170; 1st generation Mexican Americans, 60, 67, 167–168; 2nd generation Mexican Americans, 60, 167–168, 192, 264n9; 3rd generation Mexican Americans, 60, 167–168, 192; affirmative action, 187–189; American Dream, 95; Benavidas, Caitlyn, 84; cultural maintenance, 189; income, 168; intergenerational progress, 167–168, 192; Latinos, 192; low expectations for minority students, 171, 178–180, 182, 183–185; parents' education, 168; Proposition 209 (California, 1996), 187–188; racialization despite assimilation, 213; social class, 167–168, 171–172, 192; thinned attachment, 60, 189. *See also* racialization in schools employment opportunities: affirmative action, 79–80, 84, 86; biculturalism, 80, 85; bilingualism, 80, 85; race, 80, 86, 188; skin color/phenotype, 129–130; surnames, 130

English as a Second Language (ESL) classes, 183–184

English language skills, 41, 96–97, 165. *See also* bilingualism

ethnic conversion, 76

ethnic enclaves, residence in, 83, 115, 141

"ethnic option": definition, 6; Lopez, Tony, 76; Mexican Americans, 7, 208; Mexican immigrants, 21; skin color/phenotype, 129, 201; surnames, 201

ethnic pride, family memories and, 84

ethnic re-identification/resurgence, 94–106; child rearing, 102; Diaz, Samantha, 104–105, 106; higher education/college, 142; intramarriage/endogamy, 94–106, 121; Madrigal, Beatrice, 103; Madrigal, Reyna, 97–98, 100–101, 120–121, 142; Madrigal family, 102–103; risk of traditional ways dying out, 103; Schultz, Albert, 111; Segura, Yolanda, 105–106; structural assimilation, 94; women, 104

"ethnicity" (the term), 5

ethnicity: distilled ethnicity, 46–47, 58; flexible ethnicity (*see* flexible ethnicity); food, 50; Hispanics as an, 19–20, 261n3; Mexican Americans as an, 4–5, 6, 195, 231, 266n1; race compared to, 5–6; racialized ethnicity, 5, 195; sentimental ethnicity, 207; situational ethnicity, 198, 201; social context, 198; socially constructed nature, 4–5; statistical reporting standards, 261n3; symbolic ethnicity (*see* symbolic ethnicity)

"European descent" (the term), 262n4

European immigrants, 8–9, 262n5

exogamy. *See* intermarriage/exogamy

families: cultural maintenance families (*see* cultural maintenance); gender dynamics/ ideologies in Mexican families, 36–37; identity development, 15; intergenerational family knowledge, upward flow of, 28, 103; Latino families, scholarship on, 17; racial/ethnic identity, 235; racial identity formation, 163, 167, 190–191; racialization and assimilation in, 14–15; research on, 16; thinned attachment families (*see* thinned attachment); as units of analysis, 15, 262n7

family memories: assimilation, 233; cultural maintenance, 65; ethnic pride, 84; Lopez, Tony, 82; racial identity formation, 236–237; thinned attachment, 58

Feagin, Joe R., 26, 134, 149

feminism, 14, 265n14, 265n15

Fenstermaker, Sarah, 12

flexible ethnicity, 200–208; 3rd generation Mexican Americans, 200–208; definition, 194, 201; limits to, 217; racial identity, 228; racialization and, 194, 210; situational ethnicity compared to, 201; symbolic ethnicity, 225

Florida, Hispanic population, 20

food: acculturation, 165–166; ethnicity, 50; Mexican culture, 78, 82, 98, 103; Mexican food, 50, 82, 98, 103, 166; Mexican food as part of U.S., 75, 166

Freedom Summer (McAdam), 64

Freire, Paolo, 185

Fuentes, Cordelia (pseudonym), 156–158, 258

Fuentes, Marisol (pseudonym): antimachismo parenting style, 222–223; demographic information, 258; scrutiny by Mexican immigrants, 218–219; self-definition, 195–196; shopowner tailgating, 157–158

Gans, Herbert: on acculturation, 1, 2; bumpy-line assimilation, 92, 122, 239; symbolic ethnicity, 54, 208

gender: assimilation, 240; educational aspirations, 171, 172–173, 180–181; feminist scholarship, 14; influence on cultural attachments, 120; intermarriage/exogamy, 73, 121; international migration, 14; intramarriage/endogamy, 73, 121; life chances, 173; perception of Mexican Americans, 122; racial/ethnic identity, 234; racial identity formation, 191–192, 264n8;

gender (*continued*): segmented assimilation, 12; socially constructed nature, 12, 14; unitary perspective on, 14 (*see also* race; social class)

gender dynamics/ideologies, 221–225; 3rd generation Mexican Americans, 221–225; antimachismo sentiments, 221–225; Catholicism, 52; clash of cultures, 99–101; cultural maintenance, 65; intergenerational change, 223, 225; international migration, 98; Mexican culture, 38, 52, 81; Mexican families, 36–37; perpetuating static notions of, 118–119; thinned attachment, 36, 39, 58, 59

gender equality: 2nd generation Mexican Americans, 265n14; 3rd generation Mexican Americans, 265n14; adjusting to, 173; Catholicism, 52; feminist movement, 265n14; Madrigal, Reyna, 98; Mexican Americans, 59; Mexican culture, 52; Mexican immigrant women, 36–37; socioeconomic development, 98

gender oppression from cultural and religious ties, 52

generation: definition, 15; generation units, 149; intergenerational transfer of knowledge, 15, 233; racial identity style, 4

Giroux, Henry, 185–186

Goffman, Erving, 134

Gordon, Milton Myron, 8

Grebler, Leo, 3

Guadalupe Hidalgo, Treaty of (1848), 17

Guzman, Constantina (pseudonym), 258

Guzman, Gloria (pseudonym), 258

Guzman, Ralph C., 3

Guzman, Veronica (pseudonym), 184–185, 209, 258

Haney López, Ian, 13

Hernandez, Monica (pseudonym), 258

higher education/college: 2nd generation Mexican Americans, 169–170; 3rd generation Mexican Americans, 187; ethnic re-identification/resurgence, 142; Madrigal, Reyna, 142, 181–182; Montes/Rosenberg family (pseudonym), 41–43;

racial self-perception, 141; Rosenberg, Tamara, 41–43, 170, 175–176; Segura, Yolanda, 180–181; upward mobility, 141; Vargas, Elena, 142–143

"Hispanic" (the term), 197, 199, 262n9

Hispanics: as an ethnic group, 19–20, 261n3; intramarriage/endogamy, 73; percentage of Mexican origin, 21; population, 3, 20; racial classification of, 19–20

historical context: biography, 90; generational reaction to discrimination, 232; influence on generations, 85–87; Japanese Americans, 90; Lopez family, 85; political style, 85; race consciousness, 85; racial/ethnic identity, 235; racial identity, 66; racism, 236

Hochschild, Arlie, 38, 251

home ownership, 136; 2nd generation Mexican Americans, 140–141; Ramirez, Guillermo, 140; Segura, Yolanda, 140; social class, 141; upward mobility, 140–141

Hondagneu-Sotelo, Pierrette, 14, 36–37, 173

hooks, bell, 185

housing segregation, surnames and, 127–128, 262n6

human capital: acculturation, 9; understatement of gains across generations, 123

Huntington, Samuel, 6

Idaho, Hispanic population, 20

identity: Chicano/a identity, 43, 136, 195, 196–199, 227; development of, 15, 94; interactionist approach to, 12; Mexican identity, distinctiveness provided by, 57–58; theories of, 11–16

identity crisis: 3rd generation Mexican Americans, 47–48, 226; assimilation, 47–48; racial in between-ness/liminality, 57–58, 201, 205–206; upward mobility, 47–48

Illinois, Hispanic population, 20

immigrant replenishment, 9

immigration: Asian, 3, 21, 91; Latin American, 21; national patterns, 262n15; ongoing Mexican immigration, 116, 208–209, 243–244; restrictive legislation, 261n2; subjective experience of, 6

Immigration Act (1965), 9
Immigration and Naturalization Services
    (INS), 132, 266n5.ch5, 266n8.ch5, 267n2.ch6
immigration policy, 242
in-marriage. *See* intramarriage/endogamy
incorporation trajectories: assimilation, 11;
    bumpy-line assimilation, 239–240; "ideal
    types" (*see* cultural maintenance; thinned
    attachment); marriage, 93; Mexican
    Americans, 11; neighborhood context,
    240; race, 240; racial identity formation,
    93; of siblings, 108
institutional discrimination, 182
institutional racism, 138
institutions, racial/ethnic identity and, 235
intermarriage/exogamy, 106–123; 1st
    generation Mexican Americans, 73; 2nd
    generation Mexican Americans, 73, 79,
    263n1; 3rd generation Mexican Americans,
    73; 4th generation Mexican Americans,
    93; antimiscegenation laws, 91; assimila-
    tion, 60, 91, 120, 121–122, 262n6; blacks,
    262n6; children of intermarried couples,
    122; cultural maintenance, 92; gender, 73,
    121; between Hispanics and non-Hispanic
    whites, 92, 262n6; human-capital gains
    across generations, understatement of,
    123; Latinos, 62, 262n6; likelihood of, 57;
    "marrying up," 121; Mexican Americans,
    22, 23; racial awareness, 116; racial/ethnic
    identity, 116; racial progressives, 120; rates,
    92–93, 121; respondents, 266n3.ch4; as
    "taking care of yourself," 45–46; thinned
    attachment, 39, 57, 58, 60–61, 62, 72, 92,
    106–121, 110; women's view of, 121, 122
intramarriage/endogamy, 94–106; 1st genera-
    tion Mexican Americans, 65; 2nd genera-
    tion Mexican Americans, 65; 3rd genera-
    tion Mexican Americans, 65; admonition
    against, 37–38, 49, 56; consequences, 93;
    cultural maintenance, 65, 72, 79, 83; cultural
    transmission, 121; definition, 265n2; ethnic
    re-identification/resurgence, 94–106, 121;
    gender, 73, 121; Hispanics, 73; preference
    for, 73, 101, 120–121; racial/ethnic identity,
    120; women, 121

Japanese Americans, 85, 90
JCPenney, 156–157
Jewel (pop musical artist), 251
Jimenez, Michael (pseudonym), 246–247, 259
Jimenez, Ruth (pseudonym), 259

Kelly, Mary, 102
Kibria, Nazli, 46–47

"Latino/a" (the term), 195, 197, 198–199,
    262n9
Latino threat narrative, 3, 156–157
Latinos: American Dream, 160; as an invad-
    ing force, 3; blacks, distancing from, 162;
    blacks compared to, 262n6; "browning
    of America," 3; demand for immigrant
    labor, 238; deportation, 157; discrimina-
    tion, 262n6; educational attainment,
    192; intermarriage/exogamy, 62, 262n6;
    as percentage of Hispanic population,
    3; racial categorization of, 4–5, 194–195;
    racial/ethnic identity choices, 162; as
    "racial middle," 16, 160; racialized ethnic-
    ity of, 5; scholarship on Latino families,
    17, 234
law: antimiscegenation laws, 91; critical race
    theory, 12–13; race as legal construction,
    13–14; whiteness, 13, 18
Lopez family (pseudonym): bumpy-line
    assimilation, 66; civil rights movement,
    69–71; commitment to intramarriage/
    endogamy, 73; cultural maintenance,
    66; historical context, 85; marriages, 67;
    racial/ethnic identity, 85
Lopez, Juan (pseudonym), 66–67, 71–72;
    Americanization programs (1915-1929),
    66, 85; arrival in United States, 264n3.
    ch3; assimilationist outlook, 66, 85;
    Chicano Movement, 71; civil rights
    movement, 71; demographic informa-
    tion, 259; deportation programs, 67;
    discrimination experiences, denial of, 67,
    264n4.ch3; educational attainment, 67;
    intramarriage, preference for, 73; labor
    recruitment programs, 66; marriage, 67;
    parenting style, 67; political style, 72;

racial identity, 85; religious beliefs, 73; United States, relationship to, 67, 71–72, 85; work ethic, 71–72

Lopez, Marcus (pseudonym), 68–75; Brown Berets, 68, 69, 72, 85, 86, 178; career aspirations, 74–75; Chávez ,César, 69; Chicano Movement, 66, 68, 69, 71, 86; civil rights movement, 71; cultural citizenship, 68; cultural forgetting, 74, 75; demographic information, 259; education, 68; family, importance of, 71; GED, 68–69, 178, 179; healthy skepticism toward education, 177–179; household division of labor, traditional, 74–75; intramarriage/endogamy, preference for, 73; MEChA (Movimiento Estudiantil Chicano de Aztlán), 69; mother, 68; multicultural classes, 70; parents' counsel about marrying, 72–73, 75; political style, 72; presentation of self, 69–70; racial pride, 69–70, 70–71; religious beliefs, 73–74; U. S. Marine Corps, 68, 69, 178, 179; wives, 68, 72–73, 264n5.ch3

Lopez, Tony (Antonio) (pseudonym), 76–82; affirmative action, 79–80; biculturalism, 80, 85; bilingualism, 66, 80, 85; cultural maintenance inclinations, 86, 265n9; demographic information, 259; discrimination experiences, denial of, 77, 265n11; educational attainment, 179; employment opportunities, 80, 86, 188; "ethnic option," 76; family memories, 82; feelings of inclusion, 76–77; household division of labor, traditional, 77–78; maternal grandparents, 76, 77–78, 82, 265n9; Mexican food, 82; middle-class status, 76–77; military service, 179; prohibition on speaking Spanish in school, 165; racial/ethnic identity, 76; racial matching in marriage, 81–82; religious beliefs, 73; representation of Hispanic community, 80–81; skin color, 76–77; social acceptance, 77; Spanish language skills, 78–79; Ventura County sheriff's department, 79–80

Los Angeles Times (newspaper), 243

Loving v. Virginia, 91

machismo, 45, 118. *See also* antimachismo sentiments

Macias, Thomas, 115–116, 209

Madrigal family (pseudonym), 102–103, 182

Madrigal, Beatrice (pseudonym): assimilationist sentiments, 96; demographic information, 259; on discrimination, 127; ethnic re-identification/resurgence, 103; ideological resistance to discrimination, 146–148; marriage to Mexican man, 95–96; Mexican cooking, 103; parents, 95; pointed encouragement of schooling, 181

Madrigal, Reyna (pseudonym), 96–102; assimilationist tendencies, 96; demographic information, 259; English language proficiency, 96–97; ethnic re-identification/resurgence, 97–98, 100–101, 120–121, 142; gender dynamics/ideologies, 99–101; gender equality, 98; higher education/college, 142, 181–182; husband Rudy, 98–102, 266n4. ch4; intramarriage, preference for, 101, 120–121; MEChA (Movimiento Estudiantil Chicano de Aztlán), 101; Mexican identity, 98, 101; parents-in-law, 99–100; racial in between-ness/liminality, 201; racial self-perception, 198–199

Mannheim, Karl, 15, 144–145, 149–150

marriage, 91–123; 1st generation Mexican Americans, 92; 2nd generation Mexican Americans, 92–93; antimiscegenation laws, 91; assimilation, 121; bumpy-line assimilation, 28, 92, 121–123; cultural maintenance, 91, 92, 231–232; expectations of women being, 253–254; as a feedback loop, 93; identity development, 94; incorporation trajectories, 93; intermarriage (*see* intermarriage/exogamy); interracial marriage, 91; intramarriage/endogamy (*see* intramarriage/endogamy); "mythic love narrative," 37–38; "prosaic realism" framing, 38; racial/ethnic identity, 234; subjective experience of race, 91; thinned attachment, 91, 92, 231–232

"marrying up," 121

McAdam, Doug, 64

MEChA (Movimiento Estudiantil Chicano de Aztlán), 43, 69, 101
Medina, Celia (pseudonym), 259
Medina, Manny (pseudonym), 223, 246, 259
memories, appropriated, 4, 15
memories, personally acquired, 4, 15
Mendoza, Adele (pseudonym), 127–128, 170, 259
Mendoza, Ruben (pseudonym), 127–128, 170, 259
Mendoza, Tyler (pseudonym): demographic information, 259; employment opportunities, 129–130; parents' encouragement for schooling, 179–180; proving oneself through overachievement, 152–153; understanding of racial/ethnic labels, 197
"Mexican" (the term), 195
"Mexican American" (the term), 19, 195, 197, 198, 199
Mexican Americans: 1st generation (see 1st generation Mexican Americans); 2nd generation (see 2nd generation Mexican Americans); 3rd generation (see 3rd generation Mexican Americans); 4th generation, 93; 1920s-1940s, 67; affect toward Anglo-Americans, 130; as an ethnic group, 4–5, 6, 195, 231, 266n1; assimilation, 231; bumpy-line assimilation, 11; citizenship, 17, 18, 24; downward assimilation, 6; "ethnic option," 7, 208; gender equality, 59; history in United States, 17–18; identity options, 195–196; immigrant replenishment, 9; intergeneration incorporation trajectories, 11; intermarriage/exogamy, 22, 23; labels applied to themselves, 18–19; marginalized subpopulation, 240; as "mestizaje," 34–35 (see also racial in between-ness/liminality); middle-class (see middle-class Mexican Americans); passing by (see passing as non-Hispanic white); perceptions of, 122; as race, 266n1; racial categorization of, 195, 231; racial/ethnic identity choices, 162; racialization despite assimilation, 7–8, 159, 213, 237, 241; racialized ethnicity of, 195; segmented assimilation, 7; self-identification as, 130; Spanish language

skills, 265n12; upward mobility, 7, 24, 90; variety within the population, 228
Mexican cultural identification: 3rd generation Mexican Americans, 58; assimilation, 24; degree of, 240–241; socioeconomic advancement, 24. See also ethnic re-identification/resurgence
Mexican culture: Catholicism, 44, 56, 59; commitment to family, 55, 97; family structure, 55–56; food, 78, 82, 98, 103; gender dynamics/ideologies, 38, 52, 81; gender equality, 52; husbands, 36; machismo, 45, 118 (see also antimachismo sentiments); mediated experiences with, 116; men, 37–38; patriarchy, 81, 107 (see also antipatriarchal sentiments); sense of family, 47; wives, 36–37
Mexican identity, sense of: Catholicism, devotion to, 59, 83; Madrigal, Reyna, 98, 101; Ponce, Gabriel (Gabe), 107, 109; racial pride, 70–71; Rosenberg, Andrew, 264n8; social class, 264n4.ch2
Mexican immigrants, 213–225; 3rd generation Mexican Americans, 208–209, 217; assimilability of, 2–3, 4, 6, 7, 21–22, 237; California, 243; "ethnic option," 21; gender role expectations for women, 36–37; migration patterns, 262n15; racial authenticity contests, 213–225; as racial gatekeepers, 217–218; racial identity, 1; Spanish language skills, 214–215. See also 1st generation Mexican Americans
Mexican-inferiority ideology, 153
Mexicanization programs, 66
"Mexicanos" (the term), 197
middle-class Mexican Americans: discrimination, 27, 76–77; Mexican cultural identification, 24; racial/ethnic authenticity, contests of, 27; racialization, 27; segmented assimilation, 10–11
Mills, C. Wright, 64
Minutemen Militia, 3
Montes, Maria (pseudonym), 33–39; admonition against intramarriage, 37–38, 49, 56; on being interviewed, 248–249; daughter (see Rosenberg, Tamara);

Montes, Maria (*continued*): demographic information, 259; divorce, 44, 52; emigration from Mexico, 33; employment, 33–34; "excommunication" from Catholic church, 44; first husband, 37; gender roles, view of, 38–39, 53; granddaughter (*see* Rosenberg, Jillian); grandson (*see* Rosenberg, Andrew); racial pride, 34–35, 39; Spanish language skills, 36; survival mode of parenting, 35–36, 39; work ethic, 46

Montes/Rosenberg family (pseudonym): American Dream, belief in, 40; Americanization of, 34–35; commitment to family, 55; gender oppression as result of cultural and religious ties, 52; higher education/college, 41–43; Judaism, connection to, 48, 59, 264n7; members (*see* Montes, Maria; Rosenberg, Andrew; Rosenberg, Jillian; Rosenberg, Tamara); racial identity formation, 264n8; racial pride, 34–35; thinned attachment, 39, 61–62, 263n1; tight-knit, 42; upward mobility, 39

Moore, Joan W., 3

Morelos, Evelyn (pseudonym), 129, 229

Morelos, Lance (pseudonym): on affirmative action, 188; awareness of his race, 229–231; awareness of racial hierarchy, 150; demographic information, 259; on education and the American Dream, 169

Morelos, Lee (pseudonym), 229–231, 252–254, 259

multicultural education, 70, 265n7

multiculturalism: 3rd generation Mexican Americans, 227, 233; American history of, 238; civil rights movement, 90, 231; Ponce, Gabriel (Gabe), 107; Schultz, Rex, 113

"mythic love narrative," 37–38

Nagel, Joane, 102

nativism, 3, 21, 238

Naturalization Act (1790), 2, 13

Nevada, Hispanic population, 20

"Never Marry a Mexican" (Cisneros), 263n3

New Jersey, Hispanic population, 20

New Mexico, Hispanic population, 20, 21

New York State, Hispanic population, 20, 262n13

"non-Hispanic white" (the term), 262n4

non-Hispanic whites, intermarriage/exogamy with, 92, 262n6

O'Brien, Eileen, 160

Ochoa, Gilda, 217, 227–228

"off-white" racial status, 241, 244, 267n1.ch8

Office of Management and Budget (OMB), 261n3

Ogbu, John, 144

Omi, Michael, 64, 158, 163

Operation Deportation (1930–1942), 67

Operation Wetback (1954), 18, 267n2.ch6

Oregon, Hispanic population, 20

Ortiz, Vilma, 60, 123, 187

Our Lady of Guadalupe (Virgin of Guadalupe), 83, 97, 216

out-marriage. *See* intermarriage/exogamy

parenting: 1st generation Mexican Americans, 170–173; 3rd generation Mexican Americans, 176–182; antimachismo parenting style, 222–223; assimilationist style, 67; racial identity formation, 83–84; survival mode of, 35–36, 39, 58–59; thinned attachment, 58–59

passing as non-Hispanic white: being "outed," 209; Benavidas, Caitlyn, 209–210; Contreras, Renata, 202, 217; discrimination, 129, 266n1, 266n2; Dos Santos, Carmina, 204, 216–217; Rosenberg, Jillian, 51

Pattillo-McCoy, Mary, 191

personally acquired memories, 4

Pew Hispanic Center, 20–21

pigmentocracy, 87

political assimilation, 139

Ponce family (pseudonym), 107, 120

Ponce, Gabriel (Gabe) (pseudonym), 107–110; appearance, 108–109; "Chicano" (the term), dislike of, 197–198; demographic information, 259; downward cultural transmission, 109; intramarriage/endogamy, preference for, 109–110; Mexican identity, sense of, 107, 109;

Ponce, Gabriel (*continued*): movement from cultural maintenance to thinned attachment, 106; multiculturalism, 107; Spanish language skills presumed, 211–212

Ponce, Timoteo (Timothy) (pseudonym), 106–109; anglicization of his name, 164–165, 267n1.ch6; assimilation, 107; demographic information, 259; high school, 174; out-marriage with non-Hispanic white woman, 106; parents, 107; United Farm Workers, 109; wife, 108

Portes, Alejandro, 6

"prosaic realism" framing, 38

"race" (the term), 5

race, 4–7, 11–16; assimilation, 240; awareness of, 116; biological basis, 5; citizenship, 2; civil rights, 2; commonplace understanding, 5, 13; employment opportunities, 80, 86, 188; ethnicity compared to, 5–6; family-memory aspects of, 15; genetic variation within, 5; historical contingency of, 15–16; incorporation trajectories, 240; as legal construction, 13–14; Mexican Americans as, 4–5, 266n1; as negotiation between generations, 15; racial classification of Hispanics, 19–20; realization of, 164–166, 229–230; in school tracking systems, 183, 232; segmented assimilation, 12, 240; skin color as proxy for, 1, 5; social class, 34; social identity, 11–12; social weight of, 158; socially constructed nature, 4–5, 12, 135; statistical reporting standards, 261n3; subjective experience of, 91; unitary perspective on, 14 (*see also* gender; social class); upward mobility, 7

"Race and Race Theory" (Winant), 194

race consciousness, 82–83, 85

racial authenticity, 213–225; 3rd generation Mexican Americans *vs.* Mexican immigrants, 213–225; essentialization of racial identity, 220–221; generation in the United States, 217–221; racial gatekeepers, 217–218; skin color/phenotype, 215–216; social class, 219; Spanish language skills, 214–215, 219; surnames, 216

racial categorization, 194–200; of 3rd generation Mexican Americans, 194–200; imposed categorization, 40; indicators of, 112; of Latinos, 4–5, 194–195; of Mexican Americans, 195, 231; myths of race as rooted in biology, 200; "off-white" status, 241, 244, 267n1.ch8

racial/ethnic identity, 194–200; 3rd generation Mexican Americans, 193, 194–200, 226, 228, 262n8; bumpy-line assimilation, 239–240; choices, 162; factors influencing, 234–235; grandparents' influence on, 76; intermarriage/exogamy, 116; intramarriage/endogamy, 120; Lopez family, 85; "twilight" of, 243

racial/ethnic lumping, 212–213

Racial Formation in the United States (Omi and Winant), 64, 163

racial hierarchy: awareness of, 150; continuing nature of, 244; pigmentocracy, 87; scholarship, 16

racial identity: appropriated memories, 4; essentialization of, 220–221; ethnic conversion, 265n10; flexible ethnicity, 228; forces determining, 4; historical context, 66; ignorance of, 229–230; Mexican immigrants, 1; personally acquired memories, 4; social-psychological literature, 11

racial identity formation: civil rights movement, 86, 90; definition, 4; factors influencing, 231; families in, 163, 167, 190–191; family memories, 236–237; gender, 191–192, 264n8; incorporation trajectories, 93; Montes/Rosenberg family (pseudonym), 264n8; parenting style, 83–84; racial ideology of influential family members, 120; schools in, 163, 167, 190; social context, 141–142; wheel of, 234–235

racial identity politics, 241–242

racial in between-ness/liminality, 200–208; 3rd generation Mexican Americans, 200–208; identity crisis, 57–58, 201, 205–206; Latinos as "racial middle," 60, 160; Mexican Americans as "mestizaje," 34–35 racial options, 7

racial performance, 133–134

racial pride: 1st generation Mexican Americans, 149; 2nd generation Mexican Americans, 149–150; 3rd generation Mexican Americans, 149–151; Benavidas family, 83; civil rights movement, 69–70; cultural maintenance, 74; instilling Mexican culture, 34–35, 39; Mexican identity, sense of, 70–71; Montes/Rosenberg family, 34–35; as protection against discrimination, 149–151; self-conscious use of political labels, 87; success, 264n4.ch2

racial profiling, 132–133, 159

racial progressives, 120

racial self-perception, 194–200; of 1st generation Mexican Americans, 262n8; of 2nd generation Mexican Americans, 262n8; of 3rd generation Mexican Americans, 194–200; assimilation, 4; awareness of racial hierarchy, 150–151; demographics of surrounding area, 199; higher education/college, 141; imposed categorization, 40; of individual respondents, 39–40, 54, 195–196; proximity to country of heritage, 199; social context, 198; surnames, 199

racialization, 208–213; 3rd generation Mexican Americans, 208–213, 225; assimilation, 7–8, 14–15, 159, 189–193; assuming cultural knowledge based on racial stereotypes, 211–212; Benavidas, Caitlin (pseudonym), 209–210; complimentary othering, 212–213; definition, 194, 209; despite assimilation, 7–8, 159, 213, 237, 241; discrimination, 161–162, 209; expectation about linguistic abilities, 212; flexible ethnicity and, 194, 210; middle-class Mexican Americans, 27; mitigation of, 163; racial/ethnic identity choices, 162; racial/ethnic lumping, 212–213; in schools (see racialization in schools)

racialization in schools, 163–170; administrators using stereotypes, 249; anglicization of names, 164–165; classrooms segregated by race, 166; curriculum exclusions, 185–186; discouraging education in favor of work, 170; discouraging taking academic classes, 178; English as a Second Language (ESL) classes, 183–184, 249; expectation negative stereotypes will be displayed, 179, 211–212; facilities, 174–175; Jim Crow-style racism, 174, 232; low expectations for minority students, 171, 178–180, 182, 183–185; mediation of impact of, 232; prohibitions on speaking Spanish, 165; realization-of-race in schools, 164–166; school food, 166; tracking systems, 182–183, 232; at Yale University, 54. See also educational aspirations

racialized ethnicity, 5, 195

racism: color-blind racism, 137; complimentary othering, 212–213; historical context, 236; ignorance, 148; institutional racism, 138; Jim Crow-style, 174, 232; perception of, 136; structured racism, 137

Ramirez, Guillermo (pseudonym), 140, 168–169, 259

Ramirez, Pierre-Mecatl (pseudonym), 127, 133–134, 259

Ramos, Juan (pseudonym), 252, 259

Ramos, Moises (pseudonym), 148, 152, 254, 259

reculturation, 102. See also ethnic re-identification/resurgence

religious conversion, thinned attachment and, 39

research design, 23–27

research methods, 27–28, 232–233, 245–255, 263m23, 263n19, 263n24

research questions, 22–23

respondents: access to, 255; age range, 26; auxiliary (spouse) interviews, 26; demographic profile, 6–7, 26, 257–260; income breakdown, 257, 263n20; intermarriage/exogamy, 266n3.ch4; minimum age, 263n16; social class, 242, 264n11; sources of, 25; structural assimilation, 240; upward mobility, 242. See also personal names followed by "(pseudonym)" retraditionalization. *See* ethnic re-identification/resurgence

Rhode Island, Hispanic population, 20

Rosenberg, Andrew (pseudonym), 205–207; antimachismo sentiments, 223; demographic information, 260; flexible ethnicity, 205; grandmother (*see* Montes, Maria); Judaism, connection to, 48; Mexican identity, sense of, 264n8; mother (*see* Rosenberg, Tamara); racial in between-ness/liminality, 206–207; on school tracking systems, 183; segregated classes, 206–207; sentimental ethnicity, 207; sister (*see* Rosenberg, Jillian)

Rosenberg, Jillian (pseudonym), 48–58; affirmative action programs, 188; assimilationist mindset, 48–49; brother (*see* Rosenberg, Andrew); Catholicism, 56; commitment to her family, 55; complimentary othering, 212; dating, 57; demographic information, 259; discrimination experiences, denial of, 51; distancing from Mexican background, 50–51, 119; distilled ethnicity, 58; elementary school, 50–51; flexible ethnicity, 205–206; Gifted and Talented Education (GATE) classes, 49, 51; grandmother (*see* Montes, Maria); grandmother's admonition against intramarriage, 37, 49, 56; identity crisis, 57–58, 205–206; interactions with Mexican students, 217–218; intermarriage/exogamy, likelihood of, 56–57; Judaism, connection to, 264n7; Mexican culture to, 55–57; on Mexican kin, 52–53; mother (*see* Rosenberg, Tamara); passing as non-Hispanic white, 51; race, sensitivity to, 48; racialization moment, 210–211; Spanish language skills, 55; thinned attachment, 48–49, 53–57; whiteness, allegiance to, 49–51, 54, 58; Yale University, 53–54, 188, 205–206, 218

Rosenberg, Tamara (pseudonym), 39–48; Catholicism, 44; Chicana identity, 43; childhood, 40; daughter (*see* Rosenberg, Jillian); demographic information, 259; distilled ethnicity, 46–47; engagement

to a Mexican, 45; family, sense of, 47; high school counselor, 175; higher education/college, 41–43, 170, 175–176; husband Gregory, 44, 45–46; identity, racialized and gendered, 45; *machismo,* experiences with, 45; marriage to a Jew, 45–46; MEChA (Movimiento Estudiantil Chicano de Aztlán), 43; models of how women wield power, 45–46; mother (*see* Montes, Maria); race- and class-based discomfiture, 42–43; racialization, experiences of, 40; religious conversion, 44; self-definition, 39–40, 54; son (*see* Rosenberg, Andrew); work ethic, 46

Ruiz, Amalia (pseudonym), 150–151, 211–212, 260

Ruiz, Marcel (pseudonym), 174–175, 260

Rumbaut, Rubén G., 6

salsa, 226

Schultz family (pseudonym), 107, 110, 120

Schultz, Albert (pseudonym): assimilationist sentiments, 110–112; on being interviewed, 245; demographic information, 260; educational aspirations, 171; ethnic re-identification/resurgence, 111; out-marriage with non-Hispanic white woman, 106; prohibition on speaking Spanish in school, 165; wife, 111

Schultz, Rex (pseudonym), 106, 110, 112–113, 260

"Second Generation Decline" (Gans), 1

segmented assimilation: definition, 8; gender, 12; marginalized subpopulations, 240; Mexican Americans, 7; middle-class Mexican Americans, 10–11; race, 12, 240; selective acculturation, 87–88

Segura, Davina (pseudonym), 200, 260

Segura, Yolanda (pseudonym), 105–106, 140, 180–181, 260

selective acculturation, 87–88

sentimental ethnicity, 207

service industry workers, 77

shopowner tailgating, 131–132, 156–158, 159

Sikes, Melvin P., 26, 149

Simón (Mexican immigrant), 1–2

situational ethnicity, 198, 201

skin color/phenotype, 128–133; 3rd generation Mexican Americans, 228; affect toward Anglo-Americans, 130; bumpy-line assimilation, 202; cultural maintenance, 58, 65; discrimination, 128–131; employment opportunities, 129–130; "epidemiological" approach to policing, 132–133; "ethnic option," 129, 201; feelings of inclusion, 76–77; internalized inferiority, 131; negative stereotypes, 151–152; one's agency, 201; perception of Mexican Americans, 122; as proxy for race, 1, 5; racial authenticity contests, 215–216; racial categorization, 112; racial/ethnic identity, 234; racial worth, 87; realization of disadvantages of, 164; self-identification as Mexican American, 130; skin color privilege, 266n3.ch5; thinned attachment, 58, 61; white privilege, 129

social class: discrimination, 26, 159; educational attainment, 167–168, 171–172, 192; home ownership, 141; "marrying up," 121; Mexican identity, sense of, 264n4. ch2; middle-class Mexican Americans (see middle-class Mexican Americans); race, 34; race consciousness, 82–83; racial authenticity, 219; racial/ethnic identity, 234; respondents, 242; of respondents, 264n11; socially constructed nature, 12; unitary perspective on, 14 (see also gender; race)

social context: ethnicity, 198; neighborhood context, 240; racial/ethnic identity, 235; racial self-perception, 198; racialized experience, 206

social identity, race and, 11–12

social-psychological literature, 11, 16

socioeconomic advancement, 24, 98. See also upward mobility

Spanish language skills: 1st generation Mexican Americans, 78; 2nd generation Mexican Americans, 36, 78, 79, 165;

3rd generation Mexican Americans, 36, 78–79, 215; cultural maintenance, 78, 79; intergenerational decline in, 36; intergenerational importance of maintaining, 114–115; intra-ethnic prejudice, 214–215; Mexican Americans, 265n12; Mexican immigrants, 214–215; parental educational attainment, 79; presumed knowledge of, 211–212; racial authenticity contests, 214–215, 219; thinned attachment, 55, 78, 79

spatial mobility, 136

standpoint theory, 14

straight-line assimilation, 8–9, 62, 239

structural assimilation: cultural maintenance, 87; ethnic re-identification/resurgence, 94; respondents, 240; thinned attachment, 62–63, 87

surnames, 127–131; cultural maintenance, 65; discrimination, 127–128, 129–131; employment opportunities, 130; "ethnic option," 201; housing segregation, 127–128, 262n6; identification with, 266n4.ch5; internalized inferiority, 131; one's agency, 201; perception of Mexican Americans, 122; racial authenticity, 216; racial categorization, 112; racial self-perception, 199; self-identification as Mexican American, 130; thinned attachment, 48, 61

survival mode of parenting, 35–36, 39, 58–59

Swidler, Ann, 37–38

symbolic ethnicity: 3rd generation Mexican Americans, 109, 207–208, 226; flexible ethnicity, 225; Gans, Herbert, 54, 208; Morelos, Lee, 230–231; Schultz family, 107; upward mobility, 208; white ethnics, 208; white privilege, 208

Takahashi, Jere, 85

Talavera, Cristina (pseudonym), 187–188, 260

Talavera, Raymond (pseudonym), 139, 260

Telles, Edward, 60, 123, 187

Texas, Hispanic population, 20

Texas Rangers, 3

thinned attachment, 33–63; 3rd generation Mexican Americans, 89; accommodating stance, 189; acculturation, 37; assimilation, 65; bicultural homes with assimilationist orientation, 48; categorization of families as, 264n2; civil rights movement, 82; cultural maintenance compared to, 62, 64–66, 87–90, 226–227, 265n16; definition, 4, 58; differences between cultural maintenance and, 88; discrimination, 161; distilled ethnicity, 46–47; dwindling devotion to Catholicism, 59; educational attainment, 60, 189; embeddedness in American institutions, 39; factors influencing, 231–232; family memories and teaching, 58; forces driving, 48–49, 58–63; gender dynamics/ideologies, 36, 39, 58, 59; generational distance from Mexico, 39; hallmark of, 49; heterogeneous peer networks, 39; as "ideal type" incorporation trajectories, 89; intermarriage/exogamy, 39, 57, 58, 60–61, 62, 72, 92, 106–121, 110; language, 58; marriage, 91, 92, 231–232; Montes/Rosenberg family, 39, 61–62, 263n1; religious conversion, 39; representation of Hispanic community, 80; residential patterns, 88–89; Rosenberg, Jillian, 48–49, 53–57; Schultz family, 107, 110, 120; skin color/phenotype, 58, 61; Spanish language skills, 55, 78, 79; structural assimilation, 62–63, 87; surnames not identified with Latinos, 48, 61; survival mode of parenting, 58–59; upward mobility, 39, 59–60

Torres, Harry (pseudonym), 132–133, 260
Torres, Juana (pseudonym), 260
Torres, Mercedes (pseudonym), 260
Torres, Ricardo (Rick) (pseudonym), 151–152, 219–220, 223, 260
Treviño, Araceli (pseudonym), 186, 212, 222, 260
Treviño, Rafael (pseudonym): on American Dream, 166; Chicano Movement, 137–138, 139; demographic information, 260; realization of disadvantages of skin color, 164

United Farm Workers, 109, 197
U.S. Immigration and Naturalization Services (INS), 132, 266n5.ch5, 267n2.ch6
U.S. Marine Corps, 68, 69, 178, 179
University of California, 187–188
upward cultural transmission, 28, 102, 103
upward mobility, 140–143; 3rd generation Mexican Americans, 47–48; assimilation, 7; cultural maintenance, 61, 87, 94; discrimination, 140–143; disposal of minority culture, 241; higher education/college, 141; home ownership, 140–141; human-capital gains across generations, understatement of, 123; identity crisis, 47–48; Mexican American identity, 87; Mexican Americans, 7, 24, 90; Montes/Rosenberg family, 39; out-migration from homogenous Mexican-origin neighborhoods, 88; race, 7; reactions following, 241; respondents, 242; symbolic ethnicity, 208; thinned attachment, 39, 59–60
Utah, Hispanic population, 20

Valdez, Luis, 109
Vargas family (pseudonym), 250
Vargas, Elena (pseudonym), 132, 142–143, 145, 260
Vargas, Erica (pseudonym), 260
Vargas, Ramona (pseudonym), 145–146, 172–173, 260
Vasconcelos, Gustavo (pseudonym), 260
Vasconcelos, Norma (pseudonym), 260
Virgin of Guadalupe (Our Lady of Guadalupe), 83, 97, 216

Waters, Mary, 130, 199, 208, 266n4.ch5
Weiss, Robert, 245
West, Candace, 12
"white" (the term), 262n4
whiteness: "acting white," 53; expansion of, 2; law, 13, 18; mixed heritage individuals, 51; money, 27; "off-white" status, 241, 244, 267n1.ch8; Rosenberg, Jillian, 49–51, 54, 58; as set of social practices, 51; as "status property," 13; white privilege, 2, 13, 129, 208, 266n3.ch5

whites. *See* passing as non-Hispanic white

Winant, Howard, 64, 158, 163, 194

women: Beauvoir on, Simone de, 252; cultural transmission, 75, 78; as double minority, 155; ethnic re-identification/resurgence, 104; intermarriage/exogamy, 121; intermarriage/exogamy, view of, 121, 122; intramarriage/endogamy, 121; marital expectations for, 253–254; motivation in family formation, 232

work, discursive professionalization of, 77

work ethic, 40, 46, 71–72

Yale University: racialized encounters at, 54; Rosenberg, Jillian, 48, 53–54, 188, 205–206, 218

Zagada, Daniel (pseudonym), 164, 260

Zagada, Paul (pseudonym), 1–2, 260

Zavella, Patricia, 255

About the Author

JESSICA M. VASQUEZ is Assistant Professor of Sociology at the University of Kansas.

thickening: historicize, regionally specific
                   mex cul   mexico
                   Spa language   Spain, Italy, etc
                   history   united states
                   politics   chicana/o, latina/o -
                                      spanish - Hispano
                                      Puerto Rican - Boricua

thinning   Religion   local variants
                inter-marriage
                gender neighbor
border crossed us, without 711 migration
gendered expectations - change in mix too
racialization - phenotype need to problematize
internalized oppression   skin, hair, features,
                                   accent

6) how can we specify acculturation if us born?
Like DREAMERS who argue they are American by
socialization, aren't us born latinos American
+ Latino or bicultural? Isn't acculturation
an inculcation of difference, borders +
boundaries?

cultural maintenance